WEDNESDAY!
The history of Sheffield's oldest professional football club

Keith Farnsworth

Sheffield City Libraries
1982

First Published 1982.

©1982 Sheffield City Libraries,
Central Library, Surrey Street,
Sheffield S1 1XZ.

ISBN 0 900660 87 2 hardback edition
ISBN 0 900660 88 0 paperback edition

Printed and bound in Great Britain
by the City of Sheffield Printing Services.

Contents

Page

Introduction   vii

Part 1. Wednesday: the Beginning and Before

    1. The birth of a football club   1
    2. Wednesday Cricket Club, 1820-1924   6
    3. Early football days   11
    4. The Clegg brothers   15
    5. Early cup exploits   18

Part 2. The Olive Grove Era

    1. The move to Olive Grove   24
    2. Early trials and triumphs, 1887-90   30
    3. The quest for League status   35
    4. In search of Cup glory   42
    5. Olive Grove: the last act   50

Part 3. Early Years at Owlerton

    1. The trials of finding a new home   56
    2. Second Division Champions, 1899-1900   59
    3. Champions twice: 1902-3 and 1903-4   64
    4. Steps to Cup Success, 1904-1907   70
    5. Eventful years: 1907-1915   77

Part 4. Fall and Rise: 1919-1927

    1. Relegation—and Bob Brown arrives   90
    2. Years of trial: 1920-1925   93
    3. Second Division Champions, 1925-6   99

Part 5. A Golden Era: 1928-35

    1. Seven memorable seasons   105
    2. The Great Escape   107
    3. Champions twice . . . and close to the double   111
    4. End of the Bob Brown era (1930-33)   117
    5. Walker takes Wednesday to Wembley   124
    6. How Wednesday won the F.A. Cup, April 1935   131

iv

Part 6.   Downs and Ups: 1936-1958

    1. Fall from the heights: 1936-39   137
    2. A wartime interlude: 1939-46   145
    3. Struggle towards promotion: 1946-50   153
    4. The yo-yo years: (1) relegation on goal average   164
    5. The yo-yo years: (2) Dooley, triumph and tragedy   171
    6. The yo-yo years: (3) struggle and fall, 1953-55   181
    7. The yo-yo years: (4) up again. . . down again 1955-58   188

Part 7.   Wednesday After 1958

    1. The Catterick years: 1958-61   195
    2. The Buckingham style, 1961-64   208
    3. Alan Brown—man with a mission, 1964-68   219
    4. 1966 and all that   224
    5. The dark years, 1968-77   237
    6. Jack Charlton arrives, and the tide turns: 1977-82   266

For the Record—a few statistics   280

Acknowledgements   285

Illustrations

Page

1.	Sir Charles Clegg	16
2.	Heroes of Olive Grove	39
3.	F.A. Cup-winning team, 1896	49
4.	League champions 1903	68
5.	F.A. Cup winners 1907	77
6.	A Wednesday squad of 1912	84
7.	Wednesday's championship teams 1928-29	114
8.	Before the 1935 F.A. Cup final	131
9.	Jack Palethorpe scores in 1935 final	133
10.	Hillsborough players and officials, 1935	136
11.	League War North Cup final line-up, 1943	151
12.	Heroes of 1947	158
13.	Eddie Quigley	160
14.	Wednesday 1950-51	168
15.	Two Jacks. . . Marriott and Sewell	170
16.	Goal King. . . Derek Dooley	172
17.	Second Division title celebration, 1952	176
18.	Dooley: front-page news	180
19.	Second Division Champions 1956	190
20.	Wednesday 1959-60	201
21.	Wednesday in the early 1960s	216
22.	F.A. Cup final team 1966	231
23.	Hillsborough squad 1979-80	272
24.	Board of directors of the 1980s	276

Illustrations nos. 14, 17, 19, 20, 22 and 23 are reproduced by kind permission of Sheffield Newspapers Ltd.

Introduction

This is the first full-length history of Sheffield Wednesday to appear since 1926, and, after a gap of nearly 60 years, an up-dated volume has been long overdue. The job probably ought to have been undertaken at the time of the club's centenary in 1967, but, for several reasons, it was not completed at what would have been an ideal moment: Wednesday were then in the First Division and had reached the FA Cup final a year earlier. The opportunity was lost, but, perhaps, the benefits of waiting a further 15 years will be evident from the book which has now been written. Soon after 1967 the club's fortunes took a sudden and alarming dip, and the lean years hardly encouraged publication of a new history. Sadly, the period of decline proved long and painful, and there was a spell when the slide seemed never-ending. After falling into the Third Division in 1975, Wednesday dropped dangerously close to the brink of Division Four. Never had the outlook appeared so bleak. However, towards the end of the 1970s, at last the tide began to turn, and the first steps were taken on the long upward climb. In 1980 Wednesday gained promotion to the Second Division. The following season provided evidence of further progress. It seemed that finally the time was ripe to begin preparing that long-overdue history.

In fact, when the actual writing got under way in September 1981, it seemed that the book might get the happiest of endings—Wednesday's return to the First Division after an absence of 12 years. The team had started 1981-2 in excellent style, and, sitting proudly atop the Second Division, looked firm favourites to gain promotion. In the event, they didn't manage it, though they missed out by the narrowest of margins—Norwich City pipped them by a point. If only they had not let so many "soft" points slip at home; if only they had not faltered on the last lap of the race . . . so near and yet so far away from the great prize! This, of course, was the year when the Football League changed the points system, with three points awarded for a win instead of the previous two. Ironically, under the old system Wednesday would have gone up instead of Norwich. The new system devalued the draw, and, in the final analysis, Wednesday drew too many games they needed to win. It was not the first disappointment the club had suffered in 79 seasons of League football.

Wednesday's consolation was that the club was at least continuing to move in the right direction. Fourth place in Division Two represented another step forward, and this book, while it might lack the "dream" ending of a return to Division One, could conclude on a positive note nevertheless.

In telling the Wednesday story, I have been conscious that, since the club was last in the First Division in 1970, a generation of youngsters have grown up who cannot remember when the team was in the top grade. For them, perhaps, the value of this book will be that it helps set recent events in a broader context. Older supporters will remember the promise of the early 1960s well enough, and so can appreciate the full implications of the subsequent fall; and they will savour the true significance of a return to the First Division when it comes.

It seems fair to suggest that this history serves as a reminder that much of what is taking place today has happened before: Wednesday's tale extends over a span of around 160 years, and, in that time, there have been alternating periods of success and failure. The club did not make the grade and establish a great tradition without a fight, and all the days of despondency were not in the recent past. *Consilio et Animis* is the Wednesday motto—"by wisdom and courage"—and those qualities have been required in considerable measures to ensure survival, progress and success since the football club kicked off in 1867.

Generally speaking, when one thinks of the achievements of a football club, one thinks of the great players and outstanding individual performances on the field. These men have an important place in the story told in the following pages. But many of the heroes of the story never wore the club's colours or kicked a football in a League match. From John Holmes through to Bert McGee, and Arthur Dickinson to Eric England, they have a place here. One could, by the way, say a good deal about the links between local industry and Sheffield Wednesday, but perhaps it is sufficient here to note that the chairman at the time of the club's move to Owlerton (now Hillsborough) was George Senior, who later became Master Cutler; while the present chairman is a past Master Cutler, as is his fellow director, Stanley Speight. Messrs McGee, Speight and Matt Sheppard are all past Presidents of the Sheffield Chamber of Commerce.

The key figures in the Wednesday story, on and off the field, are featured in the following pages, but, of course, many who have played a part have passed from the scene forgotten, for their achievements were either not placed on record, or the record was subsequently misplaced. We shall never know the names of many who have helped the club along the way. Yet, perhaps we can imagine that they were there in the background as the drama of the years unfolded: making a telling comment at a meeting, or performing some important duty while remaining anonymous.

How interesting it is to consider some of the key moments in the Wednesday saga. With the benefit of hindsight we can see the turning points in the story, but perhaps those who were present at a particular moment were too close to the action to recognize the significance of their decisions. Take, for example, the succession of meetings in the late 1880s when the club's committee discussed the threat of profess-ionalism; and imagine the emotion in Tom Cawley's voice as he made the stirring speech which probably saved Wednesday from extinction. What, one wonders, were the feelings of those responsible for obtaining a lease on the swampy field which became Olive Grove? And how troubled must have been those men who sought so long and patiently for a new home when the club was given notice to quit Olive Grove. The full story of the move to Owlerton can only be imagined from the facts which survive, but we know enough to recognize that it was a brave step. Arthur Dickinson saw Wednesday rise from an amateur club to a famous professional organisation, and, for him, how painful must it have been to see the sudden fall from glory in that traumatic 1919-20 season. Yet someone had the wisdom to bring Bob Brown back to Sheffield; and, though success was not achieved overnight, Brown led Wednesday to some memorable triumphs. In more recent times, modern supporters can remember vividly the triumphs of Derek Dooley, the red-haired centre-forward, and the Harry Catterick years when Wednesday so nearly recaptured the glories of old; the shock of the newspaper revelations of a betting coup in 1964; the golden afternoon in May 1966 when Wednesday went close to winning the FA Cup; the wet and bitter night of 1970 when Wednesday slid to a painful defeat in their final First Division match against Manchester City.

This is a book of memories—some handed down to us by past generations of supporters, others belonging to our own time. We have memories of great players and unforgettable games. Who can but remember the story of Jimmy Seed and the Great Escape of 1928? Of those who were present, none will forget the "robbery" of the 1930 FA Cup semi-final. Remember Ernest Blenkinsop, the finest back ever to wear a Wednesday shirt? And what about Jackie Robinson? "What a player!" say all those who saw him. Who will forget that 5-4 epic against Manchester United, the European champions, in 1968? Few remain now who were present at the famous England-Scotland match at Hillsborough in 1920, but the story of the game is a part of the folklore of the Wednesday ground—as, indeed, is every one of the 28 FA Cup semi-finals staged at the ground. In recent years, perhaps, we remember the way in which Stoke lost a 2-0 lead against Arsenal in 1971, the Londoners saving the day with a last-minute penalty and going on to clinch glory in the form of a League and Cup double.

In the early days, of course, Wednesday were nicknamed "the Blades", while Sheffield United were "the Cutlers". Today United are "the Blades" and Wednesday, following their move to what was *Owl*erton, became "the Owls". How many memories are provoked by the mere mention of derby matches; what famous battles have been witnessed down the years!

In the telling of the Wednesday story, I have tried to place the emphasis on the people involved. True, the club is greater than any one individual, but many people have made a contribution on and off the field, and it is a part of the task of capturing the essence of the club's history to seek to give some indication of the stories of the various individuals: thus, where appropriate, I have sought to give the relevant background on as many as possible.

One benefit of a knowledge of the history of a club is that, in times when fortunes are at a low ebb, one can take heart from recognising that the club has survived troubled times before. The pattern of Wednesday's history lent conviction to the belief, in those dark days between 1970 and 1977, that the tide *would* eventually turn. The decline could not go on indefinitely, and, of course, it didn't. We sometimes fall into the trap of making too much of history and tradition, but, all the same, they have their place and their value—not the least of which is that they inspire a determination in some inheritors to emulate their predecessors and strive for a success which will maintain traditions and add a further proud chapter to the history of a great club.

One of the delights of having been associated with the local professional soccer clubs over the years has been the opportunity to meet and make friends with some remarkable people. Wednesday have provided their share of remarkable people in modern times, and I hope I will be forgiven if I single out one, Eric Taylor, now. When, as a new member of the *Morning Telegraph's* sports department, I was sent to cover a Wednesday away match, I was greeted by the wise-cracking general-manager.

"First time you've been with a big club, Keith?" he asked.

"Oh, no, Mr. Taylor," said I, innocently. "I went with United last week."

"Yes," said Taylor, "this is the first time you've been with a *big* club!"

Eric Taylor's wit reflected his firm conviction that there was only one *big* club in Sheffield, and it served to emphasise the loyalty and faith of the typical Wednesdayite. That loyalty and faith was severely tested in the years which followed, but, thankfully, thousands never lost those qualities and survived the darkest years to see the club turn the tide. Sadly, Eric Taylor did not live to see the revival launched.

To end on a personal note, I must say that my greatest regret is that my wife Kathleen did not live to see Wednesday begin the climb back towards the top. She was one of the staunchest of "true blue" supporters, and, indeed, played a significant part in helping me begin the compilation of club records. She hoped that one day I would write the Wednesday story at length, and perhaps it was because I wanted to do something which could be dedicated to her memory that I finally took up my pen and started writing. She would have been as proud as I am to have been associated with this book, which I hope will bring pleasure to countless Wednesdayites of today and tomorrow.

Keith Farnsworth, 1982

High Greave,
Sheffield.

Part 1
Wednesday: the beginning and before

1 The birth of a football club

It is a matter of historical record that the Sheffield Wednesday Football Club came into being towards the end of the summer of 1867, when a band of cricketers gathered one evening at a special general meeting of the Wednesday Cricket Club at Harry Sampson's Adelphi Hotel and took the momentous decision to form a football section, apparently as a means of keeping members together throughout the long months of winter.

But, of course, the seeds of the story were sown many years before. The roots were buried deep, and the football section which was destined to outlive the cricket club and become a famous name in the world of soccer did not come into being "out of the blue". The step was taken as a result of certain influences and developments which had created the circumstances and conditions in which the formation of a football club was natural and perhaps inevitable. Those responsible for creating the Wednesday Football Club may have been partly motivated by the desire to keep members together between cricket seasons, but the decision was also prompted by other considerations—not least the remarkable increase of interest in, and enthusiasm for, football in the 1860s.

In truth, the real beginning of the Wednesday story can be traced back to 1820, when the Wednesday Cricket Club was formed by six enthusiastic sportsmen. If there had been no cricket club, there may have been no football club of that name; so it is important to take note of the cricketers' story, and this will be done in more detail in the next chapter. Here we are concerned with the football, and it is fair to begin by wondering why it was suddenly decided that a club was needed to keep everyone together from September to April. After all, the Cricket Club had survived an annual shutdown for nearly fifty years, and nobody previously had suggested the need to find some means of bridging the winter gap. Plainly the step was influenced by sporting trends and fashions. It is evident that several members of the Cricket Club had begun to play football with various organisations which were springing up in the town; and perhaps it was inevitable that some of them should believe it would be preferable that Wednesday should have its own football team.

Sheffield has long had a reputation of being the birthplace of *organised* football. At this point it is probably unnecessary to trace the origins of the game in detail, other than to say there was a moment in the middle of the 19th century when the handling code became rugby and went one way, while the so-called hacking code moved in the opposite direction and emerged as soccer. Both football codes had beginnings in the old universities and public schools; and it was a group of ex-students who returned to their home town with a passion for soccer which prompted the birth of Sheffield FC, the oldest football club in the world, in the mid-1850s. The game quickly captured the imagination of local sportsmen, and, by the early 1860s, the town boasted about 15 organised clubs, playing under such names as Hallam, Norfolk, Mackenzie, Milton, Garrick, United Mechanics, and Wellington. Sheffield had its own governing body before the Football Association took responsibility for the national game in 1863; and, indeed, the national body looked to Sheffield for guidance when drawing up its original laws of the game.

It is worthy of note that Sheffield introduced the corner-kick five years before the Football Association recognised its merits; the penalty kick was initiated in the town; and Sheffield was the first place to insist on the use of the crossbar. A Nottingham man, Sam Widdowson, gets credit as being the first man to wear shinguards; but, significantly perhaps, his decision was prompted by the fact that he was due to play in a match involving Sheffield Club—and he had found from experience that Sheffielders took their football seriously and showed scant regard for the legs of opponents!

Sheffield certainly played a major role in the game's development in its pioneering days. The local FA took its responsibilities very seriously, and stuck to its own version of the off-side law until 1877. It led the way in promoting the first inter-city games, the first charity games, and, three years before the famous FA Cup competition was launched in 1871, Sheffield staged knock-out matches, with the first local trophy, the Cromwell Cup, the prize. The old cutlery town boasted the original players' accident fund; and led the way in organising local cup competitions, with the Sheffield Challenge Cup first played for in 1876-7 and the Wharncliffe Charity Cup in 1879. In later years, with the rise of the Football League and the growth of the FA Cup competition, the local knock-out fixtures began to decline in importance, but they were certainly responsible for stimulating the growth of football in the early days.

Before the dramatic rise of football, which grew in popularity at a staggering pace, cricket was the "king" of games in Sheffield, and the sporting meccas of the town were in turn the grounds at Darnall, Hyde Park and Bramall Lane. The Darnall Ground survived from 1824 until 1831; but Hyde Park was in use from 1826 until 1886, when it was acquired by the Hallamshire Rifle Volunteers. However, Bramall Lane, opened in 1854 and the venue for county cricket from 1855 until 1973, quickly became the town's most important sports arena. For many years cricket ruled supreme at Bramall Lane, and, strange though it may seem at a distance of a century and a quarter, the committee responsible for the ground did not take kindly to football. So it was a major breakthrough for supporters of the new winter game when the Lane authorities were persuaded to permit the staging of a football match in 1862. The fixture involved Sheffield Club and Hallam, and the game—which lasted for three hours and yet remained goal-less—was in aid of the Lancashire Distress Fund. Subsequently, Bramall Lane staged most of the local football finals, was chosen for an England-Scotland game, and was to be the venue for an FA Cup final replay and many FA Cup semi-finals. However, all that came about many years after the period during which the seeds were being sown for the birth of a football club called Wednesday.

The point being made is that it was amid an atmosphere of increasing football activity and growing enthusiasm for the game that the Wednesday cricketers first began to consider the advantages of playing football under the same club banner. It is appropriate, too, to note that the town of Sheffield was growing rapidly, and there was plenty of room for another football team. The population was already around 200,000 and still on the increase, with the town's metal industries expanding at an astonishing pace and adding to its fame. Naylor Vickers & Co were in the process of moving from Millsands in the town centre to establish premises in the east end, to be called the River Don Works; and while one steel giant, Mark Firth, was being installed as Master Cutler, he was succeeding another, John Brown, whose services to industry (particularly in regard to his firm's successful experiments in the rolling of armour plate) had been recognised with a knighthood. The big talking point in the summer of 1867 was the Government's decision to appoint a Commission of Inquiry to investigate the Trade Union Outrages which were then a feature of the Sheffield scene. For years non-union men in the town's tool and cutlery industries had walked the streets in fear; but, in July, William Broadhead, secretary of the Saw Grinders' Union, had been exposed as the king-pin in the network which had organised a series of outrages which had involved explosions at houses and factories, and even shootings reminiscent of the Wild West. Sheffield was, indeed, a very tough town.

How appropriate that the historic meeting at which Wednesday formed a football section should be held at the Adelphi Hotel, which stood at the corner of Arundel Street and Sycamore Street (on the site now occupied by the Crucible Theatre) until it was demolished around 1970. This hotel had a unique place in Sheffield's sporting history, for it was here in 1863 that the Yorkshire County Cricket Club was formed; and the landlord, Harry Sampson, was not only one of the great sporting heroes of the period, but a dyed-in-the-wool Wednesday man. Though he stood barely 5ft 4ins tall, he was a giant among cricketers, reputed to be one of the finest batsmen of his time. He had figured in the famous United All-England eleven, and once, in 1841, had achieved fame by defeating the legendary Tom Marsden in a single-wicket match. He also had the distinction of having made the highest individual score ever recorded in a cricket match played on ice—162, for Wednesday against Sheffield Town.

Sampson's views on the introduction of a football section were never recorded, but he was happy to see the historic meeting staged in his hotel on Wednesday September 4 1867. Brewery traveller John Pashley is best remembered as an outstanding local cricketer, and there is no record of his ever having kicked a football; but he had the distinction of being the man who stood up at the meeting to put the proposal "that a football club be formed in connection with the Cricket Club, and that no body of persons shall be empowered to sever the two clubs without the unanimous consent of a general meeting, six days notice to be given to every member of the two clubs." William Littlehales, who had previously played his football with the Mackenzie Club, seconded the motion, which was passed unanimously amid scenes of great enthusiasm. Before the meeting adjourned some sixty members had been enrolled, and they included some of the best footballers in the area.

Ben Chatterton, then aged 37 and a prominent local financial agent destined to enjoy a long spell on the Town Council, was elected the club's first President, with F. S. Chambers made Vice-President. John Marsh took on the duties of football secretary, assisted by W. B. Castleton. The initial committee included John Rodgers, John Pashley, John White, William Littlehales, Charles Stokes, William Fry, William F. Pilch, H. Bocking, T. J. Anderson and a Mr Knowles.

Ben Chatterton lived until 1902, and, therefore, saw the new club grow into a professional organisation with its own headquarters at Olive Grove, and he must have been proud to see Wednesday gain admission to the Football League in 1892 and win the FA Cup in 1896. It is not recorded if Chatterton ever saw the team play at Owlerton and, unfortunately, no evidence survives to indicate when he ceased to be a member of the club's committee. However, his successor as President was Henry Hawksley, a hatter, and one of the most popular figures in local sporting circles. Hawksley was President of both the Cricket and Football clubs from 1870 until his death in 1887—an interesting fact when it is noted that the Football Club's break with the Cricket Club occurred in 1883. The footballers claimed that they were making all the money while the cricketers were principally engaged in spending it: Hawksley was plainly a man respected by all, for he ensured that the split did not generate any ill-feeling. His death at the age of 55 was a sad loss to the club.

Perhaps the most famous of the original officials was John Marsh, the first secretary and the first captain, too; and a player of such outstanding ability that he had the distinction of captaining the Sheffield Association team in the first inter-city match with Glasgow in March 1874. Marsh was a great friend of another committee member, John Rodgers, and had come to Sheffield from his native Thurlstone to serve an apprenticeship as an engraver, the father of Rodgers being his master. Sadly, both Rodgers and Marsh died young, but each made a significant contribution to the Wednesday story—Rodgers as a cricketer, Marsh as a footballer. Marsh remained with Wednesday until the end of the 1873-4 season, when he decided to return to live at Thurlstone. Such was his zest for football, it was not long before he had organised a village team. Unfortunately, in a match in the spring of 1880, he suffered a bad fall in which he broke an arm. Medical science then was not what it is today, for the arm was not re-set properly and became infected. Poor Marsh was in dreadful pain for weeks, and eventually he was persuaded to visit a London specialist. At St Thomas's Hospital, the arm was re-set, and iron pins fixed on it in an effort to straighten what had become a twisted limb. Marsh returned home, but his friends soon recognised that he was a very sick man, and few were surprised when he died a few weeks later. He left a widow and four young children.

When Marsh left Wednesday, his successor as secretary was William Littlehales, an engraver; while William Heaton Stacey, a schoolmaster who had suddenly emerged as an outstanding footballer, took over the captaincy. Littlehales, an astute and popular official, was secretary to both the Cricket and Football clubs for ten years, until ill-health forced him to quit; and he was one of the chief figures on the committee of the Sheffield FA. Stacey played cricket and football, and contributed to both games the intelligence and dignity one might expect from a man destined to become one of the town's youngest headmasters. However, his introduction to the Sheffield Association team came about by accident. He travelled to London to watch the London-Sheffield match in January 1873, and found himself asked to make up the numbers when T. C. Willey failed to arrive on time. His performance earned him immediate recognition as an outstanding player. He was a key figure in the Wednesday side in the first of their local Cup successes.

After the departure of Littlehales, secretarial duties were fulfilled by William Fretwell, John Thompson, George Cropper and James Hoyland at different times. Hoyland, a fair footballer, was also the Yorkshire CCC's official scorer. Jack Hudson, too, had a spell as secretary whilst also captaining the team. However, for three or four years the quality of the club's administration deteriorated, and the lack of system and discipline came to a head when their application for the FA Cup was submitted too late for the 1886-7 season. This led to the appointment of Harry Eyre Pearson, the ex-Yorkshire cricketer, who restored some sense of order to the secretarial duties at a time when Wednesday were in the middle of a crisis caused by circumstances discussed in a later chapter. Here it seems appropriate to note that Pearson subsequently handed the secretary's job to one of the great figures in Wednesday history, Arthur Dickinson.

Having joined the club's committee in 1876, Dickinson was destined to play an important role in the next 50 years. He was probably the first man to merit the nickname "Mister Sheffield Wednesday", and was in the thick of the action when the club moved first to Olive Grove and then to Owlerton. Dickinson was in cutlery, but he often put the football club first in his travels in search of players; and he at least had the satisfaction of seeing Wednesday rise from an obscure amateur club to a leading professional club which won the League Championship four times and the FA Cup twice in his lifetime. But Arthur Dickinson knew some dark days, too, not the least being in the months when Wednesday looked like being homeless after losing Olive Grove, and the season of 1919-20 when so much went wrong at Owlerton.

Another important early figure was John Holmes, a big man in every way. Holmes arrived at the club in 1868, eventually took over the treasurer's duties, and, in the painful year of 1887, succeeded Henry Hawksley as club President—a position he held with flair and distinction until ill-health caused him to step down in 1899. Holmes had around him a number of men whose devotion to the Wednesday cause knew no bounds: people like Walter Fearnehough, Alfred Holmes, Herbert and Arthur Nixon, C. H. Vessey, Herbert Newbould, and Herbert, John and Alfred Muscroft. No doubt much that these men did will never now be known, and, indeed, many others may have made a major contribution without having the benefit of being remembered by posterity.

In the earliest years, it seems unlikely that anyone involved in the club's affairs could have foreseen Wednesday's eventual rise; yet people like Dickinson, Holmes and certain others were, knowingly or otherwise, responsible for taking the decisions which enabled Wednesday not only to survive while other clubs passed into oblivion, but to expand and move with the tide which washed away the old sporting world and created a new one.

The story of the ups and downs experienced in the making of Wednesday since 1867 is the story to be told in this book, but at this point it seems appropriate to devote a little space to the life and times of the now-defunct Cricket Club out of which the Football Club was created.

2 Wednesday Cricket Club, 1820-1924

The Wednesday Cricket Club was founded in 1820, and survived until 1924 when, sadly, it died through lack of support. Perhaps it sank into oblivion because, unlike the Football Club, it failed to move with the times. As older members left and died, they were not replaced; and youngsters of the later period were attracted to those clubs which played in leagues and competed for trophies, which Wednesday did not. In its time the Wednesday Cricket Club had seen its share of keen and even fierce competition, but, for many years, members were content to play friendly games. Eventually, all the remaining members were too old to play, and the end of an era spanning 104 years was acknowledged with regret.

The formal winding up of the club took place in an office at the Sterling Steel Works of E. Pearce & Co. in Rockingham Street. Lance Morley, a member for 45 years, took the chair at the meeting; while Percy Bowker, ex-captain, secretary and treasurer, was the man responsible for completing the formalities necessary to finalise the club's affairs. Bowker reported that the club's outstanding debts, amounting to around £10, had been met, and the only matter requiring a decision was the disposal of the trophies remaining in the club's possession. It was agreed that one of the trophies, the Cromwell Cup, should go to the Football Club; while the other, the Tom Marsden Cup, was to be offered to the City of Sheffield for keeping in the silver collection at the Town Hall.

So, a few days later, the final act in the Cricket Club's story was performed at a brief ceremony which followed the Football League match at Hillsborough between Wednesday and Stockport County. While supporters headed for home, enthusiastically discussing the five-goal feat of Jimmy Trotter, Percy Bowker was making a short speech in the board room, where he handed over the two trophies. Charles Clegg received the Cromwell Cup on behalf of the Football Club—though, in truth, it was theirs by right anyway. They had won it 56 years before in the first knock-out competition for which they had entered; but, after the split of 1883 the Cricket Club had retained it, and, presumably, none of the football officials had thought to ask for it. Alderman A. J. Blanchard, in his capacity as Lord Mayor of Sheffield, received the Tom Marsden Cup, a trophy associated with a man who was probably the greatest cricketer Sheffield produced in the first half of the 19th century. It had been presented to Marsden in 1831 by a group of admirers, and been placed in the club's possession by his family following his untimely death in 1843. For many years it had gone on display at the Cricket Club's annual dinner, and, on these occasions, it had been filled with ale and used for the toasts to The Game, to Wednesday, and, of course, to "Old Tom". How strange to think that, some 50 years later, this very trophy should lie forgotten among the Town Hall's silver collection. In my time as sports editor of *Morning Telegraph* I had the job of helping officials solve the "mystery" of how the Marsden Cup came to be in their keeping. It was an instance which emphasised how easily the greatest names pass into apparent obscurity, and it served to show the merit in recalling the story of the Wednesday Cricket Club for the benefit of the modern reader.

Some sources have suggested that the Cricket Club came into being in 1816, but the same Lance Morley who chaired the club's last meeting in 1924 once put on public record that he had established beyond doubt that the formation date was 1820. In a paper which Morley read to members in 1896 he stated that the six men responsible for founding the club were: William Stratford, John Southren, Tom Lindley, William Henry Woolhouse, George Dawson and George Hardisty. They chose the name "Wednesday" for the simple reason that, as local tradesmen, that was the day when they were free from their duties and could pursue sporting activities.

William Stratford was named as first President, and it is worth noting that the Stratford family were to have long links with the club: indeed, William's son, Henry, was a member for 50 years. Stratford's successor as President was Richard Gillott, who had the distinction of discovering the unique talents of the legendary cricketer, R. G. Barlow. When Gillott learned that Barlow, at that time an employee at Staveley Colliery, was not, as had been thought, a Yorkshireman, he recommended the lad to Lancashire—and, of course, Barlow achieved great fame with the Red Rose county.

Early secretaries at the club included John Tasker, famed as the pioneer of the telephone and the use of electricity in Sheffield—indeed, he was behind the first floodlit football match in 1878, as is discussed later; George Skinner; T. J. Anderson; Harry E. Pearson; journalist J. H. Stainton; and Percy Bowker, who did the job for 16 years before handing over to Charles Ellis.

Of the six founder members, perhaps the most notable was William Henry Woolhouse, who has been described as "the father of Sheffield cricket". Woolhouse and his father-in-law, George Steer, were the men behind the building of the "new" Darnall Cricket Ground in 1824; and from 1825 he was solely responsible for its management. At one time the ground had a seating capacity of around 8,000, and it was the venue for the England versus a combined Yorkshire, Notts & Leicester XI match in 1828. Woolhouse later became proprietor of the Hyde Park Ground, and, as a very useful left-handed batsman and bowler, played there in Yorkshire's first match, against Norfolk, in 1833. Sadly, Woolhouse lived for only four more years after this memorable occasion. After suffering a bad fall in 1837, he developed a serious spinal complaint and went to London in search of a cure. At the end of a long day spent chasing around the capital, he was still without a cure and suffered the additional disappointment of missing the carriage on which he had booked his journey home. He took a room at the Cross Keys Hotel. During the night he fell ill and died; and was subsequently buried in an unmarked grave in All Hallowes Churchyard, Lombart Street.

Woolhouse may be forgotten now, but he made an important contribution to the Wednesday story because it was at his Darnall Ground, and later at Hyde Park, that the club played its home matches. The Hyde Park Ground, incidentally, cost about £4,000 to build, and it extended over something like five-and-a-half acres. On the busiest days the ground could accommodate ten matches at one time: which perhaps indicates the enthusiasm and support cricket enjoyed in the 1830s. After Hyde Park was allowed to deteriorate in the post-Woolhouse era, Wednesday had a wicket at Bramall Lane from 1856 until 1893, and between 1896 and 1899. Later they used Owlerton—staging their home games there in June and July, and playing away games in May and August in order to avoid creating any problems for the Football Club.

Wednesday Cricket Club boasted many famous players over the years, and it is worthy of note that a leading local industrialist, Thomas Jessop, and Michael Ellison, agent to the Duke of Norfolk, were among the prominent members. Ellison was the man behind the founding of the "official" Yorkshire County Cricket Club in 1863, and the driving force behind the building of the Bramall Lane ground nine years earlier, in 1854. Among the Wednesday players of note were Tom Armitage, a robust batsman who toured Australia with Lilleywhite's team in 1876; William Slinn, the famous Yorkshire fast bowler; Tom Hunt, dubbed "the Star of the North" because of his great prowess with bat and ball; George Pinder, the Yorkshire wicketkeeper who also bowled a bit (often with his pads on!); and George Ulyett, who arrived on the scene in the 1870s and became one of the greatest "characters" in the history of Yorkshire cricket (and a fair goalkeeper, too). Of course, the game abounded with "characters" in the early days. One often mentioned was Reubin Hallam, who was said to have 39 trades, ranging from poet to professional cricketer, and Shakespearian actor to farm labourer. He earned local fame as the author of "Wadsley Jack", but he has a place in the story of Wednesday. Others worthy of mention include John Berry, the club's professional from 1851 to 1861; and Jimmy Dearman, who excelled at the single-wicket game.

George Dawson, one of the Wednesday men who played for Yorkshire in the famous match with Norfolk in 1833, was at the centre of a couple of controversial incidents in games with Nottingham. In one match in 1829 he disputed a run-out decision given against him, and the Nottingham team threatened to walk off if the Wednesday man refused to accept the umpire's ruling. It took some time to settle the problem, and the entry in the Wednesday scorebook made it clear how the Sheffielders felt about the business: alongside Dawson's name the scorer had written "cheated out"! In a later match with Nottingham, Wednesday lost by nine wickets, and the scorer noted: "A most disgraceful match. The Nottingham umpire kept calling 'no ball' whenever a straight one was bowled, and the Sheffielders were foolish for continuing the game when they perceived an unfair advantage was being taken."

In the light of the problems subsequently posed by the introduction of professionalism into football, it is interesting to note that up to around the end of the 1860s cricket clubs often played for money, which took preference over the mere love of the game. This was achieved in a number of ways. There were, for instance, handicap matches before which each club subscribed a certain sum into a pool; and a handicap committee decided how many men each team should be permitted to play. This usually meant that eleven leading players might face twelve or more lesser players, depending on the handicaps decreed by the committee. There were also sweepstake matches, half a dozen or so clubs putting down sums varying from £10 to £25, and then playing knock-out games, with the finalists sharing the cash. Finally, there were challenge matches, which took various forms, but usually had around £50 at stake; and these were not confined to team fixtures but often pitted one individual against another.

This was the age of single-wicket cricket; and at the time Wednesday had in their ranks the North's single-wicket champion, the legendary Tom Marsden. A great hero in Sheffield, Marsden was for some years virtually unbeatable. In 1828 he put up a £50 challenge to take on all-comers from anywhere in England, but for five years no one stepped forward to face him. Marsden's misfortune was that his life of high living and hard drinking took its toll, and by 1833, when Fuller Pilch, the champion of the South, finally took up the challenge, the Sheffield man was in decline. Pilch defeated Marsden at Norwich, and a crowd of 20,000 packed into the Darnall Ground to witness the return match. Alas, the Sheffield hero was beaten by 127 runs. Marsden remained the northern champion, however, but in 1841 little Harry Sampson defeated him by an innings and 50 runs. Marsden did not live long after that.

The greatest moment in Marsden's career came at Darnall in 1826. Batting for Sheffield & Leicester against Nottingham, he scored 227 runs and claimed six wickets to help his side to victory by an innings and 203 runs. He batted for three days, and if his double century does not seem especially impressive to the modern reader, it has to be noted that wickets then were rougher, and Marsden was only the third man to achieve the feat anywhere in England—and he was the first Yorkshireman to do it. It was as a result of this feat that Marsden's admirers presented him with the trophy mentioned earlier. The Cup was inscribed: "Presented to Thomas Marsden on 11th May 1831 by the friends and admirers of cricket in token of their estimation of his undeviating integrity in all public matches; of his first-rate talent in every department of the game; of his unwearied diligence and undaunted resolution in the field; and as a trophy of the distinguished success which has attended his exertions in that noble and manly exercise."

A small silver ball on the lid of the trophy bears the figure 227—the number of runs he scored in an epic innings which included only two boundaries. On one occasion, however, Marsden hit the ball over a 45-foot wall and it travelled 130 yards before it hit the ground. The Sheffield crowd took the 21 year-old left-hander to their hearts, and his feat prompted a local poet to compose a 13-stanza verse which included the following lines:

> Then Marsden went in in his glory and pride,
> And the arts of the Nottingham players defied.
> Oh, Marsden at cricket is nature's perfection,
> For hitting the ball in any direction;
> He ne'er fears his wicket, so safely he strikes,
> And he does with the bat and ball as he likes.

The poem concluded with these lines:

> Then homewards I trudged to our country folks,
> To tell 'em a few of the cricketing jokes;
> But that joke of Tom Marsden's will ne'er be forgot,
> When two hundred and twenty-seven notches he got.

Writers from the south frequently argued that Marsden reserved his best play for the occasions when he was playing before his home crowd, and suspected that he was over-rated by his supporters. There may have been some truth in this, but the real tragedy was that Marsden achieved his greatest fame and success before he was 25 years old, and thereafter was a victim of his own reputation. Fame was perhaps too great a burden, for he appears to have lacked the discipline to cope in his later years. Once he began to slip, he seems to have gone downhill very rapidly. He was only 38 when he died.

The period from 1820 up to the end of the 19th century provided a succession of notable Wednesday cricketers, and it is interesting to note that, on the whole, many of the more successful players did not seem to be blessed with good health. It is surprising how many of them died relatively young. Besides Woolhouse and Marsden, there was John Pashley, Harry Pearson, Henry Hawksley and W. H. Stacey, to name but a few. Yet each man in his way made a significant contribution to the club's story, and the survival of the cricket club paved the way for the introduction of football.

However, the Cricket and Football clubs remained in partnership only 16 years. Then the footballers elected to go their own way. In the event, it was probably as well that the decision came when it did, for the Football Club needed the benefits of independence to be able to face up to the challenge of professionalism. Certainly, the footballers could no longer afford to subsidise the cricketers, as it appears they had been doing. Yet the parting of the ways was tinged with sadness, and it was widely acknowledged that the now-thriving Football Club owed a debt of gratitude to the players of the summer game.

3 Early football days

Though the Wednesday Football Club came into being in the first week of September 1867, the first fixture was not completed until the last day of the following December—nearly four months later. This seems a little surprising, but one can only presume that the intervening period was taken up with the question of negotiating for a ground, arranging practice or trial matches, and, perhaps, waiting for the right moment to embark upon the adventure of a competitive game. No doubt there were good reasons for the delay, though no evidence has been handed down to help provide a full and authentic explanation. We do know, however, that one of the first decisions made by the committee was that they would adopt blue-and-white as the club's colours.

Wednesday's first recorded match was played at Dronfield on Tuesday December 31 1867, their opponents the newly-formed Dronfield FC, who persuaded a local farmer called Samuel Baggaley to let them use one of his fields. The names of the men who participated in this historic game were never recorded, but one can probably assume that John Marsh was the captain, and that a couple of wagonettes were hired to take the players and officials to the Derbyshire village a few miles beyond the southern boundaries of the town.

How difficult it is, at a distance of nearly 120 years, to imagine the scene at Dronfield on that chilly December afternoon. For a start, there were no dressing rooms, and the players changed under a hedge, probably piling their clothes and any valuables into one of the wagonettes, and leaving them in the care of a committee man. Not that there was a great deal of changing to be done. Jackets and waistcoats were removed, and workaday shirts were exchanged for the new blue-and-white jerseys. The men played in their ordinary trousers—perhaps tucking the bottoms into their stockings—and their working boots or clogs were considered good enough for chasing about a muddy field in. Some of the men declined to remove their caps—and, as the day was rather cold, one or two probably insisted on wearing mufflers around their necks!

And it was not only the players' attire which would have seemed novel to the modern observer. The goals would have been the first strange sight to greet the eye. In those days the goalposts were four yards apart and had a bar across them nine feet from the ground. But that wasn't all. At each side of the goal-posts was another goal, four yards apart and nine feet high. So the entire structure stood 12 yards wide and nine feet high. If the ball was shot between the central posts it counted as a goal, if it went between the posts on either side then it was counted as a "rouge". One goal was worth any number of "rouges". This system of counting "rouges" was discontinued in 1868, but, in the first match Wednesday ever played, Dronfield scored four "rouges"—all coming in the second half. However, Wednesday won, for they managed to get a goal after only ten minutes.

The tactics adopted in this and other early games may seen quaint and unsophisticated when compared with football as it is known in the later years of the twentieth century; but, of course, these Victorian pioneers were in deadly earnest and played football in the only way they knew how. Virtually every player on the pitch followed the ball wherever it went, the exceptions being the goalkeeper and two forwards. One of the forwards would stand close to the opposing goalkeeper, ready to give him a not-so-gentle push whenever the ball came near; while the other one laid in wait to pounce on the loose ball and kick it in between the posts. More often than not, the arrival of the ball in the goalmouth created a mighty scramble involving 17 or 18 players, and only the fittest survived a series of such melees.

The first ground used by Wednesday was the High Field, close to the junction of London Road and Abbeydale Road, on the site of the Highfield Library of today. Later they hired a field off Myrtle Road, Heeley, and had a spell at Hunters Bar. More important games were staged at Sheaf House or Bramall Lane.

Wednesday's first season, though it did not officially begin until the last day of 1867, proved very successful, for, within less than two months, they had won their first trophy—the Cromwell Cup. The man responsible for putting up this trophy for competition was Oliver Cromwell, the actor-manager based at the Theatre Royal, which stood on the site later occupied by the Crucible Theatre. Mr Cromwell limited entry to the competition to clubs which had been in existence less than two years; and four teams—Wednesday, Garrick, Exchange and Wellington—participated. Wednesday defeated Exchange 4-0 at the Mackenzie Ground in early February 1868; and week later Garrick, who borrowed seven players from Heeley, narrowly beat Wellington. The final was fixed for Saturday February 15 at Bramall Lane.

The Garrick Club had headquarters at the Garrick Hotel, which stood in Sycamore Street, just around the corner from the Adelphi. It was a popular place with local and visiting theatricals, and Mr Cromwell was one of the leading supporters of the Garrick football team. He was keen to see his favourites excel in the final.

Garrick had the advantage of a strong wind behind them in the first half, and they went desperately close to scoring soon after the kick-off.

The ball was punted hard in the direction of the Wednesday goal, and the goalkeeper, declining to stoop and save the effort, took an almighty swipe at the ball with his foot. . . . and missed! The ball rattled against an inner post, and Garrick supporters in the crowd of about 400 groaned with disappointment. At the end of normal time the match was still goal-less, so it was agreed that play would continue until someone broke the deadlock, the first team to score being adjudged the winners. Extra time had been in progress about ten minutes when, attempting to clear his lines, a Garrick defender put the ball high into the air; and, as it dropped, it caught someone on the shoulder and was deflected past the Garrick goalkeeper. Wednesday had won!

The Cromwell Cup was presented to Wednesday captain John Marsh by the donor on the latter's benefit night at the Theatre Royal on March 16 1868. Contemporary reports noted that there was only a modest attendance at the theatre until shortly before nine o'clock when the Wednesday players went on stage in football dress to receive the trophy, which Mr Cromwell described as "smaller than I would have liked to have given, but it means a lot." After a few words from him, it was the turn of John Marsh to speak; but, according to the reporter from the *Sheffield Daily Independent,* the Wednesday captain "was obviously much more at home on the football field than on the stage making a speech." The ceremony over, Marsh and his colleagues quickly left the theatre and adjourned to the Adelphi Hotel, where Harry Sampson kept his promise to fill the cup with champagne.

Here it seems appropriate to refer to the inter-city fixtures which became a popular feature of the local football scene in the game's early years. As has been mentioned, the first inter-city match was between London and Sheffield at Battersea Park in March 1866. Subsequently, Sheffield staged regular fixtures with teams from London, Notts, Birmingham, Lancashire, Staffordshire, Bucks & Berks, etc; but the annual fixture which became the most popular (and which survived the longest) was that with Glasgow.

The first Sheffield-Glasgow match was played at Bramall Lane on March 14 1874 and ended in a 2-2 draw—a result which was regarded with great satisfaction by home supporters, for nine of the Glasgow team had represented Scotland in a defeat of England shortly before. The Sheffield team was captained by John Marsh, and included such well-known local players as Charles Clegg, Jack Housley, Henry Dixon, W. H. Stacey, Bob Gregory, Jack Hunter, Tom Buttery, Harry Wilkinson, W. H. Carr and J. R. B. Owen. Players of both sides had a meal together after the match, and, according to reports in the local Press, the Glaswegians were "not only good footballers, but good singers, too." Certainly Glasgow always lined up a powerful team, for Sheffield won only one of the first 17 games. Glasgow won 9-1 in 1885 and 10-3 in 1887. Sheffield's best win in the first 20 years of the fixture was a 7-2 triumph at Olive Grove in 1893. Between 1874 and 1938 the game was played on an annual basis, except for a break between 1915 and 1919. After the Second World War the fixture was revived briefly between 1949 and 1957.

The Sheffield-Glasgow fixture was important to local clubs in that it gave them sight of some "star" players from north of the border, and the 1876 meeting was significant for Wednesday because it brought a Scottish international forward called James J. Lang to their attention. Lang was *not* the first Scot to play in England (his friend, Peter Andrews, who joined Heeley, had that distinction) but he *was* the first to leave Scotland specifically for the purpose of playing football. After helping Glasgow beat Sheffield 2-0 at Bramall Lane in February 1876, Lang returned home. A month later he played for Scotland against Wales; and then, in April, he was in the Clydesdale team that played a match against Wednesday. He made such an impression on the officials from Sheffield that they invited him to move to Yorkshire, and, in effect, become Wednesday's first professional. He agreed, and made his first appearance for the club in a match at Myrtle Road in the following October. Strictly speaking, of course, he was not a paid player: Walter Fearnehough gave him a job in his Garden Street knife-making works, but Lang did not have any formal duties. It is said that he spent most of his time reading newspapers!

Lang quickly established himself as a local hero, but it was many years later before it was revealed that he had played all his football in Sheffield with only one eye! Only when he was an old man of more than seventy did Lang disclose the secret of the handicap nobody had known about fifty years earlier. Apparently he had lost the sight in his left eye in an accident in 1869 at the Clydebank Shipyard of John Brown & Co. To the end of his life he remained on the Government list as officially "blind", but opponents were never able to take advantage because they never guessed—and even his colleagues and close friends were never told.

Inter-city games were not the only important fixtures which assisted in the development of football in Sheffield in the early days. The Royal Engineers, who played in the first FA Cup final in 1872 and the finals of 1874, 1875 (when they won the trophy) and 1878, were perhaps the best team in the country at the time. As one might expect from a team with a military background, they studied football with all the precision and concern for tactical formations that they normally gave to battle exercises; and they quickly came to the conclusion that the best way of playing football to win was by adopting the combination game, by developing the art of passing and ensuring that players ran into position to be available to accept a pass from the man in possession. In the 1873-74 season the Engineers arranged a tour of the North and Midlands. On Saturday December 20 1873 they played Sheffield at Bramall Lane, and such was their superiority that they won 4-0—the first defeat the Sheffield Association had suffered at home. The Engineers, by the way, were led that day by Major Francis Marindin, subsequently President of the Football Association and one of the great names of English football in its early days. He was in opposition to Charles Clegg on the occasion of his first visit to Sheffield, but, of course, they were destined to become great friends. Major Marindin, incidentally, was the man who refereed the first semi-final in which Wednesday played in the FA Cup in 1882, and he also took charge of the 1890 FA Cup final in which Wednesday were defeated by Blackburn Rovers.

4 The Clegg brothers

No Wednesday history would be complete without special reference to Sir Charles and Sir William Clegg. Two of the most famous and influential men of their times, they were connected with the club for more than 60 years. Charles, who was two years older than his brother, earned national fame as Chairman, and later President and Chairman, of the Football Association; being dubbed "the Napoleon of Football". William became known as "the uncrowned king of Sheffield", being leader of the City Council for many years, and Lord Mayor in 1898. It was said that the making of William was his election as chairman of the Tramways and Education committees at a vital stage in the history of Sheffield Corporation, and he was knighted in 1906. When Charles was rewarded with a knighthood in 1927, it was officially stated that it was for his services to the Board of Trade; but the honour was widely regarded as recognition for his outstanding contribution to football. Charles had the distinction of holding office as Chairman and President of both Wednesday and Sheffield United—indeed, he was one of United's founders; and he was President of the Sheffield & Hallamshire FA from 1886 until his death in 1937 at the age of 87. William was a Wednesday director from 1899 until his death in 1932, and a vice-president of the Sheffield & Hallamshire FA; and if his civic duties restricted his sporting activities in later years, he was a great supporter of the causes for which his brother worked in football—and Charles had reason to be grateful for William's loyalty and backing on a number of occasions, including the fight to avert a national strike by the Players' Union in 1909.

Charles and William were the sons of a remarkable Sheffield product, Alderman William Johnson Clegg, who had the distinction of being three times Mayor and a leading figure in the struggle to raise Sheffield's status to that of a city. W. J. Clegg came to the fore following the Sheffield Flood in 1864, when he decided to study law despite having to support a wife and six children. He achieved his goal quickly and soon established himself as one of the town's most prominent men. Perhaps it was inevitable that Charles and William should also study law and join the family practice, and it was largely through the influence and example of their father that they became militant teetotallers and non-smokers. They were, too, men of deep religious conviction, and Charles probably epitomised the Clegg philosophy with his frequently quoted adage: "nobody ever gets lost on a straight road." As a football administrator Charles fought hard and long against the introduction of professionalism, and he had a great fear that the game might be destroyed by gamblers and anyone else wishing to exploit football for financial gain. He believed that the responsibility for running the game should remain in the hands of amateurs dedicated to the principle of ensuring that football remained pure and untarnished. He argued that everything connected with administering the game should be above board, and that justice

1. Sir Charles Clegg.

should not only be done but be seen to be done. At one meeting during his 51 years on the FA Council, he said: "Let us never do anything that we cannot justify, if need be, in a court of law. We are the guardians of the game, but our zeal as trustees must not over-ride our sense of justice and our responsibility to the public. We must always do our duty without fear or favour, and retain the confidence of the people."

Yet neither Charles nor William lacked a sense of humour, and Charles often surprised youngsters appearing before him at local disciplinary meetings because he was much more broad-minded than they had expected. The Cleggs, of course, had experienced football "in the raw" in its earliest days, and they knew it was essentially a rugged, physical game likely to provoke strong emotions and crude language on and off the field. They had played in the days when facilities were few and footballers had to "rough it".

They both had a natural flair for football, playing with several clubs—including Perseverance, Broomhall, Albion and Sheffield Club— as well as Wednesday, for whom they first appeared around 1870. Both were blessed with speed, skill and enthusiasm—Charles, in fact, was an outstanding runner and won dozens of prizes on the track in such events as the 100 yards sprint and the quarter-mile. They were soon figuring in every important match played by Wednesday, and became automatic choices for the Sheffield Association in inter-city matches. They also played for England, though not at the same time. Charles had the distinction of playing in the first official international fixture with Scotland in 1872, while William was selected for the return match a year later. In 1879 William was chosen to play for England against Wales at Kennington Oval, an occasion he remembered for the rest of his life because it coincided with his appointment as defence lawyer for the notorious Charles Peace, who was on trial for the Banner Cross murder in Sheffield. In fact, William worked so late on preparations for the case on the eve of the international that he was unable to travel to London until the morning of the game. He was delayed by snow on the journey and did not take the field until the match had been in progress for 20 minutes. On his return to Sheffield he defended Peace, but his client was found guilty and sentenced to death.

An injury ended William's playing days, and when he and Charles hung up their boots both took up refereeing. For many years there were few important games played in Sheffield at which one of them was not on duty; and Charles officiated at many matches up and down the country, including internationals and two FA Cup finals. If one or other of these men could have been persuaded to write his autobiography, it would have provided a remarkable insight into football over a span of 50 or 60 years.

William's world became increasingly dominated by municipal affairs, but Charles emerged as a major figure in football. The turning point for Charles probably came in the mid-1880s, when he played a prominent role in persuading the separate Sheffield and Hallamshire associations to amalgamate and form one united body. He took the chair at the crucial meeting at the Albert Hall in September 1886, and, as head of the new association, he had a place on the FA Council. Within four years he was installed as FA Chairman, a position he held for 47 years; and, following the death of Lord Kinnaird in 1923, he was also FA President. Locally, the Clegg brothers, especially Charles, were giants, awe-inspiring figures; and they held a special place in the affections of the football people of Sheffield.

It is, perhaps, appropriate here to refer to one of the historic local games in which the Clegg brothers played—the famous floodlit match staged at Bramall Lane on the evening of Monday October 14 1878.

John Tasker, famed as the pioneer of the telephone in Sheffield and familiar as a secretary of the Wednesday Cricket Club, was the man behind this memorable event. He was having quite a battle persuading local businessmen that electricity was the coming method of providing lighting, and they declined his invitation to experiment with electric light in their works. So he came up with the notion of staging a football match at night, played with the aid of artificial light. He arranged for 22 of Sheffield's best players to participate, and, with Charles and William Clegg captaining the teams, the line-up was:

Reds—F. Stacey, J. Housley, J. Hunter, E. Buttery, F. Hinde, J. C. Clegg, W. Mosforth, A. Woodcock, C. Stratford, H. Barber, G. Anthony.

Blues—T. Lawson, W. E. Clegg, R. Gregory, T. Buttery, W. H. Stacey, G. B. Marples, A. Malpas, J. Tomlinson, F. Barber, T. Bishop, P. Paterson.

The *Sheffield Daily Telegraph* reported: "On the ground were erected wooden stagings, on top of which were placed 'points' from which the light was flashed across the field. These 'points' resembled railway semaphores, and during the evening were powered from them a steady stream of radiance—a soft, blue, clear light—under which the teams could not only see to play, but spectators could distinctly follow the match; so far as it was not obscured by the dense mass of people who seized every vantage ground from which to command a good view of the game. Behind each goal was placed an engine (of 8-horse nominal power); each engine drove two of Messrs Siemen Brothers dynamo apparatus––one machine for each light. There the electricity was generated and transmitted to the 'points' from which gleamed four broad belts of light."

The game, which the Blues won 2-0, attracted 12,000 paying spectators (receipts £300), but thousands of people climbed the walls and got in free, and the actual attendance was probably around 20,000. In truth, the floodlights they saw were far from being the sophisticated fittings introduced as standard 80 years later; and the quality of the lighting was not really very good. However, it was one of those occasions full of novelty and recognised as making a bit of social and sporting history; and a number of Wednesday men were involved. The Clegg brothers and their colleagues were not to see floodlit football become an accepted practice in their lifetime; but they at least helped John Tasker prove a point and gain the recognition which subsequently led to the widespread introduction of the electric light in the town.

5 Early cup exploits

Wednesday, having won the Cromwell Cup in the club's first season in existence, had to wait nine years before they captured another trophy, simply because there were no local competitions offering such a prize. However, football in the town was given a tremendous boost in 1876-7 when the Sheffield Association Challenge Cup was introduced; and the Wharncliffe Charity Cup arrived on the scene three years later. Wednesday had the distinction of being the first winners of both competitions, and they won one trophy or the other eleven times between 1877 and 1888.

At a distance of more than a century it is difficult to imagine the interest and enthusiasm generated by these two knock-out competitions. But, of course, none of the local teams was involved in the national FA Cup at the time, and there were no leagues. The finals of both the Sheffield Challenge Cup and the Wharncliffe Charity Cup attracted large crowds to Sheaf House or Bramall Lane, and rivalry was intense on and off the field. In later years the growth of the game and the widening of competitive horizons caused these once-prominent local competitions to lose their early importance; but it is fair to say that they made a significant contribution to the rise of the game in Sheffield.

Early in 1876 the Sheffield FA offered a prize of £5 to the students of the local School of Art for the best original design for a Challenge Cup. F. Fidler emerged the winner, and the 72-ounce trophy, valued at £50, was made by Martin Hall & Co, the Sheffield silversmiths who had five years earlier made the original FA Cup.

Wednesday beat Parkwood Springs, Kimberworth, Attercliffe and Exchange on the way to the final, where their opponents were their arch-rivals Heeley. The match, played at Bramall Lane on Saturday March 10 1877, proved to be one of the most exciting seen in Sheffield up to that time. About 8,000 spectators saw Heeley establish a three-goal lead before half-time; but in the second half Wednesday hit back. Tom and Frank Butler each got a goal, and then, amid scenes of great excitement, William Clegg snatched the equaliser. The game went into extra time, and Bill Skinner made the score 4-3 in Wednesday's favour with a goal in the closing stages. Incidentally, there were twelve players on each side in this match, a fact not then considered unusual: indeed, a year or so earlier, Wednesday and Heeley had played a 14-a-side match. A memorable final completed, players and officials retired to the Imperial Hotel in Castle Street, where Sheffield FA President, J. C. Shaw, took the chair at a celebration dinner. The teams in this first local Challenge Cup final read as follows:

Wednesday—F. Stacey, W. H. Stacey, E. Buttery, W. E. Clegg, T. Butler, H. Muscroft, J. Bingley, F. M. Butler, T. Bishop, W. E. Skinner, J. J. Lang, J. C. Clegg.

Heeley—W. Beard, T. A. Tomlinson, P. Andrews, Joe Deans, R. Martin, Joe Tomlinson, F. Brownhill, T. Leslie, J. Hunter, J. Thorpe, H. M. Barrington, J. Lindley.

Wednesday won the Sheffield Challenge Cup six times between 1877 and 1888. In 1878 they defeated Attercliffe 2-0 in the final; and they achieved notable victories over Lockwood Brothers and Sheffield Collegiate in 1883 and 1887. They chalked up their biggest victory in the 1881 final when they crushed Ecclesfield, the competition's giant-killers, 8-1. In this match Jack Hulley gave the outsiders an early lead, but Bob Gregory, one of the best players of his day, hit five goals, Mosforth got two, and Bingley the other as Wednesday turned on the style. Wednesday's team included Jack Hudson and J. J. Lang, and it is interesting to note that the Ecclesfield side included some still-familiar village names besides Hulley: the Cutts brothers, Gregory, Turton, etc. One of their forwards, incidentally, was W. H. England, who had also figured in Wednesday's colours.

In 1879 the Wharncliffe Charity Cup was put up for competition, but the fact that the first game was arranged within two days of the Earl handing the trophy to the Sheffield FA caused some alarm. The match involved Wednesday and Attercliffe, but, on the appointed day, Attercliffe could not raise a team. They felt themselves harshly treated when they were told they had forfeited the tie, and Wednesday were accused of "having friends at court". By coincidence, the first final of the new competition was a repeat of the first Challenge Cup final, with Wednesday and Heeley meeting at Bramall Lane in another exciting clash. Woodcock put Wednesday ahead after only three minutes, but Sorby soon grabbed an equaliser. Then further goals by Woodcock, one each side of the interval, gave Wednesday a 3-1 advantage. Heeley reduced arrears shortly before the end, but Wednesday held out despite facing intense pressure in the closing minutes. The line-up read:

Wednesday— F. Stacey, E. Buttery, W. H. Stacey, T. Buttery, C. L. Stratford, A. Woodcock, G. Anthony, T. Bishop, J. Bingley, W. E. Clegg, J. C. Clegg.

Heeley— H. N. Moss, J. Hunter, T. A. Tomlinson, H. Barber, R. Barringham, S. Scaife, T. A. Sorby, J. Wild, P. Andrews, J. Tomlinson, W. Moss.

Wednesday won the Wharncliffe Charity Cup four more times in the next nine seasons, playing in six finals in that period. In 1880, the second year of the competition, they lost to Heeley in the final at Sheaf House.

In 1881 Wednesday reached the semi-final and defeated Heeley 7-2; but, as a result of difficulties arising from the Sheffield Association's decision to ban players who had appeared in the Zulu novelty matches (discussed later), the final was never played. When they faced Wednesday, Heeley had been deprived of two players, Hunter and Moss, because of the local FA's ruling. They subsequently protested, and, after a formal apology from the players involved, the Association reinstated Heeley to the competition. It was arranged that Heeley would play Exchange, with the winners meeting Wednesday in the final. Exchange, however, refused to agree to the arrangement, and the trophy was withdrawn. In the event, Wednesday and Exchange staged a friendly at Sheaf House, but the large crowd found the match a pale imitation of what it might have been had a trophy been at stake. Exchange won 2-0.

There was more trouble in the Wharncliffe competition in the following season, 1881-2, when spectators at Bramall Lane on October 22 saw two matches for the price of one—and were given a major sensation into the bargain. In the first game Heeley disposed of White Star comfortably, but it was the second match which produced the fireworks, and the teams involved were Staveley and Wednesday. Within a minute of referee William Clegg starting the game, Marples put the Derbyshire side in front. Soon afterwards Bayley shot an equaliser, and Mr Clegg rejected appeals that the Wednesday man had scored from an off-side position. Without hesitation, eight of the Staveley players walked off, and the abandoned game was awarded to Wednesday. The final brought Wednesday and Heeley together yet again, and Wednesday chalked up a comfortable 5-0 win, with Cawley getting a hat-trick, and the other goals coming from Gregory and Hibbert.

In 1883 Wednesday did the "double" in capturing both Sheffield trophies. In the Sheffield Challenge Cup final goals by Newbould and Mosforth clinched a 2-1 win over Lockwood Brothers; while an own-goal, another scrambled in a scrimmage, and two in the second-half from Hudson and Gregory, helped Wednesday beat Pye Bank 4-0 to lift the

Wharncliffe Charity Cup. Incidentally, Pye Bank's best player in this match was Billy Betts, and soon afterwards he joined Wednesday to begin a long and successful spell with the club.

In those days Wednesday played regular friendly matches with some of the country's leading teams, but these matches seldom attracted the crowds in the way the local cup-ties did. As early as February 1878 Wednesday entertained Glasgow Rangers at Bramall Lane, losing 1-2; and in October 1880 Queen's Park, hailed as "the champion club of Britain", gave their Sheffield hosts a lesson in the game's finer points, winning 5-0: but, in each instance, the attendance was disappointing. It was in January 1880 that another Scottish team, Vale of Leven, faced Wednesday; and, early in the game, William Clegg fell heavily and broke an arm. H. N. Moss was allowed to take Clegg's place—the first recorded instance of a substitute being used.

It was in the season of 1880-1 that Wednesday first entered the FA Cup competition. In the first round they were drawn to visit Queen's Park, but for some reason the Scots withdrew. A few years later, Queen's Park played in two FA Cup finals, but they were dogged by financial problems, and this may explain their withdrawal in 1880; though, in this instance, travelling expenses could not have been the reason for their decision. Perhaps they could not guarantee to cover Wednesday's expenses, though it is possible that their withdrawal was because they had expected to be exempted until a later stage of the competition. Anyway, Wednesday were given a bye, and the Sheffielders had their first taste of FA Cup action when they visited Blackburn Rovers in the second round on Saturday December 18 1880. Christmas came early for Wednesday, who astonished their hosts by skating to a 4-0 victory on an icy pitch which made life difficult for the players. Wednesday's players adapted to the conditions better, and, after an even and goal-less first half, they began to get on top. Five minutes after the change of ends, Bob Gregory shot the visitors into the lead, and the same man quickly made it 2-0 following a brilliant dribble half the length of the field. Gregory finished with a hat-trick, Winterbottom getting the other goal. Jack Hunter was outstanding for Wednesday, and his performance impressed officials of Blackburn Olympic, who were at the match. Incidentally, Olympic had been KO'd in the first-round by Sheffield Club, who had won an exciting match at Bramall Lane by five goals to four; but while Wednesday were defeating Blackburn Rovers, Sheffield Club were losing heavily at Darwen.

Wednesday's team in the club's first FA Cup tie was: W. H. Stacey, T. Buttery, E. Buttery, Hunter, Hudson, Malpas, Winterbottom, Lang, Gregory, Mosforth, Newbould.

The third round took Wednesday back to Lancashire, and goals by Rhodes and Gregory gave them a 2-0 win at Turton (near Bolton). Unfortunately, having touched the peak of success, they then crashed heavily at Darwen. The Darwen forwards put five goals past Wednesday's custodian, William Stacey, who was said to have been blinded by snowflakes every time the Lancastrians shot at his goal!

Wednesday did rather better in their second campaign in the FA Cup, for they went all the way to the semi-finals. Indeed, they went within a whisker of clinching a place in the final against Old Etonians.

In the first round they defeated Providence 2-0 in a game played on Quibell's field, near Hyde Park. Cawley got the first goal, but it was the second, credited to Anthony, which provided the big talking point. Anthony did not, in fact, put the ball between the posts: a defender struck out a hand and stopped his shot on its way in. The referee, William Clegg, immediately awarded a goal instead of a penalty. This came about because 1881-2 was the only campaign in which the FA allowed referees to use their discretion in such instances. The experiment created widespread controversy, and was soon dropped.

In the second round Wednesday required three games to dispose of Staveley. After two draws (0-0 and 2-2), Rhodes became the first Wednesday man to register four goals in an FA Cup tie, and a 5-2 triumph gave Wednesday another local derby, against Heeley, in the third round. Heeley had just previously defeated Wednesday in a Wharncliffe Charity Cup tie, but on this occasion the result was reversed—and goals by Rhodes, Cawley and Mosforth clinched a notable victory.

The fourth round tie with Upton Park provided Wednesday with their first opposition from the south. The toss of a coin gave Wednesday home advantage, but there were problems in fixing a date. In the event the game was arranged for a Tuesday, and the attendance was consequently disappointing. Upton Park, who had defeated Hotspur of London 5-0 in the previous round, proved no match for the Sheffielders, who won 6-0. Cawley hit three goals, Rhodes got one; but the feature of the match was a brilliant individual effort by Billy Mosforth, who dribbled the length of the field before shooting past the goalkeeper. At the end of the game Mosforth was carried from the field on the shoulders of supporters—a form of adulation with which the little winger was not unfamiliar. Mosforth, capped by England for the first time in 1877, when he was 19, was the man who clinched a 5-4 victory over Scotland at Kennington Oval in 1879—and a section of the crowd had carried him all the way to the dressing room.

Now Wednesday found themselves in the FA Cup semi-final, and again they were paired with Blackburn Rovers. The Football Association at this time were seeking to promote football in new areas, and they decided that the game should be played at Huddersfield, a rugby stronghold. As no equipment was available there, goalposts had to be taken from Sheffield for the occasion!

The way things turned out, those posts were not needed, for the game ended in a 0-0 draw. However, Wednesday did put the ball in the Rovers goal, and, according to the match referee, Major Marindin, it should have counted. Why it didn't is one of those mysteries lost to history. As is explained more fully in a later chapter, in those days each team provided an umpire. When Wednesday put the ball in the goal, the Rovers umpire appealed for off-side, and as the Wednesday umpire did not show any disagreement with this appeal, the referee had no alternative but to disallow the goal. So the course of history was changed by a moment of hesitation, though, in a match of such importance, it is difficult to imagine why the Wednesday players accepted the decision without a murmur.

In the replay, played at Whalley Bridge, Manchester, Wednesday led after 20 minutes when a Malpas corner-kick was deflected into his own goal by Suter. Unfortunately, just before half-time Wednesday goalkeeper, Ledger, dropped the ball and presented Hargreaves with a "gift" equaliser. In the second half Rovers got on top and strode to a 5-1 victory, and Wednesday were left to ponder on what might have been. Perhaps the most disappointed man in the Wednesday side was Mosforth. In the space of ten days he had played in two semi-finals and two internationals, and had not been on the winning side in any. He played in the first semi-final on March 6 and the second on March 15; while on March 11 he had been in Glasgow in the England side beaten 5-1 by Scotland, and two days later been in the team defeated 5-3 by Wales at Wrexham.

For the record, the Wednesday team in the semi-final was: Ledger, Buttery, Wilkinson, Hudson, Stevens, Malpas, Gregory, West, Lang, Cawley, Mosforth.

This was Wednesday's last notable Cup run in the pre-Olive Grove era, but it is worthy of note that they enjoyed three splendid victories in the competition in 1882-3. In the first found they crushed Lincolnshire Cup holders Spilsby 12-2, with Bob Gregory scoring five and Cawley and Newbould three each. They defeated Lockwood Brothers 6-0 in the second round; Gregory (2), Anthony, Mosforth, Newbould and Cawley being the marksmen. The third round gave Wednesday a tough match at Nottingham Forest, but, with Billy Betts shining on his debut, they earned a replay with a 2-2 draw. The replay at Bramall Lane saw Harrison score all Wednesday's goals in a 3-2 success. When the fourth round draw paired Wednesday with Notts County they were hopeful of obtaining another good result: after all, Notts had struggled to defeat Phoenix Bessemer in the previous round. However, on the day Notts won 4-1 and went on to reach the semi-final. This was the year, incidentally, when the FA Cup was brought north for the first time, Blackburn Olympic beating Old Etonians at Kennington Oval. The Olympic team included Jack Hunter, late of Heeley and Wednesday, and his move to Lancashire provided an early hint that football was rapidly approaching the beginning of a new phase—the era of professionalism.

Part 2
The Olive Grove Era: 1887-1899

1 The move to Olive Grove: a turning point in club history

The mid-1880s were years of important industrial development and significant social progress throughout Britain. In reality, conditions were still far from ideal, at least for the majority; but advances were being made on many fronts, and they brought with them gradual changes in outlook and attitude. At this time Sheffield was the fastest-growing provincial town in the country, and by 1887—the year when Wednesday faced a crisis and the country was celebrating Queen Victoria's golden jubilee—the population was approaching 300,000. After a period of slump, trade was again picking up: the products of the town's craftsmen in toolmaking, cutlery and silverware were in increasing demand; while, with the passing of the Iron Age, Sheffield was the pioneering centre of the new Steel Era. It was not the bright industrial place we now know, but a rugged, grey and grimy town bustling with activity and bursting with energy, though somewhat insular in outlook.

Football is a game which reflects the larger world, mirroring social trends and attitudes in the way it is organised, controlled and played, and in how it is regarded within the framework and fabric of a community. In the 1880s football's popularity was increasing at an astonishing pace. This was largely due to the remarkable success of the English FA Cup competition, the entries for which had increased ten-fold in little more than a decade. The growth in the game's following had several effects, and probably even influenced trends in its tactics. For many years football had been dominated by individualistic play, with the star performers those who could dribble at speed and create goals with solo runs in which they outpaced a pursuing pack of defenders, everyone following the ball as if it were a magnet. Now there was an increasing tendency towards combination play, though not to the exclusion of individualism. But the emphasis was more and more on the team and its success. Football had not yet become a science, but it would be wrong to underestimate the tactical flair of the more experienced and perceptive players. Clearly, football was already becoming something more than a mere game, especially in the industrial centres of the north and midlands: it was developing into a kind of social ritual, a source of local pride and prestige as well as an escape, a release from the grey and drab world created by the Industrial Revolution. The quest for success in the FA Cup was somewhere at the heart of the trend towards professionalism: the search for glory and the pot of silver (made, by the way, by Martin Hall & Co of Sheffield) demanded that the best players should be obtained, and obtaining them required the offering of a greater incentive than the pride of wearing the shirt of a particular club.

Professionalism was regarded as a great evil by the traditionalists, who saw it as posing a tremendous threat to the purity of the sport. Charles Clegg, who was elected to the FA Council as a Sheffield representative during this period, was violently opposed to the trend. He said: "If professionalism is allowed it will only place greater power in the hands of the betting men, and encourage gambling. And if ever the gamblers get control of the game, I wouldn't give tuppence for it." The Football Association began by believing that, if they ignored it long enough, professionalism might prove a passing fad and fade away. When they realised it was on the increase, they tried to stamp it out, but the Victorian Canutes soon found they could not turn back the tide of progress.

Within a community where football was popular, there had been a tendency for one club to lure away a "star" player from another, and poaching was fairly commonplace. Now, however, players were not merely moving clubs within a community, but were being persuaded to uproot and transfer their affections to another town, often many miles away. Yet when the FA launched an investigation they were unable to expose any instances of professionalism, though it was widely accepted that it had been going on in one form or another for some years. The sort of thing happening was that a player would be found a non-existent job or position outside football, usually in the works of a member of a club's committee; or, as in the case of Jack Hunter, the famous Sheffield player induced to join Blackburn Olympic, he would be installed in a public house. And, incidentally, in the context of these developments, it is interesting to note that Wednesday themselves were said to have engaged the first unofficial professional when James Lang was brought from Scotland in the late 1870s and installed in a job at Walter Fearnehough's knife machine works.

The whole business could no longer be ignored by the authorities, and it was brought to a head early in 1884 when Preston North End admitted they were paying their players. Major Suddall of that club offered to provide proof that professionalism existed on a large scale, especially in Lancashire. The Football Association, faced with the prospect of being challenged by a breakaway organisation, finally bowed to the inevitable in July 1885, when they adopted professionalism—though initially in a carefully restricted form. Significantly, within three years the leading professional clubs had banded together to form the Football League so that regular fixtures could be provided to ensure the quality of competition likely to attract the kind of attendances needed to help pay the wages and costs of ground improvements and club administration.

However, professionalism did not arrive in Sheffield until 1887, and even then it was accepted with reluctance and suspicion, and, in some circles, with misgivings. But, as will be gathered, the professionalism which existed here at the outset was hardly that which became the norm within a few years.

Wednesday, as Sheffield's premier soccer club, may have been expected to take the lead, but officials were strongly opposed to the concept of professionalism, and for some time doggedly refused to even consider it. Eventually, of course, the club's committee began to realise that circumstances largely beyond their control were fashioning new attitudes and sweeping them towards a moment of decision—perhaps a date with destiny. The options open to them were: remain an amateur organisation and risk fading into comparative obscurity, perhaps oblivion; or change direction, go with the tide, and remain a force in local football in a new era.

In the beginning, of course, the alternatives did not appear quite as clear or simple as that. In retrospect, it seems obvious that, sooner or later, Wednesday would have had to face up to the problem, just as the FA had had to do in 1885. In the event, the confrontation was precipitated by an accident of forgetfulness. Wednesday's entry for the FA Cup competition of 1886-7 was submitted too late for acceptance, and this set in motion a chain of events which brought the club to a crisis point.

It is important to remember that, in those days, a player could turn out for any number of different clubs, so long as he was a paid-up member. Several of Sheffield's leading footballers were attached to two or more clubs. Billy Mosforth, for instance, once played in two cup-ties on the same day, appearing for one club in the morning and another in the afternoon. So, when it was known that Wednesday would not be appearing in the FA Cup, it was not surprising that several of their players—notably Mosforth, Jack Hudson, Teddy Brayshaw, Harry Winterbottom and Tom Cawley—should be persuaded to support Lockwood Brothers, a local works team, in the competition. In fact, Lockwood's "factory lads" (the firm was in cutlery) staggered the football world by reaching the quarter finals: and they were only narrowly defeated then by West Brom in a replayed match at Derby.

The appearance of these players in Lockwood's colours had two effects: Wednesday were often reduced to fielding an under-strength team; and the success of Lockwood Brothers in the national competition provided supporters of professionalism with further evidence that it had come to stay and was going to be a force to be reckoned with. Mosforth, Cawley, Hudson and the others probably discussed with enthusiasm the potential of a team of the best local players, attracted to the side by the "carrot" of getting paid for playing, or, at least, not being left to meet their own expenses. Naturally, perhaps, several of the Wednesday "exiles" chose to remain with Lockwood's for a number of games other than FA Cup ties; and it was while they were helping the works club win a Hallamshire FA Cup tie at Bramall Lane in January 1887 that a severely weakened Wednesday side travelled to Lancashire and were humiliated by Halliwell, who beat them 16-0. The leading players, however, knew how to organise the transfer of their allegiance to suit their own interests.

This is illustrated by the fact that they happily lined up with Wednesday to defeat Lockwood Brothers in the semi-final of the Sheffield Challenge Cup; and a few weeks later it was goals by Mosforth and Brayshaw which enabled Wednesday to come from behind to beat Collegiate 2-1 in the final. This season, incidentally, saw Brayshaw chosen to play for England against Ireland at Bramall Lane. The award of a cap so thrilled him that he afterwards insisted upon wearing it when playing in other matches—and it didn't prevent him from heading the ball when the occasion demanded!

Several of the players already mentioned—Mosforth, Hudson, Brayshaw, Cawley and Winterbottom—plus Jim Smith, Fred Thompson and T. E. B. Wilson, took the steps which were to bring the whole question of professionalism and the Wednesday club to a head. Supported by other sportsmen such as Albert Marples and Albert Chapman, and local publican Sam Hetherington, they got together and formed a football club called Sheffield Rovers. This club played a match against Eckington Works, the one step needed for them to qualify for entry to the FA Cup competition in the following season. Their entry was duly accepted by the FA, and when news of the acceptance reached Wednesday's officials, they, not surprisingly, were rather worried and alarmed. John and Alfred Holmes, Arthur Dickinson, Arthur and Herbert Nixon, and Walter Fearnehough were all Wednesday men to the core; and they quickly recognised that the club was facing the biggest crisis of its 20-year history. Its very existence was under threat.

Although most of the players already mentioned made their contribution, key figures in the drama now unfolding were almost certainly Billy Mosforth and Tom Cawley, two of the best and most influential players in local football in the 1880s. Mosforth was probably the oustanding footballer of his day, virtually a folk hero; a brilliant, fleet-footed dribbler who had gained the first of his nine international caps at the age of 19. Cawley, though he had not played for England, was a regular member of the Sheffield FA team in inter-city games, and was regarded as one of the most skilful and astute players in the district. Outstanding ball control was a feature of his style. Mosforth and Cawley serve to illustrate the point that many of the prominent footballers of the period were much more than simply players of a popular ball game, and, as the professionals they were to become, they differed considerably from the breed of paid players who followed in their footsteps in subsequent years. These two favourites in particular were respected not just for their prowess as players, but because they were thinking men, intelligent, mature and possessing qualities of leadership. The game was their passion, but they were working craftsmen first and footballers second. They and their kind did not want to play football for a living, and did not seek professionalism such as we know it today; though, no doubt, they recognised that time would create a generation of players for whom football would provide a livelihood. However, their goal was not payment for playing, but compensation for time lost from their crafts and trades, and reimbursement of travelling expenses and suchlike. This, they felt, was the least they ought to be able to expect, especially as many players in other areas were already enjoying the wider benefits of professionalism. It is significant, perhaps, that most of these players preferred to remain in Sheffield. If personal gain had been their sole aim they would surely have migrated to other areas.

People like Cawley, Mosforth and Brayshaw were, in fact, members of the club's committee, and though they were, initially anyway, in the minority in seeking the adoption of professionalism, there is not much doubt that they could talk on equal terms with such men as club president John Holmes and Arthur Dickinson. The conditions and practices of the local craft industries in which they worked had developed in them independence of spirit and a straight-forward business acumen which made them tough negotiators and plain-speaking men reluctant to endure any form of exploitation. Cawley, for instance, was a good organiser, a point illustrated when he helped create the Zulu comedy football team which flourished between 1879 and 1882, playing novelty matches and touring the country. These games helped raise funds for a number of charitable causes, but it is not difficult to imagine that the "performers" required travelling and other expenses. The colourful Zulus, playing with painted faces, may well have been the game's original professional group. Indeed, it is as a group that one tends to think of those who founded Sheffield Rovers: significantly, they were all involved in most of the major football events of the period, and it is tempting to regard them as constituting a sort of unofficial players' union long before such an organisation was dreamed of. It is, I think, very important to distinguish between these professionals and those of a later period; but, at the same time, it has to be said that these early pioneers recognised the value and potential of their talents and skills, and exploited the situation whenever the opportunity arose. They were certainly never likely to look a gift horse in the mouth; but, then, few would deny that they deserved any rewards that came their way. In this connection, there is a humorous story concerning Mosforth worthy of being recorded. One day in 1884 he was due to play for Hallam *against* Wednesday in a Sheffield Challenge Cup tie. Indeed, he was already changed and walking around wearing a Hallam jersey. A Wednesdayite in the crowd shouted to him: "Ten shillings, Billy, and free drinks for a week, if only you will change your shirt!" Mosforth quickly disappeared, and when he re-emerged from the dressing rooms he was wearing a Wednesday jersey!

Members of the new Sheffield Rovers attended a meeting at Sam Hetherington's Brunswick Hotel in the Haymarket one evening in early spring with the purpose of formally adopting professionalism. To many of those involved, it seemed obvious that, if the step was taken, it would signal the end of Wednesday as a footballing force in the town. None was more aware of this than Tom Cawley, and, just before the crucial motion was put to the assembly, he stood up and made a little speech—a speech which probably altered the course of the history of soccer in Sheffield. As someone who had been associated with the old club for more than ten years, since he was sixteen, he said, he felt Wednesday ought to be given the chance of saying a final "yes" or "no" on the question of payments. If they said no, well, the Rovers would carry on, and that would be that. He pointed out that, as those present included several members of the Wednesday club, if they all signed a requisition a special meeting could be called to have the matter thrashed out. It says much for Cawley's status among his colleagues that his suggestion was accepted with enthusiasm despite Wednesday's consistent refusal to discuss the matter seriously.

The special meeting of the Wednesday club, held at the Garrick Hotel, Sycamore Street, was indeed an historic occasion. The subject of professionalism and its implications was debated at considerable length. The telling points were the ones suggesting any rejection would mean the permanent loss of several key players to Rovers, and that failure to move with the times would mean the certain decline of Wednesday because they would be unable to compete in the chase for the area's best players. The meeting was adjourned. When it was reconvened on April 22 1887 the motion to adopt professionalism was passed unanimously, with the committee left to work out the details. Later the committee announced that players would get five shillings (25p) for home matches and seven shillings and sixpence (37½p) for away games—hardly sums, even then, which could be regarded as wages. They barely covered expenses, for, remember, players had to provide all their own gear except the jerseys. By the way, at this time Wednesday played in blue-and-white squares.

The meeting, and the subsequent announcement, were not the end of the affair. Soon afterwards Sheffield Rovers played their second and final match before being dissolved (the game was against Heeley at Sheaf House); and, in the meantime, Wednesday took steps to establish their financial affairs on a firmer basis. Arthur Dickinson was elected financial secretary. Clearly the first priority was to find a ground of their own, for they could no longer afford to lose the cut from gate money taken by the authorities at Sheaf House and Bramall Lane, where they usually played their more important home matches. It did not take Wednesday long to find a site near Queens Road, and this they obtained on a seven-year lease from the Duke of Norfolk. In truth, it was very much less than ideal, being little more than a swampy field. A stream and a public footpath ran straight across it! In all, about £5,000 was raised and spent on improvements: the path was diverted, the stream covered over, and the pitch levelled and drained. By August the ground had been enclosed, and the new Wednesday headquarters had been given the pretty name of Olive Grove. In the beginning, there was no provision for changing rooms, and players had to walk over a railway bridge and along a muddy path to change in a nearby public house!

Blackburn Rovers, FA Cup winners in 1884, 1885 and 1886, were invited to provide the opposition in the first match at Olive Grove on Monday September 12 1887. The Rovers, who were expected to prove a big attraction, had been guaranteed the sum of £10, but, half an hour before the kick-off, it seemed unlikely that sufficient spectators would be present to ensure the guarantee would be met from gate money. However, there was a late rush of supporters, and a crowd of between

1,500 and 2,000 was present to see Jack Hudson lead Wednesday into a new era. Mosforth had the distinction of getting the first goal scored at Olive Grove, but Blackburn soon equalised when Smith turned the ball into his own goal. By early in the second half the Lancastrians led 4-1, but Wednesday then staged a tremendous rally. Wilson scored twice, and, appropriately perhaps, Cawley snatched the equaliser with only a few minutes to spare before referee Charles Clegg blew the final whistle. The teams, who afterwards dined together at the George Hotel, High Street, were as follows:

Wednesday— J. Smith; F. Thompson, J. Hudson; E. Brayshaw, W. Betts, A. Beckett; H. Winterbottom, G. Waller, T. E. B. Wilson, T. Cawley, W. Mosforth.

Blackburn Rovers—H. Arthur; A. Chadwick, J. Beverley; J. Haynes, J. Hunter, J. H. Forrest; J. Douglas, N. Walton, J. Berrisford, R. Rushton, L. H. Heyes.

Incidentally, the George Waller in the Wednesday team was the man who later served Sheffield United for so many years as player and trainer; while the Jack Hunter in the Rovers side was the former Sheffield player mentioned earlier.

2 Early trials and triumphs, 1887-1890

Olive Grove may not have been the most imposing of football grounds, and as headquarters of a club with high ambitions it clearly had its limitations. However, so far as Wednesday and their followers were concerned it was quite adequate for their initial needs: it was the right place at the right time. If it was hardly as pleasing on the eye of the neutral spectator as its name might have led him to expect, the regular patrons regarded it with great affection and pride. It was, after all, convenient and practical; and, more importantly, it provided Wednesday with a base upon which they were able to lay the foundations of a professional organisation determined to prosper. The twelve years the club spent at Olive Grove saw them emerge from the shadows to gain recognition as one of the leading clubs in English football.

Those years from 1887 to 1899 were colourful and exciting, full of drama and incident. They were fraught with frustrations and disappointments, but success is never achieved without a struggle. And Wednesday enjoyed a good deal of hard-earned success. A series of triumphs in the FA Cup not only enhanced the club's reputation within the world of football, but helped put their finances on a firm footing, so enabling them to widen their horizons and seek greater goals. Not least among these goals was membership of the Football League. A year after Wednesday adopted professionalism, a group of a dozen clubs banded together to form the Football League; but, initially, the Olive Grove club could not gain membership of this exclusive set. However, such was Wednesday's determination, and their reputation among the other clubs who found themselves "outsiders", they pioneered a second league, the Football Alliance, and the club's leading official, John Holmes, was installed as its president. In the first season of the Alliance Wednesday won the championship, and they also reached the FA Cup final for the first time; and thus they provided a practical answer to the apparent threat posed by the formation of a rival professional club in the town, Sheffield United.

Wednesday had their ups and downs in the Olive Grove era, but they probably had more ups than downs. In their first five seasons at the ground—that is, the period prior to their admittance to the Football League—they played some 250 matches, of which they won almost 150 and scored more than 750 goals. At a distance of one hundred years, the brand of football may seem unsophisticated, quaint even; but Wednesday were successful in the context of their times, and, even before gaining a place in the League, they frequently showed themselves to be as good as those already regarded as among the game's elite. It is worthy of note that, in the twelve seasons at Olive Grove, Wednesday played 23 FA Cup ties at the ground, and lost only four.

In the first season at the ground Wednesday played 45 matches and won 32, losing only seven. They scored 158 goals. They won the Sheffield Challenge Cup and the Wharncliffe Charity Cup, and reached the sixth round in the FA Cup before falling to the mighty Preston North End. The national knock-out competition provided the essential drama and humour in this first campaign. For instance, after beating Belper in the first round, Wednesday visited Long Eaton Rangers, beat them 2-1, and learned that their share of the gate was £4.15s. The home secretary gave Wednesday the money before they left for home—a bag containing 1,140 pennies! The next round took Wednesday to Leyton to meet Crusaders. This time their share of the gate was eight shillings and fourpence (about 42p), and Crusaders promised to send a cheque. When the cheque arrived, the bank refused to accept it, and a dispute over one of the signatures was not settled for months. Billy Ingram scored a hat-trick in the 4-2 triumph at Nottingham Forest in the fifth round, and the draw for Round Six gave Wednesday their first tie at Olive Grove—a clash with Preston.

In the previous round Preston had defeated the Cup-holders, Aston Villa, 3-1, but Villa had completed the tie on the understanding that the result would not count; and the details of the case provides an insight into the world of football in 1888. The match was played at Birmingham, and such was the interest that the crowd was the largest ever seen at a game in the midlands city. Unfortunately, the spectators kept encroaching onto the pitch, and, amid the chaos, Villa went forward and scored. Preston immediately protested, and the referee decreed that the match would not be reckoned a Cup-tie. In the end, however, Preston won, and decided they would have the referee's earlier decision over-ruled. Amazingly, when the Football Association met at Kennington Oval to discuss the matter, they agreed with Preston's claim, awarding the match to North End on the grounds that Villa had not made proper arrangements to accommodate a large crowd.

Protest and counter-protests were the order of the day in those years, and now Preston turned their attention to the Wednesday match only to find another excuse to lodge a protest. They learned that Sheffield had been hit by a smallpox epidemic, and declined to come to Olive Grove because they claimed the lives of their players and officals would be put at risk. They succeeded in getting the game postponed, and, after a series of wrangles, it was finally fixed for Monday January 30. However, even as late as the Saturday before, Preston were still protesting. Charles Clegg, tired of the whole business, had the good sense to obtain the views of a number of local medical men, and, when he presented the evidence to the FA officials that it was perfectly safe to visit Sheffield, Preston were instructed to fulfil the fixture or face expulsion from the competition.

Preston came, and, in one of the best games seen in Sheffield up to that time, won 3-1. Wednesday, however, were far from disgraced. A crowd of around 9,000 saw the match, and the general opinion was that if Wednesday had played as well throughout the 90 minutes as they did in the last half-hour, the result might have been very different. Snow fell on the day of the game, but Preston adjusted to the conditions more quickly than the home side, and goals by Thompson (2) and Ross Jnr gave them a healthy lead by the 64th minute. Soon afterwards Ingram reduced Wednesday's arrears, and, suddenly, the mighty North End were under heavy pressure. But they held out. The teams in this first FA Cup tie at Olive Grove were:

Wednesday— Smith; Thompson, Brayshaw; Dungworth, Betts, Waller; Winterbottom, Ingram, Hiller, Cawley, Mosforth.
Preston— Mills-Roberts; Thomson, Drummond; Goodall, Ross Jnr, Gordon; Graham, Russell, Robertson, Ross Snr, Howarth.

A few weeks later Preston returned to Sheffield to meet a Wednesday Club & District side at Bramall Lane in Billy Mosforth's benefit match, and a crowd of 4,000 saw them win 8-1. The Sheffield side included the illustrious Tinsley Lindley, of Nottingham Forest and England fame, and Preston provided the goalkeeper (which may help to explain the high score!).

Wednesday's second season at the new ground was equally successful. They won 35 of their 52 matches, scoring 168 goals and conceding only 63; with high-scoring victories achieved against Park Grange (13-0), Doncaster Rovers (10-0), Heeley (9-1) and Notts Rangers (8-0). However, perhaps the most impressive wins were a 3-1 defeat of Burnley, members of the new Football League, and a 2-1 success against Preston, who were on their way to achieving the League and Cup double. They also shared a 1-1 draw with Blackburn Rovers in Jack Hudson's benefit match (receipts £53 17s 6d), and beat Heart of Midlothian 3-0. Towards the end of the season they won the Gainsborough News Charity Cup, presented to skipper Billy Betts following the 4-1 defeat of Burton Swifts in the final.

Preston, on their way to clinching a unique League and Cup triumph, returned to Sheffield in March to play in a match which was to earn a special place in the history of football in the town. This was the FA Cup semi-final with West Brom at Bramall Lane—a game which attracted the largest crowd ever seen at a football match in Sheffield up to that time:

22,688. It was a remarkable occasion, and referee Charles Clegg twice had to take the players off the field because of crowd encroachment, and even the dignified old Mayor of Sheffield, Alderman W. J. Clegg, thrust himself among the pitch invaders to try to restore some order. However, despite the problems, the overall success of the event prompted dental surgeon Charles Stokes to suggest to Charles Clegg that Sheffield United should form a football club. On the following Friday, at the Norfolk Row offices of J. B. Wostinholm, the secretary of Yorkshire County Cricket Club, the new club was founded.

Wednesday and their followers greeted the news with dismay, alarm even; and United met with a good deal of opposition in the town. John Holmes and his colleagues saw the formation of a rival professional club as a threat to their own organisation. It is said that some families were so divided on the issue that fathers ceased to speak to sons, and brother fell out with brother. United did not find it easy to recruit players at first, though, much to Wednesday's disgust, they managed to persuade both Jack Hudson and Billy Mosforth to join them. As United prepared for the 1889-90 season, they kept quiet about their plans, but, of course, all sorts of rumours sped about the town. At the beginning of August United held their first match at a supposedly secret venue; but the brake carrying the players was followed by a local newspaper reporter and Teddy Brayshaw, the Wednesday player. Not for nothing was Brayshaw the son of a famous local detective! The journey ended at the Sandygate ground of Hallam Cricket Club, where United beat Sheffield Club 3-1.

Wednesday recognised that the only way to dispel any threat to their existence was to succeed where it mattered—on the field. They made valiant efforts to gain admission to the Football League. However, despite a stirring speech by John Holmes at the League's annual meeting at the Douglas Hotel, Manchester, in early May, Wednesday failed to gain election. Six days later, Holmes was back at the same hotel, chairing a meeting at which a Northern Counties League, later known as the Football Alliance, was formed. The founding members were: Wednesday, Nottingham Forest, Crewe, Walsall Town Swifts, Grimsby Town, Sunderland Albion, Newton Heath, Bootle, Darwen, Birmingham St George's, Small Heath and Long Eaton Rangers.

Wednesday's first match in the Alliance was against Bootle at Olive Grove on September 7 1889. They went on to win all their eleven Alliance fixtures at home, and took the Alliance championship with the following record:

    P22 W15 D2 L5 F70 A39 32pts.

Their programme included 9-1 home victories over Long Eaton and Small Heath, but perhaps their most notable triumph was achieved in late March at Grimsby, where they won a rugged game 4-3 and virtually ensured themselves of finishing top of the Alliance. In fact, goals by Ingram (2), Mumford and skipper Harry Winterbottom had given them a 4-0 half-time lead; but Grimsby hit back and grabbed three quick goals. As the minutes passed, so Grimsby's enthusiasm and determination increased; and nobody in their side was more determined or aggressive than a certain Ambrose Langley, later to become a Wednesday hero.

This season is not especially remembered for the club's triumph in the Alliance, a competition now largely forgotten; but for their success in the FA Cup—a run of triumph which came to a shattering end when they were heavily defeated by Blackburn Rovers in the final at Kennington Oval.

The Cup run began with a comfortable 6-1 defeat of the star-studded London Swifts at Olive Grove in mid-January, and, a fortnight later, Accrington Stanley, one of the founders of the Football League, were beaten 2-1 before a crowd of 10,000, with Cawley and Winterbottom getting the goals that delighted the Sheffield spectators. Then came a series of three games with Notts County. Wednesday won the first match 5-0, but a protest by the Nottingham club was upheld, and a replay saw County win 3-2. This time, however, it was Wednesday who lodged a protest, claiming that their opponents had fielded two ineligible players. The third game, at Derby, ended with a 2-1 victory for Wednesday, Cawley and Winterbottom getting the goals that booked a place in the semi-final. Not surprisingly, perhaps, County again protested, and, in fact, the FA did not meet to discuss the matter until 24 hours before Wednesday were due to face Bolton Wanderers at Birmingham.

Bolton presented a tough challenge to Wednesday. They had registered a number of high-scoring wins in the Football League, and, in reaching the FA Cup semi-final, had beaten Sheffield United 13-0 and disposed of the holders Preston. In rain and hail, Wednesday held their own in the first half; but 15 minutes after the resumption Cassidy shot Bolton in front. However, Winterbottom soon equalised and Mumford got the winner.

Wednesday's opponents in the final on Saturday March 19 1890 were Blackburn Rovers, who had won the trophy three times in the 1880s and whose team included nine internationals. However, there was no lack of confidence in the Olive Grove camp—at least, not until the week preceding the game. After their famous Alliance victory at Grimsby, Wednesday travelled to Matlock to begin preparations for the final. Winterbottom was nursing a nasty ankle injury and Ingram reported sick. Winterbottom showed some signs of recovery, and resumed training in midweek; but, towards the end of the session, the captain fell awkwardly and twisted the already damaged ankle. On the Friday the Wednesday players travelled to London and booked into Haxton's Hotel in The Strand. The party included reserves "Toddles" Woolhouse and Walpole Hiller, plus Fred Thompson, who had captained the side until falling seriously ill with scarlet fever at Christmas.

On the morning of the final, Winterbottom declared himself unfit, but Ingram was persuaded to play in the skipper's place at outside-right, with Ecclesfield product Woolhouse inside, and Mickey Bennett on the opposite wing. Wednesday, wearing blue shirts and white shorts, were led out by amateur Haydn Morley, and the full line-up read:

Wednesday— Smith; Morley, Brayshaw; Dungworth, Betts, Waller; Ingram, Woolhouse, Mumford, Cawley, Bennett.

Blackburn Rovers— Horne; Forbes, James Southworth; Barker, Dewar, Forrest; Lofthouse, Campbell, John Southworth, Walton, Townley.

Just before the start of the match, a Blackburn journalist stopped R. P. Gregson, secretary of the Lancashire FA, who had visited the dressing rooms. Mr Gregson, asked for an opinion on how the game might go, commented: "Sheffield are beaten already. They are down in the dumps and sitting back there as quiet as mice. They have not a word to say. They look frightened. But the Rovers are singing and whistling and carrying on like a lot of kittens. Unless I am very mistaken, Rovers will win easily." The record books show that Rovers did, indeed, win in a canter, by a 6-1 margin. Wednesday never got a look-in during the first-half, with Blackburn scoring their first goal after five minutes and their fourth two minutes before the interval. "Clinks" Mumford reduced Wednesday's arrears after 53 minutes, but Townley completed his hat-trick soon afterwards, and Lofthouse got the sixth goal. While Rovers collected the Sheffield-made Cup from Major Marindin, President of the FA and the match referee, Wednesday's players looked as they felt—a picture of disappointment and dejection. A Blackburn player later admitted that he and his colleagues had known Wednesday were beaten before the start, because of the shakiness of the handwriting of the Wednesday players in the souvenir autograph book passed round both dressing rooms before the kick-off. It was a black day for Sheffielders in the crowd, but, at the end, some enthusiasts insisted upon carrying Morley shoulder high from the field. A few weeks later, the Cup defeat still fresh in the memory, Wednesday held a dinner at the Cutlers Hall, partly to mark having won the Alliance title, but more especially to pay tribute to Tom Cawley. During the season Cawley had been granted a benefit match, and he was now formally presented with a cheque for the total sum raised—£181 18s 3d.

3 The quest for League status

Wednesday's success in reaching the FA Cup final and winning the Alliance championship in 1890 did not appear to impress the Football League, who insisted upon keeping their door firmly closed to the Sheffield club and others. Indeed, there was not much in the way of mutual admiration passing between the clubs in the League and those in the Alliance. The League clubs evidently regarded themselves as members of the game's elite, and they tended to look down their noses at those upstarts on the outside. They did not welcome the attentions of outsiders. In 1891, for example, Blackburn Rovers complained that Wednesday had poached Tom Brandon from them, and the League clubs decided they would boycott Wednesday by refusing to play them. Significantly, nothing was said of the poaching Rovers themselves had been involved in over the years! However, John Holmes and his colleagues at Olive Grove were not unduly troubled by the League's attitude. In fact, the Alliance clubs had arrived at the conclusion that their best policy was to stick together and only accept admittance to the League as a group. They had to wait until 1892 to achieve their goal, and then only after many hours of negotiation and lobbying behind the scenes. In the meantime, much of considerable importance and interest happened in the football world; and some of it directly concerned Wednesday.

Unfortunately, after their triumphs in their first season in the Alliance Wednesday suffered a turnabout of fortunes in the following campaign. They won only four of their 22 Alliance fixtures, and finished bottom of the table. Their overall record shows that they managed 19 victories in 56 games. Yet the 1890-1 season provided a number of matches of special interest, not the least of which were the first meetings with Sheffield United, and the staging at Olive Grove of the only representative match ever played between the Alliance and the Football League. This season, by the way, also marked the arrival of the first of the Brandon cousins; Bob, a centre-forward, came from Glasgow Clyde in October 1890; and Harry, a half-back, followed soon afterwards. Tom, who came at the end of the season from Blackburn, was generally regarded as the best player among the trio, and it was as an added incentive for him to sign for Wednesday that he was installed in the Woodman Inn on Sheffield Moor.

However, the best of the Brandons in terms of service to Wednesday was Harry, who arrived just in time to make his debut in the first-ever Sheffield derby, staged at Olive Grove on December 15 1890. The day coincided with the start of "bull" week, when the local craftsmen and workers wanted to get as much time in as possible in order to ensure a maximum pay-out at Christmas. But many of the workshops were deserted on that particular Monday afternoon, for it seemed that everybody wanted to see the battle for the football championship of Sheffield. On a grey, raw afternoon a crowd of around 10,000 was present for this historic fixture. Wednesday, in the middle of a dismal run, were not regarded as favourites by the betting men—and, incidentally, there were plenty of bookmakers doing brisk business before the kick-off. Billy Whitham, the famous scorecard seller, was disposing of his souvenir programmes with astonishing speed, and still finding time to entertain the waiting spectators with his comments. In the first half of the match United had most of the play, and led at the interval thanks to a goal from Robertson after 20 minutes. However, Wednesday rallied in style following the change of ends: Woolhouse headed the equaliser, and Winterbottom (for whom this was a benefit season after 12 years with the club) shot the winner five minutes from the end. The teams were:

Wednesday— Smith; Brayshaw, Thompson; Cawley, Betts, H. Brandon; Hodder, Woolhouse, R. Brandon, Mumford, Winterbottom.
United— Howlett; Lilley, Whitham; Cross, Howell, Groves; Shaw, Bridgewater, Robertson, Watson, Calder.
    Referee: J. C. Clegg.

A month later, on January 12 1891, the return game was played at Bramall Lane. Ingram replaced Betts in Wednesday's side, but United were unchanged. Two days before this second clash, incidentally, nine of the United team, plus "Clinks" Mumford of Wednesday, had been in the Sheffield Association side which had defeated Glasgow in the annual inter-city fixture. Now a crowd of 14,000 turned up to see United avenge their earlier defeat. At one stage in the goal-less first half hundreds of spectators encroached onto the pitch, but referee William Clegg soon restored order. Ingram was responsible for breaking the deadlock, shooting Wednesday in front after 65 minutes; and, almost immediately, Bob Brandon made it 2-0. However, Arthur Watson, the inside-forward from Ecclesfield, quickly reduced United's arrears; and Rab Howell, a product of Wincobank, equalised with a long shot which took Jim Smith by surprise. United's winner came from Calder five minutes from the end, and the referee chose to ignore Wednesday's appeals for off-side.

It is interesting, and indeed amusing, to reflect that, in those days each side provided an umpire, and the duties of this official included claiming any goal scored by his team, and, where appropriate, appealing against goals scored by the opposition. Early in the 1890-1 season there was an instance when a home umpire failed to appeal against a goal scored by Crewe Alexandra at Olive Grove—and the poor man was subsequently mobbed by hundreds of irate Wednesdayites! In this particular match, Crewe won 6-4, and it was their sixth goal, coming at a time when Wednesday had been staging a tremendous rally after trailing 2-5, which caused all the trouble. However, it has to be said that the umpire, W. B. Wake, probably brought the trouble on himself, for he volunteered to act as umpire against the wishes of the Wednesday players and committee, and he seemed to take some pleasure in declining to appeal against what was (according to contemporary reports) a blatant case of off-side. The referee could only disallow a goal on appeal from an umpire.

One match in the spring of 1891 which did not arouse the partisanship associated with club games was the Alliance v Football League fixture, watched by a crowd of 5,000 who were treated to an exhibition of football from 22 of the best players in the game. Harry Davis—later to join Wednesday—scored for the Alliance, with Chadwick equalising for the League. Almost as important as the match was the fact that, afterwards, the Alliance and the League each held meetings at the Maunch Hotel to discuss the possibility of getting together to form a united league of 36 clubs. Unfortunately, what could have proved a day when football history was made ended without any basis for agreement being reached: the League would not entertain the scheme, while the Alliance said they would do so on certain conditions which were unlikely to be acceptable to the League clubs.

It is appropriate here to note the teams in this unique fixture:
Alliance— Roberts (Sunderland Albion); Rae (Sunderland Albion), Clare (Stoke); H. Brandon (Wednesday), Clifford (Stoke), McCracken (Sunderland Albion); H. Davis (Birmingham St George's), "Tich" Smith (Nottingham Forest), Devey (Birmingham St George's), Edge (Stoke), Hannah (Sunderland Albion).
League— Trainor (Preston); T. Brandon (Blackburn), Ross (Preston); Calderhead (Notts County), Dewar (Blackburn), Wilson (Sunderland); Athersmith (Aston Villa), McInnes (Notts County), Goodall (Derby County), Chadwick (Everton), Daft (Notts County).

Harry Brandon was the only Wednesday man to feature in this game, but there was significance in the fact that his cousin, Tom Brandon, was on duty in the League side. Tom was one of the outstanding stars of the afternoon, and Wednesday were not slow to indicate to him the attractions of the Olive Grove set-up. They captured his signature for the 1891-2 season, and in so doing upset Blackburn Rovers: the upshot being that Wednesday joined Stockport and Walsall Town Swifts on the Football League's "banned" list.

Tom Brandon was not the only important newcomer to the Wednesday team in 1891-2—a season in which they finished fourth in the Alliance and won 32 of their 59 competitive and friendly fixtures. Indeed, in looking back, the capture of Brandon, who did not remain long in Sheffield, seems to pale into insignificance alongside the signing of Fred Spiksley—the winger destined to become one of Wednesday's all-time greats and immortalised as "the Olive Grove flyer".

Spiksley was blessed with brilliant ball control, an astonishing burst of speed, tenacity, courage, and an appreciation of football tactics years ahead of his time: and, of course, later in life he became a successful, globe-trotting coach. He stood only 5ft 6in high, and a man of such a slight build took many hard knocks. Not surprisingly, perhaps, he regarded playing professional soccer as "like going into a bear pit"; and he said he would have preferred to earn his living by some other means than playing football. However, his reluctance disappeared when he recognised that the life of a successful footballer would give him the freedom to pursue his greatest passion, horse-racing. Many years after his playing days were over, Spiksley collapsed and died on a race-track, and his friends said he would not have chosen to end his life in any more appropriate spot.

In the season of 1890-1 Spiksley had helped his home-town club, Gainsborough Trinity, win the Midland League championship, and his fame as a maker and taker of goals attracted the attention of a number of clubs. Accrington Stanley invited him to Lancashire, and when they offered him 50 shillings (£2.50) a week and a job outside the game he was ready to join them. Fortunately, he asked for time to think things over, and, on his way home from Accington he found he had missed his connection at Sheffield station. As it was late in the evening, he decided to spend the night at the Maunch Hotel; and there he bumped into his old friend Fred Thompson, the Wednesday back. The next morning Spiksley didn't, as he had intended, catch the early train home: instead he agreed to Thompson's suggestion that he meet John Holmes and Arthur Dickinson in the Bull & Mouth Hotel in Waingate. The Wednesday officials offered him £3 a week and a berth at the *Sheffield Telegraph*, and Spiksley accepted. It was one of the greatest scoops in club history: Spiksley was to score some brilliant and vital goals for Wednesday, and play a major part in the success of the following seasons. And, of course, he also gained international recognition, with sensational performances in his first two appearances for England.

Incidentally, Spiksley's job in the composing room of the *Telegraph* conflicted with his passion for horse-racing, and he quit after a few months. He also decided that Gainsborough was a much more

2. Heroes of Olive Grove. . . (back row) W. Muscroft (trainer), H. Vessey, Tom Brandon, J. Smith, J. Darroch, John Holmes; (middle row) Harry Brandon, "Clinks" Mumford, G. Thompson, Tom Cawley, Fred Spiksley; (front row) Gemmell, Billy Betts, Richardson.

convenient place to live—and arranged with the club that he train alone at home and only travel to Sheffield on match days. Even on match days he always insisted on returning to Gainsborough the same evening, though, when the games were away, he sometimes found himself in difficulties when the team reached Sheffield. There was one famous instance when he got as far as Retford only to find the last train to Gainsborough had gone. Rather than spend the night in the waiting room, he decided to walk the 10 miles or so home, choosing the quickest route—along the railway track. Everthing went well until he reached a tunnel: half way through it he suddenly heard a train approaching, and he dived into an inlet just in the nick of time. Later that morning he arrived home and knocked loudly on the front door. An upstairs window opened, and Spiksley's father peered out. "Hey up, mother," he called into the bedroom, "have you ordered a chimney sweep?" Fred was covered from head to toe in soot!

In that 1891-2 campaign Tom Brandon and Spiksley helped Wednesday regain their old form. The team did exceptionally well at home, where they achieved ten of their 12 Alliance victories and scored 46 of their 66 goals; and the only team to beat them at Olive Grove was Newton Heath in December. However, it was the visit of Birmingham St George's for the last game of the Alliance programme which provided the most interesting and amusing story of the campaign. On the Friday, less than 24 hours before the match, Wednesday received an unexpected telegram from the Midlands club: "Stoney broke; cannot come". Arthur Dickinson quickly arranged to remit the club's travelling expenses by wire, and, thankfully, St George's arrived on time next day. Wednesday won the match 4-0, so completing only their second Alliance double of the season. When Messrs Holmes and Dickinson said goodbye to their visitors that afternoon, they probably didn't realise that they were also saying farewell to an era: for, a few weeks later, Wednesday were elected to the Football League.

Before passing onto the League era, it is, perhaps, appropriate here to mention the two meetings of the Sheffield clubs in 1891-2, for these clashes prompted the first recorded circulation of "funeral cards" in local football circles. In late October the teams met at Bramall Lane, and, to Wednesday's horror, United coasted to a 5-0 victory. The game had been in progress only eight minutes when Tom Brandon headed the ball into his own net, and two goals by Harry Hammond gave United a 3-0 lead at half-time. Sammy Dobson scored two more in the second period. Within hours of the final whistle, the following card was creating considerable mirth in the town:

In Loving Remembrance of
the
SHEFFIELD WEDNESDAY FOOTBALL TEAM
who were safely put to rest on Monday October 26th
at Bramall Lane
Poor old Wednesday were fairly done,
When United beat them five to none;
Although they lost, they did their best,
So let them quietly take their rest.
(Friends of the above club kindly accept this intimation).

Wednesday were so shocked by this setback that officials immediately debated the situation, and, according to Spiksley, promptly began the first regular training sessions in club history. The extra work paid off, for in mid-November United were beaten 4-1 at Olive Grove. Woolhouse and Spiksley each scored twice, with the legendary Ernest Needham—in his first season with United—getting the consolation goal for the team at that time nicknamed The Cutlers. Again the funeral cards came out. . .

In pitiful remembrance of
Our idols the
SHEFFIELD UNITED FOOTBALL TEAM
who departed their football life, struggling to the
end at Olive Grove on Monday November 16th 1891
When United died, they struggled hard
Enough to live a brighter and longer life:
Do as they would, they could not ward
Neat Kicks by Wednesday, and thus the strife
Ended, thus closed famous United's reign.
Sheffield now mourns their death the more,
Dying as they did—ne'er to rise again
And kick for fame at Wednesday's door.
Yes, United have lost 4 to one.

On the evidence of the above, United's consolation was that their funeral card writers seemed to have a greater flair for verse!

In May 1892, the Football League doubled in size overnight. When the League's annual meeting was held at Sunderland, delegates from the existing 14 member clubs agreed to an enlargement of the competition. Two clubs were added to the current membership, to form a First Division; and a new Second Division was created comprising 12 clubs. Wednesday, who collected maximum votes at the ballot, went straight into the top grade: Sheffield United were elected to the Second Division.

Tom Brandon, in his second and last season (he returned to Blackburn in 1893), had the distinction of being Wednesday's first captain in the Football League. Bill Allan, known to his colleagues as "William the Silent" because he had so little to say, was now the regular goalkeeper; and Albert Mumford, Billy Betts, Harry Brandon and "Sparrow" Brown were among those who survived from the Alliance team; with newcomers for the 1892-3 season including Alec Brady (ex-Sunderland and Burnley) and Harry Davis, snapped up from Birmingham St George's despite the attentions of Aston Villa.

Wednesday's first League match was at Notts County, on Saturday September 3 1892, when a crowd of 13,000 (including around 2,000 from Sheffield) packed into the Castle Ground to see the "new boys" win 1-0 with Tom Brandon the marksman. The match did not get started until well after the scheduled kick-off time. And when the players eventually emerged from the pavilion ten minutes late, they quickly retired again when it was discovered that hundreds of spectators had encroached onto the playing area. Later, owing to rain, the start of the second half was delayed several minutes. The teams on this famous day in Wednesday's history were:

Notts County— Toone; Whitlaw, Hendry; Parkes, Calderhead, Shelton; McGregor, Docherty, Oswald, Walkerdine, Daft.

Wednesday— Allan; T. Brandon, Mumford; H. Brandon, Betts, Hall; Dunlop, R. N. Brown, Davis, Brady, Spiksley.

A week later a crowd of some 9,000 turned up for the first Football League match to be played at Olive Grove. The only team change saw Dunlop going out and Rowan coming in, with Davis moving to outside-right. Wednesday did not disappoint their followers: Accrington Stanley were defeated 5-2.

Unfortunately, Wednesday suffered three successive defeats, all away, but this was followed by an unbeaten run of six matches which pushed them up into third place. Two of the games in this sequence merit a fuller note. On October 29 a crowd of around 20,000—easily a record for Olive Grove—saw Wednesday defeat the reigning champions, Sunderland. At that stage in the season, Sunderland already boasted 38 goals in nine games, and had conceded only eight. Twice Wednesday found themselves behind, but first Hall and then Brady equalised; and, 15 minutes from the end, Hall snatched the winner. It was a famous victory. Indeed, Wednesday's good run prompted the Duke of Teck and the Duke of Norfolk to attend the home match with Bolton in November; and again Tom Brandon and co. turned on the style to win 4-2.

On November 19, however, Blackburn Rovers became the first team to defeat Wednesday in a League fixture at Olive Grove; but, a week later, the Sheffield team restored Yorkshire pride with a 5-3 win at Everton. Other notable victories followed: a 5-3 defeat of Aston Villa; a 5-1 success at Newton Heath; and a 6-0 crushing of West Brom. Incidentally, it was at Newton Heath that Bruce Chalmers, a new half-back from Derby, was introduced.

Whether all this success went to the players' heads, it is not possible now to ascertain; but, for some reason, the team suddenly ran into a bad patch, suffering seven successive defeats. Indeed, in ten games they picked up only one point. The upshot was they had to win their last match, against Notts County, to avoid having to play in the dreaded test matches. The game was played on April 3 1893. County scored first, but Tom Brandon equalised (with Wednesday's first goal at home since January 2), and further goals by Harry Brandon and "Sparrow" Brown booked a 3-2 victory for Wednesday. Here it seems appropriate to note the team's overall record in their first season in the League:

	P	W	D	L	F	A	Pts
Home	15	8	2	5	34	28	18
Away	15	4	1	10	21	37	9
	30	12	3	15	55	65	27

It will be of interest to list the League appearances: Allen 30; T. Brandon 30; H. Brandon 29; H. Davis 29; A. Rowan 28; Brady 26; Spiksley 26; R. N. Brown 25; W. Betts 26; Mumford 21; Hall 17; Darroch 12; Chalmers 13; McIntosh 8; Woolhouse 5; J. Brown 2; Dunlop 1; McCorachie 1. Fred Spiksley topped the scoring charts with 14 League goals, while Rowan scored 12.

4 In search of Cup glory, 1891-96

The Olive Grove years were a time when Wednesday consolidated their status as a Football League club. However, in retrospect the period can be recognised as one in which they established a reputation as great Cup fighters. The point is emphasised when one considers that in nine successive seasons, from 1888 to 1896, they reached the quarter-finals; and, between 1891 and 1896, they won 18 of their 25 FA Cup ties, scoring 65 goals in the process. Of course, it took them some time to live down the crushing defeat of 1890, but they reached the semi-final in 1894 and 1895, and in 1896 they at last won the game's most coveted trophy for the first time in club history.

If Wednesday were still feeling sore about the drubbing inflicted upon them by Blackburn in the previous March, they got it out of their system in the very next Cup-tie they played, against Halliwell on January 17 1891. Perhaps the Sheffielders were merely avenging the embarrassing defeat suffered in a friendly at Halliwell some years earlier. In any event, they crushed the Lancastrians 12-0 before about 1,000 spectators at Olive Grove. Incidentally, the crowd was smaller than might have been the case on any other weekend, but Sheffield United were at home on the same day—and being defeated by eventual Cup winners, Notts County, who won 9-1. When the first-round draw had been made, Halliwell had got a home tie; but, for a small financial consideration, they had been persuaded to switch the match to Sheffield. It was a game Wednesday regulars remembered for a long time. "Toddles" Woolhouse scored five, Cawley and Harry Brandon each got two goals, and Bob Brandon, Albert Mumford and Billy Ingram got the others. A few weeks later Wednesday scored a memorable 3-2 win at Derby, but West Brom delivered the KO in the third round at Olive Grove.

In 1892 Wednesday started on the Cup trail with another impressive victory over a League club, Spiksley marking his Cup debut with two goals in a 4-1 triumph over Bolton. Unfortunately, for the second year running Wednesday fell at the third round stage to West Brom. However, it was the second round tie with Small Heath which captured the headlines. This tie provided another instance of Wednesday being drawn away but persuading the opposition to switch the fixture to Olive Grove—in this case the guarantee being £200. After 13 minutes Richardson headed Wednesday in front, and from that point onwards the game became more a physical battle than a clash of skills. Towards the end of the second period two Wednesday men—first Gemmell, then Richardson—were sent off. Two minutes from the end, Thompson scored a second goal for Wednesday. As a result of the referee's report, the Football Association closed Olive Grove for a fortnight, but, remarkably, it was hardly punishment, for Wednesday had no home games scheduled in that time!

The Cup campaign of 1893 was notable largely because Wednesday and Derby County required three games to decide which of them would pass into the second round. In the first match Wednesday won 3-2, Spiksley getting a hat-trick, including the winning goal in extra-time. However, immediately after the game Derby lodged a protest, alleging that Bruce Chalmers and Alec Brady were ineligible; and the FA ordered the game to be replayed. Wednesday lost 1-0 at Derby, but, taking a leaf out of their opponents' book, promptly protested. The FA ordered a third meeting, and this time Wednesday won 4-2, with Betts, Spiksley, Woolhouse and Chalmers their marksmen. When Derby lodged another protest, the FA decided enough was enough: they insisted the result should stand. So now Wednesday met Burnley at Olive Grove. Early in this tie Spiksley was knocked out in a terrific collision with an opponent, and had to be carried from the field. At half-time the Gainsborough man complained of feeling very ill, but skipper Tom Brandon begged him to turn out for the second period. Spiksley struggled onto the field, and, in true schoolboy fiction style, scored the only goal of the game. A few weeks later he needed an urgent medical check-up, and it was revealed that he had been playing all the time with two broken ribs!

The season of 1893-4 was significant not only for the fact that Wednesday reached the semi-final, but because it marked the arrival at

Olive Grove of two players destined to become great favourites—full-backs Ambrose Langley and Jack Earp. Langley arrived with a reputation as a rugged, fearless player, and, standing nearly six-feet tall with a playing weight of 14 stones, he was built to strike terror in the hearts of all but the hardiest of opposing forwards. He was to serve the club for 12 seasons with great determination and loyalty; and it is amusing to note that, when he arrived from Middlesbrough Ironopolis, many believed Wednesday had signed a "crock". The truth was that the product of Lincolnshire *did* have knee trouble, and, but for this, might have joined Aston Villa. But Villa made the mistake of insisting on a medical check before they would complete the deal. Langley, with a typical gesture of defiance, refused to let doctors examine his knee. The deal was called off, and Wednesday stepped in. John Holmes had the good sense to realise that Langley was worth taking a gamble over. Langley made his debut at left-back against Sunderland in the first match of the season. A month later Earp, a Nottingham man who had previously been with Forest and Everton, became Langley's partner, and the pair were very nearly inseparable for the next six seasons.

Langley, Earp, Jimmy Jamieson, Johnny Webster and Miller were the new names that appeared on the team-sheet in 1893-4, but they did not form a successful combination immediately. From September until the end of December Wednesday endured a lean time, and at the turn of the year they had only 15 points from 23 games. They looked strong contenders for the test matches, which in those days decided relegation and promotion. In January, a worried John Holmes called a special meeting at which the matter was discussed, and afterwards he revealed that if the team won five of the remaining six League fixtures the players would be given an extra £50 to share between them. Wednesday beat Newton Heath, Darwen, Preston, Nottingham Forest and Burnley, scoring 12 goals and conceding only one in the process; and they finished seven points clear of the danger mark. Ten players shared the £50—the odd man out being Earp, at that time an amateur.

If proof were needed that success breeds success it was provided by the fact that the revival in the League coincided with the Cup run which took Wednesday into the semi-final. Indeed, the team's record in League and Cup between January 6 and the trip to Burnley on March 23 reads: P10 W8 D1 L1 F21 A8—a 100 per-cent improvement on what they had achieved in twice as many matches in the first half of the season. And one presumes that John Holmes felt that success in the Cup had provided an unexpected return on his club's £50 outlay!

Wednesday were blessed with a little Cup luck in the first-round tie at Royal Arsenal, when Spiksley got both goals in a 2-1 win. A soilitary goal from Woolhouse gave them victory in the second-round clash with Stoke; and the reward was a home pairing with Aston Villa, who, at the time, were running away with the League Championship and strongly fancied for the League and Cup double. A crowd of 22,100 (at the time an astonishing gate) paid £741 12s to see what proved to be an unforgettable match. After ten minutes Woolhouse shot Wednesday in front, but Villa drew level before half-time, and midway through the second half Hodgetts gave the visitors the lead. As full-time approached hundreds of spectators, convinced they had seen the last of the scoring, began to drift away from the ground. However, with barely two minutes left, Webster dashed down the wing and thumped the ball into the middle: and there was Spiksley flying into the goalmouth to push home a sensational equaliser. The game went into extra-time, and for 25 minutes neither side could break the deadlock. Then Spiksley produced another flash of brilliance. Collecting the ball on the left, he jinked past a couple of defenders, drew the goalkeeper to the near post, and placed his cross so precisely that Woolhouse had the easiest of tasks in scoring the goal that clinched a great victory.

It has to be said that at this time Spiksley was probably the most talked-about player in the game. Capped for the first time in 1893 against Wales and Scotland, he scored a hat-trick in each game; and in 1894 he collected caps against Ireland and Scotland. Features of his play were his speed and his almost uncanny anticipation; and he was denied many perfectly legitimate goals because referees insisted he had been off-side when he wasn't. One instance when Spiksley's speed deceived the referee was in the 1894 semi-final with Bolton at Fallowfield, Manchester.

Wednesday's party travelled to the ground in a drag drawn by four horses, and, on the way, a black cat ran right across their path. "That's good luck for us today!" someone exclaimed. In fact, it proved to be an afternoon when they had only bad luck. Just before half-time Jamieson was adjudged to have handled the ball, though he claimed it had hit him on the chest; and from the free-kick the ball reached Bentley, who shot Bolton into the lead. Early in the second half Spiksley "read" a Brandon free-kick splendidly, speeding forward to head the ball into the net. . . only to be given off-side. Soon afterwards, Allan, trying to keep out a long shot from Bentley, only succeeded in turning the ball into his own net. Five minutes from the end Woolhouse reduced Wednesday's arrears, but it was too late to save the day. The same afternoon Notts County were beating Blackburn in the other semi-final at Bramall Lane.

Wednesday played the same team in the matches with Aston Villa and Bolton: Allan; Earp, Langley; H. Brandon, Betts, Jamieson; Webster, Davis, Woolhouse, Brady, Spiksley. Incidentally, towards the end of the season, skipper Billy Betts, "the old war horse", had a benefit match against Liverpool, and a sum of £56 10s 9d was raised. The occasion marked the end of an era, for by the time the new season came round Wednesday had found a new centre-half and future captain: a young man called Thomas Henry Crawshaw.

Tom Crawshaw, a typical Sheffielder in style and character, was to emerge as one of the giants of the local football scene. A product of the old Park district, he served his football apprenticeship playing alongside his brother, George, in the Attercliffe team which was then a power in amateur circles; and it was after a spell at Heywood Central that he returned to Sheffield to join Wednesday. He made his debut at the start of the 1894-5 campaign, and by the end of the season had gained the first of his ten England caps and also been chosen to represent the

Football League against the Scottish League at Glasgow. In fact, the only club match he missed in his first season at Olive Grove was a trip to West Brom—and, in his absence, Wednesday could not prevent Albion getting the 6-0 result they needed to avoid having to play in the test matches.

Crawshaw was not the only player making his debut when Wednesday kicked off the season at Everton. Three Scots—Bob Petrie, Archie Brash and Bob Ferrier—were also on duty for the first time. Ferrier, who was to make his name as a half-back, was initially used as an inside or wing forward.

Wednesday collected 28 points from their 30 League games, which was a disappointing performance considering they had 25 points in hand after 20 matches. They won only one of their last 11 League fixtures, and in the second half of the season seemed to reserve their best form for the FA Cup. They started on the Cup trail in brilliant style, defeating the holders Notts County 5-1 at Olive Grove, where Brash (2), Davis, Spiksley and Ferrier got the goals which made the result the sensation of the round. In the second round Wednesday thrashed Middlesbrough 6-1, with Harry Davis getting a hat-trick and Spiksley a double. Only 4,000 spectators went to Olive Grove for this match, for Sheffield United were playing West Brom at Bramall Lane on the same day.

There was no counter attraction when Wednesday, playing in the quarter-finals for the eighth successive season, faced Everton, and a crowd of 28,000 cheered the Sheffield side to a memorable 2-0 victory. Brady gave Wednesday the lead after 25 minutes, but soon afterwards Davis went off injured. To add to their woe, Ferrier was so badly injured that he hobbled helplessly on the wing. Yet it was Ferrier who limped in to score the second goal just before the interval; though playing on was to prove costly to the Scot, for he missed the semi-final at Derby.

Wednesday, facing West Brom, recalled Woolhouse, thus giving the Ecclesfielder the distinction of playing in his third semi-final. However, the lone survivor from the 1890 team had a disappointing afternoon, and the gamble failed. Hutchinson put Albion ahead after 20 minutes, and nine minutes before half-time Wednesday went further behind when Williams scored from the penalty spot. In those days the penalty line extended the full width of the pitch, and the incident which led to the spot-kick actually occurred close to the corner flag! Langley tackled Billy Bassett, and the Albion man fell to the ground as if poleaxed. Langley was bitter about the incident for months afterwards, and, when Wednesday later visited Albion in the last League match of the season, he vowed they wouldn't get the six goals they needed to avoid the test matches. "They'll do it over my dead body!" he said. Alas, Albion achieved their target, but Langley survived to fight another day. Albion went on to lose to Aston Villa in the first final played at Crystal Palace, but Villa subsequently lost the Cup. . . literally! The treasured trophy was put on display in the window of a Birmingham shop, and one night it was stolen, never to be recovered. A new trophy was introduced for the 1895-6 campaign; and, of course, Wednesday were to be the first winners to collect the second FA Cup.

In retrospect it would seem that Wednesday's Cup triumph dominated the 1895-6 campaign, but it is appropriate to note that they also enjoyed reasonable success in the League. They finished in seventh place. Unfortunately, their away form left much to be desired, for on their travels they won only twice—at West Brom and Preston— and suffered heavy defeats at Wolves (0-4), Bury (1-6) and Stoke (0-5). However, they did not lose a home match until Derby visited Olive Grove and put four past them at the end of December.

In the team the chief changes were at centre-forward, where Lawrence Bell, a 21 year-old from Third Lanark, was introduced; and in goal, where Jim Massey, formerly of Doncaster Rovers, replaced Allan. It has to be said that Allan, having played in 16 consecutive FA Cup ties, was desperately unlucky to be sidelined just at the moment when Wednesday started on the run that took them all the way to the final. However, the goalkeeper probably contributed to his own misfortune. Playing at Burnley in early January, he took a heavy knock on a leg, but never mentioned it to anybody. A week later he played against Blackburn, and had the good fortune not to be put under any serious pressure. Even so, he did little more than aggravate his injured leg, and when he turned up for the game with Aston Villa on January 18 he could barely walk. The only other goalkeeper available, Massey, was nursing a broken finger; but he was pushed into action. In fact, Massey's early form was not very impressive, but he gradually improved and remained the first-choice goalkeeper for the next six seasons; and one of his best performances came in the Cup final against Wolves.

A fortnight after making his debut, Massey was facing Southampton St. Mary's in the first round of the Cup. A goal down early in the game, Wednesday hit back; two goals by Alec Brady put them in front before half-time, and they emerged 3-2 winners. Against Sunderland in the second round, Spiksley set up the first goal for Bell, and the centre-forward's tenacity later created the opening for Spiksley to get the winner, Wednesday going through by a 2-1 margin. In the third round Wednesday were again paired with Everton (who had previously KO'd Sheffield United), and a 12,000 crowd at Olive Grove saw goals by Brash (2) and Bell (2) clinch a fine victory on a pitch made heavy by continuous rain. Langley missed this game through injury, and Spiksley complained of feeling ill before the kick-off, but it turned out to be a memorable day. The fourth goal was the best seen at Olive Grove for years. Archie Brash, the smallest man on the field, jinked round two men and fed Spiksley, who exchanged passes with Davis before presenting Bell with a simple scoring task.

The semi-final at Goodison Park brought Wednesday up against Bolton again, and when Tannahill put the Wanderers in front after only seven minutes it looked as if another disappointment was in store for the Sheffielders. However, Brash shot Wednesday level early in the second half, and, with the score 1-1 at the end of 90 minutes, the teams met again a week later at Nottingham. In the replay Wednesday began in sensational style, with Crawshaw hitting the target from 25 yards in the opening minutes. Soon afterwards, however, "Sparrow" Brown, late of Olive Grove, levelled the scores. Things didn't look good for the

Sheffielders when, early in the second half, Langley took a heavy blow on his troublesome knee; by the end of the game the knee was swollen to the size of a football. However, after 60 minutes Bolton were punished for bringing down Spiksley; and from Petrie's free-kick Davis headed the second goal. Three minutes from the end Spiksley made the score 3-1, so ensuring Wednesday of a place in the second FA Cup final to be played at Crystal Palace.

At this point it may be appropriate to reflect on how the team used to prepare for special matches in those days. Matlock was a popular place, but, on the whole, Wednesday preferred to remain at home. They usually trained at Olive Grove, or sometimes at Owler Bar, in the mornings, afterwards taking the train to Dore. They would then walk to the Peacock Inn, and there they would tuck in to a hearty meal of steak and onions. After resting awhile they would set off back to Olive Grove, where they would remain until quite late in the evening, passing the time singing and talking. Occasionally, trainer Billy Johnson would take them to the theatre—though, after complaints from the regular patrons, the footballers only took in a show on those days when onions were not on the menu at the Peacock!

It was after a week spent training at home that the Wednesday party travelled to London for their Cup final date with Wolverhampton Wanderers. However, when they arrived at their overnight headquarters, the Queen's Hotel at Upper Norwood, the team for the big game had not been finalised. Ambrose Langley was still being troubled by his knee. The committee had decided he would only be risked if the ground was firm: in the event of it being heavy, Brandon would switch to left-back with Jamieson playing at left-half (as he had done in four of the previous ties). That Friday night neither Langley nor his room-mate Fred Spiksley got much sleep. One or the other kept slipping out of bed to check that the weather was still fine. Meanwhile, in another room, Jamieson was also wide awake. . . praying for rain! When the players took breakfast, the clouds were dark and threatening, but, in the event, the day remained fine. Langley played and the teams took the field as follows:

Wednesday— Massey; Earp, Langley; H. Brandon, Crawshaw, Petrie; Brash, Brady, Bell, Davis, Spiksley.

Wolves— Tennant; Baugh, Dunn; Griffiths, Malpass, Owen; Tonks, Henderson, Beats, Wood, Black.

Within 30 seconds of Lieutenant Simpson setting the game in motion, Wednesday had scored. A quick throw-in by Brash put the ball at the feet of Spiksley, and though the Wolves goalkeeper got a hand to the winger's shot he could not stop the ball reaching the net. However, less than ten minutes later Black equalised for Wolves with an overhead kick which caught Massey off guard. The game was only 18 minutes old when Spiksley got what proved to be the winning goal. Davis won the ball in a tackle, his pass found Spiksley, and the winger cracked in a shot which had so much force that the ball went into the net and rebounded out again. And, in the excitement, Tennant promptly punted it upfield, thinking it was still in play. At the end of the game the Wolves goalkeeper walked off the field alongside Jack Earp. "When do we replay?" he

3. F.A. Cup winning team, 1896. . . (top) Earp, Langley, Bell, Spiksley; (middle) Brandon, Massey, Petrie; (bottom) Crawshaw, Brash, Brady, Davis.

asked. "There's no replay," replied the Wednesday captain, "We've won 2-1." Tennant looked at him in disbelief. "You can't have," he said, "for only one shot went past me." He was not convinced of the truth until he saw Earp receive the new Cup from Lord Kinnaird.

The men who had brought the trophy to Yorkshire for the first time were given a tumultuous welcome by thousands of joyful Sheffielders when they returned home a few days later. The area around the Midland Station was so densely packed with people that the start of the victory parade was delayed for nearly half-an-hour. Eventually, led by a band playing "Hail the Conquering Heroes", the brake bearing the team began its journey; but the four gallant horses were unable to proceed at much more than a snail's pace. The situation was chaotic in Commercial Street, and, subsequently, the parade was cut short. When they reached the corner of Exchange Street and Waingate, the players climbed from the brake and disappeared into the Royal Hotel, where Councillor George Senior and Arthur Nixon had arranged a celebration dinner. Later, the band reassembled and the parade resumed. Eventually, the players found themselves at the Empire Theatre in Charles Street. Of course, they were top of the bill, and their appearance on stage was the highlight of the evening. It all added up to a great day in the history of the club. Alas, it was to be the last day of its kind for a few years. In the period immediately following, Wednesday were to be outshone in the

League and Cup by their neighbours and rivals, Sheffield United; and they were to endure some painful days as the end of the Olive Grove era drew near.

5 Olive Grove: the last act

Within less than three years of winning the FA Cup for the first time, Wednesday's world had turned upside down, and delight had turned to despair as a result of a remarkable turnabout of fortunes. After two seasons in which they enjoyed a fair measure of success and a climb up the League table, they suddenly found themselves in a desperate plight—under notice to quit Olive Grove, and at the same time fighting to avoid relegation from the First Division. It was the crisis of 1887 all over again, only worse, for this time there was much more at stake. There was a spell when it seemed that everything that could go wrong *did* go wrong, and things appeared to be going only in one direction—from bad to worse. Ironically, just when Wednesday were enduring the bleakest phase in club history, rivals Sheffield United were enjoying great success, winning the League Championship in 1898 and the FA Cup in 1899.

The prospect of losing Olive Grove came as a mighty shock to everyone connected with the club, and members of the committee were stunned when initial efforts to find a new home met with failure. Certainly the situation was viewed with a degree of disbelief, it all had an air of unreality about it; and it is fair to say that the atmosphere of uncertainty and near-panic affected the form of the team, whose lack of confidence and success added to the woe. Naturally, perhaps, there was a good deal of uninformed talk and misguided speculation abroad in Sheffield; and there were many who believed that Wednesday would cease to exist if they found themselves without a home.

Wednesday's lease on Olive Grove was scheduled to expire on September 29 1898, but officials believed that its renewal was a mere formality. The committee had no thought of leaving a ground regarded with so much affection by so many, and, indeed, a few years previously, they had rejected the chance to move to new headquarters. When they learned that the lease on their ground would not be renewed, the news left John Holmes and his colleagues staggered. The Midland Railway Company, who owned one small but important piece of land, said they could no longer delay plans to expand; while Sheffield Corporation, who owned the bulk of the area, said the land was required for purposes other than sport: both, however, intimated that they were unlikely to seek possession before the end of the 1898-9 soccer season.

If Wednesday's committee thought that finding a new ground was going to be a simple task, they soon had a rude awakening. A number of possible sites were considered, but all proved either unsuitable or, for one reason or another, unobtainable. Despite the urgency of the situation, members of the committee were determined not to take anything on a short-term basis, and they wanted no part of any arrangement by which they might be evicted from their home again at any time in the near or distant future. They would *buy* a piece of land, and if that meant the club would have to be reconstructed into a limited liability company in order to raise the necessary capital, then so be it. Unfortunately, time was not on their side, and as the weeks and months quickly rolled by they got no nearer to solving the problem. The situation became tense, even desperate. It was as late as the third week in March 1899 that a site at High Bridge, Owlerton, became the subject of negotiations, and the deal was not signed and sealed until early April—by which time Wednesday knew they would be embarking upon a new era as members of the Second Division.

Here it is, perhaps, appropriate to quote a letter from William Clegg, the Lord Mayor of Sheffield, read at the special meeting held at the Maunch Hotel in April 1899, when members heard for the first time full details of plans for the reconstruction of the club. Mr. Clegg's comments give some impression of the way many people felt about the club's situation.

"As an old member of the club," he wrote, "and one who still takes an interest in its doings, I sincerely regret the present aspect of affairs. A series of unavoidable and unfortunate circumstances, for which neither the officers of the club nor the team are in any degree to blame, have very largely contributed to the club's present position. Bad luck and other causes have dogged the steps of the club and the team almost from the commencement of the season, for which I am quite sure they have the sympathy of all the true sportsmen of Sheffield.

"I suppose we may now consider it inevitable that the club will be relegated to the Second Division of the League, but I hope that none of the present members and subscribers or the public will desert it in its present time of trouble and depression. I am quite sure that no effort will be spared by you or your colleagues, and I hope by members of the team, during the next football season to recover your position and work yourselves back into the First Division. If you succeed in doing so I am quite sure you will receive the warm congratulations of every true lover of sport in Sheffield."

Prior to this period of acute crisis, Wednesday's world had been aglow with promise and bright with optimism, and in the two seasons following the 1896 Cup triumph the team enjoyed reasonable if unspectacular success. It was disappointing that they should have gone out of the Cup at the first-round stage in 1897, and that they lost at West Brom in the second round in 1898 after a memorable victory at Sunderland in the previous round; but they had more than compensated for these setbacks with much-improved performances in the League. In 1896-7 they finished in sixth place, and fifth in 1897-8—their highest positions in their six seasons as members of the First Division. The period had seen the departure of Harry Brandon and Lawrence Bell of the team that had won the Cup; but the conversion of Bob Ferrier from inside-forward to half-back had proved an outstanding success, while the discovery of an outstanding local product, Albert Kaye, had, or so it seemed, solved the problem at centre-forward. Kaye scored 10 goals in 1897-8, and only

Spiksley (17) got more.

Wednesday's strength in their Football League days at Olive Grove had been their respectable home form. Their weakness was the apparent inability to string together any reasonable sequence of results on their travels. In 1896-7, for instance, they won only once away, and only three away victories were achieved in the following season. They owed their high placing in the table to good home results. In 1896-7 only Liverpool and Aston Villa beat them at Olive Grove—Villa in that season having the distinction of clinching the League and Cup double. In 1897-8 Wednesday lost three times at home—in one instance Nottingham Forest beat them 6-3—but the loss of six home points compared favourably with the record in previous seasons. Unfortunately, in the season of disaster, 1898-9, Wednesday not only failed to register a single away victory, but suffered seven defeats and dropped 16 points at home.

Yet, though 1898-9 was a campaign enshrouded in gloom, it did not begin badly, and the early weeks offered no hint of the fall to come. After losing at Liverpool in the opening fixture, Wednesday collected seven points from their next four games, and at the end of September stood second in the table. However, a series of heavy setbacks quickly pushed them into the relegation zone (this was the first season of relegation and promotion as we know it today); and there may be some significance in the fact that the team's performances deteriorated dramatically just at the time when the problems created by the failure to find a new ground had pushed the club's crisis to its most critical stage. In February the committee, concerned about the collapse of form, doubled the players' bonuses to £2 for an away win and £1 for a home win; and the players were promised £200 to share between them if relegation was avoided. Sadly, Wednesday won only eight games all season, and only two of those victories were achieved between February and the end of the season—with one of those two wins (in the home game with Aston Villa) having been virtually sealed in November, as will be explained shortly.

It is often said that nothing goes right for a struggling team, and Wednesday were certainly dogged by misfortune not always of their own making as they slipped to 18 defeats in their 34 League games. At different times they had Spiksley, Davis, Earp, Langley and the fast-improving Layton on the injury list. In defence Massey, Crawshaw and Ferrier managed to avoid serious knocks, and contributed some degree of stability; while Ruddlesdin was an immediate success when he was introduced into the half-back line. However, the fact that backs Earp and Langley played together in only 14 games was significant, for their absences created weaknesses which opponents were always ready to exploit. But it was in attack that Wednesday had their biggest problems. Only 32 goals were scored. They failed to find the net in 15 games, and managed only eight goals in away matches. Bill Hemmingfield, who scored on his debut against Nottingham Forest in September and claimed six goals in his first seven matches, seemed at first a great discovery; but though he finished the season as leading scorer, his final tally was a mere eight goals. Dryburgh (5) and Crawshaw (4) were the next highest scorers; while Spiksley and Kaye, who had scored 27 between them in the previous season, this time managed only three each. Kaye's three, by the way, all came in the game against Wolves in late October.

During the season no fewer than 18 players were tried in the five forward positions (and bear in mind that Spiksley missed only four matches); and six different men appeared at centre-forward. In one game Wednesday tried a local amateur, Harry Potts of Sheffield Club, at inside-forward, and they even experimented with Jack Earp in attack. In November Wednesday paid Bolton £200 for John Wright, an experienced forward with a big reputation as a marksman; but he did not produce his best scoring form until the following season.

Wright made his debut in the famous match with Aston Villa—the game which earned a permanent place in the record books because the first 79½ minutes were played on November 28 1898 and the remaining 10½ minutes were completed on March 13 1899! Incredibly, 29 players participated in the fixture, and Wednesday used 16 men. This astonishing and novel piece of football history is remembered when it is forgotten that it was at the abandoned match that a ballot was held to enable supporters to indicate where they would like Wednesday's new ground to be.

The visit of Aston Villa was, as always in those days, a big event on the local football calendar, and the crowd on that late November day in 1898 included William Clegg, in his capacity as Lord Mayor, Charles Clegg, chairman of the Football Association, J. J. Bentley, President of the Football League, and local Member of Parliament, Batty Langley. How unfortunate that the match referee, A. Scragg, of Crewe, should choose this particular occasion to arrive late. Mr Scragg missed his train connection at Manchester, and in his absence the game was started seven minutes late under the control of the well-known local official, Fred Bye. Mr Scragg arrived in time to take the whistle for the start of the second half, but he had been on the field only 34½ minutes when he abandoned play because of failing light. But for the delay at the start, and a brief hold-up before the second period began, the game could have been finished. Wednesday were leading 3-1 when the match was halted, and they added a fourth goal when the final 10½ minutes were completed nearly four months later. Villa, not surprisingly, wanted the entire game replayed, but, to the astonishment of many, the League said no. The loss of those two points did not prevent Villa from taking the Championship at the end of the season, but the gaining of them did not save Wednesday from relegation.

For the record, Wednesday's team in the first 79½ minutes was: Massey; Earp, Layton; Ruddlesdin, Crawshaw, Jamieson; Dryburgh, Davis, Hemmingfield, Wright and Spiksley. For the last 10½ minutes Massey, Earp, Crawshaw, Ruddlesdin, Wright and Spiksley were still there, with Langley, Ferrier, Bosworth, Richards and Pryce filling the other positions—and, presumably, claiming the increased win bonus for their 10-minute contribution to the victory!

It was in this season that Harry Davis—soon to depart the scene and be replaced by a man with the same name—was granted a benefit. A match was arranged with Notts County at the end of January, but such was the depression at the club and among supporters that only a few hundred people turned up, and barely £18 was taken at the gate. So, when the Villa game had been completed, spectators stayed on to see a friendly match between the teams in aid of the popular player's benefit.

Because the Villa game was put into abeyance until March, Wednesday actually went from the start of November until the middle of January without a win. Indeed, the 1-0 defeat of bottom-of-the-table Bolton on January 14 was their only win in 17 games between November 5 and March 11. After beating Wolves at the end of October, Wednesday registered only three more victories all season, and, not surprisingly, finished at the very foot of the table.

It was in late January that Wednesday suffered what was at the time the heaviest League defeat in their history—a nine-goal crushing at Derby. The team had prepared for the game at Matlock, but the Derbyshire air failed to put any sparkle into their play. They were simply over-run. As well as scoring nine times, Derby had another effort disallowed, they hit the bar, and Archie Goodall missed a penalty. The legendary Steve Bloomer scored six goals—three in each half—and so made the best possible impression on the watching members of the International Selection Committee. The heavy ground (a thunderstorm occurred before the kick-off) did not suit Wednesday; though it has to be noted that, soon after Bloomer had opened the scoring in the third minute, the Sheffielders were reduced to ten men when Spiksley limped off with a leg injury. One of Derby's goals was deflected into the net by Earp, Oakdon got one, and the ninth came when Massey was bundled into the net (along with the ball!) by two home forwards.

After this disaster, little went right for Wednesday in the remaining months of the season. They were deserted by good fortune, and, as often happens in times like this, a number of crucial refereeing decisions went against them. On March 4 they led Everton 1-0 early in the second half, and looked to have sealed victory when Spiksley scored what seemed a perfectly good second goal. But the referee adjudged the Wednesday man to be off-side. Everton rallied and won 2-1. A week later Notts County beat Wednesday 1-0, and the referee rejected claims that Fletcher's goal had been headed from an off-side position. Then, when Wednesday had the chance to salvage a point from the penalty spot, Crawshaw put his shot a foot the wrong side of the post.

At the end of March Wednesday played a rearranged game with Stoke. As the visitors had been unable to fulfil the fixture on the original date because they had been playing in the FA Cup semi-final, they had to pay Wednesday £75 compensation for loss of gate money. They arrived at Olive Grove with the cheque, but that was all they were prepared to give away. Stoke won 3-1.

A Wright penalty gave Wednesday their last victory at Olive Grove, against Burnley on April 1, but the club's relegation was already an accepted fact. A youngster called Hutton, playing in only his second League game, had the distinction of scoring Wednesday's last League goal at Olive Grove on April 15; but the visitors, Newcastle United, took the points with a 3-1 win. The Wednesday team on this occasion was: Massey; Earp, Langley; Ferrier, Crawshaw, Ruddlesdin; Bosworth, Pryce, Hutton, Wright, Spiksley.

On the day Wednesday played their last League game at Olive Grove in an atmosphere of deep melancholy, their neighbours Sheffield United were enjoying a moment of triumph at Crystal Palace, where they beat Derby County 4-1 to win the FA Cup for the first time. In ten short years United had achieved a great deal. In a dozen years as a professional organisation, so had Wednesday, but, for them, the best years were just around the corner. . . or, to be more precise, they were a few miles down the road at a place called Owlerton!

Part 3
Early Years at Owlerton: 1899-1915

1 The trials of finding a new home

In modern times Sheffield Wednesday's ground has been widely recognised as one of the country's premier soccer stadiums, and for many years the club led the way in terms of improving spectator facilities. Hillsborough (it was called Owlerton until 1913) has been the venue for many top matches—internationals, World Cup games, Inter-League fixtures, FA Cup semi-finals, etc.—and the attendance record stands at 72,841, set in 1934. Nowadays the capacity is 50,174, but what has made Hillsborough special is that almost half the capacity is in seating—in the South Stand, and the terracing in front of it; in the 1961 Cantilever North Stand; and in the West Stand, built for the World Cup matches in 1966. On a big match day the Wednesday ground certainly presents a magnificent spectacle.

In this context, and at a distance of more than 80 years, therefore, it is hard to imagine the place as it was in 1899—and even harder to imagine the heartache and the mounting frustration endured by club officials in the months after Wednesday had been served with notice to quit Olive Grove. For a long time they faced the growing likelihood of being without a permanent home, and the fact that this glum prospect coincided with the team's relegation to the Second Division only added to the gloom. At one stage the club's future hung precariously in the balance, and, but for the determination of a group of Sheffield businessmen who were football fanatics, there might have been no stadium at Hillsborough today.

Finding another ground to replace Olive Grove was no simple matter, and officials suffered a series of setbacks and disappointments. The deal which gave Wednesday the site on which the present ground stands was not finally completed until a few months before the start of the 1899-1900 season.

When the Midland Railway Company said that Olive Grove was needed for development, they indicated that Wednesday would be allowed to complete their 1898-99 programme, but could give no firm promises. So club officials took the precaution of discussing their problem with members of the Bramall Lane Ground Committee, who agreed that Wednesday could play any outstanding League matches at United's home should they lose possession of Olive Grove before the scheduled April 30, seven months after the lease expired.

As was mentioned in the previous chapter, Wednesday's home game with Aston Villa in November 1898 earned a place in the record books because it was abandoned after 79½ minutes' play, with the remaining 10½ minutes completed nearly four months later. However, this fixture had a place in club history for another reason—supporters participated in a poll to indicate their preference for the area where they would like to see Wednesday establish new headquarters. The ballot boxes were borrowed from the City Council, courtesy of Ald. William Clegg; and, of some 9,000 votes cast, 4,767 favoured Carbrook while 4,115 preferred Owlerton.

In the great debate about Wednesday's future, all sorts of suggestions were voiced. Some people felt that the Sheffield clubs should share Bramall Lane for first-team matches, with reserve games played at Sheaf House. The idea of ground sharing was to be revived at regular intervals in the next 70 years—right up to the early 1970s when United decided to get rid of County Cricket and turn Bramall Lane into a four-sided soccer ground; but, for one reason or another, it was never pursued as a genuinely practical proposition. Even in 1899, in the face of a near-desperate situation, Wednesday's officials recognised that the only realistic solution was to have their own home and the independence that went with it.

Wednesday took a long hard look at Sheaf House, but negotiations proved inconclusive. Attempts were made to buy land in Ecclesall Road, but the price quoted was too high; and then a site at Hillfoot Bridge gained attention until talks broke down. A move to Carbrook looked on the cards when a piece of land became available at £5,000, but, before the deal could be formally agreed, the owner accepted a larger offer from someone else. Efforts to bargain for land at Owlerton owned by Burgoyne's trustees also fell through, and, for a time, Wednesday officials began to despair of ever finding a new home.

At this stage the Lancashire & Midland Railway Company offered them a temporary ground at Tinsley, but it did not entirely suit the club's requirements. Wednesday officials acknowledged that it would do in an emergency, but they hoped something better and more permanent would turn up. And, fortunately, it did. James Willis Dixon, head of James Dixon's, the famous firm of silversmiths, indicated that he was ready to release a 10-acre site on the north bank of the River Don at High Bridge, Owlerton. Mr Dixon, a past President of the Sheffield Chamber of Commerce and, until 1892, occupant of Hillsborough Hall (which he had since given to the City for use as a public library), accepted a price of £5,000 plus costs. Wednesday paid a deposit of £500, and, as soon as the paperwork was completed, the job of turning meadowland into a football ground began in an atmosphere of haste and high enthusiasm.

It is difficult now to appreciate how great a gamble Wednesday took in moving to Owlerton, which was then miles beyond the city boundary and poorly served by public transport. The area later became a thriving and busy suburb heavily populated and well within the boundaries of a great industrial borough; but in 1899 there were hardly any houses beyond Hillsborough Barracks, and only the most dedicated followers seemed likely to undertake the long walk from the city centre to the new ground on the worst days of winter. Fortunately, as events proved, Wednesday had plenty of loyal and determined supporters—and, in fact, the average attendance in the first two months of the first season at Owlerton was 3,000 up on the average for the last term at Olive Grove.

Wednesday were also blessed with a team of officials who were determined to ensure that the club would not only survive but thrive and make a mark in football at large in the 20th century. Many people made significant contributions in terms of time and dedication, and what some of these unsung heroes did has been forgotten. However, what has not been left unrecorded is the fact that the key figure in the Wednesday story at this stage was undoubtedly Arthur Dickinson, the astute honorary secretary who kept his head while many around him went dangerously close to losing theirs.

At the time of the serving of the notice to quit Olive Grove, Wednesday were an incorporated club with fewer than 50 members and a capital of £250, run by an enthusiastic and energetic committee. With a considerable amount of money being required to purchase and equip a new ground, it was obvious that changes would be necessary to raise capital. In May 1899 the committee, with Charles Clegg in the chair, met at the Maunch Hotel to arrange a voluntary winding up of the old club, with Arthur Dickinson appointed liquidator. At a further meeting the resolution was passed that a limited liability company be formed, to be called The Wednesday Football Club Ltd. Articles of association were drawn up (they contained the names of George Senior, Charles and William Clegg, Alfred and John Holmes, Col. Herbert Hughes and A. J. Dickinson), and, with the issuing of shares, £7,000 was quickly subscribed. A new era was about to begin.

It is appropriate at this point to list the 22 men who were named as the club's first directors. Their names alone serve to indicate that Wednesday had the practical support of some of Sheffield's most famous, knowledgeable and influential men, people involved in a wide range of industrial, commercial, civic and sporting activities. They included the Lord Mayor, the immediate past holder of that office, and three others destined to hold the position; a future Master Cutler; and the Official Receiver. The occupations ranged from being heads of firms in steel, cutlery, gold and silver refining, building construction, jewellery, pawnbroking and accountancy. One director was a veterinary surgeon, another an estate agent, another a wine merchant, four were solicitors, and two were schoolmasters who were also League referees.

George Senior, a man who had begun his working life as an apprentice nailmaker and became the self-made man who owned Pond's Forge, was elected chairman, a position he was to hold until his death in 1915. A plain-speaking man, typical of his time and place, Senior was one of the giants of local industry. His fellow directors were: Charles and William Clegg, George Franklin, Herbert Hughes, Bernard Firth, William Turner, Walter Fearnehough, Joseph Mastin, Henry Wood, Tom and Herbert Nixon, A. Muir Wilson, A. G. W. Dronfield, J. R. Wheatley, John and Alfred Holmes, William Tasker, Fred Bye, Joe

Cowley, Herbert Newbould and the faithful Arthur Dickinson.

Wednesday did not retain such a large board of directors for long, but these were the men who launched the club on its new era. Charles Clegg, as is mentioned elsewhere, was one of the great figures in the Football Association; while A. G. W. Dronfield had links with a club which had preceded Wednesday—he had been a founder and once captain and secretary of Sheffield Albion, a famous local club in the 1860s and 1870s until it was eclipsed by the rise of Wednesday. Colonel Hughes was Law Clerk to the Cutlers Company, as well as being secretary and later President of the Sheffield Chamber of Commerce. William Turner was later succeeded on the board by his son, W. G. Turner, a club chairman in later years; and people like the Holmes boys, the Nixons, Fred Bye and Herbert Newbould were among those who had been committed to the club since the early days of Olive Grove and before.

June, July and August 1899 were hectic months for everyone connected with Wednesday. The ground was levelled and enclosed; the old stand was removed from Olive Grove and transported to Owlerton, and, while things were far from perfect, everything was made ready in time for the start of the new season on the first Saturday in September.

Wednesday embarked upon their new era with enthusiasm, full of hope that it would bring a return of brighter days. Their confidence was tempered with caution, but they believed that a huge gamble would soon pay dividends. Proof that the sun soon began to shine on the famous old club is evident from a study of the team's record in the first eight seasons at Owlerton:

1899-1900	Second Division Champions
1902-3	First Division Champions
1903-4	First Division Champions & FA Cup semi-finalists
1904-5	FA Cup semi-finalists
1905-6	Third in First Division
1906-7	FA Cup winners

2 Second Division champions, 1899-1900

The 1899-1900 season merits a special place in the history of football in Sheffield, for in this year the city of steel and cutlery was the talk—and the envy—of the football world. Both Wednesday and United scaled the heights in terms of performances and achievement, and the rivalry between the clubs touched new peaks of intensity, epitomised in the fierce and full-blooded FA Cup second round battles which were an unforgettable feature of an extraordinary campaign.

In the first half of the season both Sheffield clubs were unbeaten: Wednesday did not lose until December 31; while United's run extended over 22 League games, and they equalled Preston North End's record of ten years earlier before falling to their first defeat on January 20—when the "funeral cards" greeted their return from Bury. United, holders of the FA Cup, led the First Division for much of the season, but, after the Cup duels with Wednesday, they faltered on the last lap of the chase for the Championship, and Aston Villa pipped them for the crown by a mere two points. Wednesday, however, made no mistake in achieving their goal of a quick return to the top grade with the minimum of delay; and though they ultimately took the Second Division title by only a two points margin from Bolton Wanderers, they finished eight points clear of third-placed Small Heath (now Birmingham City). Wednesday's 25 wins and the haul of 54 points (from 34 games) were both Second Division records at the time.

Wednesday, who called upon 21 players (including six survivors from the 1896 FA Cup-winning side) during this campaign, actually had the distinction of being the first team to defeat United, doing so in a club match at Bramall Lane on Boxing Day. United, however, had the consolation of being the only visiting side to lower Wednesday's colours at Owlerton—achieving this in the bitter Cup replay of February 1900.

Jim Massey missed only five games in goal, Willie Layton replaced Jack Earp at right-back after the first match, and Ambrose Langley, who took over the captaincy, was absent only through suspension in March. The half-back line of Bob Ferrier, Tom Crawshaw and Herrod Ruddlesdin came into its own in this season, and this trio were to emerge as popular and locally famous as the Strange-Leach-Marsden line of thirty years later. It is interesting to note that Ferrier and Ruddlesdin, like Strange and Marsden, started out as inside-forwards before being tried at wing-half. Ferrier had arrived from Dumbarton in 1894, but it was not until 1898 that he became a regular; while Ruddlesdin, a product of Birdwell, had been signed in 1898, and was to gain three England caps, the first in 1904.

The key to Wednesday's success lay partly in their strength in defence—they conceded only 22 goals (a mere seven at home)—and partly in their power in attack. Of 84 goals scored, 61 were registered at home; and "Jock" Wright (25), Millar and veteran Spiksley (10) bagged nearly 50 between them. The left-wing partnership of Wright and Spiksley was the team's outstanding feature; while right-wing partners Brash and Pryce also made a significant contribution. Late in the season Wednesday signed Harry Davis, a versatile forward, from Barnsley; and, as well as contributing seven important goals in his 14 Second Division outings, he was to emerge as one of the "stars" of the period: a future England player and a man whose courage and tenacity earned him the nickname of "Joe Pluck".

The new season kicked off on Saturday September 2 1899. With First Division football available close to the town centre at Bramall Lane, Wednesday's directors knew the team would have to pull out all the stops to maintain support at a ground so far from the heart of the city. In the event, right from the outset they got the backing of their followers, as a crowd of 12,000 turned up to see the club's first match in the Second Division.

Chesterfield, newly elected to the Football League, provided the opposition, the teams lining up as follows:

Wednesday— Massey; Earp, Langley; Ferrier, Crawshaw, Ruddlesdin; Brash, Pryce, Millar, Wright, Spiksley.
Chesterfield— Hancock; Pilgrim, Fletcher; Ballantyne, Bell, Downie;

Morley, Thacker, Gooing, Munday, Geary.

William Clegg, in his capacity as Lord Mayor, kicked off. The game was barely ten minutes old when Wednesdayites were stunned to silence as Munday shot Chesterfield in front. However, Wednesday quickly recovered: by half-time they led 2-1, and they finished victors by 5-1, the goals having come from Millar (2), Spiksley, Ferrier and Brash.

A week later Wednesday visited Gainsborough Trinity, and it was in this game that Layton began his long run as the regular right-back. He had joined the club in 1895 and was to remain with them until 1909. After his playing days were over, he emigrated to Australia, but the most interesting story concerning Layton is the one of how he came to join Wednesday. In those days he was working at Blackwell Colliery, Derbyshire; but he decided not to turn in for the night shift on the day before he was due to play in a trial at Olive Grove. In his absence seven of his colleagues were killed in an explosion at the pit. "I saw the hand of fate in that," he said later, "and I vowed that if Wednesday signed me I would never play for any other club."

Wednesday dropped only three points in their first 14 matches, their 11 victories including a 5-0 win at Burton Swifts and comfortable home successes against Small Heath (4-0) and Luton (6-0)—Spiksley getting the first hat-trick scored at Owlerton in the defeat of Luton. The team's fifteenth match was at Chesterfield—and it was there that a solitary goal from that man Herbert Munday ended Wednesday's unbeaten run. The Sheffield side was on top for most of the game, but couldn't convert superiority into goals; and, just before half-time, Chesterfield broke away down the left and Munday shot past Massey following an accurate cross from Geary.

On the following day, January 1, Wednesday met Grimsby at Owlerton, and found themselves a goal down at half-time. It was not until the 68th minute that Langley shot an equaliser; and seven minutes from the end Wright hit the winner. Five days later Millar hit four goals in a 5-1 win over Gainsborough, but Wednesday followed this with a narrow defeat at Bolton—a Bob Jack goal giving Wanderers a victory which put them three points clear of Wednesday at the top of the table. A fortnight after losing at Bolton, Wednesday met their promotion rivals again in the first round of the FA Cup; and this time it was a goal by Wright which gave the Sheffielders the victory which brought them the famous Cup dates with their Bramall Lane neighbours. Just prior to the Bolton tie, by the way, Wednesday defeated Loughborough 5-0, with Wright grabbing a hat-trick; but, at the start of February, they suffered an unexpected setback at Newton Heath (now Manchester United). This was the game in which Harry Davis made his debut, but he didn't get much chance to shine in a rugged match of many free-kicks; and Bryant sent Wednesday crashing to their third defeat of the season with a 70th-minute goal.

Now came "the match of the season"—the FA Cup clash with city rivals, United, at Bramall Lane. When the draw for the second round paired the Sheffield clubs it provoked a great wave of enthusiasm, excitement and debate. There were few neutrals to be found in the pubs and taverns of the town, but those who regarded themselves as such believed that United were the likelier winners—because they had home advantage and were holders of the trophy, and because Wednesday had lost their last three away games.

United prepared for the tie at Lytham, while Wednesday trained at home. On the day of the game Wednesday were at full strength while United were without injured forward Fred Priest. A crowd of 32,381 paid £1,183, but they saw no goals and less than 50 minutes' play; for a violent snowstorm hit Bramall Lane, and shortly after half-time referee John Lewis abandoned the match. Wednesday were disappointed by the decision because they had played into the snowstorm for much of the first half.

The tie was scheduled to be replayed the following Thursday, but, that morning, another heavy fall of snow caused a further delay in settling the issue. The game finally got under way on the Saturday, though only after dozens of volunteers had worked long and hard to remove the snow from the pitch. Many people apparently anticipated another postponement, for only 28,374 (receipts £917) turned up to see the teams share a 1-1 draw.

This was the match which gave a broad hint of the prolonged ill-temper that was to come later and make this series of Cup duels one of the most unsavoury in the history of the Sheffield clubs. The ground was very heavy and muddy and hardly suited good football. Perhaps the conditions helped induce the ill-feeling; though the tension had obviously been building up to a peak long before the kick-off, and early frustrations brought it all into the open.

In the first half Hedley had the ball in the Wednesday net, but his effort was disallowed because he was adjudged to have handled. United's supporters disagreed strongly, and their mood was hardly brightened when, after 20 minutes, Wednesday snatched the lead. Wright and Spiksley were involved in a smooth move down the left, and from Spiksley's cross Brash shot past Foulke. The ill-temper flared up in the second half, and what probably started it was an injury to Massey, who was kicked when attempting to pick up the ball and had to leave the field for treatment. Then Spiksley was carried off with a knee injury. Both players returned, but by now the mood of the match had become rather ugly. Fouls, one report said, were almost too numerous to record, but, eventually, something positive happened. United got an equaliser. It came ten minutes from the end, when Beers and Bennett set up an opening for Jack Almond to shoot past Massey.

Because the third-round ties were scheduled for the following weekend, the replay was fixed for the Monday, February 19, at Owlerton. Two days hardly seemed long enough for tempers to cool. On the morning of the game the *Sheffield Daily Telegraph* made a valiant plea for both teams to "bury the hatchet". The appeal fell on deaf ears. While United were at full strength, Wednesday were without Massey, Millar and Spiksley. Mallinson deputised in goal, with Lee and Topham filling the gaps in attack. The line-up was:

Wednesday— Mallinson; Layton, Langley; Ferrier, Crawshaw, Ruddlesdin; Brash, Pryce, Lee, Wright, Topham.

United— Foulke; Thickett, Boyle; Johnson, Morren, Needham; Bennett, Beers, Hedley, Almond, Priest.

Many people could not get to the match, and there were only 23,000 spectators (receipts £641 18s) to witness a clash which was described as "a disgrace. . . a game of wild excitement that sadly tarnished the image of Sheffield football." Wednesday had one man carried off with a broken leg, and two sent off by referee Lewis; while United had two players off injured for spells. Wednesday actually finished with eight men on the pitch, United with nine.

United won 2-0, but the *Telegraph* commented: "Under the circumstances there was no very great glory attached to the victory, for one goal was scored when Wednesday had ten men and the other when they had only eight." As in the previous game, the aggression and anger exploded into ugliness in the second half. Wednesday, no doubt, began the match feeling somewhat aggrieved, but whatever restraint might have been apparent in the early stages was thrown to the winds after the 38th-minute incident which saw Lee break a leg in a tussle with the mighty Harry Thickett. Two minutes after half-time Wednesday suffered a further blow. Langley tripped Walter Bennett in the penalty area, and Needham made no mistake with his spot-kick. Then, after 71 minutes, Wednesday were reduced to nine men when Pryce got his marching orders for kicking Hedley, who had to be helped off. Fourteen minutes later Langley, in one of his many clashes with Bennett, got a bit too rough—and Mr Lewis sent him off. Bennett went off at the same time, and took no further part in the match. Soon after this incident Beers shot United's second goal.

Five days after their Cup exit Wednesday travelled to Small Heath, and, not surprisingly considering they were without Massey, Wright, Millar, Spiksley and Lee, tumbled to their heaviest defeat of the season. Stand-in centre-forward Davis marked the occasion with his first goal, but the Birmingham side hit four. Wednesday dropped to fourth place in the table.

However, Wednesday suddenly recovered their best form, dropping only three points in their remaining 12 games. In the space of 17 days between the end of February and mid-March they scored 15 goals in three successive home fixtures—defeating Barnsley (5-1), New Brighton Tower (4-0) and Burton Swifts (6-0). Wright was on target in all three games, claiming a hat-trick against Barnsley; while Earp, recalled as deputy for the suspended Langley, marked his return with one of the goals in the defeat of Burton.

Wednesday's only defeat on the last lap of the campaign came at Barnsley in late March—ironically on the day that Massey returned in goal after a five-match absence. By now, however, Wednesday had the bit firmly between their teeth, and a run of five successive victories saw promotion clinched by mid-April—in fact on the day Wright grabbed another hat-trick in the 4-0 defeat of Port Vale. In one game—at Grimsby—Wednesday struggled before scoring twice in the last six minutes; and Langley salvaged a vital point with a timely goal at Walsall.

A last-day victory over Middlesbrough clinched the Second Division title.

It was a triumph for everyone connected with the club—from chairman George Senior to the humblest reserve, for, to complete a happy season, the reserves won the Sheffield Challenge Cup, the Wharncliffe Charity Cup and the Sheffield Association League championship. An outstanding backroom worker in this season, by the way, was Paul Frith, the trainer.

At the club's annual meeting in June, a loss of £579 3s 8d was hardly sufficient to cast any gloom over proceedings. Bonus payments to players had increased from £127 10s in 1898-9 to £533; but the directors felt that Langley and co. had earned every penny. As for various other expenses, most had been incurred through fees paid for professional services in connection with negotiations for a new ground. These would not be repeated, for Wednesday had found a permanent new home where they were destined to enjoy further triumphs in the next few years.

3   Champions twice—1902-3 & 1903-4

Wednesday did not exactly set the First Division ablaze as soon as they returned to the top grade, but the fact that they finished in eighth place in their first season and ninth in the second indicated that they had the potential to climb higher. It was, after all, a period of consolidation, and a time when the team was gradually being re-shaped. Wednesday were fairly successful at home—indeed, between February 16 1901 and March 8 1902 they won 14 and drew four of their 18 games at Owlerton—but they showed disappointing form on their travels. In 1900-1 they did not register a single away victory. When they won at Liverpool on October 12 1901 it was their first away success for 19 months; but in the following March and April they chalked up three successive away wins, and if they had won their last away game (at Derby, where they drew after leading 2-0) they would have finished the 1901-2 season in the top six.

Those first two seasons back in Division One were not lacking in incident or interest, but, in the context of the history of the period, the chief developments were the changes in personnel which created the team which went on the capture the League Championship twice and, later, the FA Cup. Of the team which shot Wednesday back to the top grade in 1900, six players figured prominently in the triumphs of 1903 and 1904: Layton, Langley, Ferrier, Crawshaw, Ruddlesdin and Davis. Spiksley made an important contribution in 1902-3; but the second title-winning season marked the end of an era for him and Langley. Massey, Brash, Pryce, Millar and Wright had all departed by mid-1902, and several newcomers had arrived. Most important among the new men were Andrew Wilson (from Clyde), Jack Lyall (Jarrow), Harry Chapman (Worksop), Harry Burton (Attercliffe), Jock Malloch (Brighton), and George Simpson (Jarrow); while Jimmy Stewart and William Bartlett, who arrived from Gateshead NER in the spring of 1902, were to prove capable deputies before establishing themselves as regulars. Amateur Vivien S. Simpson, who also played with Sheffield Club, was another man who made his mark in this period.

Initially, the most important new boys were Wilson, probably the greatest centre-forward Wednesday ever had; Lyall, the Dundee-born goalkeeper who was to be a "fixture" in the team for eight seasons; and Chapman, the 5ft 6in Kiveton Park product who emerged as perhaps the finest uncapped inside forward of his day. Malloch came to the fore, too, after a spell in the reserves: initially, the ex-Dundee and Brighton man was Spiksley's deputy, but he later displaced Wright at inside-left, and George Simpson, the plucky little Geordie, subsequently qualified as Spiksley's successor.

Wilson was probably not the first great hero of the Owlerton era, but he was certainly the man who wrote his name large in the history of the club's first two decades at the new ground. A bustling, determined but even-tempered man, he made some 530 appearances in League and Cup and scored well over 200 goals, being leading marksman in eight of the 15 seasons when he was a regular. Wilson was capped six times for Scotland. Chapman, despite being dogged by knee trouble, played in some 300 League and Cup matches and scored 100 goals, including 93 in the League. But for the brilliance of Derby's Steve Bloomer, he would surely have played for England. He was a bundle of enthusiasm and energy, and a fine tactician; and he "made" Harry Davis, the 5ft 4in winger. Davis and Chapman were dubbed "the marionettes", but they were far from delicate and took some rough treatment in their stride.

Lyall played in some 300 League and Cup games between 1901 and 1909, but, following Massey's departure, Frank Stubbs, a giant in the Willie Foulke mould, had the first chance to become the regular goalkeeper. However, after a run of 16 games in which he had done well, Stubbs had an astonishing experience in the first away match of the 1901-2 season. At half-time Wednesday led Notts County 1-0. Then, soon after the resumption, Stubbs took a heavy blow on the head in a fierce scrimmage; but, despite being plainly very dazed, insisted he could continue. Almost immediately, he punched the ball into his own net. . . and proceeded to present County with five more goals by gently placing the ball over the line, much to the amazement and consternation of his colleagues! He was replaced by Lyall for the next match.

Wilson (13) and Wright (10) led Wednesday's scoring charts in the first season back in the top grade, but they did not enjoy consistent success: Wilson took time to settle, while Wright, so long the supporters' favourite, began to fade. Both men started the 1901-2 season well, but then ran into a lean spell: Wilson losing his place to Vivien Simpson for a few games, Wright being allowed to move to Bolton.

In both 1900-1 and 1901-2 Wednesday finished higher than their city rivals, United, in the table, though the honours were evenly shared in League games between the clubs. However, United had the consolation of reaching the FA Cup final in both seasons: in 1901 they lost to Spurs in a replay at Bolton; but in 1902 Southampton were defeated at the second attempt at Crystal Palace. After their Cup triumph, United returned to

Sheffield to meet Wednesday in a match at Owlerton in aid of the Ibrox Disaster fund: Wednesday won 3-0, but United were without five of their Cup-winning side.

Wednesday began the 1902-3 campaign with a visit to Bramall Lane for a derby clash notable for two reasons: the fixture marked the debut in United's colours of Herbert Chapman, brother of Harry, the Owlerton favourite; and it saw Wednesday register their first-ever League win on United's ground. On that September evening, a crowd of 20,113 saw Priest shoot United ahead after only four minutes; but goals by Spiksley and Wilson enabled Wednesday to lead 2-1 at the change of ends. Harry Davis made it 3-1 to Wednesday, and Lipsham scored a second goal for the home side. A few weeks later, however, United got their revenge, for on October 11 they became the first team to beat Wednesday at Owlerton; on this occasion Priest got the only goal, shooting past Lyall after the goalkeeper had saved his penalty kick.

October 1902, incidentally, saw Owlerton stage its first inter-city fixture, Glasgow beating Sheffield 2-0. The Sheffield side included seven Wednesday players, and the Chapman brothers formed the right wing.

The 1902-3 season produced an exciting chase and a dramatic finish in the Championship. West Brom were the early leaders, but Wednesday's chief rivals were Sunderland and Aston Villa. Wednesday kicked off with three wins, Wilson and Davis scoring in each game; but they did not look much like potential champions on many occasions in the first half of the season, when they suffered heavy defeats at Newcastle, Liverpool and Stoke. The highlights of the early weeks were a 3-0 win at Notts County (Spiksley's hat-trick inspired his admirers to present him with a new hat!), and a 4-1 triumph at Nottingham Forest. Wilson claimed a hat-trick in the 4-1 defeat of Everton in early December, and fine victories at West Brom just before Christmas and in the home match with Aston Villa on January 1 saw Wednesday start the New Year in second place, one point behind Albion. Harry Davis scored all the goals in the 3-0 defeat of Bolton in the next game, but defeats at Middlesbrough and Wolves (goals were conceded in the last few minutes in both games) kept Wednesday trailing in the title race until the end of February.

Langley had the distinction of scoring five times from the penalty spot in this season, and two of these goals in February helped push Wednesday into top spot. In the home game with Grimsby his spot-kick salvaged a point, and his goal against Nottingham Forest earned Wednesday the points which put them ahead of West Brom on goal-average.

Wednesday's most important win of the season was achieved at Roker Park on March 21. Sunderland had not lost since the visit to Owlerton the previous November, and stood in third place but only two points behind Wednesday. It was a tense, closely-fought match, settled by a 55th minute goal from Wilson. The victory put Wednesday three points clear of West Brom. Sunderland's supporters did not take kindly to defeat, and, amid astonishing scenes, the Wednesday party was attacked and stoned as they left the ground. The team's brake was followed for some distance by a howling mob of home supporters. Later, as a result of the trouble, Roker Park was closed for two weeks and Sunderland had to play at Newcastle.

Unfortunately, Wednesday did not take the fullest advantage of their lead in the table. The team was plagued by bouts of the jitters. Another Langley penalty was needed to salvage a point at Everton on the first Saturday in April; but Bury and Derby County, that season's FA Cup finalists, both defeated Wednesday (Bury won 4-0), and, for a time, it looked as if the Sheffield side had thrown away their hopes of taking the title.

Wednesday concluded their programme on April 18 with a 3-1 victory over West Brom—Wilson, Langley (pen) and Spiksley were the scorers. This left them with a one-point lead over Sunderland, but the Roker men had one more game to play—and it was at Newcastle, where they had never been beaten by United. With the fate of the Championship out of their hands, Wednesday set off on a West Country tour. On the day the Championship was decided, Wednesday were playing Notts County in an exhibition match designed to promote association football in South Devon. At the home of newly-created Plymouth Argyle, Langley and co. won 2-0 with goals by Malloch and Ruddlesdin, and this earned them the Plymouth Bowl, which was presented to the Wednesday captain on the stage of the Plymouth Theatre Royal by Football League President, J. J. Bentley. But, of course, Wednesday were more concerned with events at Newcastle, and their jubilation that evening was not because they had collected the Plymouth Bowl but a result of learning that Newcastle had defeated Sunderland 1-0, thanks to a 49th-minute goal by McColl. Incidentally, news of Newcastle's win reached Owlerton during a Midland League match between Wednesday's reserves and Worksop Town, and when Billy Whitham put the score on the board the crowd's enthusiasm was such that the game was held up for several minutes. The top of Division One at the end of the season looked like this:

	P	W	D	L	F	A	Pts
1. Wednesday	34	19	4	11	54	36	42
2. Aston Villa	34	19	3	12	61	40	41
3. Sunderland	34	16	9	9	51	36	41
4. Sheff Utd	34	17	5	12	58	44	39

When Wednesday's party returned from their tour—from Plymouth they had gone to Bristol and then to South Wales—they were met by a huge crowd at Sheffield Midland Station, and after a triumphant ride up Commercial Street and High Street they were given a celebration dinner at the Carlton Restaurant before being taken to a variety show at the Empire Theatre. Later the club organised a formal celebration banquet at the Masonic Hall, where, in the absence of Langley, Fred Spiksley made a short speech on behalf of the players. Perhaps there was something symbolic in that, for a feature of the season had been Fred's return to fitness and something like his old form. Unfortunately, the campaign was to prove his Owlerton swan-song: injuries kept him on the

*4. League Champions 1903. . . (back row) Ferrier, Hemmingfield,—; (middle row)
Davis (asst. trainer), Layton, Langley, Lyall, Crawshaw, Ruddlesdin, Paul Frith (trainer);
(front row) V. S. Simpson, H. Davis, H. Chapman, A. Wilson, Malloch, Spiksley,
G. Simpson.*

sidelines throughout 1903-4 and he eventually joined Glossop before
embarking on a coaching career which was to take him to Sweden,
Mexico, America, Germany and Spain.

The triumphant 1902-3 season had seen Wednesday capture five
trophies—in addition to the Championship Cup and the Plymouth Bowl,
there was the Sheffield Challenge Cup, the Midland League Cup and the
Wharncliffe Charity Cup, all won by the reserves. The first-team's
success was based on a fine defensive record (only seven goals
conceded at home) and consistency of team selection. Langley,
Ruddlesdin and Wilson did not miss a match; Lyall, Ferrier, Crawshaw
and Malloch were absent only once, and Chapman and Spiksley only
twice. Chapman (14), Davis (13), Wilson (12) and Spiksley (8) were the
chief marksmen.

In the season of 1903-4 Wednesday again won the League
Championship: they also reached the FA Cup semi-finals. Again
defensive strength was the base upon which success was built: they
were unbeaten at home, and only four teams managed more than one
goal in a match against them all season. Layton and leading scorer
Chapman (16 goals) were the only ever-presents, but Lyall, Ferrier,
Crawshaw, Ruddlesdin, Davis and Wilson did not miss many games. An

injury at Sunderland in mid-October signalled the end of Langley's long run at left-back (he did, in fact, play against Newcastle in December, when he scored from the penalty spot); and Burton, a local product, seized the chance to make the position his own. George Simpson established himself at outside-left; and this season saw players like Bartlett, Stewart and V. S. Simpson begin to show promise.

Wednesday lost only one of their first 11 games—at Wolverhampton in early October. Their second defeat, at Stoke in mid-November, cost them top spot in the table, and they had to wait until the end of January before claiming it back. After that, however, they did not falter, and a seven-match run which brought 13 points gave them a four-point lead over their chief rivals, Manchester City. A notable feature of the season was that, between September and January, the two leading sides in Division One were the Sheffield clubs. However, when Wednesday were beginning to strike their best form in the second half of the campaign, United fell away and finished in seventh place. Wednesday shared a 1-1 draw at Bramall Lane in December, but won the return fixture in April with goals from Chapman (2) and George Simpson. April was the month when Wednesday suffered bad defeats at Everton and Newcastle, but, completing their programme with victories over Aston Villa (4-2) and Derby County (2-0), they landed their second League title with three points to spare. In fact, Wednesday clinched the Championship five days before their final fixture, for Everton's defeat of Manchester City meant City could not catch up. Final positions at the top:

	P	W	D	L	F	A	Pts
1. Wednesday	34	20	7	7	48	28	47
2. Man City	34	19	6	9	71	45	44
3. Everton	34	19	5	10	59	32	43

Pipping Manchester City in the race for the League title was some consolation for Wednesday, for City had defeated them in the FA Cup. The Cup trail had started at Plymouth, where the Southern Leaguers scored a last-minute equaliser to force a replay; but at Owlerton goals by Davis and Chapman (pen) gave Wednesday victory. In the second round Vivien Simpson was in dazzling form and scored three in the 6-0 defeat of Manchester United. Two matches were needed to dispose of Southern League Tottenham in the next round, but again Davis and Chapman proved the matchwinners.

The Goodison Park semi-final with Manchester City saw Wednesday play badly and pay the price. Wilson, out of the side injured for six weeks, was rushed back before he was fully recovered from a head injury; and it was a gamble which failed. City took the lead after 20 minutes. Lyall did remarkably well to stop a fierce shot from the legendary Billy Meredith, but he could not hold the ball, and Gillespie pounced to put the rebound into the net. Turnbull scored the second for City after 40 minutes, and added a third 22 minutes after half-time; and, but for some superb goalkeeping by Lyall, Wednesday's defeat might have been much heavier.

Wilson, by the way, finished the season with 12 League and Cup goals, and survived a rumour that he had died from the injuries which had kept him out of the team in the weeks before the semi-final. One local shopkeeper actually announced Wilson's death with a notice in his shop window, but the Wednesday centre-forward proved that the rumours were greatly exaggerated by appearing in the last six games of the season; and though he did not score in any of them, he was fit enough to collect his second Championship medal!

4 Steps to Cup success, 1904-1907

Wednesday began the 1904-5 campaign in champion style, as if intent upon completing a hat-trick of title triumphs with the minimum of delay. They won their first seven games, and led the First Division until the beginning of November—successes in this period including victories at Middlesbrough (3-1) and Bury (4-1), and a 3-2 defeat of Aston Villa at home after trailing 0-2 at half-time. The bubble burst at Sunderland in late October. And on the following Saturday Woolwich Arsenal became the first team to put three goals into Wednesday's net at Owlerton: indeed, the Londoners were the first visiting side to defeat Wednesday in 32 home matches. These setbacks marked the start of a run which saw Wednesday win only one of 11 games: they never quite recovered, and ended the season in ninth place.

It was during that glum autumn period that Wednesday staged one of the greatest recovery acts in club history—in the home match with Everton on November 12 1904. Trailing 1-5 until the 63rd minute, Wednesday hit back to earn a point in an astonishing rally.

Goalkeeper Jack Lyall was absent with an injured foot, and Jarvis came in for only his second League outing. Just two minutes after the kick-off, the youngster was beaten by Young. Harry Davis soon equalised, but then goals by Settle (2), Hardman and Abbott gave Everton a 5-1 lead at the interval. The second half was 18 minutes old when Wednesday began their recovery. George Simpson was tripped in the penalty area, and though Stewart's spot-kick was stopped, the inside forward rushed the rebound into the net. With 22 minutes remaining George Simpson scored a third goal, and after 80 minutes Vivien Simpson snatched number four. Tension and excitement touched a peak, and, with Wednesday pushing forward furiously in search of an equaliser, Davis clashed with Hardman. The Wednesday man struck his rival a blow with his fist: and referee Heath promptly gave him his marching orders. With the minutes ticking away, Wednesday mounted a succession of attacks; then, with barely 30 seconds remaining, Ferrier hit a free-kick into the goalmouth, and, somehow, in the resulting melee, the ball was rushed into the net. A point had been salvaged in the nick of time!

Wednesday won only six of the 17 League games in the second half of the season, their best results being home victories against Middlesbrough (5-0) and Bury (4-0). The Bury match, on January 14, was notable for two reasons: Stewart scored the club's only hat-trick of the season, and Wednesday introduced a new signing from Stockport

County, Tom Brittleton, who was to enjoy a long and largely successful run at Owlerton as a half-back or inside-forward. Brittleton made well over 300 League appearances and remained with the club until 1920, when, at the age of 41, he began a spell with Stoke, whom he helped win promotion from the Second Division in 1922. He was capped five times for England, though it is amusing to note that, in 1910, he declined an invitation to tour South Africa with the F.A. party because he said he would rather spend the summer fishing!

There was a time during the 1904-5 season when it seemed that the FA Cup might provide Wednesday with some consolation for disappointments in the League. They started on the trail to Crystal Palace with a 2-1 win at Blackburn, where Chapman and Hemmingfield got the goals. In the second round Portsmouth were KO'd thanks to.an 88th minute goal from Davis. Then came a hard-earned draw with Preston at Deepdale, but Wednesday won the replay 3-0, Wilson (2) and Stewart getting the goals. Unfortunately, Chapman was so badly injured in the Preston replay that he missed the semi-final with Newcastle, and his absence was probably the difference between success and failure. At Hyde Road, Manchester, Wednesday enjoyed precious little Cup luck: Howie gave Newcastle the lead after 18 minutes, and the Sheffield side may have realised that it wasn't going to be their day when a United defender handled but the referee ignored strong appeals for a penalty.

Newcastle did rather well out of Wednesday in this season. In December they had defeated the Sheffielders 6-2; in March they put them out of the Cup; and in late April they visited Owlerton and won 3-1 after trailing to a George Simpson goal until 11 minutes from the end. This last win was especially vital, for it set Newcastle on their way to the League Championship: the Geordies clinched the title by winning at Middlesbrough a week later in their last game of the campaign.

If Wednesday had failed to reach the Cup final they at least had the consolation of playing at Crystal Palace by invitation in late April—and they collected a trophy. As reigning Champions they were asked to play the Corinthians for the Sheriff of London's Charity Shield. They won the game 2-0, both goals coming from Andrew Wilson. Incidentally, another feature of the season was the appearance of Ruddlesdin and Lyall on opposing sides in the England-Scotland match.

Wilson (15), Stewart (13) and Davis (12) were leading scorers, but it was probably significant that not one player was an ever-present. Burton missed only one game, and Crawshaw, Lyall, Wilson and Davis were seldom absent; but Layton suffered a loss of form and was out of favour in mid-season, Slavin taking his place; while Ferrier, Ruddlesdin, Bartlett and Chapman were all dogged by injuries.

Wednesday's record was generally regarded as disappointing, and supporters who had become accustomed to success were not slow to express their dismay. The club's annual meeting in June was a lively affair, noteworthy because it saw a newly-formed Shareholders' Committee put up candidates to oppose the retiring directors. In fact, there was one vacancy on the Board, caused by the death of Joseph Mastin, and the directors invited his son, Arthur Mastin, to stand for election, offering W. F. Wardley as a second choice. The retiring directors standing for re-election were A. J. Dickinson, W. Fearnehough, H. Nixon, B. A. Firth, Tom Nixon, C. Ellis, W. L. Angell and W. J. Solesbury. The Shareholders' Committee nominated Percy Bowker and J. H. Thackray. At the meeting, held in the Masonic Hall, the voting saw the re-election of all the retiring directors with the exception of Ellis, with Wardley gaining a seat on the Board and Messrs Bowker, Thackray and Mastin all defeated. It was at this stage that A.G. W. Dronfield, quoting Article 59, proposed that a ballot of *all* shareholders be conducted by post. This was agreed, and when the results were announced in July they showed that both the directors' nominees, Wardley and Mastin, had been elected; but Messrs Bowker and Thackray had again failed, while W. J. Solebury and Wilf Angell, the two directors who had opposed the wishes of their colleagues by not supporting Mastin, both lost their seats. Angell, a well-known local fruit and potato merchant, failed to gain re-election by only seven votes.

After this off-the-field drama, it was probably a relief to get back to the football; and in 1905-6 Wednesday showed a marked improvement in that they finished third in the First Division and also reached the quarter-final of the FA Cup. This was the season which saw the two grades of the Football League increased to 20 clubs each, with 38 games instead of 34. Wednesday had a spell at the top of the table from September to late November, but, in the end, finished seven points adrift of Champions Liverpool and three points behind runners-up Preston North End.

Wednesday lost only one of their first 11 games, and their seven wins included a 3-0 success at Newcastle and a 1-0 victory at Preston. But they lost five of the next seven matches, and soon slipped to fifth place. A Boxing Day victory over Wolves—Jimmy Stewart got four of the five goals—pushed Wednesday level on points with leaders Aston Villa, but a six-match run without a win between December 30 and the end of February virtually killed off hopes of a push for the Championship. Stewart, who had an excellent season with 22 League and Cup goals, claimed hat-tricks in the late-season wins against Arsenal (4-2) and at Nottingham Forest (4-3); but a heavy defeat at Birmingham in mid-April proved costly for Wednesday. If there was some consolation for Wednesdayites, it was probably provided by the fact that their favourites did the double over Sheffield United, thus reversing the results of the previous season.

Late April saw a local lad, Frank Bradshaw, make his senior debut in the home fixture with Everton—and he celebrated with two goals in a 3-1 win. Bradshaw, a big, well-built inside-forward, had emerged a "star" in Wednesday's Midland League title-winning side of 1905-6, and he was to have a run of nearly 90 League appearances and score 37 goals before a knee injury apparently ended his career in 1910. I say apparently, because when Wednesday said he was finished and let him join Northampton for £250, Town's manager, Herbert Chapman, sent him to a specialist whose treatment gave Bradshaw a new lease of life as a player. In fact, Bradshaw not only made a big impact at Northampton, but was later sold (at a profit) to Everton, and was still playing with Arsenal 13 years after he had been told that his playing days were at an end!

The 1905-6 campaign, however, is not remembered for the introduction of Bradshaw, nor for the fact that Wednesday finished in third place. If it is mentioned at all it is because of two games: the quarter-final Cup clash with Everton in March, and the League duel with Preston a few weeks earlier.

In reaching the last eight in the FA Cup, Wednesday had defeated Bristol Rovers 1-0, Millwall 3-0 (after a 1-1 draw), and Nottingham Forest 4-1. Then came the pairing with Everton at Goodison Park. What a game it turned out to be! Everton began with a tremendous burst, and, thanks to Sharp and Taylor, were two-up after only six minutes. In the space of the next four minutes Wednesday missed a penalty—Scott brilliantly saved a spot-kick by Davis—and reduced arrears through Simpson. Then, in the closing stages of the first half, Everton bagged two more goals and led 4-1 at the interval. After 55 minutes Bartlett scored a remarkable goal, jinking past four men before beating Scott to make it 4-2. Wednesday now struck top form, and, dominating proceedings, put their supporters in mind of the great revival of 16 months earlier. Ten minutes from the end Davis made amends for his earlier miss by scoring Wednesday's third goal from the penalty spot. The closing stages of a pulsating Cup-tie were full of thrills and spills, but Everton held out—and they subsequently defeated Newcastle in the final at Crystal Palace.

The League fixture with Preston in January 1906 earned a place in club history not for the football but as a result of incidents which occurred afterwards involving home supporters and visiting players and officials. The match, in fact, was the kind of uninspiring if rugged clash which deserved to be forgotten: Chapman had given Wednesday the lead soon after half-time, and Preston had equalised from the penalty spot after 80 minutes. The penalty incident was probably the spark which fired the trouble which followed; for home supporters felt Lyall had been harshly penalised for one harmless-looking collision with an opponent, while Preston had escaped punishment for a succession of infringements.

Why it happened is a purely academic point at this distance in time, but the fact is that, as soon as the game was over, a large and noisy crowd gathered outside the players' entrance. If the Preston party had tried to get away quickly and quietly, things might have not got out of hand. However, arguments abounded and heated words were exchanged by the crowd outside and the visiting players standing at the dressing room windows; and, as the party prepared to leave, a longer debate followed. The Prestonians at last boarded the wagonette taking them to the Royal Hotel in the city centre, but that was not the end of the affair. Scores of spectators pursued the brake on its journey along Penistone Road; and, despite the presence of two mounted policemen, stones and mud were thrown at the Preston party.

It was, of course, a foolish business, and nobody would claim that the spectators involved were genuine sportsmen or representative of the

Wednesday club's supporters or the majority opinion. A few misguided persons allowed their feelings to get the better of their judgement for barely half-an-hour, and it brought criticism and disgrace on the name of the club and the city. The incident provoked considerable correspondence in the local newspapers, with various people, including J. C. Clegg and Preston director Thomas Houghton, expressing their views in public; and evidence was provided to show that the visitors had fuelled the flames of fury with comments best left unsaid.

Within three weeks the Football Association's specially appointed Commission of Inquiry sat at the Royal Victoria Hotel in Sheffield to consider the facts of the case. After five hours they announced their findings. They decided that: (a) the match had not been played in the proper spirit, the conduct of both teams having been calculated to bring discredit upon the game; (b) the match had not been properly controlled by the referee, and there had been a want of alertness on the part of the linesmen; (c) T. Houghton, a Preston director, had conducted himself improperly towards spectators in the neighbourhood of the dressing room at the close of the match; (d) the Preston players had conducted themselves in a vulgar manner at the dressing room windows at the close of the match. The Commission censured the players of both teams and the referee; Mr Houghton was suspended from management for one month; each of the Preston players was fined £1; and the Wednesday ground was ordered to be closed for 14 days, though the Commission noted that the club had done all it could to ensure the proper conduct of the match. "But," said the FA Commission's statement, "spectators must be taught that their misbehaviour at the close of the game cannot be tolerated."

The season of 1906-7 saw Wednesday finish in their lowest position in the First Division since their move to Owlerton. Six defeats at home, where they dropped 17 points, contributed to their fall to thirteenth place. In fact, they lost only one of their first 16 games, and in December stood second in the table; but they won only one of their next 11 League games, and only four of their First Division fixtures between December 8 and the end of the season. Their last League victory was the 5-2 defeat of Manchester United in mid-November; but they crashed 1-5 at Newcastle after leading 1-0 at half-time, Manchester United put five past them in April, and Aston Villa defeated them 8-1 at Villa Park in early February. The period from January 19 to April 4 was nothing less than a nightmare as nine defeats were suffered in 10 games.

Of course, in retrospect the season is not remembered for the dismal League record but for a triumph in the FA Cup. Certainly in 1907 Wednesday were blessed with a little Cup luck, though they earned it with some remarkable performances in which they showed great fighting qualities. In the first round, for instance, they trailed by two goals at one stage in the home tie with Second Division Wolves; but goals by Tummon, Stewart and George Simpson gave them a dramatic victory. At Southampton in the second round, Wilson was the hero with an equalising goal 20 seconds from the end: Wednesday won the replay 3-1, the goals coming from Wilson, Stewart and Chapman.

The third round brought Wednesday up against Sunderland at Owlerton. They went into the match without Wilson, and Bradshaw made his Cup debut. A tight, tense game ended in a goal-less draw. The replay at Roker Park was a tremendous affair, and skipper Tom Crawshaw later described it as the hardest game he ever played in. George Simpson was the man who broke the deadlock when he scored for Wednesday after 67 minutes; but, a few minutes later, Harry Davis, careering forward in pursuit of the ball, tripped over McConnell's outstretched leg and crashed heavily to the ground. "The crack was heard all over the ground," Crawshaw recalled later. "I ran across, and Harry held up his foot. 'It's broke' he said without a trace of emotion. Later, in the dressing room, when they were getting him ready to take to the hospital, he said only one thing: 'give us a cigarette, captain.' I think he sensed that his playing days were over." The loss of Davis at a crucial phase in the replay left Wednesday under great pressure for the final 20 minutes. Sunderland players swarmed around the Sheffield goalmouth, but, miraculously, Wednesday held out for a memorable victory.

The fourth round draw paired them with Liverpool, the reigning Champions, at home. Vivien Simpson deputised for Davis, while Stewart displaced Bradshaw. Chapman got the only goal of the afternoon early in the second half, and, at the final whistle, the Owlerton regulars rushed out and carried the little inside forward shoulder high from the field.

The semi-final—Wednesday's third in four seasons—brought a clash with Woolwich Arsenal at St Andrews, Birmingham. For this game Chapman moved to outside-right, Bradshaw returning as his partner. Arsenal, enjoying a good run in the League, were full of confidence, and their goalkeeper and captain, James Ashcroft, told Crawshaw before the match: "I feel sorry for you fellows today. You simply won't be in it." The game was only nine minutes old when Wednesday fell behind: Lyall stopped but could not hold a shot from Satterthwaite, and Garbett pounced to shoot the loose ball into the net. Was it to be another case of Wednesday falling at the last hurdle before Crystal Palace?

Fortunately, after 21 minutes the Sheffielders equalised. Crawshaw floated the ball into the Arsenal goalmouth from a free-kick, and Wilson darted in to prod it past Ashcroft. Soon after half-time Stewart thundered the ball against the Arsenal crossbar, and Wilson caught the rebound on the volley to crack home Wednesday's second goal. In the last minute Stewart made it 3-1.

Crawshaw later told an amusing story concerning Dr and Mrs Bishop of Buxton, who were great supporters of Wednesday. Dr Bishop had attended to Davis when the winger had broken his leg at Sunderland. Mrs Bishop always carried an old umbrella to matches, and this came to be regarded as a lucky mascot. "I thought it wasn't going to help us today," said Crawshaw after the Arsenal game. "I thought we weren't going to get here," said Mrs Bishop. "By the time we had reached the ground Arsenal had scored. Fortunately, you got an equalising goal soon after we had reached our seats!"

Wednesday were not entirely surprised to find that their opponents at Crystal Palace would be Everton, the Cup-holders; and the fact that everyone seemed to think the trophy would go to Merseyside for the second year in succession did not trouble Crawshaw and his colleagues. Wednesday's captain—at 34 the oldest man in the side, and the lone survivor from the 1896 Cup-winning team—knew it would be a very tough match: Everton stood third in the First Division and were fielding ten of the team that had won the trophy a year earlier. Asked for his views on the game, Crawshaw commented: "Now look here, I'm not going to say we are going to win, and I'm not going to say we shall lose. We are going to try to win. We shall go all the way, and while the ball is rolling you can bet we have a chance. We shall keep going to the end."

There was some doubt about Wednesday's line-up until the day of the game, Maxwell had played at outside-right in the four League games preceding the Final, but Wednesday decided to revert to the team which had defeated Arsenal, with Chapman on the wing and 22-year-old Bradshaw, after only 14 senior outings, getting the inside-right position. Everton sprang a surprise by leaving out Scottish international inside-forward, George Wilson. The teams were:

Wednesday— Lyall; Layton, Burton; Brittleton, Crawshaw, Bartlett; Chapman, Bradshaw, Wilson, Stewart, G. Simpson.
Everton— Scott; W. Balmer, R. Balmer; Makepiece, Taylor, Abbott; Sharp, Bolton, Young, Settle, Hardman.

Both sides went close to scoring in the opening stages: Abbott headed against Lyall's crossbar, and an error almost let in Young; while Simpson had the ball in Everton's net but was adjudged off-side. After 20 minutes, however, Wednesday took the lead. Stewart and Chapman were involved in a move which led to Everton's goal being put under heavy pressure: twice Scott punched the ball out, but Chapman then put in a fierce shot which the goalkeeper couldn't hold; and while Chapman was appealing that the ball had crossed the line, Stewart nipped in to head the ball into the net. Wednesday immediately found themselves facing a series of attacks from a determined opposition, and once Bartlett cleared off the goal-line with Lyall beaten. Everton's persistence paid off just before half-time when Jack Sharp levelled the scores. After that the play was fairly even, and a draw was looking likely. Then, with just four minutes left before the final whistle, Wilson chased a long pass down the right wing. He caught the ball in the nick of time (Crawshaw said later that he felt sure it had gone out of play), screwed in a cross, and Simpson, close to the far post, headed into the net. The Cup was bound for Sheffield!

Crawshaw later recounted two memories of that weekend in London. Concerning the game, he recalled how Chapman's loose cartilage had come out twice, but the Kiveton man slipped it back each time without most people noticing. After the final, the team stayed in London for a few days, and were invited to the Canterbury Music Hall, where George Robey, known as "the Prime Minister of Mirth", was topping the bill. Naturally, perhaps, Robey had the Cup-winners on stage during his act; and, as the players went up, Crawshaw asked "Shall I have to say owt?" and was relieved when Robey shook his head. Then, when the audience stopped applauding, the comedian suddenly said: "And now Tommy

5. F.A. Cup winners 1907. . . Players, officials and directors. (back row) A. G. W. Dronfield,
John Holmes, Arthur Dickinson, J. C. Clegg, H. Nixon, J. Thackray, C. Ellis, T. Lee,
W. Turner, W. F. Wardley; (middle row) J. Davis (asst. trainer), H. Newbould, Davis,
Brittleton, Layton, Lyall, Bartlett, Slavin, Burton, Foxall, Paul Frith (trainer); (front row)
Bradshaw, Chapman, Wilson, Crawshaw, Stewart, G. Simpson, Maxwell.
Note: Davis, injured in an earlier round, appeared in this picture on crutches.

Crawshaw will tell us all about how Wednesday did it." Crawshaw remembered: "I was lost for words. But I managed somehow. Mind you, I think they were mostly amused by my Yorkshire accent, and probably didn't understand much of what I said!"

On the following Tuesday the Wednesday party arrived home to be greeted by thousands of cheering supporters who lined the route from the Midland Station to the Town Hall, where the Lord Mayor, Ald. Styring, gave them a civic reception. A few hours later the team found themselves on stage again—this time at the Empire Theatre in Charles Street. The next day, however, it was back to business: they travelled to Bristol City; and, after that game, they called at Birmingham to complete their away programme. On the Saturday they played their last game of the season, at home to Everton, the team they had defeated at Crystal Palace the previous week; and this time the honours were shared in a 1-1 draw.

5 Eventful years: 1907-1915

After enjoying considerable success in their first eight years at Owlerton, Wednesday endured leaner times in the eight years which followed—the period from mid-1907 to 1915, when League and Cup football was suspended owing to the Great War. However, if major honours eluded them, this phase was not lacking in interest: on the contrary, it contained lots of incident and drama on and off the field, and much of significance occurred, Of course, it *could* be said with some justification that the Cup triumph of 1907 marked the end of an era, for Wednesday were not to capture another top prize until 1926 with the Second Division championship, and they did not win the FA Cup again until 1935. Indeed, after 1907 Wednesday ran into a spell when little went right for them in the Cup, and they suffered a number of unexpected and embarrassing defeats in this competition. However, if their record in the League was hardly sensational, they did remain among the First Division's leading clubs until the end of the period under discussion in this chapter; and, by the time the war began in 1914, Owlerton had become Hillsborough, and Wednesday's ground had become recognised as among the best in England.

These eight years brought many changes in the playing staff, and only Brittleton and Wilson of the Cup-winning side survived until 1915. However, the 1907 team did not break up overnight, and the bulk of the changes were gradual and spread over a long period. Crawshaw, who went to Glossop via Chesterfield, and Stewart, who moved to Newcastle, were the first to go, both leaving in the summer of 1908; George Simpson and Burton were involved in an unexpected double transfer to West Brom towards the end of 1908-9, and soon afterwards Jack Lyall left for Manchester City; and, later, Bradshaw, Chapman, Layton and Bartlett departed. The newcomers were many, and while some did not survive for long, others remained to make significant contributions to the Wednesday story in these years. The names which began to appear regularly on the Wednesday teamsheet included Davison, Spoors, Campbell, McLean, Glennon, Robertson, McSkimming and Blair; and it is appropriate here to mention also McConnell, Weir and the Burkinshaw brothers.

Wednesday's Cup record in these years was depressing. In four successive seasons from 1908 to 1911 they were defeated by non-League opposition, three of the setbacks coming at Owlerton. In the League they did better, for they finished outside the top seven only twice. However, in 1914 they went dangerously close to relegation, an alarming turn of events when it is noted that this same season had supposedly signalled the beginning of a bright new dawn with the completion of the new South Stand.

Wednesday climbed up to fifth place in the table in 1907-8, but, in truth, the season ended on a disappointing note. For much of the campaign they had kept close on the heels of eventual champions Manchester United, and they would have finished in second place but for the fact that only one of their last six games ended in victory. They had started the season in style, winning six of their first eight games; but then they faded, and a lack of consistency had cost them the chance of a place among the honours.

Their record included splendid victories against Bolton (5-2), Arsenal

(6-0) and Manchester City (5-1), and they beat Sheffield United twice; while the best performance of the season was probably the home defeat of leaders Manchester United on November 30, when a record crowd of 38,397 saw victory achieved with goals from Bartlett and Stewart. Yet the same side which could rise to the occasion brilliantly on some days could so easily suffer a sudden loss of form and lose at home to teams struggling at the foot of the table—a point illustrated in the home defeats suffered at the hands of Sunderland (who won 3-2 in December) and Birmingham (4-1 winners in April). Heavy defeats at Aston Villa (0-5) and Middlesbrough (1-6) emphasised how easily they could be punished by a team catching them slightly off-colour.

However, the biggest setback of all in 1907-8 came in the FA Cup. Wednesday, the holders, were KO'd by Norwich City of the Southern League. Attempts were made to persuade the Norfolk club to switch the tie to Sheffield, but Norwich insisted on retaining ground advantage. Of course, they had everything to gain and little or nothing to lose; and, on the day of the game, the pitch was so frozen and slippery that superior skills alone were no advantage. The match had been in progress about 25 minutes when Wednesday's luck ran out: Layton, attempting to make a tackle, slipped on a patch of ice, and Beauchap was presented with a gift he could hardly fail to take. Norwich increased their lead in the second half when, surprisingly perhaps, a 30-yard effort from Allsopp completely deceived Lyall. So, Tom Crawshaw's 48th and final FA Cup appearance for Wednesday was numbered among his most disappointing. A few weeks later the old skipper bowed from the scene; and perhaps it was symbolic that his last outing in Wednesday's colours was in the Sheffield derby with United at Owlerton.

The departure of Crawshaw and Stewart at the end of the season coincided with the arrival on the scene of two of Wednesday's best signings of the pre-war period—goalkeeper Teddy Davison, and Jimmy Spoors, who came as a centre-half but later emerged as an oustanding back. Both hailed from the North East, and both were to give long and loyal service—Davison remaining with the club until 1926; Spoors until 1920, when he joined Barnsley. Davison, who in 1922 became the smallest goalkeeper ever to play for England, made 424 League and Cup appearances in his 18 years with Wednesday; and, of course, he earned a unique place in Sheffield football history because he later spent 20 years, from 1932 to 1952, as secretary-manager of United. By coincidence, his first senior appearance for Wednesday was in the annual charity match with United.

Davison made up for his lack of inches with his remarkable agility and clever positioning, but he emerged as the natural successor to Lyall only after surviving a period of keen competition from Henry Kinghorn. A product of junior football in his native Gateshead, he distinguished himself by making a brilliant penalty save in his trial with the reserves in a Midland League match against Lincoln at Owlerton on Good Friday 1908. A quiet, serious man, he kept a comprehensive record of his playing career, and, when I visited him on his 80th birthday in September 1967, he told me that saving penalties had been something of a speciality of his. He faced 86 spot-kicks, and the penalty-taker failed to find the net on no fewer than 33 occasions; and Davison saved two penalties in a match three times.

Much could be said about this remarkable little man. It is, for instance, interesting to note that, as manager of Chesterfield, he was responsible for discovering World Cup goalkeeper, Gordon Banks; and he took the legendary Jimmy Hagan to Sheffield United. One story about Davison the player somehow sums him up. In November 1911 when United and Wednesday drew 1-1, Joe Kitchen's equaliser for United was hotly disputed by "honest" Teddy. Davison, who didn't usually protest, claimed that Kitchen had used his arm to help the ball into the net. The referee wouldn't believe him, but a critic of the day commented that if Davison said it was so you could be sure that it *was* so, because this was one man not given to telling lies. On the following Monday Davison received a postcard: it was addressed "George Washington, Wednesday FC, Owlerton"! It is worth recording that Davison was on the losing side only three times in 23 games for Wednesday against United.

The season of 1908-9 saw Wednesday again finish in fifth place. Andrew Wilson, again leading scorer with 21 League and Cup goals, took over the captaincy role vacated by Crawshaw; and the old captain's successor at centre-half was English McConnell, the experienced Irish defender signed from Sunderland. Unfortunately, McConnell, largely due to injuries, was limited to 44 appearances in his two seasons at Owlerton; and, in the long term, Spoors and later McSkimming proved the more consistent pivots. This season saw Davison make his League debut in the home game with Bristol City in October, and Spoors against Middlesbrough in November. Of the regulars only Wilson, Bartlett, Brittleton, Bradshaw and Chapman topped 30 appearances; but Billy Lloyd, the ex-moulder who had been on the club's books since 1906, established himself at outside-right, while Fred Foxall's success at outside-right and Walter Holbem's consistency at left-back led to the decision to part with Simpson and Burton.

Yet again Wednesday started the season well—they lost only one of their first 13 games—but let themselves down with a mere four victories in their last 14 fixtures. They won only two away matches, at Nottingham Forest in September and Liverpool in April; but it was home defeats against Bradford City, Sunderland and Blackburn in the last weeks of the campaign which dashed their hopes of a place in the top three. Ironically, perhaps, the defeats by Bradford City and Sunderland came in benefit matches—the Bradford game being given over to Burton and Bartlett, the Sunderland fixture to Simpson. Sunderland beat Wednesday 5-2, and it was at the conclusion of this match that Simpson and Burton signed for West Brom.

The season produced a number of notable victories. In the defeat of Manchester City in November, Harry Chapman got a rare hat-trick; Wilson hit three goals in the 6-2 defeat of Arsenal in late December; and Frank Rollinson, deputising for Bradshaw in the March clash with Chelsea, scored twice in a 5-1 win. However, perhaps the most dramatic success was the 4-3 defeat of Bury on December 19 1908. Two goals up after 30 minutes thanks to Lloyd and Bradshaw, Wednesday found themselves trailing 2-3 early in the second half. Bradshaw then equalised, but immediately afterwards Chapman was carried off. With ten men Wednesday battled furiously, and a draw seemed inevitable until Wilson snatched the winner with virtually the last kick of the game.

Three weeks after this game Wednesday started on the Cup trail again. A crowd of only 7,893 turned up to see them defeat Stoke 5-0 in the first round. Stoke had just resigned from the Football League owing to financial problems. In the second round Wednesday travelled to Portsmouth, where they were shocked to find themselves trailing 0-2. Their saviour was a young reserve, Oliver Tummon, who scored twice in the last 12 minutes. In the Owlerton replay goals by Rollinson, Brittleton and Wilson saw Wednesday safely through to the third round. Alas, this tie produced another sensational defeat for the Sheffielders. It was a game of three penalties—one converted by Glossop, the non-Leaguers, just before the interval; and two missed by Wednesday in the second half. Brittleton missed the first, and Burton (who had conceded the penalty from which Glossop had scored) put the second spot-kick against the crossbar.

In 1909-10 Wednesday again lost at home to non-League opposition in the Cup. This time they fell victim to Southern League Northampton Town, whose manager was Herbert Chapman, brother of Wednesday's Harry. Despite playing against ten men for most of the first half, Wednesday could manage no more than a 0-0 draw at the County Ground; and Northampton won the replay on an Owlerton pitch ankle deep in mud. It was not a happy season: Wednesday slipped to eleventh place in the table, and the club suffered a loss of £2,067. That loss, incidentally, provoked much debate at the annual meeting, and the club put the blame down to three factors: the team's poor playing record; the purchase of several new players; and the threat of a national football strike by the Players' Union before the start of the season. The strike was called off at the eleventh hour, but Wednesday felt that the uncertainty which had prevailed for much of the close-season had seriously affected the sales of season tickets.

Wednesday certainly made every effort to strengthen the team after a terrible start to the season. They collected only two points from their first six games and conceded 12 goals in their first three home fixtures, Middlesbrough scoring five, Bury four, and Everton three. When they lost on their first-ever League visit to Tottenham in late September, Wednesday found themselves bottom of the table. First victim of the bad start was Willie Layton, whose first-team career came to a sudden end. Spoors was switched to right-back, and the return from Ireland of McConnell gave the defence some of the stability it badly needed. However, it was plainly time for new faces to be introduced, and, in the following months, so they were. They included Finlay Weir, from Maryhill; Bob McSkimming, from Albion Rovers; Sam Kirkman, from Carlisle; James Murray and George Robertson, from Motherwell; and Patrick O'Connell, from Belfast. In addition, two youngsters, Stringfellow and Hamilton, were given a run in a forward line often weakened by injuries to Bradshaw and Chapman. The most successful of the forwards brought in were Kirkman, who quickly established himself at outside-right, and Rollinson, the local lad who, as Bradshaw's deputy, enjoyed one run of seven games in which he scored eight goals.

It was not until the first Saturday in October that Wednesday chalked up their first win, a 4-1 success against Preston. This victory marked the start of a home sequence which produced six wins in seven games, including a fine 3-2 defeat of eventual champions Aston Villa. McSkimming, who was to be a regular for the next seven seasons, helped strengthen the defence; but it was not until the arrival of Murray and Robertson in March that the forward line began to look capable of better things—and, significantly, the two Scots claimed four of the goals in Wednesday's best win of the season, a 6-0 triumph at Nottingham Forest in late April.

The most memorable match of the 1909-10 campaign was the Sheffield derby at Bramall Lane in November. This 31st League meeting between the city clubs was described by local soccer writers of the time as one of the greatest: a game full of incident and good play, with fortunes ebbing and flowing, the 30,000 crowd (receipts £821 9s 3d) thoroughly entertained by the 3-3 draw. Though Wednesday began well, United found themselves two goals in front after only 18 minutes; and, after Wednesday had bounced back to lead 3-2 soon after the interval, United earned a draw with a third goal ten minutes from the end. United's first goal, coming from a long effort by Brelsford, was the result of a rare error by Davison, who let the ball slip from his hands into the net. However, Davison could not be blamed for United's other goals—both snapped up by Simmons from crosses by Evans—for they were the result of splendid opportunism. Chapman was responsible for Wednesday's second goal, set up by Wilson; while the first and third goals were due to the individual brilliance of man-of-the-match Sam Kirkman, playing in his first Sheffield derby. The first goal came when Kirkman beat three men in a solo run from the half-way line before shooting past a surprised Leivesley at an acute angle. In scoring the third goal, Kirkman's anticipation of the flight and direction of a long clearance by McConnell paid off; for while Benson held back, the winger dashed forward, prodded the ball with his head, and ran on to put an unstoppable shot past the goalkeeper. The teams on this occasion were:

United— Leivesley; Benson, Brooks; Brelsford, B. Wilkinson (capt), Sturgess; Walton, Simmons, Kitchen, Hardinge, Evans.

Wednesday— Davison; Spoors, Holbem; Brittleton, McConnell, Taylor; Kirkman, Chapman, Wilson, Rollinson, Foxall.

Wednesday had a slightly better season in 1910-11: at least, by gaining three more points than in the previous campaign, they climbed into sixth place in the table. However, the team's performances failed to generate much enthusiasm among supporters. An outlay of £1,654 on transfers resulted in a loss of £1,096 on the season; and, at the annual meeting, Charles Clegg complained about the apathy of the Sheffield football public. But could they really be blamed? Wednesday again made a bad start: by the end of November they had only nine points, and just after Christmas their tally was 14 from 19 games. The New Year did not begin well, for in mid-January they made another unexpected exit from the FA Cup in the first round. Non-League Coventry visited Owlerton and won 2-1, Wednesday paying dearly for missed chances in the early stages, and then being handicapped by an injury which reduced Spoors to the role of passenger. If only substitutes had been introduced 60 years sooner!

It was in February that the tide began to turn, and perhaps the most significant steps taken by the directors were spending £1,000 to get Preston's unsettled centre-forward David McLean and a smaller sum to capture Leith left-half Jimmy Campbell. Wednesday had tried no fewer than nine men at centre-forward before McLean's arrival, and the team had failed to score in eight of their 15 games prior to his introduction. McLean had one of the hardest shots in football, and, once he settled, made a very significant contribution to Wednesday's success. However, his outstanding abilities made him a difficult man to deal with whenever financial rewards were discussed, and he was to prove a controversial figure. He quickly became a firm favourite with the supporters, as did Campbell, who had arrived in Sheffield with a reputation as the best young half-back in Scotland. Campbell was one of the many players at their peak just when the war brought League football to a halt; and, afterwards, he was past his best. In 1920 he was allowed to join Ambrose Langley's Huddersfield, but this talented and popular Scot was already being dogged by the illness which led to his untimely death in 1925 at the age of 38.

Campbell and McLean were introduced into the side together in the home game with Bury—Brittleton's benefit—on February 18, and, whether it was a direct result of their influence or not, Wednesday were beaten only once in the remaining 13 games of the season. Against Bury, Wednesday claimed their first goal for a month, but, ironically perhaps, the scorer was defender Spoors. However, McLean opened his account with the goal that brought a 1-0 win over Sheffield United at Bramall Lane on February 25; and though this was one of only two goals he managed up to the end of the season, his presence gave Wilson the freedom to recapture his scoring flair after nearly four months without a goal.

McLean rediscovered his own scoring touch in his first full season, 1911-12, when his 25 League goals helped Wednesday finish in fifth place. In fact, 14 of McLean's goals came in a run of seven successive home games between late November and the end of February; and the centre-forward's tally for the season included four goals in the sensational defeat of Sunderland on Boxing Day, one hat-trick (in the 5-1 win at West Brom), and five doubles. Wilson managed 11 goals, while Teddy Glennon, the Denaby product who later made a name for the goals he got in the war years, collected his best haul of League goals, 14.

The Sunderland match was a real Christmas cracker. Wednesday won 8-0, led 7-0 at half-time, and bagged six goals in an 18-minute spell. The goals came as follows: Kirkman (4 min), Kirkman (25), McLean (30),

6. A Wednesday squad of 1912. . . (back row) Davis (asst. trainer),—, Brittleton, Worrall, Davison, Spoors, O'Connell, Campbell, Ted Kinnear (trainer); (front row),—, Kirkman, Glennon, McLean, Wilson, Robertson, Weir.

Glennon (35), McLean (37), Glennon (40), McLean (43), and McLean (55). It has to be said that Sunderland were down to ten men after 25 minutes, Thompson being injured. Then, after 80 minutes, they lost goalkeeper Scott, who was hurt in a collision with Robertson. Holley went in goal. Wednesday's team in this remarkable game was: Davison; Worrall, Spoors; Brittleton, Weir, Campbell; Kirkman, Glennon, McLean, Wilson, Robertson. This win, incidentally, came early in an unbeaten run of 12 League matches; though, in the middle of the sequence, Wednesday again went out of the FA Cup in the first round, losing at home to Middlesbrough.

The season of 1912-13 saw Wednesday finish in third place—their highest position since 1906—and only five points behind Sunderland, the champions. At one stage in mid-season Wednesday actually led the table by three points; and, as late as March, they climbed back into top spot briefly following an excellent 2-0 win at Bramall Lane, where McLean and Robertson were the marksmen. In fact, Wednesday lost only three of their last 12 games, but Sunderland, with 21 points out of 24, took the title in style. In the later stages of the season Wednesday had a run of four games in which they scored 16 goals: at home they beat Chelsea 3-2 and Bradford City 6-0, and won 4-1 at Derby and 5-2 at Arsenal.

Sunderland had started the season badly, picking up a mere two points from their first seven games. However, by the time they visited Owlerton on Christmas Day they were enjoying an excellent run. A crowd of 38,000 saw Robertson shoot Wednesday in front after only 30 seconds, but Sunderland rallied and goals by Mordue (penalty) and Holley gave them a vital victory. Next day, however, Wednesday visited Roker Park and, with McLean and Kirkman on target, won 2-0—the first team to win at Sunderland since mid-September.

Aston Villa were the team who dashed Sunderland's hopes of a League and Cup double in this season, for they defeated the Wearsiders 1-0 in the FA Cup final. Villa also left a mark on Wednesday's history in 1912-13, for on October 5 they beat the Sheffielders 10-0. Villa Park has never been one of Wednesday's luckier grounds, and, before this particular fixture, they had won only twice in 19 visits. However, there was nothing in the form book to suggest such a huge Villa win, for both teams were on nine points, and, if anything, Wednesday's record was slightly better. In fact, Wednesday had as much play as their hosts. Looker On, writing in the *Sheffield Daily Telegraph,* commented: "The heavy score was entirely due to some of the most remarkable shooting I have ever seen." Five goals were scored by Hampton, Stephenson and Bache each claimed two, and Halse got the other. Wednesday's team that day was: Davison; Worrall, Spoors; Brittleton, McSkimming, Campbell; Kirkman, Lloyd, Wilson, Wright, Robertson.

Another match worth mentioning briefly from this season was the home game with Derby County in January. After 65 minutes Wednesday found themselves trailing by three goals, and they did not get their first goal until the 75th minute. Only four minutes remained when McLean got his second goal, and barely two minutes were left when Kirkman snatched the equaliser.

Consistency of team selection was the key to Wednesday's improved form. Davison and Campbell did not miss a game, while Kirkman, McSkimming, McLean, Spoors and Worrall were absent only twice, and Wilson only once; with Glennon and Brittleton missing only four games. The big individual success was McLean, who scored a record 30 League goals, plus eight in the FA Cup. McLean hit two goals in a match nine times, but did not manage a hat-trick in the League; though, in the Cup, he scored four in the 5-1 defeat of Grimsby and three in the 6-0 triumph over Chelsea. Unfortunately, the Scot's outstanding success led to problems when the time came for him to be offered terms for the following season.

The close season of 1913 was notable for a number of reasons. Success on the field had brought the crowds back, and with match receipts up by nearly £4,000, the club announced what was then a record profit of £5,382. Wednesday decided that the money should be invested in ground improvements; and the Olive Grove stand was displaced as the main enclosure by a splendid new South Stand with seating accommodation for 5,600. The stand, built at a cost of £18,000, included new offices, dressing rooms, refreshment rooms and a billiard room. Terracing was built in front of the stand, and, in addition, the banking at the Penistone Road end (now known as the Spion Kop) was substantially raised. Plans included the provision of a roadway between the back of the new stand and the river, and the Sheffield City Council intimated that they would widen the High Bridge and the Leppings Lane bridge to improve access to the ground. Wednesday announced that their headquarters would henceforth be known as Hillsborough.

The rest of the close-season news concerned individuals. Ambrose Langley, after a spell with Hull City, returned to Wednesday as assistant to A. J. Dickinson, his responsibilities largely connected with team affairs. Unfortunately, Langley's return was overshadowed by the news that McLean had rejected terms for 1913-14 and had signed for his home-town club, Forfar Athletic. The facts of the McLean case were that Wednesday had offered him the maximum wage of £4.10s a week and promised him a benefit, with a guarantee of £350. McLean wanted a three-year contract, but Wednesday's policy was to give all their men one-year contracts. Subsequently, the club discussed the possibility of giving him a two-year contract, but McLean said he would only accept this if he could have a guaranteed benefit of £400. Wednesday said no, and the player went off and virtually consigned himself to non-League football by signing for Forfar, who were then a Scottish junior club. It was said that McLean was intending to marry, and had been offered a lucrative position outside the game by a soccer-loving Forfar businessman.

With McLean gone, the debate about the loss of such a favourite dominated the local football scene; and it was at this point that director A. G. W. Dronfield took the step which was to cost him his place on the Wednesday board. Mr Dronfield wrote to the *Sheffield Daily Telegraph* to give his personal views and to explain why he disagreed with his fellow directors over the handling of the affair. He felt that more should have been done to keep McLean. It was a bold but foolish gesture, and, at the annual meeting a few weeks later, Mr Dronfield failed to gain re-election—and largely because he declined to give assurances to shareholders that he would never again discuss the private business of the club in public. How ironic that, while Mr Dronfield's principles caused him to disappear from the scene, the man he had defended, McLean, should subsequently have a change of heart: six months later the centre-forward returned to Wednesday and re-signed on the very terms he had previously rejected!

As McLean was not available at the start of the campaign, Wednesday signed J. D. Burkinshaw from Swindon. A native of Kilnhurst, he thus joined his brother, Laurie, at Hillsborough. Other newcomers included George Streets, a goalkeeper from Mansfield Mechanics, and Jimmy Gill, a young forward who had played with Sheffield Boys. Streets made his debut in the opening game of the season, at Bolton, for Davison had been injured in a practice match. The newcomer played brilliantly, and a goal by Glennon gave Wednesday a 1-0 victory.

Five days later, with Davison fit again, Wednesday faced Manchester United, and a crowd of 29,000 turned up to see the team—and the new stand, which was not quite complete. Unfortunately, Wednesday lost 1-3. Indeed, they lost five of their first nine home games, and six of their first twelve, and when Burnley beat them 6-2 at Hillsborough on January 2 the Sheffield side found themselves perilously close to the foot of the table. The Burnley match saw Streets making his second appearance in goal, and it was to be his last. He had a nightmare afternoon.

McLean returned in time to play at Preston in mid-January, but Wednesday lost 0-5. The centre-forward marked his return with nine goals in 15 outings up to the end of the season, but Wednesday won only five games and finished third from the bottom of the table—four points clear of relegated Preston.

Much of the interest in the second half of the 1913-14 season centred on the FA Cup, which produced an eventful crop of matches as Wednesday reached the quarter-finals for the first time since 1907.

The first round tie with Notts County would merit a place in club history in any event, because it was the occasion upon which the new South Stand was fully used for the first time by players, officials and directors as well as spectators. However, the game is largely remembered because, after Wednesday had won 3-2, County lodged a formal protest and urged the FA to order a replay. Wednesday went into the match without Robertson, Kirkman and Glennon, all injured, and McLean, who was ineligible. However, they began well, and J. D. Burkinshaw shot them in front after 10 minutes. Then Second Division County hit back; Peart levelling the scores from the penalty spot, and Flint shooting them in front with only 27 minutes played. Laurie Burkinshaw equalised shortly before half time. It was Wednesday's third goal, three minutes after the interval, which prompted County's protest. The incident followed a corner-kick. Iremonger, the County goalkeeper, caught the cross, but, as he fell to the ground with the ball, found himself at the centre of a tremendous scrimmage. He ended up in the net, still clutching the ball. The referee signalled a goal, but, before play could resume, Iremonger was carried off unconscious. County's protest was discussed by the FA at a meeting at the Royal Victoria Hotel, Sheffield, but they lost their case.

In the second round Wednesday went to Wolverhampton, where a McLean goal earned a replay—and another tie which prompted a protest and earned a place in club history. The game attracted a crowd of over 43,000 and record receipts of £1,669 12s. Kirkman headed Wednesday in front after 15 minutes, but the game's major incident occurred 12 minutes from the end. Suddenly, and without warning, a newly-erected retaining wall at the Penistone Road end collapsed, and huge chunks of concrete, plus scores of people, fell onto spectators in the area beneath the wall. Some 70 people suffered injuries. The referee held up the game while the injured were treated and transported to the Infirmary; and, for a time, the corridors beneath Hillsborough's new stand resembled a casualty ward. When the referee took the players back onto the field, the visitors did not want the match to continue. Pears, Wolves' Welsh international goalkeeper, had fainted at the sight of so many injured spectators outside the dressing rooms, and was unable to resume. Wednesday did not add to their score, but Wolves promptly lodged a protest. However, like Notts County, they failed to impress FA officials.

So the third round brought Wednesday a home pairing with Brighton, a tie which they won without much difficulty, thanks to goals by McLean, Gill and J. D. Burkinshaw. An unexpected bonus from this game was the "discovery" of David Parkes, who shone at the heart of Brighton's defence and so impressed home officials that they quickly negotiated his transfer. He played in Wednesday's last ten games in that season, with McSkimming switching to right back.

Wednesday's quarter-final tie with Aston Villa, the Cup-holders, was another historic occasion. The crowd of 57,143 was the biggest ever seen up to that time at a football match in Sheffield, and receipts of £2,302 were another record. Unfortunately, Wednesday lost 0-1, the only goal of the game coming from Edgeley two minutes before half-time. Sheffield's dreams of having both clubs in the semi-finals were dashed, though United got through by beating Manchester City.

The Villa match at least served to show that Hillsborough, now fully developed, was suited to the big occasion, and a tradition which has survived into the mid-1980s was established. Even before the building of the South Stand, Wednesday had been asked to stage the 1912 FA Cup semi-final between Blackburn Rovers and West Brom; and now the ground was chosen as the venue for the 1915 England-Scotland match—though, in the event, the game was cancelled, and Hillsborough had to wait until April 1920 to get the fixture.

The 1914-15 season was overshadowed by the outbreak of the Great War, and the football authorities were criticised for allowing League and Cup soccer to continue. However, having begun the campaign, both the Football League and the Football Association decided it should be completed. As things turned out, the FA Cup was brought to Sheffield by United, who beat Chelsea in the "khaki final" at Old Trafford; and either United or Wednesday might have clinched the League Championship with a little more consistency. Wednesday finished in seventh place with 43 points, but only six points separated Everton, the champions, from 10th-placed Bradford City.

When Wednesday beat Bolton 7-0 on March 1—the game was watched by a crowd of only 7,000—they went top of the table, but a mere two points from their next five games cost them the initiative; and, despite a 1-0 win at Everton at the start of April, they failed to exploit their advantage. Everton took the title with only 46 points. Apart from the defeat of Bolton, Wednesday's other victories of note included a 5-2 success against Aston Villa and a 6-0 win over Bradford (McLean got a hat-trick in each match); but they lost heavily at Oldham (2-5) and at Tottenham (1-6).

Perhaps the most interesting feature of the 1914-15 season for Wednesday was the signing of Jimmy Blair, at the time regarded as the best back in Scottish football. Blair, who had come into prominence with Ashfield, a Glasgow junior club, was snapped up by Clyde, and it was with them that he had attracted the attention of Everton and the two Manchester clubs. Clyde had refused to part with him, and it came as a major surprise when it was revealed that Ambrose Langley had travelled to Glasgow and succeeded in signing him for Wednesday. The fee was around £2,000.

Blair's career with Wednesday was, unfortunately, marred by misfortune, shortened by the war, and, as in the case with McLean, dogged by contractual troubles. Before he could make his debut, Blair was injured in a motor-cycle accident, and his first outing was not until the Bradford game in late September. Then, after nine appearances, he was involved in another road accident, and was on the sidelines until mid-January. In his first season he played in only 18 League games, and then, with League football suspended, he went home to Glasgow, and was hardly seen in Sheffield during the war years. When the war ended he refused to return to Wednesday because he said he was better off financially in Scotland. He eventually decided to resume his Hillsborough career, but did not remain long before he was transferred to Cardiff City. Despite everything, Blair was recognised as an outstanding talent, and played for Scotland in both the "victory" international against England in 1919 and the famous England-Scotland game at Hillsborough in 1920. Ironically, the man who had been so keen to leave Sheffield spent the later years of his life in the city, and died there in 1964.

It is probably of interest to record the Wednesday team which played in the last match at Hillsborough before League soccer was finally suspended owing to the war. The game, against Burnley, ended in a disappointing 0-0 draw, and the line-up was: Davison; Spoors, Blair; Brittleton, Parkes, McSkimming; Capper, J. Burkinshaw, McLean, Wilson, Robertson. None of these men could have known that they were seeing the end of an era in club history, for it was to be many years before Wednesday again finished in such a high position in the First Division.

Part 4
Fall and Rise: 1919-1927

1 Relegation—and Bob Brown arrives

Crisis, despair, gloom and doom were well-worn words in the Wednesday vocabulary in the years following the end of the Great War. The campaign of 1919-20 was one of the most disastrous in the club's history, and, after the fall from the First Division, the struggle to rise again proved long and painful. Not for another 50 years were Wednesday to endure a spell of comparable bleakness in terms of failure on the field and disappointment, frustration and fierce criticism off it. The collapse of the team's fortunes in that first post-war season prompted Arthur Dickinson to give up his duties as honorary secretary, bringing the appointment of Bob Brown as the club's first professional secretary-manager in June 1920. Brown, an astute and canny North Easterner, eventually guided Wednesday to great heights, building one of the club's most successful teams; but he had to endure a succession of setbacks and several years of struggle and troubles before he attained his goal.

In that black season of 1919-20 Wednesday won only seven games and suffered 26 defeats. They won only one of their first 13 matches, and just one of the final 16; and a haul of a mere 23 points left them 14 adrift of the safety mark. Notts County, who were relegated with them, finished with 36 points and scored 56 goals—finding the net twice as many times as Wednesday. For months the club's officials were in constant state of depression and desperately searched for a solution to mounting problems. Supporters could hardly believe what was happening. A staggering total of 41 players were called up in the quest for a winning formula, and only three—Brittleton, Blair and Gill—managed more than 25 appearances. Despite trying 21 different men in the five forward positions, only 28 goals were scored in 42 League games. To add insult to injury, Wednesday made a sensational exit from the FA Cup, falling 0-2 at home in a first-round replay against Darlington, then of the North Eastern League. To say it was a season when nothing went right is probably an understatement. Only twice did Wednesday score three goals in a match—at home to Burnley in late January; and in registering their only away win, ironically against the eventual League champions, West Brom, in November.

Wednesday's failure was partly due to the misplaced loyalty which prompted them to stand by so many of the players who had served them well before the war. No fewer than 14 of these "old hands" were used;

but, significantly, after the fall into the Second Division, all but two—goalkeeper Davison and defender Blair—were released. Eleven of Wednesday's 26 defeats were by a one-goal margin, and disaster might have been averted if they could have found one consistent marksman. Gill (8) and Welsh (4) contributed half the paltry haul of goals, and the side failed to find the net in 22 matches.

The biggest blow was undoubtedly the loss of David McLean, the Scottish ace who had so often been a matchwinner in the years before the war. In 1919-20 McLean figured in only three games, but did not add to his pre-war tally of 88 goals. There was friction off the field, McLean again being dissatisfied with his terms. In 1913 he had eventually accepted the club's offer after a long dispute, but this time Wednesday decided to let him go. In October McLean's transfer to Bradford Park Avenue was completed in a Sheffield cinema.

The gap left by McLean was never adequately filled. Soon after the Darlington debacle, Fletcher Welsh, leading scorer in the Scottish League,was signed from Raith Rovers, but after scoring three goals in his first two games he made only seven more appearances before being dropped. He never showed the form which had prompted Wednesday to buy him, and, when he reached the stage whereby he couldn't even command a place in the reserves, he was allowed to return to Scotland.

Arthur Dickinson scoured the country for players. In October he was among the hundreds of football people who attended the unique "auction" of players which followed the sensational expulsion of Leeds City from the Football League. There he acquired two forwards, Arthur Price and J. Edmundson, for £1,000 and £750 respectively. Other newcomers in this season included Johnny McIntyre, a half-back, from Fulham, Colin Mackay and W. H. Harvey. None, however, made any significant impact.

Only one of the many signings in this painful season was to pay dividends in the long run. That was George Wilson, who cost what was then a huge sum, £3,000, from Blackpool. Wilson, a stylish centre-half and one of the best headers of the ball in the game, quickly became a favourite. He went on to gain nine international caps in his time with Wednesday, and on one occasion in 1921 he and Sheffield United's Billy Gillespie were the opposing captains in the England v Ireland match. Unfortunately, Wilson's arrival in March 1920 came too late to prevent Wednesday's fall into the Second Division. In any event, Wilson did not stay long enough to help the club climb back to the First Division: a dispute over terms at the end of the disappointing 1924-5 season led to his transfer to Nelson.

The strain caused by the succession of setbacks began to tell on Dickinson. In 44 years with the club, including 28 as honorary secretary, he had never known such pressures and frustrations. No matter how hard he tried, nor how far he travelled in the search for players, things seemed to go from bad to worse. Halfway through the season he tendered his resignation. His colleagues, however, declined to accept it, and successfully urged him to remain in office until the end of the season.

The end of the campaign saw Wednesday immediately release or make available for transfer some 20 players. The last balance sheet upon which Dickinson worked showed an overall loss of £1,677 5s 3d; with match receipts of £25,000 offset by a wage bill of £8,300 and a £5,000 deficit on transfers. At the annual meeting in June such was the atmosphere of criticism that two of the retiring directors were unseated by candidates nominated by the newly-formed Shareholders' Association. Towards the end of the meeting, chairman Charles Clegg made an announcement which prompted little immediate enthusiasm among shareholders: a new secretary-manager had been appointed. His name was Robert Brown.

Brown was not entirely unknown at the club—nor was he unfamiliar with Hillsborough. Unlike Herbert Chapman, the legendary manager of Huddersfield and Arsenal, with whom he was later to be compared, Brown never played League soccer, though the game had long been his passion, and in his teens he had played with Hebburn Argyle. He had served his time in the shipbuilding industry, but a flair for administration had led to his move to Sheffield around 1901, and he joined Wednesday as assistant to Arthur Dickinson. As a figure in the background he saw Wednesday win two League Championships and the FA Cup; then, in 1911, he became secretary-manager of Portsmouth, at the time struggling near the bottom of the second division of the Southern League. In the space of a few years he piloted Pompey to the Southern League championship. A rival manager at this time was Chapman, who subsequently left Northampton to join Leeds City; and Brown also had his sights on the management of a League club when the news reached him that a vacancy was about to arise at Hillsborough.

Though Brown's appointment was not officially revealed until late June, it seems highly likely that he had been lined up for the job as much as two or three months earlier; and though Wednesday went through the formality of advertising the post it seems probable that Dickinson already knew the man he wanted for the job. It is interesting to note that Fred Kean, one of the first players signed in the Brown era, came from Portsmouth—and was told of Wednesday's interest by Brown *before* Brown left Fratton Park. Yet Brown resigned his position with Portsmouth in March. Kean, who had joined the Hampshire club in 1919 after being spotted while playing with Hallam, travelled back to his native city to discuss terms with Arthur Dickinson. When the deal had been completed, Kean was invited to meet the new Wednesday manager. . . and, to his surprise, into the room walked Bob Brown.

Kean, who came as an inside-forward, did not make an immediate impact, but, following his conversion to half-back, he became a big favourite and was to make nearly 250 League and Cup appearances. Right-half was his best position, but he had a spell at centre-half immediately after Wednesday's return to the First Division in 1926. A product of the Carlisle Street and Ellesmere Road schools, and the son of a Sheffield craftsman who became first secretary of the National Union of Gold, Silver and Allied Trades, Kean went on to gain nine England caps. He remained at Hillsborough until 1928 when Bolton paid

£5,600 for him shortly before selling David Jack to Arsenal for the game's first five-figure fee.

Kean, of course, was only the first of a string of significant and sometimes inspired signings Brown made in the first half of his period in charge at Hillsborough. As will be noted in detail in the following pages, others included Jack Brown, Billy Felton, Ernest Blenkinsop, Frank Froggatt, Rees Williams, Billy Marsden, Jimmy Trotter, Tommy Walker, Sam Taylor and Sid Binks in the years leading to the Second Division championship success in 1926, and Alf Strange and Mark Hooper soon afterwards.

2 Years of trial: 1920-25

Brown's first five seasons as Wednesday's secretary-manager were fraught with difficulties on and off the field. In two of these campaigns the team finished as high as eighth place, but never began to wear the look of serious promotion candidates. Several times during these troubled years Wednesday found themselves in the relegation zone, and as late as 1924-5 only a brief revival in the closing weeks of the season lifted them out of danger and into 14th position.

It was a time of many failures and few successes; a period in which directors, staff and players endured harsh criticism from frustrated supporters and commentators. It did not help that, in three of these seasons, rivals Sheffield United reached the FA Cup semi-final (1923), finished fifth in Division One (1924), and won the FA Cup (1925). The outcry among Wednesday's followers touched a peak in the autumn of 1923. The *Sheffield Daily Telegraph* posed the question: "The Wednesday—What's Wrong With The Old Club?" Not surprisingly, perhaps, the anonymous writer of the article appearing under that headline could not supply the answer. He pointed out that the club had spent around £25,000 on transfers in four years (how paltry that figure seems at a distance of some 60 years!), but it had not brought any improvement in Wednesday's fortunes, which had been on the wane since the end of the war. If only, he said, Wednesday had gone as near to success as had Barnsley (pipped for promotion to Division One on goal-average in 1921-2), the discontent might not have been so great; but, alas, they had never even been in the running.

Of course, the article provoked a flood of correspondence. Much of the comment was lacking in any authentic appreciation of the realities of the situation, but it indicated the great feeling for the club among supporters who were baffled by the team's failures. The club remained silent on the matter, but officials were provoked into making a public statement early in November 1923, following an article in a London publication, *All Sports Weekly*. The article alleged widespread friction in the dressing room: skipper George Wilson was said to be upset because he wasn't getting the support on the field, and it was claimed that he felt the strain was shortening his playing career; with Fred Kean named as the chief target of Wilson's criticism. The club issued the following statement: "The directors have made a full inquiry into matters affecting the club and find that there were some minor matters which have caused friction. These have now been satisfactorily dealt with, and, it is believed, will not recur. The directors desire to express their strong condemnation of the paragraphs suggesting the probability of George Wilson and Fred Kean leaving the club, as there is no foundation for such suggestions, which can only cause mischief." The air was cleared, but it was to be a long time before the team began to enjoy success. The experience of having their affairs discussed in the Press prompted Wednesday's management to issue strict instructions to players, who were warned not to discuss club business in public. As late as 1926 two reserve players who spoke out of turn were given their cards and told they were not wanted at the ground.

Wednesday began the 1920-1 campaign with three goal-less draws. Then, following the transfer of Welsh to Third Lanark, Johnny McIntyre was switched from half-back to centre-forward, and he promptly scored 10 goals in his first six games in his new position. Unfortunately, his success induced closer attention from opposing defenders, and, in the home game against Birmingham in late October, McIntyre retaliated and got himself sent off. The experience caused him to lose his scoring touch for several weeks. However, McIntyre ended the season with a tally of 27 goals—more than all the goals scored by the rest of the team put together. But it was a performance he was unable to repeat, and he subsequently moved to Blackburn Rovers, with whom he rediscovered his scoring flair.

After winning only one of 15 games between October and January, Wednesday began to climb rapidly following the start of a run which brought only one defeat in their last 15 games. Jimmy Blair was transferred to Cardiff City in November 1920, to be replaced by Harry O'Neill; and, in the following January, Sam Taylor, an inside-forward, was signed for a substantial fee from Huddersfield Town. Taylor helped McIntyre recapture his scoring flair, and contributed eight goals in 19 games—including two in Wednesday's best win of the season, the 6-0 defeat of Wolves in early April. In his four-and-a-half seasons with the club Taylor scored 36 League goals. He later played with Mansfield and Southampton.

The campaign of 1921-2 saw Wednesday bedevilled by injuries and illnesses, and, at one point, more than half the team went down with 'flu. They began with only one win in their first seven games, but an unbeaten run of eight matches at the end of the season left them in tenth place—eight points behind Stoke, who pipped Barnsley for promotion on goal-average. Their best wins, both at home, came against Blackpool (5-1) in November and Bury (4-1) in April. This was the year when Davison touched the peak of his form and saw his consistency at last recognised by the selectors; his choice for the game against Wales at Liverpool giving him the distinction of being the smallest goalkeeper to play for England.

If little that was memorable was achieved in 1921-2, it is worth noting that the season saw Bob Brown complete a number of signings which were to pay dividends within a few years. Jimmy Trotter was brought from Bury for £2,500; Charlie Petrie arrived from Stalybridge Celtic; Arthur "Darkie" Lowdell came from Ton Pentre; and Frank Froggatt, a Sheffielder, was snapped up after impressing with Denaby United. Trotter, Lowdell and Froggatt all took a long time to establish themselves. Trotter was dogged by misfortune in his early years, but this product of Newcastle was to bag a century of goals for the club, including 37 in 1925-6 and again in 1926-7. Lowdell made over 100 League appearances in six seasons, enjoying his best spell in the Second Division championship campaign of 1925-6. Froggatt started out in the shadow of George Wilson, but made the centre-half position his own long enough to captain the side on its triumphant climb back to the First Division.

In recalling the 1921-2 campaign, reference has to be made to the FA Cup. In the first round Wednesday beat West Ham thanks to a remarkable goal by Arthur Price, who scored with a speculative shot from the half-way line. The Londoners had Arthur "Ted" Hufton, an ex-Atlas & Norfolk Works player, in goal that day: the same A. E. Hufton who was to play in the 1923 FA Cup final and appear in England's goal in 1928 when the famous "Wembley Wizards" gave Scotland an astonishing 5-1 victory. Anyway, Wednesday's defeat of West Ham in 1922 gave them a trip to Everton, where, thanks to a Sam Taylor goal, they deservedly earned a replay. The second game attracted a crowd of 62,407, paying £4,445 (both records); but, sadly, Wednesday lost 0-1.

The campaign of 1922-3 began and ended brightly, but Wednesday lacked consistency. However, they finished in eighth place, and six more points would have been enough to see them promoted; so narrow is the margin between success and failure. They lost at home to Notts County, Barnsley, Blackpool and West Ham. The defeat against Barnsley came only a week after they had recovered from a 0-2 deficit at Oakwell to win 4-2. The fall against West Ham in the last home match gave the Londoners the two points which enabled them to pip Leicester City on goal-average in the chase for promotion.

It was a disappointing season, but, again, one which provided a number of individual successes. Kean, called up to play against Belgium in March and Scotland in April, became the first Sheffield-born player to be capped by England since Tommy Crawshaw 19 years earlier; and Ernest Blenkinsop, one of several newcomers introduced to the Wednesday side, was to emerge in due course as the club's most capped player—and a future captain of England.

Blenkinsop was one of seven major signings made during 1922-3—and one of four newcomers destined to make a big impact over a long period. The others were goalkeeper Jack Brown, full-back Billy Felton, and outside-right Rees Williams. Bob Brown also bought Sid Binks, Horace Henshall, and Andy Smailes.

Binks was a big, well-made and remarkably fast centre-forward—indeed, he was an outstanding sprinter on the track. In the beginning he seemed likely to provide the solution to one of Wednesday's problem positions. He had just helped Bishop Auckland win the Amateur Cup and gained amateur international honours when Brown persuaded him to turn professional. In 1922-3 he was one of three Wednesday forwards to score 13 goals (the others were Taylor and Smailes), and in 1923-4 was leading marksman with 16 goals; but, subsequently, his dashes down the middle failed to catch out the opposition, and, in November 1924, he moved to Huddersfield in the deal which took Edward Richardson, a winger, to Hillsborough. For a time Binks was a great favourite, the subject of a supporters' song "Binks Is Always Scoring Doubles" (to the tune of "I'm Forever Blowing Bubbles"), but his success was short-lived; though, fortunately, Trotter then discovered his best form, and the catch-song of the supporters then became "Trot-Trot-Trotter, score a little goal for me!"

Andy Smailes, later to become a great servant to Rotherham United as player, trainer and manager, was another player who began well at Hillsborough but faded. Signed from Newcastle, he had a spell in December 1922 when he scored seven goals in five matches; but then he lost his touch, and in October 1923 moved to Bristol City in the deal which gave Wednesday another centre-forward, W. B. Walker.

Rees Williams, who came from Merthyr Tydfil, was a much more successful signing. A clever winger with brilliant ball control, he scored only seven goals in his five years at Hillsborough, but he made many goals for others in his 160 League outings, and his skills earned him four caps. He was eventually displaced by Mark Hooper, and went to Manchester United in 1927. Another successful signing was Billy Felton. In fact, Felton was on his way to play for Grimsby at Accrington in January 1923 when he was called from the train to sign for Wednesday. A few hours later he was making his debut at left-back against Southampton at Hillsborough. Felton was to remain in Sheffield until March 1929, when he joined Manchester City; and, in 1925, he was capped by England against France. Felton was quickly switched to right back soon after joining Wednesday, the move being made to accommodate perhaps the most notable signing Bob Brown made in all his 13 years with Wednesday—Ernest Blenkinsop.

Blenkinsop, a product of Cudworth, was playing with the village team and working underground at Brierley Colliery when he got the chance at the age of 19 to become a professional footballer. He was spotted by Hull manager, Percy Lewis, who is reputed to have paid £100 and 80 pints of beer to get his man. When Lewis visited Blenkinsop at the pit, the youngster quickly accepted the offer of a £10 signing-on fee and a week's wages, £5, in advance. At the time he was earning 30 shillings (£1.50) for a 48-hour shift, but he offered to work a week's notice. However, the colliery manager wouldn't hear of it. "No, lad," he said, "thee go. Owt might 'appen down t'pit in a week." Blenkinsop packed his bags and went to Hull, but he stayed there only 15 months; and, in view of subsequent developments, it is amusing to reflect that Hull spent some of that time trying to convert him into a dashing centre-forward!

The turning point in Blenkinsop's career came on the day he played at left-back for Hull reserves against Wednesday reserves at Hillsborough. Bob Brown went up into the stand intent on taking a close look at Hull's other back, Matt Bell; but he quickly decided that Blenkinsop was more to his liking. Hull were paid £1,100 for the man who was to become one of the classiest defenders in English football; and "Blenkie" became an idol of the supporters in making 426 League and Cup appearances for the club as well as playing 26 times for England.

Blenkinsop made his debut at right-back in Wednesday's game at Bury in late January 1923. His home debut was a week later at left-back in the famous FA Cup second-round tie with Barnsley. A crowd of 66,103 saw Wednesday fall behind three minutes before half-time, but second-half goals by Smailes and Binks brought them a memorable victory. Blenkinsop was not the only man getting his first taste of a big Cup-tie atmosphere: another was defender Joe Sykes, a local lad who never really got a chance to shine at Hillsborough because of Wilson's consistency. In fact, Sykes enjoyed his best years in the game after moving to Swansea Town.

It was through the FA Cup—though not in a tie involving Wednesday—that Bob Brown discovered another promising youngster who was to write his name large in Hillsborough history. Jack Brown was playing with Midland League Worksop Town in 1923 when they reached the first round and were paired with Tottenham Hotspur—winners of the competition in 1921, and defeated semi-finalists in 1922. In the first match the non-Leaguers from Nottinghamshire held mighty Spurs to a goal-less draw, and goalkeeper Brown turned in a magnificent performance. Brown was equally brilliant in the replay (both games were played at White Hart Lane) despite conceding nine goals. Wednesday paid £300 for Brown, and it was a bargain. He was to establish himself as a regular within a couple of seasons, and went on to make over 500 League and Cup appearances as well as gaining six England caps—five of them between February and May 1927. Incidentally, one of the scorers in that 9-0 Spurs victory in 1923 was Jimmy Seed, later to become a colleague of Brown's at Hillsborough.

The 1923-4 season saw Wednesday make the bad start which sparked off the public criticism mentioned earlier. They won only two of their first 11 matches and were third from the bottom of the table in early October. Their first away match, at Port Vale on Monday August 27, provided an example of the sort of misfortune which dogged them—and probably served as an indication of an easy-going attitude which was undermining discipline in the team. Billy Felton and Rees Williams missed the train taking the team to the Potteries, and Wednesday arrived at Vale Park with only ten men. Petrie, originally selected as reserve, stepped in at right-half, Kean was switched to right-back, and Jerimiah Jackson, the 46-year-old trainer, had to play as an emergency outside-right. In fact, Jackson was so exhausted after 35 minutes that he had to retire, and the depleted Wednesday side probably did well to escape with a two-goal defeat. Felton and Williams were later each fined £5 by the Football League's Management Committee.

After the bad start, Wednesday went into a 10-match run which saw them lose only once. Brown was dropped and Davison returned to play brilliantly. A 5-0 defeat of Nelson in late October—newcomer Walker got two of the goals—lifted Wednesday out of the bottom four. Petrie enjoyed a run of seven goals in seven games, including two in the 6-0 defeat of Crystal Palace on December 22, when Binks scored the other four goals. As the season progressed Wednesday enjoyed a number of other important wins: Taylor scored three times in the 5-0 defeat of South Shields, while Binks claimed a hat-trick in the team's only away win—a 3-2 success at Bristol City. Bristol, by the way, finished bottom of the Second Division, and Wednesday did the double over the club which Andy Smailes had joined: but City caused an upset by putting Wednesday out of the FA Cup in a second-round replay.

The season of 1924-5 was probably the toughest Bob Brown experienced in his time at Hillsborough. Of course, with the benefit of hindsight, we can see that events illustrated the proverb which says it is always darkest just before the dawn. However, as the months from August 1924 to May 1925 passed slowly by, it was no doubt beyond the wildest imaginings of anyone connected with the club that promotion and success could be little more than a year away. As late as April 1925, while rivals Sheffield United were preparing to play in the FA Cup final, Wednesday found themselves in the relegation zone, desperately fighting to avoid a fall into the Third Division. In the event, they finished 14th, but only four points clear of Crystal Palace, who went down with Coventry.

This was the campaign which saw Binks depart and Trotter suddenly show signs of becoming Wednesday's most successful centre-forward since David McLean. Trotter scored 16 goals in 24 League outings, including a record five in the home clash with Portsmouth in early December. While Trotter was emerging as the new hero of Hillsborough, it is interesting to note that an unsung reserve, Ronald Eyre, was being transferred to Bournemouth. Eyre, who made only one senior appearance with Wednesday, was to become the darling of Dean Court with a haul of 259 goals in the next eight years.

Newcomers to Wednesday's colours in 1924-5 were Harold Hill, from Notts County; Arthur Prince, from Port Vale; and Billy Marsden, from Sunderland. Hill's ten goals were to make him second highest scorer; Prince displaced Harron at outside-left; and while Marsden did not enjoy immediate success, he was destined to make a significant contribution to the Wednesday story between 1925 and 1930. Marsden was to play in more than 200 games, and, but for a spinal injury suffered while on England duty in 1930, would surely have gained more than three international caps.

Two signings in March were especially important in that they gave Wednesday the impetus which earned them vital points in their final seven games. Sam Powell arrived from Leeds and Matt Barrass cost £1,950 from Blackpool. Powell's five goals in those final matches (including a hat-trick against Fulham) were invaluable; and Barrass was on target in the 5-0 defeat of Hull at the end of April. By coincidence, shortly before leaving Blackpool, Barrass had been involved in Wednesday's biggest home upset for years—a 2-6 defeat on Christmas Day, when Barrass hit a hat-trick for Blackpool. That game was a nightmare for Fred Kean. Long after the match rumours persisted that Kean had been drinking heavily before the game. Years later Kean said in an interview: "It was too daft to laugh at really, but the rumour wouldn't go away. It got so bad that in the end the directors called a special inquiry, and I had to attend. I told Charles Clegg that I wanted to know the name of the man who had said he had seen me drinking. Clegg asked 'What for?' I said 'because I'll sue him, that's what for.' Then old man Clegg said 'Forget it, Kean. As far as we are concerned it never happened'."

To add to Wednesday's dismay at such a poor season, their rivals Sheffield United won the FA Cup—and they had beaten Wednesday on the way to Wembley. This second-round tie, played at Bramall Lane at the end of January 1925, was watched by a crowd of over 40,000, and was described as one of the greatest Sheffield derby clashes of the period between the wars. The game was played on a pitch ankle deep in mud, and the rain continued during the match, so that the teams turned straight round at half-time and did not leave the field. Trotter scored twice for Wednesday in the first nine minutes. At the time they had the wind and rain behind them as they attacked the Shoreham Street goal. However, after 18 minutes, Tommy Sampy reduced United's arrears, and, two minutes later, George Green made it 2-2. A minute after the change of ends Sampy put United in front, where they stayed. Wednesday were without Kean and Blenkinsop at this time—Blenkinsop missed 28 games through injury. The teams lined up as follows:

United— Sutcliffe; Cook, Birks; Pantling, King, Green; Mercer, Sampy, Johnson, Gillespie, Tunstall.

Wednesday— Brown; Inglis, Felton; Toone, Wilson, Powell; Lowdell, Hill, Trotter, Taylor, Richardson.

United went on to beat Everton, West Brom and Southampton to reach Wembley, where a goal by Tunstall saw them defeat a Cardiff side which included ex-Wednesday favourites Jimmy Blair and Gill. Wednesday's sole consolation was that they had been the only side to score against United in this Cup run.

3 Second Division champions, 1925-6

The summer of 1925 was not one in which the sun shone on Wednesday and their supporters. The outlook was decidedly dull, the close-season atmosphere less than happy; and only a blind optimist would have suggested the team was likely to make a serious challenge for promotion in the coming season. If anyone had been brave enough to predict that Wednesday would win the Second Division championship in 1926 he would have been laughed off as a fool.

The club reported a loss of £3,265—not a large sum by the standards of the 1980s, but at the time little less than a disaster. What made matters worse was the apparent unrest in the dressing room. Several players—including Kean, Williams, Wilson, Inglis, Taylor and Collier— rejected the terms offered for the new season. Kean and Williams eventually re-signed, but others were transferred. George Wilson, so recently England's captain, went to Third Division (North) Nelson, and Sam Taylor (Mansfield), Inglis (Manchester United), Collier (Kettering), and Petrie (Swindon) left. True, Wednesday acquired several new-comers during the summer, including George Whitworth (Crystal Palace), Ernest Cook (Pontypridd), Fred Marson (Wolves) and Lewis Bedford (Walsall); but, in the event, none was able to make any significant or lasting impact. Indeed, Whitworth, leading scorer with Palace in the previous three seasons, got into the first team only once—for a County Cup tie—and moved on to Hull in November. Wednesday's success was achieved with those players already on their books, plus a number signed as the new campaign progressed.

So, in the summer, little happened to inspire any optimism. The mood of disappointment and gloom was reflected by Charles Clegg when he spoke at the club's annual meeting, held at the YMCA in late June. "I think," he told shareholders, "it is a very long time since we have had to submit such an unsatisfactory report of the club at the end of a season. So far as the first team is concerned, I have no hesitation in saying that their displays have been most disappointing and unsatisfactory." He admitted that this had been partly due to a lack of harmony within the club, and said the directors had done their best to remedy the situation but had not succeeded to the extent they had desired. Later, when one shareholder suggested that the club might have solved its problem now that Wilson had been transferred, Clegg replied: "I am not saying you are wrong, but it will do no good discussing the matter."

Frank Froggatt was subsequently named as successor to Wilson as captain—the first Sheffield-born player to be given the job on a permanent basis since Crawshaw—and Matt Barrass became the new vice-captain. After one season as first-team trainer, George Utley, the former Barnsley and Sheffield United captain, left to become coach to Fulham; and Chris Craig, after a successful year in which he had guided the reserves to fourth place in the Central League, was promoted, with William Hodgkiss brought from Rotherham Town as the new assistant trainer. Between the annual meeting and the eve of the new campaign, the atmosphere in the dressing room improved considerably, and Bob Brown, discussing the team's prospects with the reporter from the *Sheffield & Rotherham Independent*, said: "It's no good making rash statements, but we are hoping to be in the First Division at the start of the 1926-7 season."

There is not much doubt that a vital clue to the success which followed was the appointment of Chris Craig, who, virtually overnight, instilled in the players a spirit and a quality of endurance which provided the basis for a positive, determined attitude. If the side included no players nationally ranked as "stars", they became a team of great triers, 90-minute men who refused to accept defeat. In his time Bob Brown made many astute signings, but the appointment of Craig was one of his happiest choices. Craig, a Scot from Forfarshire, had the football and medical knowledge, and the personality, which earned him the respect of the players. Brown had known him for many years, and did not hesitate to give him full responsibility when Utley quit. Craig and Brown had first met when they were both based at Portsmouth—Craig arrived there after a long spell in the Royal Army Medical Corps. As a half-back Craig was given a few games in Portsmouth's team, and later played with Reading, Southend and Merthyr. When he gave up playing he became trainer to Aberdare, and it was from there that Brown brought him to Sheffield.

By coincidence Wednesday began the season with a home game against Fulham, whose training staff included not only Utley but former Olive Grove idol, Fred Spiksley. The game was only four minutes old when Arthur Lowdell gave Wednesday the lead from the penalty spot. Bedford—the only newcomer on show—and Sam Powell scored further goals to clinch a 3-0 victory. The team that day read: Brown; Felton, Blenkinsop; Lowdell, Froggatt, Marsden; Williams, Barrass, Trotter, Powell, Bedford.

Brown, Froggatt and Marsden went on the play in every match; Blenkinsop, Trotter and Williams missed only one game; and Barrass missed only two. Felton played in the first 35 games at right-back; Prince displaced Bedford in late October and was the regular outside-left from then until the end of March; and Lowdell and Kean shared the right-half spot, with Lowdell having a 21-match run there in mid-season before finishing the campaign at inside-right.

The chief threat to Wednesday in the promotion race came from Middlesbrough, Chelsea and Derby County. Middlesbrough made the early running and were the first team to defeat Wednesday—at Ayresome Park on September 19—but they faded and eventually finished in ninth place. Chelsea, from whom Wednesday took three points out of four, stayed in the race until near the finish; but Derby, who achieved the double over Wednesday, were the most consistent challengers, and they ultimately finished runners-up, three points behind Wednesday and five in front of Chelsea.

Wednesday lost only one of their first 10 matches. In September they touched peak form in scoring 15 goals in three successive home games—beating Preston 5-1, Stockport County 6-2 and Portsmouth 4-2. Trotter suddenly found his scoring boots, hitting four against Preston and equalling his five-goal feat of the previous December in the game against Stockport. In this match four of his goals came in a seven-minute spell just before half-time.

Wednesday suffered their first home defeat on October 17, when Derby County (at the time in the middle of a run which brought 16 goals in four games) visited Sheffield and won 4-1. Trotter had given Wednesday an early lead, but Derby exposed the home side after the interval, when an injury reduced Marsden to a virtual passenger. Unfortunately, when Wednesday visited Nottingham Forest a week later, Kean was away on England duty, and Blenkinsop was ill. Lowdell was recalled, Len Williams deputised at left-back; and Prince and Powell displaced Bedford and Ayres respectively: but a poor display cost Wednesday the points.

The next game was at home to Barnsley, and the most significant team change was not the return of Blenkinsop or Kean, but the decision to give Harold Hill his first outing of the season. Hill, a tenacious Tom Thumb of a player, celebrated by scoring twice in a 3-0 victory; but of greater significance in the long run was the fact that he immediately established a left-wing partnership with Prince which was to be a key feature of the side until mid-February. Hill scored 12 goals in 21 matches.

Wednesday began November with a setback at Port Vale, the home side winning 4-3. Kean was injured in this game, with the result that he was to miss the next 21 games—not because the injury was serious, but by virtue of Lowdell's outstanding form as his deputy. Darlington paid their first League visit to Sheffield on November 14, and Trotter bagged a hat-trick in a 4-0 win. This was followed by a 1-0 win at Hull (for whom Whitworth was making his debut), and then came a significant 4-1 victory in the home game with Chelsea. Hill was at his brilliant best in this match, and his hat-trick helped take Wednesday to the top of the table on goal-average.

In December Wednesday collected nine points from a possible 12, but Derby collected one point more—and the difference cost Froggatt and co. the top spot. A 2-1 win over Southampton put them back on top on December 12, but defeat a week later at Blackpool (ex-Hillsborough favourite Sid Binks got the game's only goal) pushed them down to third. The Blackpool trip, incidentally, saw McIlvenny, an Irish international signed from Cardiff, make his only senior appearance, deputising for Trotter. Fortunately, Trotter was back for the Christmas fixtures, and he bagged six goals in the three matches which saw Wednesday beat Bradford City 4-1 and 5-1 and Oldham 5-1. The left-wing partnership of Hill and Prince shared seven of the 14 holiday goals which put Wednesday on the same points as leaders Derby but with an inferior goal-average.

After losing at Fulham on January 2, Wednesday chalked up five successive victories which shot them back to the top of the table. Then, on the last Saturday in February, some 5,000 Sheffielders travelled to the Baseball Ground to see the return game with Derby. Again Derby triumphed, Harry Bedford (who had scored twice at Hillsborough in October) getting a hat-trick. Despite the defeat, Wednesday stayed top, but, on the first Saturday in March, scheduled opponents, Nottingham Forest, were playing in the FA Cup quarter-finals, and Derby took advantage of Wednesday's blank to regain the leadership following a win at Stoke.

Though Wednesday did not have a League fixture that day, March 6, they did, in fact, have a game which, while only a friendly with Kilmarnock, was significant in that it marked the first appearance of a player who was to make an important contribution to the club's story—Tommy Walker. Walker had been signed a fortnight earlier from Bradford City at a cost of £1,900. A Scot who had originally been "discovered" playing with Vale of Grange 18 months earlier, Walker was to make more than 250 League appearances for Wednesday, and, like his new colleague Sam Powell, was later to join the club's training staff and give long service after hanging up his boots. After his outing in that Kilmarnock friendly, Walker went back to the reserves—but not for long. Wednesday won only one of their next five games, and while they regained the lead in the table after drawing 1-1 at Barnsley on March 13, a home defeat against Port Vale and a heavy setback at Darlington prompted wholesale changes.

The defeats at the hands of Port Vale and Darlington had immediate effects, but it is appropriate here to point to their long-term significance. Vale visited Sheffield and won 2-0, and one of their outstanding performers was an inside-forward by the name of Alf Strange. Strange scored one of Vale's goals, and he plainly made an impression on Bob Brown, for, less than a year later, he was brought to Sheffield. Strange was to make some 380 League appearances for Wednesday, gaining two Championship medals and 20 England caps.

Darlington caused a real stir when they thrashed Wednesday 5-1 on March 27. The Sheffielders scored first when Trotter converted a penalty, but after that it was all Darlington, and the star of the home team was a wee winger called Mark Hooper. Within ten months he was signed by Wednesday for £2,000, and between 1927 and 1938 he was to make 423 League and Cup appearances for the club, scoring 136 goals. Hooper, talking many years later, recalled that Wednesday boss, Bob Brown, had known about him long before he scored two goals in that 5-1 triumph. "But he'd told me that I was too small to play League football. I told him he was making a mistake, and said that one day I hoped I would play against Wednesday and show him. When the day came I gave Ernest Blenkinsop a real hard time!" Brown didn't sign the 5ft 5½ins. Hooper immediately, but the little man knew the Owls manager would soon be knocking on his door.

Brown had other things besides Hooper on his mind when the team returned to Sheffield to prepare for the three-match Easter programme. The Wednesday manager sensed that, if something wasn't done quickly, the team's promotion dreams might disappear. For the home match with Hull City, Brown took the bold step of dropping Felton, Lowdell, Hill and Prince: Walker was introduced at right-back, Kean was recalled at right-half, Brough Fletcher was brought in at inside-right with Barrass switching to inside-left, and Jack Wilkinson, an 18 year-old from Wath, was given his debut at outside-left. Wilkinson had been signed earlier in the season along with another youngster, Tony Leach; and the boy had been playing exceptionally well in the reserves. Fletcher, a veteran, had been signed from Barnsley in early February specifically to captain the reserves and coach the youngsters; but now Brown decided that Fletcher's "old head" was just what was needed to steady a first-team plagued by promotion "nerves".

The changes paid off immediately. Fletcher had a hand in the first goal, scored by Trotter; and Wilkinson, playing with all the poise of a veteran, grabbed a second goal to clinch victory. On Easter Monday and Tuesday Wednesday completed a double over Stoke City: a Trotter penalty earned the points in the away game, and Powell and Wilkinson were on target in the return. Fletcher, his mission completed, retired from the first-team scene leaving them sitting pretty with a two-points lead at the top of the table. Wilkinson quickly became a favourite with the Hillsborough crowd, and was to remain so until losing his place to Rimmer in 1928.

At Chelsea on the Saturday after Easter, Wednesday salvaged a vital point thanks to a last-minute penalty save by Jack Brown. A week later Wilkinson was again on target in the 3-0 defeat of Clapton Orient; but Derby were still only a point behind with a match in hand. When Trotter scored both goals in a 2-1 win at Southampton on April 24, promotion was finally clinched—but Derby, having taken 13 points out of 14 since the end of March, were still capable of taking the Second Division title.

Then, however, Chelsea did Wednesday a favour by defeating Derby at Stamford Bridge in midweek; and, on the season's last day, Saturday May 1, Wednesday concluded their League programme with a 2-0 win over Blackpool while Derby lost at Stockport. The Second Division championship was Wednesday's, and the top of the table looked like this:

	P	W	D	L	F	A	Pts
1. Wednesday	42	27	6	9	88	48	60
2. Derby	42	25	7	10	77	42	57
3. Chelsea	42	19	14	9	76	49	52

Trotter's goal in that final game brought his tally for the season to 37—well ahead of the previous club record for a season, 30, held since 1913 by David McLean; and the team's tally of goals (88, including 61 at home) and points (60) were also records. When the annual meeting came round the directors reported a profit of £3,402.

On the Monday after winning the Second Division title, Wednesday met city rivals United in the final of the Sheffield & Hallamshire County Cup at Bramall Lane. A crowd of 39,698 (then a record for the competition) saw United win 3-1, with Harry Johnson claiming a hat-trick—a feat he was to repeat in a much more important game, an FA Cup tie, two years later.

The conclusion of the 1925-6 season marked the end of an era for the club's long-serving goalkeeper, Teddy Davison, who left to join Mansfield Town and begin his apprenticeship in management. Several players were placed on the transfer list, among them Oliver Levick and Len Williams, who went to Stockport; George Ayres, who joined Blackpool; and, notably, Matt Barrass, who, after scoring 14 goals in the run to promotion, was dissatisfied with the terms offered for 1926-7 and was transferred to Manchester City. It is, perhaps, appropriate to mention that Froggatt, after such a memorable season, was to play in only six more League games, losing the centre-half spot to Kean early in the first season back in the top grade; and, in November, 1927, he joined Notts County. More than 30 years later, in 1959, Froggatt's son, Redfern, was to complete a family double by also leading Wednesday to the Second Division championship.

Part 5
A Golden Era: 1928-1935

1 Seven memorable seasons

In the seven seasons between 1928 and 1935 Wednesday enjoyed a period of success and consistency probably unparalleled in any other phase in their history—though, no doubt, it had old-timers drawing comparisons with the achievements of the great years from 1896 to 1907. Wednesday captured the League Championship twice, in 1929 and 1930; the FA Cup was brought to Sheffield in 1935; and only once, in 1933-4, did they finish lower than third place in Division One. Indeed, in 1930 they went very close to achieving a League and Cup double: they took the League title by a margin of 10 points, but fell in the FA Cup just one step from Wembley, suffering defeat in the semi-final when two controversial refereeing decisions went in favour of their opponents, Huddersfield Town.

It was a period when Wednesday had strength, skill and character in every position in the team. They had as many as 15 or 16 internationals on their books in these years, plus some outstanding players who never gained recognition from the selectors but remained consistent favourites with the Hillsborough supporters. On one occasion, in 1930, Wednesday had four men—Blenkinsop, Strange, Marsden and Rimmer—away playing for England against Scotland, but the supposedly weakened side still won 3-1 at Liverpool; and, in the same year, with three men in the England side facing Wales at Wrexham, depleted Wednesday went to Leicester and won 5-2: two examples to emphasise that they had reserve strength in depth.

In defence the team enjoyed the consistency of Jack Brown in goal, with Jack Breedon, signed from Barnsley in 1930, a capable and patient deputy; and Tommy Walker and Ernest Blenkinsop regulars at full-back. Wednesday had one of the best half-back lines in the country in Alf Strange, Tony Leach and Billy Marsden; though Marsden's playing days were prematurely ended by injury suffered while on tour with England in 1930, and he was later succeeded by Gavin Malloch and then Horace Burrows. In attack there was Mark Hooper and Ellis Rimmer providing contrasting styles and shooting power from the wings, and such outstanding marksmen as Jack Allen, Jack Ball and Harry Burgess. The conversion of Allen into a centre-forward was one of the outstanding individual success stories of the period. Jimmy Seed, hero of Wednesday's remarkable escape from relegation in 1927-8, remained to make a significant contribution to the two Championship triumphs before moving into management, first with Clapton Orient but more successfully with Charlton Athletic; and the later years of the period saw the arrival of a younger hero in Ronnie Starling. Other figures of note in the same years as Starling included backs Joe Nibloe and Ted Catlin; and Walter Millership, who began as an inside forward before being successfully converted to centre-half.

To say that Wednesday won 146 of the 294 League games in the seven seasons under review, and won 16 of their 28 FA Cup ties, may not convey much to the modern reader. However, an indication of the team's consistency is provided by the fact that, in six of these seasons, they lost only 10 home games. The team scored more than 670 goals, including 100-plus in Division One in both 1929-30 and 1930-1, and 109 in League and Cup in 1931-2. On their best days they were apt to crush the opposition, and they scored five or more goals in a match on no fewer than 20 occasions; including their biggest-ever League win, the 9-1 defeat of Birmingham City (who had the legendary Harry Hibbs in goal) in December 1930. In 1930-1 they enjoyed one seven-match run which brought a haul of 36 goals; while they kicked off the 1931-2 campaign with 20 goals in their first four games. Of course, they had their bad days, too. In October 1931 they conceded nine goals at Everton, for whom Dixie Dean hit five; and Derby County, Huddersfield Town and Wolves each put six goals past Jack Brown; while Liverpool and West Brom each had the distinction of scoring five on visits to Hillsborough.

It is probably of particular interest to note that more than 450 of the 670 goals scored in these seven seasons came from just five players. Wingers Rimmer and Hooper accounted for 207 between them, and Ball hit 94, including a record 11 from the penalty spot in one season, 1932-3. Burgess claimed 77; while Allen, whose 76 came in only 92 League and Cup games, was leading scorer in both Championship-winning seasons.

Off-the-field tragedies of the period included the sudden death of A. J. Dickinson, who collapsed in a London hotel in November 1930 while on Football League business; and the death in April 1934 of Chris Craig, trainer since 1925. Dickinson, and Sir William Clegg (who died in August 1932), were survivors from the club's amateur days.

The man who took much of the credit for Wednesday's rise back to the top after the lean years of the early 1920s, Bob Brown, suffered a sudden decline in health in 1933, and resigned in September of that year. Sadly, he did not live to see Wednesday achieve the FA Cup success which had eluded them in 1930, for in March 1935, while going on a scouting mission for another club, he collapsed on Leeds railway station, and died soon afterwards. Joe McClelland, the old manager's assistant since 1931, took temporary charge of the team after Brown's departure. Initially, Tom Muirhead was appointed as Brown's successor, but had to withdraw from the arrangement when his club, St Johnstone, refused to release him. So the job went to Billy Walker, the former Aston Villa and England player, and, after seeing Wednesday climb from close to the foot of the table to eleventh place in his first few months, Walker guided them into third place and to an FA Cup final triumph over West Bromwich Albion in his first full season in charge.

2 The Great Escape

Wednesday's period of success between 1928 and 1935 was immediately preceded by one of the most remarkable seasons in the club's history: 1927-8, the year of the Great Escape. After spending most of the season at or very near the bottom of the First Division and looking certain to be relegated, Wednesday staged an astonishing recovery, the story of which has passed into the folklore of football in Sheffield. With 10 games left Wednesday were stuck at the foot of the table, seven points adrift of the nearest club. The situation seemed hopeless. But, taking 17 points out of a possible 20, including two from a dramatic victory on the last day of the season, they scrambled to safety.

Looking back on this season in the context of the period as a whole, we can now see that amid all the trauma and the drama something very significant was happening. Behind the gloom and despair the basis for future success was being shaped. New players arrived, others were switched about the team or brought back from the reserves, and, slowly but surely, partly by accident and partly by experiment that succeeded, a blend was achieved which was to prove the foundation on which successive League Championship triumphs and a period of success were built.

The man most readily associated with this astonishing season is Jimmy Seed, the inside-forward acquired from Tottenham Hotspur in the summer of 1927. Spurs threw him in as a makeweight in a cash-and-player deal which took Darkie Lowdell to London. Seed was turned thirty at the time, and was all set to hang up his boots and become manager of Aldershot; but Spurs refused to release him because they wanted to transfer him to Sheffield. The details of the move were completed over the telephone, and Seed did not see a Wednesday official until he was met by manager Bob Brown at the railway station on the day he arrived in Sheffield.

What Seed did not know until later was that Brown had been trying to sign him for more than a year—in fact, since Wednesday's promotion from the Second Division in 1926. In Wednesday's first season back in the First Division, it was apparent that the team needed a player of experience: an "old head" to take responsibility and give guidance on the field. In that 1926-7 campaign they had finished in 16th place. The team had lacked consistency, and had failed to win a single away game, suffering heavy defeats at Tottenham (3-7), Arsenal (2-6) and Derby (0-8).

Ironically, Seed might not have been considering leaving Tottenham at all but for the fact that the London club had chosen to cut his wage by £1—from £8 a week to £7. This made Seed determined to go into management, but, fortunately for Wednesday, he was persuaded to continue playing. He admitted later that the move to Sheffield gave him a lease of life as a player. He spent four seasons with Wednesday and made a very significant contribution to the team's success; though, writing in his autobiography in 1957, he reflected: "To be honest, I did not surpass myself as a player (at Sheffield), but they wanted my experience, and I was fortunate in having a bunch of boys who were as loyal as I could wish for. Their keenness was a joy to watch."

However, Seed's impact was less than immediate, and, indeed, it was not until the later stages of the season that he began to exert the influence that was to make him the idol of the Hillsborough regulars and which was to prompt Brown to suggest that the mere presence of the ex-England man on the field was enough to inspire the rest of the team. "If you're not fit, Jimmy," Brown would say, "just throw your shirt onto the pitch."

But Seed did not settle quickly, and the many obvious weaknesses in the team were exposed with alarming regularity in the early months of the season. Seed was tried at inside-right, inside-left and left-half, and found himself sidelined for a month after fracturing a rib at Manchester United in early September. Wednesday won only two of their first 15 games. Jack Brown was dropped after conceding six goals in the first two matches, but his deputy, Mellors, was beaten 19 times in the next nine games.

At the end of November Wednesday achieved their first away victory—a 6-4 success at Derby, notable because it marked the debut of a new centre-forward, Ted Harper, who celebrated with a hat-trick. Harper, then 25, arrived from Blackburn Rovers with an impressive reputation as a marksman, but he made only 12 appearances before losing his place to old favourite Trotter. Harper left Hillsborough in 1929 to join Spurs. A five-goal defeat in the home game with Huddersfield on December 27 pushed Wednesday back to the bottom of the table, where they were to remain for much of the rest of the season. By mid-March they were seven points adrift of Portsmouth in 21st place, and it seemed that only a miracle would save them from falling into Division Two.

However, around this time there was just the slightest hint that things were beginning to drop into place. Bob Brown kept trying different permutations. Some paid off, some didn't. In February, for instance, he made two signings: one was an immediate success, the other a disappointment. The success was Ellis Rimmer, an outside-left signed from Tranmere. Rimmer, tall for a winger, settled in quickly, made an important contribution to the battle for survival, and was to emerge as a leading figure in the success story in subsequent years. He was to make 382 League appearances, in which he scored 119 goals; and, within two years of signing for Wednesday, he had gained international recognition. Charles Wilson, unfortunately, did not have the same impact. A former Sheffield schoolboy, he had made his League debut at 16 in the colours of West Brom, but he made only five senior appearances in his first season after his move to Hillsborough. It was to be 1930 before he established a regular place, as the first replacement after the loss of Marsden; but he moved to Grimsby in March 1932. Meanwhile, in March 1928, Wilson was displaced at inside-left by Jack Allen. Allen, who had been out of the team since October, scored four goals in Wednesday's last 10 matches.

The return of Allen and Trotter in attack, and the switch of Tony Leach from wing-half to centre-half: these were key pieces in the jigsaw of this campaign. Another was the recall of Alf Strange at Easter, and moving him from inside-forward to wing-half for the home game with Spurs proved a masterly stroke. It meant that at the end of April, at Sunderland, the great half-back line of Strange, Leach and Marsden played together for the first time; and Wednesday's 3-2 victory in this game proved crucial in the struggle for survival.

However, probably the most important single change in the team in that final phase of the 1927-8 campaign was probably the passing of the captaincy from the long-serving Fred Kean to Jimmy Seed. Kean lost his place at centre-half after the Bolton game in late February, and could not get back. Ironically, a month later while unable to get into Wednesday's first team, Kean captained the Football League against the Scottish League in Glasgow. After some 230 League appearances for Wednesday, he was transferred to Bolton later in 1928, and was in Bolton's FA Cup winning side of 1929. Leach, who had been with Wednesday since 1926, was an instant success at centre-half; and so was Seed as skipper, even though he often played when not fully fit.

Despite a good 4-0 home win over Liverpool and a 2-2 draw at Leicester at the end of March, Wednesday went into April still six points adrift at the foot of the table. However, over Easter they achieved what were to prove two particularly significant victories over Seed's old club, Tottenham, to chalk up their first League double for two years. On Good Friday at White Hart Lane, Wednesday won 3-1, Hooper scored twice and Seed once; and, four days later at Hillsborough, a hat-trick by Hooper and another goal by Seed gave them a 4-2 victory. In between these two fixtures, Wednesday dropped a home point against Derby County, with Hooper missing two penalties—an indication, perhaps, of the tension in the team.

However, on April 14 Wednesday went to West Ham and won 2-0, Jack Allen scoring both goals; and this was followed by a home victory over struggling Portsmouth, with Trotter and Allen the marksmen. Then came that win at Roker Park on the last Saturday in April, a vital victory because it meant that Sunderland had to win their final game to escape relegation, and, if they did that, they would doom their opponents, Middlesbrough, to the Second Division. Wednesday were still bottom and favourites to fill one of the relegation places. But on May 2 they played a midweek game at Arsenal where, thanks to a late equaliser from Seed, they salvaged a point which pushed them into 19th place. Now they knew everything depended on their final game against Aston Villa.

The last day of the 1927-8 campaign provided one of the most intriguing relegation situations in the history of the First Division. No writer of fiction could have dreamed up a finale so full of possible permutations and been believed. But fact is often stranger than fiction, and on the morning of May 7 only two points separated Liverpool in twelfth place from bottom club Manchester United. It was a tense and exciting situation involving several clubs, with four of the day's 10 games being relegation battles.

Wednesday, watched by a crowd of around 40,000, failed to score in the first half against Aston Villa—whose team, incidentally, included Billy Walker. However, three minutes after the interval, Seed made the pass from which Jack Allen shot Wednesday in front; and, on the hour, Trotter got a second. The Owls were safe! At the final whistle the crowd invaded the pitch, and the hero among heroes was the veteran Jimmy Seed. Earlier in his career Seed had known many great moments, and later, in his long years as manager of Charlton Athletic, he tasted glory many times: but few occasions compared with that afternoon in May 1928 for a touch of triumph tinged with a sense of personal justice.

Seed studied the day's other results. Manchester United had saved themselves with a 6-1 win over Liverpool, while Sunderland had sent Middlesbrough back to Division Two with a 3-0 victory at Ayresome Park. Middlesbrough's relegation companions were. . . Tottenham! No doubt Seed savoured the irony of the twist of fate which had caused that to happen. Spurs did not play on that last day. They had completed their programme a week before and gone off on a tour of Holland, not expecting for one moment to return home a Second Division club. When Wednesday had been bottom and seven points adrift, Spurs had been in twelfth place. However, they had lost eight and won three of their final 14 games. Wednesday's final position was 14th, and they had not only come through their ordeal with flying colours but had found a blend which would, with a few more touches, enable them to enjoy a long spell at the top of the First Division in the immediate future.

Though the 1927-8 season is best remembered for Wednesday's dramatic relegation escape, it is worthy of note that the campaign also included two memorable FA Cup fifth-round meetings with Sheffield United. After beating Bournemouth 3-0 and winning 2-1 at Swindon, Wednesday were rewarded with a home tie against their city rivals. On a very heavy Hillsborough pitch, the clubs shared a 1-1 draw, Wilkinson having given Wednesday the lead and Partridge grabbing the equaliser. However, the talking point among the 57,076 spectators was "the lost ball incident", which occurred in United's goalmouth 12 minutes from the end. Following a corner-kick from Hooper, the ball fell loose only two or three yards from goal; and Seed, seizing upon it, hammered a shot which United goalkeeper Alderson managed to block with his body. The ball shot into the air. . . and disappeared! At least, nobody could find it for perhaps 20 or 30 seconds, despite the fact that eight or nine men stood in the goalmouth. Suddenly, the crowd behind the goal roared: they had spotted the ball stuck in the mud, slap bang in the centre of the goal, barely six inches from the goal-line! It needed only the slightest touch to put it into the net, and Seed was standing almost touching it, but with his back to the goal. Len Birks, the United back, was the first man to spot the ball, and he rushed forward and kicked it to safety just a fraction of a second before Seed stepped back. It was an astonishing escape for United, an amazing miss by Wednesday!

The replay, which took place at Bramall Lane on the following Wednesday, earned a place in the record books because United centre-forward, Harry Johnson, became the first man to score a hat-trick in an important match between the Sheffield clubs. Johnson's treble, shot in the space of 18 minutes in the second half, transformed an ordinary game into a memorable one. United won 4-1, with Hooper getting Wednesday's lone consolation from the penalty spot five minutes from the end. The attendance at the replay was 59,447, bringing the aggregate gate for the two games to 116,523.

3 Champions twice. . . and close to the double

In their Championship-winning seasons of 1928-9 and 1929-30, Wednesday relied largely on the same men who had contributed to the dramatic rescue of 1928. Manager Bob Brown had suddenly created a successful blend of talents, and the team went from strength to strength as the players grew in confidence—a point emphasised by the fact that while the first Championship triumph was clinched by a mere one point, the second was won by a margin of 10 points—the biggest winning margin since Aston Villa had finished 11 points ahead of Sheffield United 33 years earlier in 1897. In 1930 Wednesday also established a League record by scoring 105 goals, an increase of 21 on the previous campaign.

The only significant change from the side which had escaped relegation was the remarkably successful switch of Jack Allen from inside-forward to centre-forward, with Allen's previous role passing first to Bob Gregg and later to Harry Burgess. Gregg, signed from Darlington in May 1928, had a 30-match run in his first season, but then lost his place to Burgess and moved on to Birmingham City in January 1931. Burgess came from Stockport County in the summer of 1929. He was one of Brown's costliest signings, but he quickly became a favourite with the crowd and proved an astute acquisition. He went on to make 234 League and Cup appearances and scored 77 goals before moving to Chelsea in March 1935. Not surprisingly, the man who persuaded Chelsea manager, Leslie Knighton, to sign Burgess was Brown—by that time acting in a scouting capacity for the London club.

In these two seasons of triumph, Mark Hooper was an ever-present, and the little winger was unlucky not to win international recognition. It was said that on one occasion the selectors put his name alongside Hulme (Arsenal), Adcock (Leicester) and Crooks (Derby), but Hooper was passed over on the casting vote of Sir Charles Clegg, who did not like pushing too many players from his own clubs! Jack Brown and Alf Strange missed only one game for Wednesday; and Walker, Blenkinsop, Leach, Marsden, Allen and Rimmer were rarely absent. Brown was recalled to the England side, while Blenkinsop, Strange, Marsden and Rimmer were all capped for the first time in this period. Blenkinsop, in fact, won 13 of his record 26 caps between May 1928 and May 1930. And the England team which defeated Scotland in April 1930 included four Wednesday men, with Rimmer getting two of his side's five goals.

Wednesday's success, therefore, was largely due to the fact that the team virtually picked itself, and the players developed an extremely close understanding as well as a spirit which enabled them to bring out the best in each other. Goalkeeper Brown and backs Walker and Blenkinsop were survivors from the 1926 promotion side; Strange, Leach and Marsden quickly gained recognition as one of the best half-back lines in the country; wingers Hooper and Rimmer contributed 33 and 22 goals respectively; and Seed, as well as providing astute leadership, scored 17 goals and helped create many more. But there is little doubt that the move which gave Wednesday the final flourish was switching Allen to centre-forward, where he proved such a success that neither Trotter nor Harper could reclaim a regular place. Allen dominated the team's scoring charts in both seasons, and then, as suddenly as he had become a hero, he went out of favour. One of his last games for Wednesday was in that controversial FA Cup semi-final against Huddersfield Town, when he scored "the goal that wasn't". Ironically, following his transfer to Newcastle United in June 1931, he was involved in a more famous Cup controversy when he scored against Arsenal in the 1932 final after the ball had allegedly gone out of play.

Allen, who started his career with Leeds United, joined Wednesday from Brentford in March 1927. In 28 League games prior to his switch to centre-forward he had notched 11 goals, which, on paper at least, looks reasonable. However, he had been in and out of the side and had not exactly set the Don alight. Then, in the early weeks of the 1928-9 campaign, Brown was looking for a way of putting some sting into the Owls' attack. The team had begun the season respectably, with four wins in the first eight matches, including a 5-2 victory over Sheffield United. Now, however, both recognised centre-forwards, Trotter and Harper, were nursing injuries, so Brown had little choice but to experiment. Allen was probably the most obvious candidate, and when Wednesday travelled to Portsmouth on October 6 1928 he was chosen to lead the attack. Allen marked the occasion with a goal, but Wednesday still lost 2-3. However, in the next home match, against Birmingham City on the following Saturday, the new centre-forward grabbed a hat-trick; and a week later he scored all Wednesday's goals in a 4-0 win at Bury. In his first 14 matches at centre-forward he scored 22 goals, and went on to score 64 goals in 70 League games, leading the club's scoring charts by a mile in both title-winning seasons. His record included two fours, three hat-tricks and 13 doubles.

Wednesday did not lose at home throughout the 1928-9 campaign. Interestingly, though Allen was so often the hero, he only scored once in Wednesday's biggest victory of the season, the 6-0 defeat of West Ham in mid-April (Hooper 2, Strange 2, and Rimmer got the others); and he was absent injured when Derby County were beaten 5-0 in mid-February, Harper re-appearing to score three.

The Hillsborough side hovered close to the top of the First Division from September until early November, and it was following a seven-match run which brought 13 points that they finally climbed into number one spot on November 24. Between mid-December and early January they extended their lead to as much as five points, but, largely through poor away form, they were unable to consolidate their place at the top, and the pressure remained on them until the final week of the season. However, despite the expected tension, team-spirit was sky-high, and the fighting qualities of the side are illustrated by a story told to me by Ernest Blenkinsop, speaking of the match at Bolton in February 1929. "Before the game started," he said, "we knew that Jack Allen had a suspect ankle. Well, in the very first minute, Jimmy Seddon tackled him, and Jack was carried off. Then Blackmore scored for Bolton. A minute later, I'm chasing a through ball from one of the home half-backs, and I get a knock on my thigh. So I go off for treatment. By the time I return, Blackmore has made it 2-0 to Bolton. We've ten men on the field, and I'm hobbling on the wing. Just before half-time I manage to hobble into Bolton's penalty area just in time to get my 'good' leg to a cross from Rimmer, and I score one for us. Later in the game, Allen limps back on; and, with about five minutes left, he stumbles in to get an equaliser. We returned home to Sheffield in agony, Jack and me, but we were all grateful for a hard-earned point." Fortunately, Blenkinsop was fit for the next game, but Allen was on the sidelines for three weeks. While Allen was absent, Harper and Charles Wilson were tried in his place. And, incidentally, it was around the same time that Jack Whitehouse, a signing from Derby County, displaced Gregg for four games. But Whitehouse could not establish himself and soon left for Bournemouth.

In that first Championship-winning season Wednesday's chief failing was an inability to make any consistent impact in away games. On their travels they only won three times—at Bury in October, Leeds in November, and Burnley in December. Defeats in six of their last seven away games kept the destiny of the title in doubt until the end of April. But Wednesday, with 52 points, finally finished ahead of Leicester (51) and Aston Villa (50). On the last day of the season Villa beat Wednesday, but Leicester took the runners-up spot by virtue of a 6-1 win over Bolton the same afternoon. Bury, one of only two clubs over whom Wednesday achieved a double, were relegated along with Cardiff City—the Welsh club going down despite having the best defensive record in the First Division.

In 1929-30 Wednesday's away form improved dramatically. They won 11 games and collected a total of 26 points on their travels, compared with 13 points in the previous season. By early February they had won eight and lost two of 13 away games, and their notable victories included those at Portsmouth (4-0), Burnley (4-2), Everton (4-1) and Grimsby (5-0). There was special merit, too, in the 3-1 victory at Liverpool, where, because of the absence of four men on international duty, Wilson and Norman Smith were brought in along with Millership and Jones, who were making their first senior appearances.

Wednesday, however, began their home programme with two defeats in their first three games, losing to Arsenal and Leeds. After that, though, they didn't lose again at Hillsborough. Indeed, as if to make quick amends for those early setbacks, they chalked up six successive home victories which produced a haul of 24 goals, including 10 for Allen. The centre-forward scored three in the 4-0 defeat of Leicester, and four in

7. *Wednesday's Championship teams 1928-29. . . (back row) Hopkins (asst. trainer),*
A. Francis (director), E. G. Flint (director), S. H. Nixon (director), A. J. Dickinson (director);
(second row) W. G. Turner (vice-chairman), T. Hodgkiss, W. Webster, G. A. Johnson,
T. Neale, J. Brown, C. Dodds, L. Hargreaves, R. D. Mellors, E. Mills (director),
W. Fearnehough (director), Dr. Ian Rhind; (third row) W. F. Wardley (director), T. Jones,
C. Hooper, E. Harston, J. Whitehouse, T. Leach, E. Blenkinsop, H. Burgess, W. S. Smith,
B. Pardon, R. W. Trotman, J. B. Gunstone (director), A. J. Blanchard (director); (fourth row)
Bob Brown (secy-manager), M. Hooper, A. Strange, T. Walker, Sir Wm. Clegg (director),
Sir Charles Clegg (chairman), J. Allen, E. Rimmer, R. Gregg, C. Wilson, N. Smith, J. Dean,
S. P. Stephen (asst. secy.); (fifth row) Chris Craig (trainer), G. Beeson, J. Seed,
W. Marsden, E. Hatfield, C. P. Goddard, R. J. H. Burridge; (front) J. Wilkinson, J. Trotter,
Trophies on show: Sheffield Challenge Cup, Football League Championship trophy,
Central League Cup, and Sheffield County Cup.

the 7-2 win against Manchester United.

In the early part of the season Wednesday's chief rivals in the title race were Leeds United and Manchester City, who had the edge for a time. But in late December, following a Christmas double over struggling Everton, Wednesday slipped into top place, and consolidated their position with a 3-3 draw at Manchester City on New Year's Day and a 3-2 win at Arsenal three days later. By early February, following a five-goal win at Grimsby and a 4-1 home victory over Burnley, Wednesday completed a ten-match run worth 17 points to lead the table by six points. Then, albeit briefly, they found themselves under threat from Derby County. A 1-4 defeat at Huddersfield and a narrower setback at Leicester, combined with a growing pre-occupation with the FA Cup, saw Wednesday concede top spot to Derby. However, on March 15, goals by Rimmer (2), Allen and Burgess gave Wednesday a 4-2 win over Newcastle, while Derby dropped a home point to Manchester United. This meant that Wednesday went into their semi-final duel with Huddersfield Town on March 22 as First Division leaders on goal-average, with four games in hand over Derby.

Between January and March Wednesday gradually emerged as strong contenders for the League and Cup double, which had not been achieved since Aston Villa's feat in 1897. In 1929 Wednesday had suffered the ignominy of a fourth-round defeat at Second Division Reading; but now, in 1930, they enjoyed their best Cup run since 1914. In the third round a goal from Allen disposed of Burnley; Allen hit two and Seed and Hooper one each in the 4-3 win at Oldham in round four; and this was followed by a 5-1 home victory over Bradford, a crowd of 53,268 seeing Seed, Rimmer, Allen and Hooper set up Wednesday's biggest Cup win for 17 years. In the quarter-final Wednesday shared a 2-2 draw with Second Division Nottingham Forest; and a crowd of 59,205 was present at the Hillsborough replay to see Seed, Allen and Burgess on target in a 3-1 victory.

Then came the historic semi-final with Huddersfield Town, defeated finalists in 1928, losing semi-finalists in 1929, and still one of the most powerful sides in the First Division after a decade of success under first Herbert Chapman and now Clem Stephenson. A crowd of nearly 70,000 packed into Old Trafford, and they saw Hooper give Wednesday the lead with a spectacular shot after 21 minutes. Just before half-time, however, Huddersfield snatched an equaliser—the first of two controversial moments in the game when Wednesday's luck ran out.

Ernest Blenkinsop once told me his view of that first Huddersfield goal: "Town's winger, Billy Smith, got the ball and chased down the left flank before crossing it into the middle. Lewis, their centre-forward, went up to meet the ball, and I was just about to go up with him when I realised he was going to miss it. As I expected, he *did* miss it—with his head. But, in desperation perhaps, he lunged at the ball with his fist, punching it in the direction of Alex Jackson." The *Sheffield Daily Telegraph* described what happened then: "It was obvious from Jackson's attitude when he received the ball that he was doubtful about something. His hesitation was the hesitation of a player who expected the whistle to go for an infringement." But Mr Lines, the referee, did not blow. So Jackson went forward and put the ball into the net. Mr Lines promptly signalled a goal, and though he was persuaded by the protesting Wednesday players to speak to a linesman, he stood by his decision, and at the interval the scores were level.

Despite this disappointment, Wednesday continued to have most of the play. But, midway through the second half, Jackson got away and shot Huddersfield into the lead. The dream of a League and Cup double for Sheffield was fading fast until the dying moments of the game. Then, in a last desperate fling, Hooper burst down the right wing and centred the ball to Allen. The centre-forward shot. . . and the ball sped like a rocket towards the net. Just as it was crossing the line, the referee blew the final whistle. Wednesday were denied an equaliser by a fraction of a second. The referee is the sole timekeeper, and he said it was full-time the moment Allen was in the act of shooting; and Wednesday's protests that Mr Lines had played short time fell upon deaf ears. Blenkinsop, recalling the incident nearly 40 years later, said that Percy Bowker, soon to become a director, had kept a stopwatch and had claimed that the game had ended after a second-half lasting only 43 minutes. However, the history books show that Huddersfield won the game 2-1 and went on to play at Wembley , where they were defeated by Herbert Chapman's Arsenal.

Wednesday recovered quickly from their Cup setback, and promptly showed their determination not to slip in the race for the Championship. On the day of that unhappy semi-final defeat, Wednesday's struggling Sheffield rivals, United, did them a favour by defeating Derby 2-0 at Bramall Lane. Wednesday went on to win eight and lose only two of their final 12 matches. Derby, in contrast, won only three of their last 10 games, and it was probably appropriate that the title was clinched on April 22 when Wednesday defeated Derby 6-3 at Hillsborough. On the previous day Derby had beaten Wednesday 4-1 at the Baseball Ground, but, though they narrowed the gap at the top to three points, Derby knew they had to complete their first double over the Owls for five years to keep their title hopes alive. In the event, they failed. With 17 goals in their last five games Wednesday took their second successive Championship in style.

Allen claimed a hat-trick in the defeat of Derby and eventually finished the season with 39 League and Cup goals. Hooper, with five goals in the last two games—a 4-2 win at Sunderland and a 5-1 defeat of Manchester City—finished with a tally of 21. Burgess had a haul of 20 League and Cup goals (he also scored four in one County Cup match with Rotherham), and Rimmer scored 17.

While Wednesday were enjoying another year of outstanding success, Sheffield United had been fighting desperately to avoid relegation; and, in fact, only escaped the drop into the Second Division on goal-average thanks to a 5-1 victory at Manchester United on the last day of the season. Ironically, two days later United met Wednesday at Bramall Lane in the final of the County Cup—and the League Champions were defeated 3-1. However, Wednesday's pride was only slightly dented. A blow of greater consequence occurred five days later in Berlin, where Billy Marsden suffered a spinal injury while playing for England against Germany. The accident did not involve an opponent, but Marsden's colleague, Roy Goodall of Huddersfield Town. Goodall described the incident to me thus: "I had moved across to cover a German attack. The ball was coming towards me, and just as I was about to take it on my knee, someone came flashing across me. It was Billy, coming in low with the idea of heading the ball. We were both committed, and, before I knew what was happening, my knee caught Billy on the back of the neck." Marsden never played League football again. Six months later he tried to make a comeback in the reserves, but a further knock persuaded him to hang up his boots. The loss to Marsden and to Wednesday was considerable, and many supporters felt that none of his successors ever quite matched their favourite; though Gavin Malloch and, later, Horace Burrows were to establish themselves with the Hillsborough crowd. Marsden, meanwhile, took up coaching and had a spell in Holland before having a brief stint as part-time manager of Doncaster Rovers in the war years.

4 End of the Bob Brown era (1930-33)

In each of the next three seasons Wednesday finished in third place in the table. They remained among the front-runners in the First Division every kick of the way, but the top prize invariably proved to be well beyond their grasp. This was despite the fact that, in two of the seasons, they actually won more games than in their first Championship-winning season; and, in the other, they finished with one point more than had carried them to the title in 1929. In two of these three seasons they were outpaced by the outstanding team of the 1930s, Herbert Chapman's Arsenal; and, in the other campaign, they lost out to an Everton side inspired by the devastating marksmanship of Dixie Dean.

However, if the period brought no trophies to Hillsborough, it could hardly be regarded as less than successful. There were several powerful teams around at this time, and, as well as Arsenal and Everton, the likes of Aston Villa, Huddersfield and West Bromwich Albion touched a peak of consistency which made competition extremely keen. In two of these seasons Wednesday again topped a century of goals—102 in the League in 1930-1, and 109 in the League and Cup in 1931-2. But Aston Villa, Everton and Arsenal also bagged 100-plus in two seasons, with Villa's 128 in 1930-1 enabling them to wrest the League scoring record from Wednesday.

Viewed from a distance of more than 50 years, the seasons immediately following Wednesday's Championship triumphs of 1929 and 1930 can be seen to hold special interest in that they marked the final phase of the Bob Brown era. Brown, it is clear, did not depart the scene as a result of his or his team's failure: in the end he was defeated by personal misfortune and ill-health. He left behind a number of players who were to serve his successor as well as they had served him; and, to the end of his long stay at Hillsborough, Brown maintained a happy knack of snapping up players who would make a significant contribution to the Wednesday story.

In his final phase, for instance, he produced another outstanding goalscorer in Jack Ball; and he signed three of the players who would later help bring Cup glory to the club—Ronnie Starling, Horace Burrows and Ted Catlin. Within less than a year of joining Wednesday from Newcastle in 1932, Starling was called up by England to face Scotland, and he became a big favourite with the club's supporters. Both Burrows, signed from Mansfield, and Catlin, brought down from the Middlesbrough area, gained international recognition—ironically *after* Brown had left the club. Other notable signings in this period included goalkeeper Jack Breedon from Barnsley, and George Stephenson, Tom Davison and Gavin Malloch from Derby County. Departures of significance included Jimmy Seed and Jack Allen.

In the 1930-1 campaign Wednesday barely got a sniff at the title, and finished with 14 points fewer than Arsenal, who collected a record 66 points (and, incidentally, also beat Wednesday 2-1 in the FA Charity Shield match at Stamford Bridge). True, as late as early February, the Owls were within one point of Arsenal, but, with only one defeat and 13 wins in their last 19 games, the North London club had all their rivals gasping for breath long before the end of the campaign.

This was the season in which Jack Ball, signed from Manchester United in the summer, displaced Allen. Ball stayed just over three years before being transferred back to Manchester United, and in that time he scored 94 League and Cup goals, many of them from the penalty spot. He scored 17 goals in his first 14 games for Wednesday, and his introduction to the side coincided with one of the most remarkable goalscoring sequences in club history. Between November 1 and December 13 1930 Wednesday had a run of seven games in which they scored 36 goals. The sequence included the record 9-1 defeat of Birmingham City. Harry Hibbs, the legendary England goalkeeper, was in City's side that day, but, between the 16th and 73rd minutes, he was busier picking the ball out of the net than making saves. Ball (2), Burgess, Rimmer and Hooper gave Wednesday a 5-0 lead before half-time, and Seed and Hooper helped themselves to two apiece in the second half. Birmingham's lone goal came from Briggs, the brother-in-law of Sheffield United favourite Freddie Tunstall. The seven-match sequence is worth detailing:

Sunderland (h)	7-2
Leeds United (a)	3-2
Arsenal (h)	1-2
Leicester (a)	5-2
Blackpool (h)	7-1
Portsmouth (a)	4-2
Birmingham (h)	9-1

The 36 goals came from Ball (11), Hooper (7), Burgess (6), Rimmer (5), Seed (3), and Wilson and Walker (2 each). Four of the seven goals against Blackpool came in a 21-minute spell; while the victory at Leicester was achieved with three men absent playing for England.

A 12-match run without defeat between September 6 and November 8 kept Wednesday close on the heels of Arsenal, but the Londoners came to Sheffield and ended Wednesday's unbeaten sequence. Four wins on the trot followed, but as the season wore on, home defeats against Sheffield United and Liverpool, and heavy defeats at Blackburn, Manchester United and Sunderland left Wednesday trailing in the title chase. Jack Brown broke a thumb at Middlesbrough on Boxing Day, but Breedon proved a capable deputy, though the ex-Barnsley man was beaten five times when Liverpool visited Sheffield on February 14. Winning only two of their last six games, Wednesday finished well out of the running for the Championship, and the top of the table at the end of the season looked like this:

	Wins	Pts
1. Arsenal	28	66
2. Aston Villa	25	59
3. Wednesday	22	52

Wednesday kicked off the 1931-2 season in great style—George Stephenson got four goals in the 6-1 win at Blackburn; Grimsby Town (4-1) and Bolton (7-1) were defeated at Hillsborough; and Chelsea were beaten 3-2 at Stamford Bridge. However, Wednesday then lost four away matches on the trot and conceded 20 goals. Their heaviest defeat was at Everton, the home side winning 9-3. That day Wednesday had Blenkinsop and Strange absent on England duty, while Leach was out injured. Ted Catlin was making only his second senior appearance as Blenkinsop's deputy; but it was Tom Davison, deputising for Leach, who had the toughest time, for Dixie Dean eluded him five times to score. At half-time Everton's lead was only 2-1, with Stein (22 min) and Dean (42) the marksmen, Rimmer replying after 44 minutes. Goals by White (46), Dean (49 and 55) and Critchley made it 6-1 on the hour. Hooper (61) and Ball (65) reduced Wednesday's arrears, but further goals from Dean (73 and 75) and Johnson (88) completed another great day for Everton. The Goodison Park club, League Champions in 1928, relegated in 1930, and Second Division champions in 1931, were a powerful outfit. A week before putting nine past Wednesday they had scored five at Sheffield United, and their 116 League goals in 1931-2 included nine against Leicester, eight against Newcastle, seven against Chelsea and six against West Ham.

Six games without a win just before the turn of the year proved costly for Wednesday, for though they were to have a sequence of five victories in six matches in March and early April, they were unable to make up the ground lost earlier in the year. Malloch arrived from Derby in December and seemed to solved the problem at left-half; but, despite impressive wins over Blackburn (5-1) and West Ham (6-1), Wednesday had too many disappointing results to look likely to overhaul Everton at the top. They conceded six goals at Huddersfield in January and five in the home clash with West Brom in March; Dean got another two goals when Everton completed the double over Wednesday at Hillsborough in February, and Arsenal also did the double by beating the Owls at Hillsborough in mid-April. At the end of the season, the top of the First Division read:

		Wins	Pts
1.	Everton	26	56
2.	Arsenal	22	54
3.	Wednesday	22	50

Arsenal had drawn four matches more than Wednesday and suffered four fewer defeats, and at one stage the London side had looked set for the League and Cup double. In the FA Cup final they lost to Newcastle United, for whom ex-Wednesday man Jack Allen scored twice—the first following the famous "over the line" incident.

Wednesday's leading scorers were Ball (23) and Rimmer (21). Hooper's tally, 12 in 40 games, was his smallest in his five full seasons at the club; and, in missing the last two matches of the campaign, the little winger ended a run of 189 consecutive League and Cup appearances.

In the close season of 1932 there were a number of talking points of interest to Wednesdayites. Three of the club's former players obtained new managerial appointments—Teddy Davison at Sheffield United, Andrew Wilson at Stockport, and W. H. Harvey at Chesterfield. In fact, Harvey succeeded Davison at Saltergate, Davison having taken over as secretary-manager at Bramall Lane following the tragic death of John Nicholson, killed in a road accident outside Sheffield Midland Station in late April. In the space of less than a year Sheffield soccer had lost two "backroom" giants in A. J. Dickinson and John Nicholson, and, in August 1932, Sir William Clegg died.

However, the chief talking point among Hillsborough regulars in the summer of 1932 was probably the team's chances in the 1932-3 campaign. Of several newcomers to the playing staff, the most important was the 22 year-old Ronnie Starling, an inside-forward signed from Newcastle in June. A product of Tyneside, Starling had made a big impact as a schoolboy player, and had spent four years at Hull City. He had helped Hull reach the FA Cup semi-final in 1930, when, despite struggling at the foot of the Second Division, they held mighty Arsenal to a 2-2 draw at Leeds before falling 0-1 in the replay at Villa Park. Hull were relegated at the end of that season, and Starling was sold to Newcastle for £4,000—a substantial fee at the time. In his first season on Tyneside, Starling made 36 League appearances, but fell out of favour in the following term, and, for the second time in three seasons, Cup glory eluded him—this time because he could not maintain a regular first-team place. Wednesday stepped in and got him at the bargain fee of £2,500.

Starling, a ball-player, did not think his style would suit Wednesday, but, in fact, the man with the wavy hair and the clever feet settled in quickly. He missed only one game in his first season—and that was because he was making his England debut against Scotland in Glasgow. Starling and Sheffield United's Jack Pickering gained their first caps after starring for The Rest in a 5-1 defeat of the England team in the trial match at Portsmouth.

Wednesday enjoyed a nine-match run which brought 17 points between mid-October and early December—including a 5-3 victory at Wolverhampton (where Ball got four goals) and a 6-3 win at Aston Villa (Ball and Starling got two goals each). In fact, after losing at Bolton on December 17 and ending the sequence, Wednesday embarked on another undefeated run of nine games extending into February. However, eventual champions Arsenal were never less than two points in front of either Wednesday or Aston Villa from December to the end of the season. The Hillsborough club's hopes of landing the title were dashed by an uncharacteristic sequence of setbacks in April. They won only one of their last nine matches, and successive defeats at Huddersfield and Arsenal, followed by a two-goal setback in the home game with Villa on April 15—their first home defeat in 24 matches—put paid to any hopes of not just the title but the runners-up spot, too. It was probably of significance that only 5,017 spectators turned up to watch Wednesday's final home fixture against a Bolton side already virtually doomed to relegation. The top of the table at the end of the season read:

	Wins	Pts
1. Arsenal	25	58
2. Aston Villa	23	54
3. Wednesday	21	51

Jack Ball again led the scoring charts, and of especial interest was the fact that his 33 League goals included 11 from the penalty spot—a record for a season until it was overhauled 40 years later by Francis Lee of Manchester City. None of the other forwards reached double figures, with Hooper, Burgess and Rimmer each scoring eight. Rimmer was the only ever-present, though Strange, Ball and Starling each missed only one game. George Beeson, on the club's books since 1929, began his best run of appearances at right-back in this season, and he not only kept Tommy Walker out but, in October 1933, was to win a place in the Football League XI against the Irish League.

When the final whistle blew on the 1932-3 season, nobody could have foreseen that the end of an era was close at hand and that major changes would be made at Hillsborough over the remaining months of the year. In fact, the tide in the affairs of the club turned on a personal setback suffered by manager Bob Brown—a blow which seriously affected his health and subsequently prompted him to decide that he no longer had the will or the energy to face the stress and pressures of football management.

Brown was a man totally committed to his work and dedicated to a club which had become to him a way of life. A tough, strict disciplinarian who expected and got respect from his players, he drove nobody harder than himself. He lived for football and his job. As is often the case with a successful man deeply engrossed in his profession, Brown had the support of a woman whose devotion was absolute, and whose presence in the background was a constant source of strength and encouragement. Mary Brown, like her husband a product of the North East, loved her football, and she understood his passion for the game. Over the years she had shared in his trials and triumphs, and she knew her man found it difficult to relax even when success had been achieved. When the 1932-3 season ended, Brown promptly got down to the task of preparing the annual report and all the various tidying-up jobs necessary at the end of a nine-month campaign. In May he set up and completed a number of signings, including Tom Brolly from Glenavon, and Jackie Thompson, an 18-year-old centre-forward from Blyth Spartans; and fixed the details for the transfer of George Stephenson to Preston. Then, in July, he and his wife went to Blackpool for a holiday.

Mrs Brown was as much in need of a rest as her husband. A few years earlier she had had a major operation, and she had not been in good health for some time. However, on the day the Browns left for the Lancashire coast, she was in fair spirits. Halfway through the holiday she had a sudden seizure, and, on the day before they were due to return to Sheffield, she died. To say that the Wednesday manager was shattered is probably an understatement. After the funeral he returned to Hillsborough determined to bury himself in his work. But it was soon evident that he had been knocked right off his stride by the blow, and those close to him feared that his sense of loss was so deep that it might be many months before he could come to terms with his situation. He was a mere shadow of the man he had been only a few weeks earlier, and it seemed that the purpose had gone from his life. His health began to suffer. In early September he fell ill at a match, and his doctor ordered a complete rest. After a fortnight of being confined to bed at his Wadsley Lane home, Brown submitted his resignation to Wednesday chairman, W. G. Turner; and it was accepted without argument because it was obvious that the old manager was seriously ill.

After a few months Brown had made sufficient progress to begin seeking some alternative form of employment. At nearly sixty, he was content to look for something light and not too strenuous, preferably in football. His knowledge of the game and his ability to assess players were qualities widely recognised, and several managers engaged him to perform scouting duties. One of the first people to give him work was Chelsea manager, Leslie Knighton, a product of Sheffield and a man who in his time had been associated with Huddersfield Town, Manchester City, Arsenal and Birmingham. There was a note of irony in Knighton's gesture, for, years before, Brown had often had to be quite severe in his dealings with the man now employing him. When Knighton was scouting prior to his move into management, he often spent time in the Wednesday dressing room talking football gossip with the players. Brown frequently had to ask him to leave. However, Knighton had great admiration for Brown, and it was largely due to Brown's recommendation that Chelsea took Harry Burgess from Wednesday for a £5,000 fee, though the deal was not completed until a week after Brown's death.

It was in early March 1935—only a month before Wednesday won the FA Cup under the management of Billy Walker—that Brown collapsed when about to board a train for Hartlepool at Leeds. Barely 24 hours later he died in Leeds Infirmary without having regained consciousness. A few days later he was buried at Wadsley, and the mourners included his former office boy, Eric Taylor, his old assistant, Joe McClelland, and the former Wednesday player and Sheffield United trainer, George Waller.

Before the shock departure of Bob Brown from the Hillsborough scene, Wednesday's 1933-4 campaign had begun normally. They kicked off with a 3-2 victory at Manchester City. Then came two home defeats, at the hands of Aston Villa and Arsenal. When Villa completed a double with a 1-0 win at Birmingham on September 4, Wednesday had two points from their first four matches—their worst start for eight years. Goalkeeper Jack Brown, who had missed the start of the season through injury, displaced Breedon for the next game, at Everton, where Wednesday won 3-2 with goals by Burgess (2) and Ball. The team was beginning to slip into top form. On September 16 they registered their first home win, and the manner of their 3-0 defeat of Middlesbrough had the pundits suggesting that Wednesday were again showing flashes of their old brilliance. It was in the week following this match that the news of Brown's resignation emerged. On the Wednesday evening there was a reserve match at Hillsborough, and this was probably the occasion on which the directors were given confirmation of Brown's decision to quit. The board's formal acceptance of Brown's resignation was announced to the Press the next day. Surprisingly, perhaps, no reference to the developments was made in the official programme for the next home match.

Wednesday's supporters immediately appealed to the directors to approach Jimmy Seed, but the old hero had just settled himself at Charlton following a difficult initiation into management at Clapton Orient. Seed was flattered to be remembered with such affection in Sheffield, but he did not want to return now as Brown's successor. Arthur Fairclough, who had made his name at Barnsley, was another candidate for the job. However, the first man to be offered and formally accept the position was Tom Muirhead, the former Glasgow Rangers favourite, now managing St. Johnstone. The appointment was finalised in a Newcastle hotel before the England-Wales match in November, but no sooner had the news been released to the Press than it was followed by an announcement that the deal was off. Muirhead telephoned Hillsborough to say that his club had refused to release him from his contract. Three years later, in 1936, Muirhead achieved his ambition to manage an English club when he joined Preston North End.

While the directors pondered on the problem of finding a new manager, Joe McClelland was put in temporary charge. However, Wednesday won only two of their next 11 matches, and by the end of November stood third from the foot of the First Division. They beat Newcastle and Chelsea at home, but lost five successive away games and two at home. After the home defeat by Portsmouth on November 18 (the game was watched by a crowd of only 8,810), Starling was dropped, and a week later Ball was axed. Youngsters Alex Law and Jackie Thompson were tried in the forward line. Beeson and Leach found themselves out of favour, Leach being displaced at centre-half by Walter Millership, originally an inside-forward but converted initially at the suggestion of Bob Brown. Alf Strange was moved back to his old inside-forward position, but, though it was not recognised at the time, his long run as a regular was virtually at an end. All in all, it was a gloomy period, and the best result achieved by Wednesday in these weeks was the rather unimportant 6-1 win at Barnsley in the County Cup semi-final at the end of October.

When it was known that Muirhead was unable to obtain his release to move to Sheffield, one man who reacted to the news was the Aston Villa and England forward, Billy Walker. At 36 Walker was still good enough to command a place in the Villa side, but, after some 480 League appearances, he was looking for a move into management. As recently as the previous December he had captained England to gain his 18th cap, but he admitted to Villa secretary, Billy Smith, that he was getting tired of playing, and fancied a new challenge. He discussed the Wednesday vacancy with Smith and Villa's directors, and they said they would not stand in his way. He posted his application to Hillsborough, and in early December was joined by Smith and director F. Normanton at a meeting with Wednesday chairman, W. G. Turner. On the following day, December 8, it was officially announced that Walker was hanging up his boots to have his first crack at management with Wednesday.

Whether the news of Walker's appointment was responsible we do not know, but the fact is that the next day, December 9, Wednesday went to Liverpool and turned in a courageous performance which earned them a 3-1 victory despite the loss of Strange in the second half. Strange broke a bone in his right foot, and, after hobbling on the wing, went off to leave Wednesday with 10 men for the final 15 minutes.

Walker was given an official reception when he took up his appointment on the following Tuesday. A special tea was laid on, and the directors, players and staff were present to hear chairman Turner deliver an enthusiastic speech, followed by a reply from Walker in which the new manager noted that in his first season as a player Aston Villa had won the FA Cup: he hoped that in his first season in management Wednesday would win the trophy. As it turned out, the new chief was not to achieve his target quite as soon as he wished, but he was to do it in his first full season, at the end of a 16-month spell during which he made a number of unexpected and controversial changes at the club.

5 Walker takes Wednesday to Wembley

Billy Walker's top priority when he moved in at Hillsborough was to raise the team-spirit that had been sagging for months and to steer the club away from the foot of the First Division. He achieved both—and quickly. Within weeks there was a dramatic improvement in the atmosphere in the dressing room, and Walker's first 12 League matches in charge saw Wednesday undefeated with 18 points from a possible 24. At that stage they had climbed into sixth place. Later, they suffered several setbacks, but finished the 1933-4 campaign comfortably situated in mid-table. Indeed, four points more and they would have been in the top six. However, while Wednesday had been making good progress, neighbours Sheffield United suffered the frustration of being relegated from Division One for the first time in 41 years.

The day Walker started work at Hillsborough coincided with the draw for the third round of the FA Cup. It was widely known that the new manager (he became secretary-manager in February 1934) had his sights on a long Cup run, and a pairing with Rotherham United at Millmoor gave rise to high hopes of a promising start on the Wembley trail. When the tie was played Wednesday won 3-0, with goals from Dewar, Leach and Hooper. In the fourth round Wednesday were held 1-1 at Oldham; but won the replay 6-1, Dewar getting a hat-trick. The fifth-round tie with Manchester City made a piece of Hillsborough history, for a record crowd of 72,841 (receipts £5,566) saw the teams share a 2-2 draw. In his autobiography, City's goalkeeper, the late Frank Swift, described this as one of the most amazing games he ever played in. "After we had changed and were ready for the field," he wrote, "we found the narrow tunnel from the dressing room to the pitch was blocked by ambulance men tending groaning casualties. After forcing my way through with the other players, I had to stand aside to let pass a stretcher bearing a man crushed to death on the Spion Kop.

"The early play was in keeping with the atmosphere, and, five minutes after the start, Sam Cowan missed his kick, Neil Dewar nipped in and passed for Rimmer to crash the ball past me. Then our lads settled down, and midway through the first half we scored a unique goal. Alex Herd received a short pass from a free-kick in our half, and started a long, lazy dribble. On and on he carried the ball, with the Wednesday defence falling back, every man seemingly expecting Alex to pass. He went on until he was about 25 yards from goal, suddenly let fly—and we were level.

"Dewar put Wednesday in front after the interval, and the crowd settled down to cheer their favourites into the sixth round. But they didn't know our lads—25 minutes to go and Herd snapped in the equaliser."

City won the replay 2-0 and, having been defeated in the final the previous year, made no mistake by going on to beat Portsmouth at Wembley. But Swift remembered the first game with Wednesday as City's hardest match. And Wednesday returned to their League programme having generated some colour and atmosphere among their supporters in the space of a few short weeks.

Walker was destined to remain in football management for nearly 30 years, achieving his greatest success with Nottingham Forest; and, right from the start, it was recognised that he was a man with a natural flair for leadership. He possessed a deep fund of practical knowledge and experience, could communicate effectively with his players, and was probably unsurpassed as a technician. In his first 16 months at Sheffield he made a big impact and achieved much. However, he did make a number of decisions which were highly controversial and, at the time, heavily criticised by the club's supporters. Chairman Turner had said that Walker "would be manager from top to bottom", and the manager was left to do whatever he considered best; though there were times when, privately at least, even some of the directors and senior players questioned the wisdom of some of his decisions.

The first important move Walker made was to recall Ronnie Starling to the first team, persuading him that he had an important role to play and that he was too good a player to be squandering his rich talents in the reserves. This step won widespread approval, and Starling emerged as the key figure in the success the team achieved in this period. He was subsequently made captain, and a forthright spokesman he proved to be for the players.

However, when the long-serving Ernest Blenkinsop, the idol of the Hillsborough regulars, was suddenly transferred to Liverpool in March, supporters and even some of the players were staggered. The stylish back had played for the Football League against the Scottish League in Glasgow only the month before, and had captained England in the previous April. Later, when Walker transferred Tony Leach to Newcastle and Harry Burgess to Chelsea, Wednesdayites wondered if the new manager was making mistakes he would later regret. But the results obtained by the team at this time were good, and supporters consoled themselves that perhaps there was method in his apparent madness.

Walker plainly knew what he wanted, and was determined to get it. He held firm views on how a football club should be managed, and pursued his goal with the same single-mindedness and directness which had brought him so much success as a player. Not surprisingly, perhaps, he rubbed some people up the wrong way. But others were probably more conscious than he that this was his first managerial position, and there were times when they were apt to compare his lack of experience and his bluntness with the quieter style and authority of Bob Brown. However, so long as success was achieved on the field, Walker was allowed to have his way.

The new manager's first signing was Neil Dewar, the guardsman-like centre-forward acquired from Manchester United at the end of December 1933 in a part-exchange deal which took Jack Ball back across the Pennines. Dewar was not unknown to local football enthusiasts, for he had scored a hat-trick for Glasgow in the inter-city match with Sheffield in 1932. In February 1933 Manchester United had paid Third Lanark £6,000 for him. But he did not settle at Old Trafford, and was delighted to join Wednesday. Dewar was to score 48 goals in 95 League and Cup appearances for the Owls, and he began in style; but he had a spell out of favour when he lost his place to a later signing, Jack Palethorpe, in the months leading up to the 1935 Cup final. It is, perhaps, of interest to note that Dewar's first goal for Wednesday came in his second game, against Arsenal at Highbury on January 6 1934—that day having a place in history of English football because it was darkened by the news of the death of Herbert Chapman, legendary manager of Arsenal, and, of course, a product of South Yorkshire whose brother, Harry, was a one-time Wednesday favourite.

One of Walker's boldest gestures in his first months at Sheffield has long been forgotten, but it is worth recording the fact that he attempted to sign Stanley Matthews from Stoke. At the time wing-wizard Matthews had not yet gained the first of his 54 England caps, but was already such a favourite with the Victoria Ground regulars that the Stoke directors said they dare not consider parting with him. Some time later, in February 1935, Walker heard of another promising teenager, not yet old enough to turn professional. He brought him to Sheffield for an interview, but the lad returned to Lancashire and subsequently signed for Burnley. His name was Tommy Lawton, later to become one of the game's greatest centre-forwards.

Walker's first months were not without their disappointments. After that 12-match run mentioned earlier (it was an 18-match run counting Cup-ties and two games prior to Walker's arrival), Wednesday lost at home to Leeds and Huddersfield; and then Blenkinsop returned with Liverpool and helped them defeat the Owls 2-1. In early March Wednesday suffered a 1-5 defeat at Bramall Lane, where United's Billy Boyd, making his derby debut, scored the first hat-trick in 60 League meetings between the city clubs—equalling Harry Johnson's three-goal feat in the FA Cup in 1928. That derby day of 1934 was saddened for Wednesday by another event: before the game it was learned that long-serving trainer, Chris Craig, had been admitted to hospital with a serious illness. Craig, who underwent two major operations in the following weeks, died in early April.

At the end of the season Billy Walker made further changes. He transferred Tony Leach, and let Tommy Jones (a Welsh international so long in Mark Hooper's shadow) go to Manchester United; while George Beeson moved to Aston Villa in the deal which brought Scottish international back, Joe Nibloe, to Sheffield. Other signings included Wilf Sharp, originally a centre-half, from Airdrie; and Bernard Oxley, a forward, from Sheffield United. After the start of the 1934-5 season Walker further strengthened his squad with the capture of Preston centre-forward, Jack Palethorpe, and inside-forward, Jack Surtees, who made a quick impression after being given a month's trial at the request of his brother, Albert, a former colleague of Walker's at Villa Park.

So the Wednesday team began to bear a re-shaped look as the club progressed towards that memorable spring in 1935. Jack Brown remained in goal, heading for his 400th senior appearance. Tommy Walker, Catlin and Nibloe competed for the full-back positions, with Nibloe settling at right-back from late January onwards, partnered by Catlin, to the exclusion of Walker. The half-back line at the start of the season read Burrows-Millership-Malloch, but Burrows was switched to left-half in December and Sharp established himself at right-half. In the forward line wingers Hooper and Rimmer were still automatic choices, though injuries caused Hooper to miss 13 League games, and Oxley was usually the deputy. Centre-forward Dewar lost his place to Palethorpe. Starling eventually switched to inside-left to make way for Surtees at inside-right, with Burgess losing his place. It was a remarkable year for Surtees, for, having failed to make an impact with four previous clubs, he was all set to emigrate to America when Walker was persuaded to take a look at him. A few bright performances in the reserves earned him a contract, and, such is the unexpectedness of football, his 25th senior appearance for Wednesday was in the Wembley final. On the other hand, Harry Burgess, having played in 19 Cup ties for the Owls, missed out on Wembley in his last season with the club.

There is one name which appeared on the Wednesday team-sheet only once in the 1934-5 season, but the occasion held special significance because the player in question was to become one of the idols of Hillsborough—Jackie Robinson. Early in the season manager Walker went to watch another player in a junior match in the North East; but found he could not keep his eyes off the dark-haired youngster whose special qualities stood out like a beacon light on a black night. He brought the youngster to Sheffield. On Easter Monday—five days before the FA Cup final—Wednesday rested Starling and gave the 17 year-old Robinson his first taste of League football in the match at West Bromwich. Robinson was not told that he was playing until shortly before the game, and he had to borrow a pair of boots from Starling; but he "played like a veteran", scoring Wednesday's goal in a 1-1 draw. (At the time of his debut, it was thought that Robinson was not quite 16, and it was not until the outbreak of the war in 1939 that his birth certificate showed him to have been born in 1917 and not 1919 as original club records had indicated).

Wednesday did not lose a home game throughout the 1934-5 campaign and dropped only seven points in front of their own supporters. However, after victory at Chelsea in the first match of the season, they did not win another away fixture until they beat Leicester on December 8. When Walker returned to Aston Villa for the first time as Wednesday's manager, his old team beat his new one 4-0, and Pongo Waring gave a superb display at centre-forward, scoring twice. How Walker longed to have a leader in his attack like Waring! Dewar was scoring with decreasing frequency, and Oxley and even Rimmer had been tried at centre-forward.

Indeed, the game in which Rimmer was first tried in that position holds a special place in Wednesday's history, for it marked the first visit to Sheffield of a famous Continental side. FC Austria arrived at Hillsborough on December 16 1934 having defeated Liverpool and drawn with Fulham and Birmingham. A crowd of 12,445 saw Wednesday become the only side to beat the slick and colourful Austrians: they did so with three second half goals—two from Rimmer (one a penalty) and the other from Millership. This game marked the first appearance in Wednesday's goal of amateur international H. H. C. Hill, who told me of the occasion: "At the time, I was studying for a maths degree at Sheffield University, and I was doing some training at the Wednesday ground. On the morning of that match Billy Walker telephoned to ask if I would be going to the game. When I said yes, he said I had better bring my boots because I was playing! Brown and Breedon were both injured. I was dead scared at the start. After about five minutes the Austrians hit the bar. Fortunately, we got on top, and in the end won comfortably. But it was a memorable occasion." The Austrians were entertained to a meal at the King's Head Hotel after the match, and Walker presented each member of their party with a Sheffield-made pen knife—though he had difficulty explaining the tradition of giving a coin in return as a means of ensuring friendships were not cut!

At this time, incidentally, Hill was on the books of both Wednesday and Sheffield United, and Teddy Davison, United's manager, was disappointed when the goalkeeper chose to transfer his registration to Hillsborough. Later, in April 1935, Hill played in two League matches for Wednesday, and there were those who thought that if Jack Brown did not recover from injury in time the amateur might be the surprise choice for the Wembley final. Several newspapers decided to cover themselves against that possibility by making a special journey to Hill's Derbyshire home to take photographs for their files!

After that game with the Austrians, Walker signed Jack Palethorpe in time for the next League match, at home to Everton. Palethorpe, then 24, had been at Preston only 10 months, but he had an impressive record. Previously he had been successful at Reading, and in 1933 had helped

Stoke win the Second Division championship. The tall centre-forward failed to score in his first three games, but, on Boxing Day, he claimed a hat-trick in the 4-0 win at Birmingham City. His first goal was a piece of luck, his second came from the penalty spot, and his third was scored with his head: an all-round performance! He scored eight goals in his 20 League matches that season, and though he was not destined to remain long in Sheffield he earned himself a place in club history with a number of vital goals along the road to Wembley.

By coincidence, on the day Wednesday entertained the Austrians the draw was made for the third-round of the FA Cup, and Wednesday's pairing with Oldham Athletic was one of the talking points at the reception afterwards. Oldham were bottom of the Second Division, and in the previous year's competition Wednesday had crushed them 6-1: so, on paper at least, Billy Walker had a good reason to be confident.

Those with long memories noted that the referee for this tie was Mr Lines—the same official who had been at the centre of the controversy in the 1930 semi-final duel with Huddersfield. On the day, however, there were no difficult decisions, and no dispute about the result. Despite the fact that the light covering of snow made conditions less than ideal, Wednesday recorded a comfortable 3-1 victory. Palethorpe headed them in front after only six minutes. Rimmer made it 2-0 twenty minutes into the second half; and, though Walsh pulled one back for Oldham a minute later, Tynesider Surtees booked Wednesday's place in the fourth round with a third goal soon afterwards.

Wednesday then faced a tough game at Molineux. At the time Wolverhampton Wanderers were in mid-table in Division One and had scored 25 goals in the five home games preceding this tie. Before the kick-off Billy Walker surprised his team's followers and the pundits by dropping Tommy Walker and replacing him with Joe Nibloe. Walker had played in all but one of Wednesday's previous 29 FA Cup ties, and had not missed a game since mid-November. Many years later, he revealed that he had been getting changed for the game when he was told he wasn't playing. The incident virtually marked the end of his career as a senior player. Nibloe, by the way, had been in the Kilmarnock side which had won the Scottish Cup in 1929.

Again Palethorpe gave Wednesday an early lead, heading in from a Rimmer cross after 13 minutes. Wolves did not draw level until 14 minutes after half-time, through Harthill; but Rimmer quickly put Wednesday back in front when he got his head to a cross from Hooper. After the game the Wednesday party learned that neighbours Sheffield United's Cup trip to the midlands had ended in a seven-goal defeat at West Bromwich.

The fifth-round draw paired Wednesday with Leeds United or Norwich City, away; and they confidently expected to be visiting Elland Road on February 16. However, when Walker took his men to Leeds to watch the replay, they saw Second Division Norwich score a shock 2-1 victory. The result prompted old-timers to recall that Norwich had shaken Wednesday in the competition back in 1908, defeating the then Cup-holders in East Anglia after declining to switch the fixture to

Sheffield. Now, in 1935, all the talk was of City's tight and peculiar ground, known as The Nest and said to be worth a goal start to the home side. Norwich, managed by former Arsenal captain, Tom Parker, were looking for another First Division "scalp", and the game promised to be a test of Wednesday's character.

By now Billy Walker had established a pattern of taking his team to Cleveleys for special training a fortnight before a Cup-tie, with the week before the games usually spent doing normal training at Hillsborough. However, on this occasion when Wednesday began final preparations at home in advance of the tie, Walker made special arrangements to help accustom his players to the unique conditions they would face at the Norwich ground. On the Tuesday before the tie he held a public practice match, reducing the width of the Hillsborough pitch by five yards and inviting supporters to come and pack themselves around the touchline. A crowd of around 8,000 turned up, and Walker declared the experiment a success. On the big day all the preparations paid off—just. But for the brilliance of Brown, who made three incredible saves, Wednesday might have gone out of the competition. However, 16 minutes from the end, Rimmer popped up to emerge the match-winner.

In the quarter-finals Wednesday were drawn to face Arsenal at home. At the time the Gunners stood top of the First Division, three points better off than fourth-placed Wednesday and all set to complete a hat-trick of Championship wins. Earlier in the season the teams had shared a goal-less draw at Hillsborough, but, just a month before the Cup clash, Arsenal had defeated Wednesday 4-1 at Highbury in a game remembered because it saw Alex James score the first hat-trick of his career. On March 2 this eagerly-awaited sixth-round tie attracted a crowd of 66,945 to Hillsborough, and home supporters were stunned to silence after only seven minutes when Ted Drake put Arsenal in front. Wednesday's equaliser was probably the best goal Mark Hooper ever scored, and it prompted an astonishing display of enthusiasm from the crowd. Copping handled just outside Wednesday's penalty area, and Nibloe's long free-kick found Hooper, who went forward and whacked the ball into the net from 15 yards. Inevitably, the winning goal came from Rimmer. Hooper and Sharp were involved in the move, but it was Rimmer's ability to seize a half-chance which made all the difference. Taking Male completely by surprise, the winger had the ball in the net before you could say Alex James. Arsenal could hardly complain at defeat, for Drake had fluffed at least two chances of putting the game beyond Wednesday's reach.

So Wednesday found themselves through to their tenth FA Cup semi-final, and the draw saw them facing Second Division Burnley before a 56,600 crowd at Villa Park on March 16. It is interesting to note that when Burnley's players visited Hillsborough to watch the Owls play Huddersfield in a League match on March 9, Wednesday turned out in blue shirts with white collars and sleeves. However, Walker promised that the stripes would be back for the trip to Villa Park.

In their quarter-final match with Birmingham City, Burnley had shown great fighting qualities by recovering from being two goals down and

8. *Edward, Prince of Wales, is introduced to Jack Surtees by Wednesday skipper Ronnie Starling before the 1935 F.A. Cup final.*

winning 3-2. So Wednesday knew that they must not go into the game with the slightest hint of over-confidence. Even after Rimmer had headed them in front as early as the fifth minute, Starling and Co. proceeded with caution. It was not until 12 minutes into the second half that Wednesday increased their lead and began to relax. Much of the credit for this goal went to Hooper, for when Burnley's goalkeeper, Scott, collected a long punt from Surtees, the little winger followed up with a heavy challenge. And when Scott, perhaps surprised by Hooper's audacity, let the ball slip from his grasp, Rimmer pounced to notch his second goal of the game—his sixth in the competition that season. Rimmer was also involved in the third goal, scored by Palethorpe after 73 minutes. Wednesday were through to their first FA Cup final for 28 years.

6 How Wednesday won the FA Cup, April 27 1935

In the six weeks between Wednesday's semi-final triumph and their appearance at Wembley, no doubt the thoughts of everyone at

Hillsborough were dominated by the exciting prospect of the FA Cup final and the dream of lifting the game's most coveted trophy for the first time since 1907. (In fact, the Cup at stake now was not the one they had won in 1907, for this had been replaced in 1911). However, while the twin towers of Wembley beckoned, in the meantime there was the more immediately important matter of gathering League points and consolidating the team's high position in the First Division.

The record books show that while Wednesday won only two of the seven League games played in this period, by collecting 10 points from their last nine matches (including two after Wembley) they were able to squeeze into third place, one point ahead of Manchester City and nine points behind Arsenal, the champions.

When they clinched their place in the final, Wednesday did not know immediately who their Wembley opponents would be. However, within a few days West Bromwich Albion beat Second Division Bolton Wanderers in a replay of the other semi-final, and Hillsborough regulars knew that their favourites now faced a tough task. Albion's 2-0 defeat of Bolton brought their tally of Cup goals to 18—seven more than Wednesday —and their greater scoring power in League and Cup suggested to many that they would have the edge in the final. On the way to Wembley they had scored seven against Sheffield United and five at Stockport; and six against Leeds and Middlesbrough in the League. Both teams were strong in defence, which prompted pundits to predict a single goal would probably decide the destiny of the Cup; but many favoured Albion because the team they chose included nine of the men who had figured in the Wembley defeat of Birmingham City four years before.

Subsequent events emphasised the truth that no game, least of all a Cup final, is won on paper, nor can it be judged in advance on facts and figures alone. A match which was expected to be negative was so positive that it produced six goals; while Albion's previous experience of Wembley was no real advantage on the day. In the event, superior stamina and the flexibility of their forward line swung the balance in Wednesday's favour, though they also had a slice of the necessary good fortune, too. In fact, the fate of the Cup in this year of the Royal Jubilee was probably determined by two decisions made by Albion before a ball was kicked.

For a start they elected to leave Arthur Gale out of their attack. Gale, who had scored in all but one of the previous rounds, was replaced by Tommy Glidden, called up for his first Cup appearance of the season. At outside-right, Glidden never escaped the attentions of Catlin, and he lacked the support he might have expected from his partner, Joe Carter. Playing Carter was a gamble which failed, for the 34 year-old inside-forward (described as Albion's equivalent of Jimmy Seed at Wednesday a few year earlier) had not played since the semi-final because of ligament trouble. Ten minutes after the referee had set Wembley's thirteenth FA Cup final in motion, Carter suffered a recurrence of his injury and was little more than a passenger by half-time. Indeed, when the score was 2-2, he missed the kind of chance he would have converted with ease if he had been fully fit—and the

9. Jack Palethorpe (right, white shirt) shoots Wednesday into the lead in the 1935 final against West Bromwich Albion at Wembley.

course of Cup history was probably altered in a moment of drama so painful to the Albion veteran. Carter, coincidentally, almost became a Wednesday player a year later, but the transfer was called off after he suffered an injury in an accident at home.

Among the spectators in the Wembley crowd of 93,204 were such old Wednesday Cup heroes as Billy Betts, who had played in the 1890 final; Tommy Crawshaw, twice a winner, in 1896 and 1907; and Frank Bradshaw, a key man in the 1907 success. Before the game Ellis Rimmer, seeking to maintain his record of having scored in every round, received a letter from one of the scoring heroes of the 1907 final, George Simpson, who reminded him that an outside-left had scored in each of Wednesday's two previous Cup final wins.

The teams lined up for the 1935 final as follows:
Wednesday— Brown; Nibloe, Catlin; Sharp, Millership, Burrows; Hooper, Surtees, Palethorpe, Starling, Rimmer.
West Brom:— Pearson; Shaw, Trentham; Murphy, W. Richardson, Edwards; Glidden, Carter, W. G. Richardson, Sandford, Boyes.

The game got off to a sensational start, Wednesday taking the lead after only two minutes. It is worth noting that an astute piece of refereeing contributed to the goal. Catlin took a knock and lay injured as the Sheffield side repelled an attack. Mr Fogg chose to let play continue as the ball was swept upfield, and, all in the space of a few moments, Hooper played the ball to Palethorpe and the big centre-forward hit a low shot past Pearson into the net. Catlin knew nothing about it until the interval.

It took Albion 20 minutes to equalise, and they did so with the best goal of the game. Ironically, it was scored by a former Sheffield schoolboy, Wally Boyes—the smallest and, at 22, the youngest player on the field. Boyes, who had joined Albion as a 16-year-old, collected a pass from Carter, sped forward and unleashed an unstoppable rising shot. Brown, the oldest man on the field, probably felt his age as he stooped to pick the ball out of the net!

The second half was the best part of the match: full of excitement and pace, flashing raids at both ends, and some remarkable misses. Starling missed one good chance and had another effort cleared off the line before Wednesday regained the lead after 60 minutes. Starling it was who produced the pass, but Hooper provided the finish: the little winger beating two men before scoring with a shot which went in off a post. The broad smile on Hooper's face as he ran back to shake hands with his colleagues was one of the endearing memories of a happy and unforgettable day.

However, within five minutes Albion were again level, when a 20 yards shot from Sandford was inadvertently deflected past Brown by the head of Millership; and, when they lined up for the re-start, the tension in the faces of the Wednesday players was a painful indication that they feared the fates might be turning against them. It was in the period immediately following their second goal that Albion went desperately close to going in front for the first time. Carter put the ball against a post, then missed a golden opportunity. Boyes pounced on a slip by Nibloe to lay on a wonderful opening for W. G. Richardson; but the Albion centre-forward, with eight Cup goals to his credit that season, took so much care in placing his shot that he rolled the ball wide of the goalkeeper and a fraction wide of the post, too. If he had blasted the ball he might have been more successful.

This is the moment to reflect that, so far in the game, Rimmer had been having a lean time in the shadow of Shaw and Murphy—and to tell the amusing story of his missing mascot. Before the start of the Cup run someone had given the Wednesday winger a lucky horseshoe, and he had hung it on his dressing room peg before every tie. Unfortunately, when Wednesday had gone to their Cup headquarters at Bushey Wood two days before the final, the horseshoe had been overlooked. However, reserve trainer Sam Powell discovered it just before leaving for Wembley on the morning of the game. He arrived at the ground after the players had gone onto the field; so it was half-time before Rimmer was given his mascot and placed it on his peg.

Superstitious nonsense, probably. Certainly, the arrival of the mascot did not have an immediate effect. But Rimmer did suddenly burst to life in the closing stages of the game—indeed, just when everyone was resigned to extra-time. Barely four minutes remained when Sharp sent the ball bouncing in the direction of Albion's goalmouth. Rimmer went chasing after it. Pearson ran from his goal-line. The odds were on the goalkeeper getting his fist to the ball first, but Rimmer's head was there just a fraction sooner. . . and Wednesday were again in front. Two minutes later the Albion goalkeeper failed to hold a hard drive from Hooper, Rimmer pounced, and Wednesday now led 4-2.

The Cup was on its way to Sheffield! There it was in the hands of skipper Ronnie Starling. Five years earlier, as a Hull City player, he had known the bitterness of defeat one step from Wembley—in the same year that Wednesday had also fallen at the last hurdle in that controversial tie with Huddersfield. Of the Wednesday team from that day in 1930 only Hooper, Rimmer and Brown remained, though Tommy Walker was somewhere inside Wembley looking on. At last glory had returned to Hillsborough, and a triumph had been achieved which was to prove the high point of Billy Walker's four-year spell as manager of Wednesday.

10. F. A. Cup winners: the Hillsborough club's players, officials and directors in 1935. . .
(back row) Tommy Walker, —, Jack Surtees, Sam Powell (trainer), Wilf Sharp, Jack Palethorpe, —, Jackie Robinson;
(second row): Eric W. Taylor, Ellis Rimmer, Les Fenwick, Jack Brown, Ronnie Starling, Joe Nibloe, Ted Catlin, Walt Millership,
George Irwin (trainer), George Ainsley, Horace Burrows, W. H. Walker (secy-manager); (third row) W. F. Wardley, E. G. Flint,
S. H. Nixon, P. Bowker, W. G. Turner, Sir Charles Clegg, W. Fearnehough, A. J. Blanchard, E. Mills, Dr. Ian Rhind, J. Swallow;
(front row) Mark Hooper, —, Sedley Cooper, Harry Grange, George Drury, Jack Thompson.

Part 6
Downs and Ups: 1936-1958

1 Fall from the heights: 1936-39

The period following their FA Cup triumph was decidedly glum for Wednesday. Suddenly and unexpectedly, the golden years were gone, and with them the magic that had pervaded a very special era in club history. Of course, it is true that the margin between success and failure is very narrow; and it would be unfair to suggest that the turnabout of the club's fortunes was quite as dramatic as it may seem in retrospect. However, the decline was soon apparent, though, in the beginning, few could recognize the signs indicating that the years in the wilderness would be long and at times painful—and not always because of circumstances within the club.

Now came a time of struggle, and a spell which seemed dull and ordinary when compared with what had gone before in the first half of the 'thirties. Wednesday fell from the First Division. And, for a while, things went from bad to worse as the team stumbled to within sight of the Third Division (North). Billy Walker left, and Jimmy McMullan came; and, all the time, a remarkable sense of optimism prevailed among the club's supporters, many of whom firmly believed that success was largely a matter of waiting for the cycle to turn again. Unfortunately, just when Wednesday appeared to be building a side capable of taking them back into the top grade, they were pipped for promotion by Sheffield United—and then their ambitions were thwarted by the outbreak of the Second World War. Six years later when peace returned and football began to get back to normal, Wednesday had to start all over again as the 'grey' years continued. The old favourites were gone, and the future was largely in the hands of a new generation of players who had emerged in the war years, guided by one or two whose best years were now behind them. The wartime period had brought to the fore a young man called Eric Taylor, once Bob Brown's quick-witted and energetic office boy but now the secretary-manager responsible for shaping Wednesday's post-war destiny. After the war, the club had a tough beginning, and again the spectre of the Third Division (North) threatened. At last, however, promotion was achieved, but relegation quickly followed. In the 1950s Wednesday went up to the First Division and down again to the Second with such regularity (as, indeed, did neighbours Sheffield United) that Taylor dubbed these "the yo-yo years". It was frustrating but it was fun; and the Wednesday manager's sense of humour was not lost on the footballing public of Sheffield. The first dozen years after the war were not without their trials, but they brought their triumphs, too. As a phase in the club's history, it may not seem to compare with the heady days of the early 'thirties, but these were vital years which were to provide the base upon which the entire British game was to build a new era. So it was a time of change, a period in which developments began which were to transform the face and image of football—and when the changes in the game were to reflect those in the world at large. Things that happened in the first 15 years or so after the end of the war period pointed to the kind of game we were to know in the 1960s and beyond—and to conditions which would be unrecognisable to the supporters and players of the pre-1939 era.

✱ ✱ ✱

Within a year of winning the Cup in 1935, Wednesday were in the doldrums, struggling to avoid the drop into the Second Division. They escaped by a margin of a mere three points. The reprieve, however, was only temporary. A year later they finished bottom of the table. Down they went. Worse was to follow. In their first campaign in the lower grade, they struggled desperately in the relegation zone. To play in the Third Division was unthinkable, yet, in the end, they finished only two points clear of 21st-placed Barnsley. Things began to improve in the next season, 1938-9, but promotion eluded them by a point—Sheffield United, thanks to a high-scoring win on the season's last day, pushed them out of second place. Four months later, just as the 1939-40 campaign was getting under way, the war began.

The season of 1935-6 provided a remarkable contrast with the previous campaign. The Cup holders struggled to defeat Crewe in their first defence of the trophy, succeeding only in extra time in the Hillsborough replay; and Second Division Newcastle United delivered the knock-out in the following round. However, it was in the League that Wednesday's slide gave the most cause for alarm. Their fall from the top end of the table was reflected in declining attendances: three games in February attracted fewer than 7,000—and this after 35,244 had been at the October clash with Derby County, and 34,700 at the Arsenal match in January.

Wednesday lost only four games at home, but 16 points were conceded to visiting teams; and they did not manage to make up the lost ground on their travels, for they suffered 13 defeats and conceded 54 goals. They won only one of their first seven games, but this at the time did not give rise to any undue concern, for, in fact, only two of the fixtures were lost. Yet some serious flaws had begun to appear. Just when things appeared to be looking up, they crashed to three successive defeats in which 17 goals were conceded—five at Sunderland, seven at Leeds, and five in the home game with West Brom. They achieved notable victories against Aston Villa (5-2) and Arsenal (3-2); but, overall, lacked their old consistency, and their inability to score became a source of concern to manager Walker as the second half of the season progressed.

Walker was not slow to try to recapture the old fluency and stability, but his excursions into the transfer market were largely unsuccessful— as well as being the cause of the £16,000 loss suffered by the club in this season. A number of the 1935 Cup heroes went out of favour: Palethorpe was transferred to Aston Villa, and Sharp (remembered for the tenacity with which he had snuffed the threat of Arsenal's Alex James on the way to Wembley) and Surtees were dropped. Even Mark Hooper had a spell in the reserves. Walker bought a new half-back, Dick Rhodes, from Wolves; plus forwards George Bargh (Preston), Bob Bruce (Middlesbrough), Tommy Grosvenor (Birmingham) and Charlie Luke (Huddersfield). The only man signed in this period destined to make a lasting impression was Harry Hanford, the Welsh international defender captured from Swansea City. One important deal which fell through involved the West Brom veteran Joe Carter.

However, despite a number of heavy defeats in the later part of the season, Wednesday's chief weaknesses were in attack—and particularly at centre-forward. When Walker dropped Palethorpe at the start of October, Dewar was recalled and proceeded to score 16 goals in 19 games. Unfortunately, he then managed to find the net only twice in the next 11 matches. The chief criticism of Dewar was that he did not use his weight enough, and Walker decided it was time to introduce someone with some bustle. Albert Ashley, a dour Derbyshire collier signed from the Clowne area, was told he would be making his League debut at Stoke. Dewar travelled as reserve. Ironically, when the team reached the Potteries, defender Ted Catlin was discovered to have developed a painful boil on a leg. Walker, left without much choice, switched Ashley to left-back and Dewar got a reprieve. The young back played exceptionally well against Stoke's brilliant winger, Stanley Matthews, but the hero of the day was Dewar. The centre-forward scored two goals in a 3-0 victory which clinched Wednesday's safety and doomed Aston Villa and Blackburn Rovers to relegation.

Wednesday's escape was not, unfortunately, a prelude to a revival of fortunes. On the contrary, they slipped into deeper gloom, and, with only four wins in their last 22 matches in the 1936-7 campaign, sank to bottom place and were relegated to the Second Division with Manchester United. It was a season marked by some poor performances, especially in away matches, and by injury problems which at one stage saw no fewer than 15 players under treatment for injuries.

Ironically, at the half-way stage of the season they had 18 points from 21 games, and, in fact, were better placed than they had been at the same time in the previous season. When they beat the ultimate Champions, Manchester City, 5-1 just before Christmas, they hardly looked relegation candidates; but then they lost five games on the trot, and registered only one win between December 25 and the end of February.

The root of their troubles was an inability to field a consistent line-up. Only Catlin at left-back managed 40 appearances, with Rimmer (30) the next most regular performer. Jack Brown's long run as first-choice goalkeeper came to an end, and two newcomers, Derek Goodfellow (ex-Gateshead) and Roy Smith (ex-Selby) were tried as replacements. Rhodes, Burrows, Millership, Hanford and Moss (signed from Aston Villa) shared the half-back positions; but, yet again, the most serious shortcomings were in attack. No fewer than eight different men filled the wing positions, eight men were tried at centre-forward, and a string of different players were permutated in the inside-forward roles. Significantly, Wednesday managed only 53 goals, and leading scorer Dewar's haul for the season was a mere nine.

Jack Surtees was transferred to Nottingham Forest in October, while Ronnie Starling left for Aston Villa in January. Catlin provided one of the few individual success stories in that his consistency earned him the left-back spot in the England team against Wales, Ireland and Hungary between October and December. Another success in a generally unsuccessful season was teenager Jackie Robinson, who at last established himself in the first-team and did so well that he was selected to play in an international trial, and, in May 1937, was capped by England in the game with Finland in Helsinki. This campaign also saw Jackie Thompson enjoy his longest run to date, and George Drury, a product of Hucknall, did enough in his 21 outings to indicate that he was a star of the future.

Not for the first time in Wednesday's history, the games with Everton provided the most memorable matches of the campaign. After starting the season with a 2-0 home win over Sunderland, Wednesday visited Goodison Park. That they lost 1-3 is forgotten now, but what is remembered is that when Everton captain Dixie Dean headed his side into the lead after 29 minutes he scored his 353rd goal in League football, so beating the record held by the legendary Steve Bloomer. The return game was played at Hillsborough eight days later, and a crowd of 16,677 witnessed an astonishing 10-goal thriller which Wednesday won 6-4. Dewar put Wednesday in front after only six minutes, but a slip by Brown allowed Miller to equalise 13 minutes later. However, Rimmer quickly restored Wednesday's advantage, heading in from a Luke cross. Starling, having his best game since the Cup final, set up his side's third goal, converted by Dewar; and then Brown prevented Coulter from reducing Everton's arrears when he saved a penalty kick. Two minutes after half-time Luke made the score 4-1 in Wednesday's favour, but then Everton scored twice in the space of the next five minutes, Gillick the marksman on both occasions. Rimmer got Wednesday's fifth, and Dewar completed his hat-trick with the sixth. The final goal, Everton's fourth, came from Stevenson five minutes before the end. It will be of interest to recall the teams:

Wednesday— Brown; Ashley, Catlin; Rhodes, Hanford, Burrows; Luke, Starling, Dewar, Hooper, Rimmer.

Everton— Sagar; Jackson, Cook; Britton, Gee, Mercer; Gillick, Miller, Dean, Stevenson, Coulter.

Despite suffering relegation—and a mere two wins in their last 12 games sealed their fate—Wednesday reported a profit of £8,286 on the season; and, thanks largely to the sale of Starling and Surtees, they received £10,442 more from transfers than they spent.

Later in the season, incidentally, Wednesday were asked to stage an FA Cup sixth-round second replay between Sunderland and Wolves. The game, which Sunderland won 4-0, attracted a crowd of 48,960, and, subsequently, the staff at Hillsborough were congratulated on the efficiency of their organisation. So pleased were the Football Association they promised that the Sheffield ground would be seriously considered as a neutral venue for more important fixtures in the future. It is, perhaps, appropriate to mention at this point that the newest recruit to the Wednesday office staff had arrived on the scene in the previous October. His name: Eric England.

In their first Second Division campaign since 1926, Wednesday finished six places from the bottom, only two points better off than relegated Barnsley. It was their lowest-ever League placing; and it didn't help that, in the same season, neighbours Sheffield United were only pipped for promotion on goal-average by Manchester United—the club relegated from the top grade with Wednesday a year earlier.

Before the start of the season, Sam Powell was promoted to first-team trainer following George Irwin's departure for Crystal Palace; and Neil Dewar left for Third Lanark, while Grosvenor joined Bolton. When Wednesday began their League programme with a visit to Chesterfield, the team included two newcomers: Harry Ware, a centre-forward from Newcastle, and Sid Chedgzoy, an outside-right from Runcorn. Unfortunately, both these signings proved disappointing: Ware made 12 appearances and moved on to Norwich in November; while Chedgzoy returned to Cheshire in October having had only four senior outings. Soon after the start of the season, Ernest Matthews, another centre-forward, was acquired from Bury, but he, too, failed to make a lasting impact, though his seven goals in 16 games made him joint top scorer with Robinson. It is relevant to note that, in only his fifth match for Wednesday, Ware suffered a fractured jaw in an off-the-ball incident which was later the subject of an FA inquiry which resulted in Burke of Norwich being cautioned as to his future conduct. Ware missed the next three games, and when he returned he played for a while at right-half. In the light of what had occurred only a matter of weeks before, it was something of a surprise when he moved to Norwich. However, the Norwich officials had admitted how impressed they had been by the vigour of Ware's play!

Overall, 1937-8 proved an acutely disappointing season. Wednesday never seemed able to field a consistent team: some 32 players were called upon, and only five—Goodfellow, Ashley, Catlin, Millership and Burrows—topped 30 appearances. Ashley played in 35 games, ending Nibloe's reign; and two other members of the Cup-winning side, Hooper and Rimmer, reached the end of the road. It is, perhaps, worth recording that the last time Hooper and Rimmer played together in a home League match was against West Ham at the beginning of October; and another feature of this fixture was that the opposition included a half-back called Joe Cockroft, an admirer of Hooper and himself destined to become a Wednesday man in later years. Wednesday continued to have problems at inside-forward, where Thompson was again dogged by injuries; and the quest for the right blend saw Robinson, Driscoll, Curry, C. Walker and Drury as well as Thompson fill the positions.

Wednesday collected only eight points from their first 14 matches, with just two wins—against Fulham and West Ham. In mid-October a crowd of 52,523 was at Hillsborough for the first-ever meeting of the Sheffield clubs in the Second Division; but it was a sad day for the home side, as a 67th-minute header from Arthur Eggleston gave United the points. Another dropped point in the home match with Stockport County a fortnight later left Wednesday in 21st place; and when Barnsley, thanks to two goals each from Hunt and Bray, beat them 4-1 at Oakwell on Saturday November 6, they found themselves bottom of the table. Before the weekend was over, Billy Walker had resigned.

It took Wednesday a little under two months to find a successor. In the meantime, the team played eight matches, of which four were won and two drawn, thus increasing their tally of points from eight to 18. Their best wins were a 4-0 defeat of Luton at home on November 13 and a 4-2 success at Plymouth on Christmas Day. Towards the end of December it was revealed that the managerial vacancy had been offered to former Manchester City and Scotland player, Jimmy McMullan. Remembered as one of Scotland's 1928 "Wembley Wizards", McMullan had been Notts County's manager for about a year, and, before that, team-chief at Oldham and Aston Villa. County agreed to McMullan's release in time for him to watch his new club in action for the first time in the home match against Chesterfield on New Year's Day. Wednesday celebrated his arrival with a 1-0 win, the goal coming from Clipstone product, Allenby Driver, making his League debut at inside-right in place of the injured Thompson.

If McMullan's top priority was pulling Wednesday out of danger and escaping the drop into the Third Division (North), he achieved his aim—but it was a desperately close call. Under his direction Wednesday averaged a point a match from 20 games; but safety was only clinched thanks to successive 2-1 victories in the last two fixtures of the season, against Burnley (home) and Spurs (away).

McMullan sold Luke to Blackburn and Drury to Arsenal. Of several important signings, the most astute were Douglas Hunt from Barnsley and Charlie Napier from Derby County. Hunt, formerly of Winchester and Tottenham, had been at Oakwell exactly a year. He cost Wednesday £3,000, but his six goals in 12 games, including three in those last two vital matches with Burnley and Spurs, made the investment worthwhile; and, subsequently, he made a significant contribution with many more important goals. Napier was another experienced forward, a Scottish international who, after six years with Celtic, had made 90 League appearances for Derby County. Napier's skills soon established him as a firm favourite at Hillsborough, and he was given the captaincy. Other newcomers to the side in the second half of the 1937-8 campaign included Irish forward Bill Fallon, signed from Notts County; Len Massarella, an ex-Denaby winger who had impressed in trials; and Frank Westlake, a young back acquired from Thurnscoe Victoria the previous summer.

In a bid to strengthen the side further for the 1938-9 campaign, McMullan returned to the transfer market during the summer of 1938 and obtained Dave Russell, a half-back from East Fife, and Idris Lewis, a

Welsh international winger from Swansea Town. Lewis was to make only 18 senior appearances and was subsequently replaced by veteran Ernest Toseland, signed from Manchester City in March; but Russell quickly settled at right-half, and was to share with long-serving Horace Burrows the distinction of being an ever-present in an eventful season. Russell's career had begun in 1932 with Dundee United, and later he helped East Fife win the Scottish Cup.

Wednesday made an excellent start to the 1938-9 season. A week before the League programme started they defeated Sheffield United 4-1 in a special Football League Jubilee match at Hillsborough: Hunt scored three goals, and Robinson turned in a brilliant performance. Then Wednesday collected nine points from their first five Second Division matches. In one of these games Arnold Lowes, a Durham-born youngster, joined the ranks of those Wednesday men who have scored when making their League debut. In this instance, Lowes helped his side to a 2-0 defeat of Tranmere, a success which put Wednesday top of the table.

However, Wednesday managed only one victory in their next seven games, and slipped into mid-table. They lost at Chesterfield, Bradford and Southampton—Napier got a hat-trick at The Dell, but still finished on the losing side—and a home defeat against Newcastle followed by a five-goal setback at West Brom left Hillsborough shrouded in gloom. When Wednesday faced Norwich City at home on November 19, McMullan announced three changes: Ex-Gillingham man Fred Lester returned at left-back in place of the promising local lad, Bill Pickering; Hanford took over from Millership at centre-half; and Massarella displaced Lewis at outside-right. The result was that a re-vitalised Wednesday romped to a 7-0 victory, with Douglas Hunt earning himself a place in the record books by scoring six goals. Hunt's goals came after 17, 25, 39, 44, 65 and 87 minutes. A week later the centre-forward scored three more goals in a 5-1 triumph at Luton.

Despite home defeats at the hands of Plymouth in December and West Ham in January (the last match was a nightmare for Goodfellow), Wednesday now ran into a spell in which they won 10 matches out of 13. This sequence included a 5-1 defeat of Fulham before a Hillsborough crowd of 46,743; a 4-2 success at the home of Second Division leaders Blackburn Rovers; and 4-1 victories over Burnley and Tranmere. A lone goal from Hunt gave Wednesday a victory at Swansea, where the home side missed a penalty—the penalty-taker being John Harris, later destined to become manager of Sheffield United, and, of course, an assistant manager at Hillsborough. Incidentally, when Wednesday beat Bradford Park Avenue at home in early February, the visitors had two men sent off.

On the first Saturday of March, a crowd of 48,963—Hillsborough's biggest gate of the season—saw a tension-packed clash with Sheffield United. On the morning of the game, United stood in second place in the table, four points ahead of Wednesday, though the Owls had two games in hand. Wednesday badly needed a win, and, fortunately, they got it—Bill Fallon scoring the only goal after 78 minutes when he pounced as

United defenders Cox and Jessop hesitated over which one of them should make a clearance. The teams lined up thus:

Wednesday— R. Smith; Ashley, Catlin; Russell, Hanford, Burrows; Dillon, Robinson, Hunt, Napier, Fallon.

United— J. Smith; Young, Cox; Jessop, Johnson, Settle; Hagan, Hampson, Dodds, Pickering, Reid.

Wednesday could hardly have made a stronger bid for promotion. They lost only one of their final 12 games, and but for home points conceded to Chesterfield and Nottingham Forest they would surely have succeeded in returning to the top grade. At Easter they managed only three points out of six, losing at Millwall and drawing at Plymouth. A double by Napier helped Wednesday win the Millwall return 3-1, but, on the following Saturday, Wednesday were held at home by Forest. Hunt brought his tally of League goals to 24 with a double in the 2-1 win at Burnley on April 22—a success which put the Owls in second place in the table. Four days later a Napier goal earned a point at Manchester City.

Wednesday's last match of the season was at home to Tottenham, and a crowd of 27,639 saw Napier get the only goal to clinch a victory which left the Owls still second-placed with 53 points from their 42 games. They were one point in front of Sheffield United, but the Blades had one match still to play—and, by coincidence, it was at home to Tottenham. The fixture was completed on the following Saturday, and United made no mistake, crushing the Londoners 6-1, with Hagan (3), Henson (2) and Hampson getting the goals that shattered Wednesday's promotion dream.

It is worthy of note that, in the 1938-9 season, Wednesday had a marathon run in the FA Cup, playing in eight matches in just three rounds. In the third round they were held to a 1-1 draw by non-League Yeovil at Hillsborough. Goals by Lewis and Napier gave them a narrow victory in the replay. In the fourth round Wednesday needed three games to dispose of Third Division Chester, goals by Robinson and Hunt breaking the deadlock in the second replay, staged at Maine Road, Manchester. An aggregate attendance of 160,000 was registered for the three fifth-round ties with Chelsea. At Stamford Bridge in the first clash, Wednesday were held to a 1-1 draw because of a disputed penalty converted by their former player, Burgess; a goal-less draw followed at Hillsborough; and goals from Burgess(2) and Joe Payne gave Chelsea a 3-1 win in the second replay, at Highbury.

Whether these Cup-ties contributed to Wednesday's failure to gain promotion is difficult to establish for certain. It seems doubtful, though it has to be said that it was in this period that they suffered vital setbacks at Coventry and Newcastle. In the end, it was a source of much dismay that Wednesday had failed so narrowly, but Jimmy McMullan had every reason to be optimistic that the team's return to the First Division would not be much longer delayed. The team was looking good. Goalkeeper Roy Smith had kept Goodfellow out since the turn of the year; Ashley and Catlin looked solid at the back; Russell, Hanford, and Burrows made a very useful half-back line; and there was strength in depth with forwards such as Toseland, Robinson, Lowes, Hunt, Napier and Fallon to call upon. Robinson had scored 15 goals, Fallon 10 and Napier nine to add to Hunt's 24 in the season just ended. Young Pickering was developing, and, with Millership and others on hand, there was reason to believe the future could be very bright.

Unfortunately, Prime Minister Chamberlain's "peace in our time" promise was soon to be shattered by Hitler's invasion of Poland. The 1939-40 season came along, bringing with it the novelty of players having to wear numbered shirts; but it survived barely a week before the blow fell. Wednesday kicked off with a three-goal defeat at Luton; they beat Barnsley 3-1 at home two days later; and then lost by a single goal (scored by Glover direct from a corner) at home to Plymouth on Saturday September 2. The next day Britain went to war. Football (and indeed life in general) was not to be the same again for many years. When "normal" football resumed in 1946 a good deal had happened in the meantime . . .

2 A wartime interlude: 1939-46

When the second World War began in September 1939, the Football League, FA Cup and other leading competitions were immediately suspended. They remained six years in cold storage. Everyone had much more serious things on their minds; important matters involving life and death and the business of survival. Yet it did not take long for people to recover from the initial shock of finding the country at war and to adapt quickly to the dramatic changes in circumstances. Perhaps there is something in the character of the British which brings out previously untapped depths of spirit and determination at such times of crisis; but, anyway, it was soon decided that "the show must go on", and the belief was that the best way to raise morale in wartime was to try to live as normal a life as conditions allowed. Sport provided a vital link with a saner world and an outlet for emotional frustrations. So football was resumed, albeit in restricted form; and, continuing throughout the war, the game made an important contribution towards the raising of spirits by encouraging people to relax and re-charge those war-weary batteries. Certainly football enjoyed increased popularity and was welcomed by those who wanted, for a brief 90 minutes or so once a week, to escape the drudgery, discomforts and dreadful realities of a war which threatened extinction. Most people left at home spent long, tiring hours in factories, and passed countless evenings and nights in air-raid shelters; and football provided a release which acted as a kind of national safety valve.

In retrospect, playing statistics and records for those years may seem of little consequence, and, admittedly, the nature of the times meant that many of the games were makeshift affairs. But, all the same, it would be wrong to simply dismiss these games. In one sense, perhaps, the matches in themselves were more important than the results, though the results were hardly insignificant to those involved; but what really mattered was that the clashes brought a splash of colour to a very dark world, providing entertainment the value of which could never be measured in terms of goals or points or prizes.

Petrol shortages and other restrictions on travel made it necessary for the game to be organised on a regional basis. The team line-ups were often conditioned by circumstances, with those men available at kick-off time playing—many of them having come straight off the morning shift, or dashed from some military camp on a weekend pass. The clubs virtually closed down; grounds were deserted most of the week, being opened up perhaps on a couple of evenings for training sessions, and otherwise only coming to life on match-days. Managers, secretaries and other senior staff found themselves seconded into essential wartime work, while the younger staff seldom remained long out of uniform. Soccer took a back seat, and administration became a matter of doing what was really necessary and no more.

Of course, many players quickly found themselves called up, too. Some, because they had joined the Territorial Army in the previous summer, were in khaki within a matter of days of war being declared. Many were never to play serious football again, while many failed to recapture the form or the promise of pre-war days. Those who remained in home bases managed to retain some links with the game, playing whenever they could get leave, and often guesting with a club near to the camp at which they were stationed. In this way, some clubs, by virtue of an accident of geography, found themselves with an abundance of famous and talented players to call upon; while others struggled to field an adequate team because they could not replace their "lost" stars. Some players remained at home in reserved occupations, working on munitions or in factories on special wartime production. These men were more regularly available to their old clubs, though some were still restricted by shift-work. It should be said that some clubs, despite the absence of famous names, managed to build up formidable and successful teams, largely because the war years produced a succession of talented local lads who seized the opportunity, recognising that circumstances had provided them with the chance of a longer and earlier run in the first-team than might have been the case in normal times. Many of these wartime "discoveries" survived to make a name in the game in the post-war era.

Wednesday's wartime story was, for the most part, fairly typical of the average leading club of the period. On the whole the years passed without any major sensations, though the club parted company with one manager and eventually appointed a successor; and much local enthusiasm was generated when the team reached the final of the League North War Cup in 1943. Apart from that, the only spectacular success was achieved in 1946 when the reserves broke records in winning the Central League championship. The later years of the wartime period were the best years for the club, for the team began to play with more consistency from around 1942 on, and several bright youngsters began to blend with the remaining older players. And when the FA Cup competition was resumed in 1945-6, Hillsborough, having staged a number of wartime representative games, finally gained long-awaited recognition when it was chosen as the venue for a semi-final—the first at the ground for 24 years.

These were troubled years, and it was a period fraught with frustration and difficulties, life at large overshadowed by uncertainty and upheaval and an unreal, nightmarish atmosphere in which many felt it wisest to live for the day and let tomorrow take care of itself. The pressures, peculiar to the times, altered the course of many lives; and chance played an important part in fashioning a number of soccer careers while finishing others. Some saw their best years played out in a world dominated by conditions over which they had no control; while others, mainly the younger players, had a unique opportunity to develop and mature.

Wednesday began the wartime period less than well, though it is, perhaps, relevant to note that 1940 and 1941 were very tough years for the people of Sheffield, with the city the constant target of Hitler's bombs. For some time after the blitz of December 1940 it was difficult to believe that life could ever be normal again, and activities such as football seemed at one stage to be on the point of coming to another halt.

Unfortunately, the first victim of Wednesday's lack of success and consequent decline in income was Jimmy McMullan. With the outbreak of war, he took a full-time job in a local factory, and, in effect, became a part-time manager. He was given a temporary contract, and when this expired in the spring of 1942 the directors decided to discontinue the engagement. Vice-chairman William Fearnehough said: "We've not fallen out with Jimmy, but feel our decision is in the best interests of everyone in the present circumstances." Naturally, it was a sad blow to McMullan, who felt he had been desperately unlucky. "I believe," he commented, "that if there had been no war I should have remained with Wednesday for many years. After all, I had a good side together, and I had some promising youngsters ready to bring out. Then the war came. A good deal was achieved between January 1938 and May 1939, and we had every reason to look forward with high hopes."

McMullan lost a number of his best players as soon as the war started, and the man he missed most was Charlie Napier, who returned to Scotland within days of League football being suspended. (In fact, Napier was brought back to Sheffield for a short time in 1943, but his stay was not very successful. In Scotland he had been guesting with Falkirk, but, after being sent off in a match in early 1941, was banned by the Scottish FA. Eric Taylor had the ban lifted, but, soon after re-appearing in Wednesday's team, Napier was sent off in a game against Grimsby, and, sadly, a further ban was imposed. It was not lifted until the end of the war—too late for Napier to re-establish his career.) McMullan found it extremely difficult to run a team in wartime. "There are many problems," he said. "Some clubs have players available, but others—and some equally as famous as Wednesday—have had a bad time. All things considered, I doubt if any other manager could have done better."

McMullan, it has been said, was not tough or aggressive enough, and he found that the managerial philosophy which had served him well in peacetime was inappropriate to wartime conditions. He never dictated to his older players, only asking that they made the best use of their skill and experience. He always told his younger players to follow the lead of their senior colleagues. "Use your energy to support the old 'uns," he would say. "Remember that the last 15 minutes of a game are more important than the first 15. Take time to size up the opposition, then harry and chase the old-timers on the other side. Tire them out and let our own older players conserve their energy, and then you'll be poised to take full advantage towards the end of the game." Had McMullan had a Napier to call on, the course of Wednesday's history might have been altered; but the manager suffered, too, because he was unable to give his undivided attention to football.

McMullan's successor was Eric Woodhouse Taylor, whose appointment as secretary with effect from April 14 1942 and subsequent elevation to secretary-manager in June 1945, were probably the two most significant and far-reaching decisions made by the club in the war years. Taylor, who had joined Wednesday as an office boy in September 1929, had been assistant secretary since 1934; and, in fact, had been chiefly responsible for overall administration for some years. A chirpy, quick-witted extrovert, he had been greatly influenced by his first boss, Bob Brown, but he was a man with his own mind and ideas and he had great ambitions for Wednesday. In the war years he had to spend most of his working hours in Howell's tube works, but he was confident that, once peace returned and football got back to normal, he could put Wednesday back at the top and transform Hillsborough into a great stadium fit for the best the game could offer. Significantly, he had been secretary-manager less than a year when Hillsborough was chosen to stage its first semi-final since 1922; and Taylor ensured that, in making the arrangements for this important event, he had his former colleague Eric England released from RAF duties to complete the backroom team.

Initially, however, Taylor performed his secretarial duties in tandem with his job at Howell's. At the outset he kept a watchful eye on playing matters, but did not directly involve himself in team talks, tactics, and suchlike. Wisely, perhaps, he left this side of the business to trainers Sam Powell and Tommy Walker, and, more especially, to such experienced players as Ted Catlin and Walter Millership, and, to a lesser extent, Joe Cockroft and Jackie Thompson. Between them these men had an abundance of knowledge and experience, and Taylor recognised that they would not only bring out the best in each other but guide the youngsters, too.

As fortune would have it, Taylor's first season as secretary was probably the club's best in the wartime period. By this time the team had a fairly consistent and solid look about it, and the blend of experience and youth helped them reach the final of the League North War Cup.

A number of players who had been with the club before the war were available: as well as Catlin and Millership, there was Albert Morton in goal, Ashley at back, Russell had returned at half-back, and Robinson and Thompson at inside-forward. Reynolds, a winger who had been playing with Rochdale, had returned to his native Sheffield to work on munitions; while Frank Melling, a well-known local amateur footballer-cricketer, lent speed and scoring power to the front-line; and Hugh Swift, a former Burngreave schoolboy with strength and speed, had emerged as perhaps the first outstanding wartime "discovery".

Circumstances had also brought Joe Cockroft, an experienced half-back, home to South Yorkshire. Cockroft, a native of Barnsley, had moved via Rotherham United and Gainsborough Trinity to West Ham; and, with the London club, had established a club record of 217 consecutive League and Cup appearances between 1932 and 1937. He had also played in an international trial for England against The Rest. Joe might have remained in the south, but in 1941 his home was blitzed and he brought his family north. After two or three games with Chesterfield he began playing with Wednesday. At the end of the war Cockroft's formal transfer from West Ham was negotiated, and he remained at Hillsborough until 1948.

The war years saw Jackie Robinson touch his peak, and many were left pondering what he might have achieved if there had been no war. In wartime and transitional seasons, Robinson scored 93 goals, and his haul of 35 in the 1942-3 campaign included six hat-tricks. At his best, he was breathtakingly brilliant. Ideally built, he had superb ball-control and a natural body swerve, plus an apparent ability to run as fast with the ball as without it. He also had a terrific, strong shot, and many of his goals were scored from outside the penalty area. Like many players of genius, his chief fault was his tendency to be selfish, but when he played for the team he had the capacity to lift the side to great heights. It was said that if Jackie got a goal early in the game he would invariably proceed to play brilliantly, and on such occasions he was the idol of the crowd. His tragedy was that he did not look after himself as well as he might, and, by the time the war ended, he was only a shadow of his old self. Incidentally, when war broke out, Robinson and the other players had to produce birth certificates, and he was found to be two years older than had been thought!

Midway through the 1942-3 season Wednesday began to knit as a unit and gave warning that they were likely to be strong contenders for honours. In mid-February they qualified for the League North War Cup tournament "proper" by thrashing Sheffield United 8-2 before a crowd of 18,232 at Hillsborough. United hardly got a look-in, and goals by Robinson (12 and 20 min), Thompson (15, 40), Melling (25) and Reynolds (35) gave Wednesday a 6-1 half-time lead; United's goal having come from Nightingale. In the second period, Robinson completed his hat-trick and Melling scored again before Jack Pickering got United's second.

In the first-round proper, Wednesday beat Bradford City 2-1 on aggregate; and they followed this with a 5-2 aggregate win against Nottingham Forest—Melling claiming four goals in the 5-1 victory at Hillsborough. This was followed by an exciting 3-2 triumph over Sheffield United in the first leg of the third round. United led twice, first through Albert Nightingale and then Pickering; but, on each occasion,

Robinson snatched an equaliser. Melling scored the winner nine minutes from the end—an ironic touch for a man who was later (because of his cricket interests) to become a United director. Incidentally, this match attracted a crowd of 37,500; at the time a wartime record for Sheffield. The second-leg at Bramall Lane ended 0-0, and Wednesday now faced York City in the semi-final. They drew 1-1 at Bootham Crescent, where Thompson was the marksman; and won 3-0 at Hillsborough, where Robinson got two of the goals. It is worthy of note, perhaps, that Jack Smith of Sheffield United guested in Wednesday's goal in the semi-finals.

The final brought Wednesday up against Blackpool, one of the most successful teams of the period. In the first leg, at Bloomfield Road, the teams lined up as follows:

Blackpool— Savage; Pope, Jones; Farrow, Johnston, Powell; Matthews, Dix, Dodds, Finan, Burbanks.

Wednesday— Morton; Ashley, Catlin; Russell, Millership, Cockroft; Reynolds, Robinson, Melling, Thompson, Swift.

Robinson played throughout with a damaged ankle, and Wednesday were reduced to 10 men five minutes after half-time; but the Sheffield team rose to the occasion magnificently, and were desperately unlucky to have to settle for a 2-2 scoreline. A stroke of Matthews magic set up Blackpool's first goal 10 minutes before half-time, Finan heading in; but five minutes later Cockroft levelled the scores from the penalty spot. Soon after half-time former Sheffield United centre-forward, Jock Dodds, fouled Catlin and the Wednesday man was found to have badly damaged knee ligaments. After an absence of 15 minutes he limped back onto the field, but was a helpless passenger. Swift switched to left-back, and, to everyone's surprise, took the challenge of Matthews in his stride. Of course, Swift, *was* a back, only playing on the wing because Wednesday lacked a natural outside-left. Things looked good for Wednesday when Robinson, cashing in on some good work by Thompson, shot them in front. However, in the final seconds of the game Eddie Burbanks somehow scrambled an equaliser after Matthews had for once eluded Swift and pumped a low cross into a crowded goalmouth.

The second-leg, played at Hillsborough on May 8 1943, proved something of an anti-climax for the record crowd of 47,657 (receipts £5,965). Blackpool were without Matthews, away on England duty; while Gadsby deputised for Catlin in the home side. But perhaps the key to the game was Blackpool's decision to switch Johnston to left-half; and he and Farrow were instructed to push forward to put pressure on their Wednesday counterparts, so creating greater freedom for Dix and Finan. Wednesday's inside forwards did not react to this change of tactics, and, overall, their performance was disappointing. The turning point of the game, however, was a free-kick conceded by Millership for a foul on Dodds after 24 minutes. Dodds was still regarded as the "villain" of the piece, and there was a cruel twist in the way the Blackpool leader hammered the free-kick into the Wednesday net from 30 yards, the ball glancing off Millership and speeding past Morton. Gardner got another

*11. Wednesday's line-up for the second leg of the League War North Cup final,
v Blackpool, at Hillsborough, 1943. . . (back row) Eric Taylor (secretary), Russell, Ashley,
Millership, Morton, Gadsby, Cockroft, Catlin; (front row) Reynolds, Robinson, Melling,
Thompson, Swift, Powell (trainer). Note: Catlin played in the first leg.*

for Blackpool after 76 minutes, and Robinson headed Wednesday's
consolation four minutes from the end. A smiling Dodds collected the
trophy from H. V. Alexander, First Lord of the Admiralty. This game
marked the end of Melling's spell with Wednesday: he returned to his
studies and later qualified as an architect.

Catlin's senior career was virtually ended by his injury, but he was
later to play an important role with the reserves when the Central League
competition was resumed in 1945-6. In this campaign the second-team
had the distinction of enjoying a record run of 25 games without defeat,
and they took the title with 63 points from 40 matches, heading the table
with six points more than runners-up Aston Villa. The team included
Tommy Ward, a centre-forward whom Wednesday had signed from
Crook Town in 1937; Alex Wands, another product of the North East; and
Frank Westlake, Laurie Mackenzie, Jimmy McCarter and Ralph Stewart.

The 1945-6 season also provided a number of highlights for the
first-team, who finished fifth in the League North table (12 points behind
champions Sheffield United) and reached the fifth round of the revived
FA Cup.

By now the senior squad included a number of new faces: Jack
Lindsay, a centre-forward from Greenock Morton; Charlie Tomlinson, a
Sheffield-born winger acquired from Bradford; Redfern Froggatt, a
promising forward and the son of a former Wednesday captain; Birley
Carr product Alf Rogers; and defenders Tom Gale (ex-Gateshead), Cyril
Turton (ex-Frickley Colliery), and Edgar Packard, a product of Mansfield

who had, in fact, been on the club's books since before the war.

In this season the FA Cup competition was played on a two-leg basis. Wednesday started on the Wembley trail with a 5-0 aggregate win over Mansfield Town; and followed this with an 11-2 aggregate triumph over York City, with goals coming from Tomlinson(3), Driver(3), Thompson(2), Froggatt(2) and Aveyard.

Stoke City provided the opposition in the fifth round, and Wednesday's line-up when they visited the Potteries for the first leg was: Goodfellow; Swift, Pickering; Cockroft, Gale, Wands; Driver, J. Thompson, Aveyard, Froggatt, Tomlinson. Freddie Steele headed both goals in Stoke's 2-0 win, and the Midlanders went into the second leg, played at Hillsborough two days later, with a considerable advantage. A staggering crowd of 62,728, paying £5,698, turned up for the game. Wednesday's only change was the return of Jackie Robinson after a month's absence through injury. But the old hero had a poor day. Indeed, though Bill Pickering excelled against Stanley Matthews, and Hugh Swift again shone, Wednesday's overall performance was something of a let-down. Stoke held out for a 0-0 draw and went through to the quarter-finals.

Wednesday's consolation was that Hillsborough was chosen to stage the FA Cup semi-final between Birmingham City and Derby County, a game which attracted a crowd of 65,000 (receipts £14,250) and ended in a 1-1 draw. Derby won the replay at Maine Road, Manchester, and went on to win the FA Cup by defeating Jimmy Seed's Charlton Athletic at Wembley.

Representative and other big matches staged at Hillsborough are featured in detail elsewhere, but here it seems appropriate to note that in the war years the Wednesday ground was the venue for three important representative games. On January 18 1941 a Football League XI defeated an All-British XI 5-3, but, because of a blizzard which blew up just before the start, the attendance was only 4,409. In the following May an RAF XI beat an Army XI 5-2; and, on April 4 1942, England beat Scotland 4-1 in an Army international, with Tommy Lawton scoring a hat-trick which delighted the 28,567 spectators.

These matches, forgotten now, were significant in that they laid the foundations for Hillsborough's future use as a venue for big games; and they provided Eric Taylor with the opportunity to exhibit his remarkable flair for organising a major event and ensuring that, on the day, all went smoothly. Taylor knew how to put on a big match, and Football Association officials soon recognised that here was a man to whom they could leave everything. In future years the choice of Hillsborough for FA Cup semi-finals and other major fixtures ensured extra income for the club. Taylor must take much of the credit for that, but it is necessary to add that Eric England in particular, and others, contributed to Wednesday's success in this direction.

If Eric Taylor had one disappointment in the last of the war years, it was that, in 1945, he was unable to persuade the famous Moscow Dynamos to include Hillsborough on their British tour programme. However, in the long-term, this was a minor setback.

3 Struggle towards promotion: 1946-1950

When League football finally returned to normal in 1946, the enthusiasm with which the public greeted its resumption was truly astonishing. Soccer suddenly had a greater following than ever before, and, like the cinema, enjoyed a remarkable boom in popularity for the next 10 years or so. The first post-war season, 1946-7, coincided with one of the worst winters in living memory, when heavy snow and a prolonged spell of freezing weather delayed completion of the League programme until early June; and yet attendances totalled more than 35½ million. In each of the following three seasons attendances topped 40 million, and the aggregate remained above 36 million until the mid-1950s.

Social historians have called the immediate post-war period the Age of Austerity, because, generally speaking, it was a time of many shortages. Essentials like fuel, food, clothing and similar commodities were rationed, and luxuries seemed to cease to exist for the ordinary person. A motor car in every family and a television in every home were dreams a long way from fulfilment. In football the maximum wage was raised to £10 a week in 1946, but even players on the top rate travelled by bus or tramcar. Ground admission charges were reduced from 1s 6d to 1s 3d, thanks to a cut in Entertainment Tax, but cheaper football was not the sole reason for the dramatic increase in attendances. The increase came about largely because, as in the war years, the game was one of the few entertainments which offered a splash of colour and a dash of drama and excitement in times that were generally rather grey.

It was a good time for football. Within the game people accepted the boom with surprise and delight. Despite the huge crowds, there was virtually no trouble among spectators: on the whole, supporters were easy-going and good-natured, happy simply to see soccer back to normal. On the playing front, English football was still regarded as the best, and the 1953 Hungarians and the ultimate rise of the Continental and South American nations were developments beyond the imagination of the average supporter in the late 1940s. If, in retrospect, the English game can be seen to have been introverted and complacent, it should be said that there *were* people with the vision to look to the game's future and foresee big changes ahead. A few, indeed, could envisage the eventual expansion of the game into a European affair even at club level, and could see, too, the need for ground developments and the improvement of spectator facilities as soon as circumstances permitted. However, for the moment, there was no foreign travel on the scale subsequently taken for granted, and horizons were limited by the conditions of the times. In any event, most people were pre-occupied with what was happening in their own backyard and down at their local club.

Eric Taylor, now firmly established as secretary-manager of Sheffield Wednesday, was one of the men with an eye on the future, and he lacked neither opinions nor plans for the years ahead. But, in 1946, his first priority was to guide Wednesday back to the First Division. This task proved more difficult than many might have anticipated.

Wednesday spent the first four post-war seasons in the Second Division. In 1946-7 they went desperately close to a fall into the Third Division, but escaped by a mere three points. However, having survived, their fortunes improved considerably: they finished fourth, then eighth, and finally, in 1949-50, clinched promotion by the narrowest of margins—pipping Sheffield United and Southampton on goal-average. These were tense and sometimes traumatic years, but they were certainly never dull for the club and its supporters.

In this period Eric Taylor quickly emerged not only as a clever and imaginative administrator with a flair for organising the big occasion, but as an astute football manager, too. His knowledge of the game and an ability to recognise talent were soon apparent: while his excursions into the transfer market, to buy or to sell, earned him a reputation as a canny negotiator and hard bargainer. In the earliest of the post-war years, the signing of players like George Hunt, Doug Witcomb, Eddie Quigley, Eddie Kilshaw, Eddie Gannon and others highlighted his astonishing knack of buying the right man at the right time—and at the right price. Significantly, he knew when to sell, too, as was illustrated by the moves which took Jackie Robinson to Sunderland in 1946, Joe Cockroft to Sheffield United in 1948, and Quigley to Preston (for a record £26,000) in 1949.

In putting his rebuilding plans into operation, Taylor's first priority was the strengthening of his backroom staff. He began by seeking to persuade Dug Livingstone, a tough but respected member of Sheffield United's training staff since 1936, to become team-manager at Hillsborough. The deal fell through when negotiations had reached an advanced stage. Within a few weeks, however, Bill Knox was recruited from Huddersfield Town, taking up the post of trainer-coach in late February 1947. Knox, who had played with Celtic, Burnley and Luton Town in the inter-war years, made an important contribution towards improving the team's fortunes; but, sadly, he died suddenly just before promotion was achieved in 1950.

At this point a few statistics may serve to spotlight some of the principal players in the story of this important phase. In these first four seasons Wednesday played 168 League matches, and four men figured in most of them: Hugh Swift (160), Redfern Froggatt (142), Doug Witcomb (132), and Frank Westlake (109). In 161 of those games the centre-half spot was filled by either Cyril Turton or Edgar Packard; while Roy Smith was first-choice goalkeeper to begin with, but, subsequently, Girvan-born Scot, Dave McIntosh, held the position with greater regularity, with Albert Morton the usual stand-in. It is of interest to note that, of 263 League goals scored by Wednesday in these four seasons, 180 were contributed by six players: Quigley (50), Froggatt (35), Clarrie Jordan (28), Dennis Woodhead (24), Jimmy Dailey (24) and Tommy Ward (19). Quigley's goals came in only 74 games, and, when it is remembered that he was bought for £12,000 and sold at more than double that figure two years later, it serves to emphasise Taylor's business acumen. Froggatt, on the other hand, was a home product; a clever, skilful player who was to give long and loyal service, gain four

England caps, and establish what was then a post-war scoring record of 140 League goals by the time of his retirement in 1960. Clarrie Jordan and Jimmy Dailey were contrasting centre-forwards in style, but each in his own way made a useful contribution; and while Jordan might have achieved more but for the knee trouble which eventually ended his career, Dailey, having cost only a £10 signing-on fee in the beginning, was subsequently sold for a substantial fee.

Wednesday tried a number of wingers in those years, including Oscar Fox, Charlie Tomlinson, Jackie Marriott, the unlucky Frank Slynn and the popular Dennis Woodhead. Woodhead (the grandson of Billy Betts) proved the most consistent, and the fact that he scored 73 goals in 213 League appearances does not adequately reflect his vital contribution in two or three key spells in certain seasons. Marriott, who cost £2,000 from Midland League Scunthorpe United, spent nine seasons at the club. In December 1948 Wednesday paid £20,000—at the time a record for a winger—for Bury's Eddie Kilshaw; but this clever and seasoned campaigner played in only 17 games before suffering the injury which ended his career.

✳ ✳ ✳

The 1946-7 season saw Wednesday struggling right from the first match, for they lost 1-4 at Luton on the opening day and then conceded four more goals in the home game with Barnsley. They won two of their first five matches—one was a 5-3 triumph at Leicester—but only three of 21 games played between mid-September and mid-January. Not surprisingly, they went into the New Year close to the foot of the table, and the second half of the season saw them struggling desperately to avoid relegation, with Millwall, Swansea Town and Newport County their rivals in the battle for survival. In fact, Newport were doomed long before the end of the season, but Swansea and Wednesday kept their supporters on tenterhooks until near the end of May.

The main changes in the first half of the season saw the departure from the scene of Driver, Robinson, Lindsay and Aveyard; with George Hunt and Jimmy Dailey the first important arrivals. Hunt, signed from Bolton in early November, was unable to turn the tide immediately, but the 37-year-old former England forward was to prove a major influence in the season as a whole, lending much-needed experience and leadership to the side. Dailey, a dashing, energetic 19-year-old who had been an amateur with Wolves before returning to Scotland and Third Lanark, was not everybody's ideal centre-forward, but he contributed 13 vital goals in the fight to avoid relegation. Indeed, Dailey scored on his debut at West Brom in mid-November, and claimed seven goals in his first eight games.

By the time the third round of the FA Cup came round in early January, Wednesday's desperate League position took the edge off the traditional dreams of a good run on the Wembley trail. Ironically, the Owls reserved two of their best performances for the Cup; and, after beating Blackpool 4-1, defeated Everton 2-1 before a crowd of 62,500 at Hillsborough. Jock Dodds, who led Everton's attack, did not have as happy a day as had been the case when he captained Blackpool in 1943;

and early goals by Froggatt and Tomlinson put Wednesday on the victory path. The much-postponed fifth-round tie with Preston finally went ahead in late February; and when two second-half goals gave the visitors a place in the quarter-final, there were no complaints from anyone at Hillsborough. Eric Taylor and his colleagues simply hoped that some of the form shown in the Cup games would now be seen in the remaining Second Division fixtures.

It was around this time that Bill Knox joined the staff, and, soon afterwards, Doug Witcomb was signed from West Brom for a £6,000 fee. Witcomb, already capped several times for Wales, was a strong-tackling half-back who was to enjoy a long run at Hillsborough; and, happily, his debut coincided with Wednesday's biggest win of the season—a 5-1 defeat of Tottenham. In this game Dailey snatched a goal in the first minute and went on to get a hat-trick. The following Saturday, Wednesday were scheduled to face Swansea Town, and the result against Spurs had put them in the ideal mood to meet their great relegation rivals; but, unfortunately, at the end of a 12½-hour journey to South Wales, the Sheffield party learned that the game had been postponed.

April was a crucial month in the relegation struggle, with Wednesday's hopes fluctuating from match to match. On April 5 they crashed to a five-goal defeat at Coventry, for whom Lowrie got four; while Swansea won 3-1 on the same day. However, on the following Monday, Wednesday went to Fulham, and, thanks to goals by Hunt (14 min) and Ward (25), won 2-1; with Swansea losing at home to Coventry. The next day Coventry again defeated Swansea, and Lowrie, the "villain" four days earlier, was now the hero so far as Wednesday supporters were concerned, for he bagged a hat-trick.

However, for both Wednesday and Swansea it was still touch-and-go. When Wednesday, with Marriott setting up goals for Ward and Slynn, beat Nottingham Forest on April 12, their delight was tempered by news of Swansea's win at Leicester; but a week later, when the Owls lost at Southampton, they didn't feel quite as badly about it when they learned that Chesterfield had won at Swansea.

When Wednesday beat Newport County 2-1 at the end of April, they found themselves needing six points from their last five games to ensure safety. Unfortunately, they lost first at West Ham and then in the re-arranged game at Swansea. Now Wednesday and Swansea stood level on points, though Wednesday had a match in hand. On the following Saturday, while Wednesday were without a game, Swansea visited Barnsley. Never can Wednesdayites have been so pleased to see the Oakwell club win, as they did by a margin of 3-1.

When Wednesday started the Whitsun weekend with a home game against Newcastle United, the players wore black armbands as a mark of respect for W. G. Turner, club President, and, from 1931 until 1945, chairman. He had died three days earlier. This was a match Wednesday badly wanted to win, for they felt that two points would just about clinch safety. But though Ward shot them ahead after 33 minutes, Hair equalised for the visitors after 70 minutes. On Whit Monday a crowd of

33,390 turned up in weather more suited to a Roses cricket match than a football game between Wednesday and Manchester City, the club already assured of the Second Division championship. A lone goal from Ward—his 18th of the season—clinched a home victory. . . and Wednesday were safe at last! Ironically, now came the news that Swansea had lost their last match, going down at home to Millwall: that final victory of Wednesday's had not made any difference to the relegation issue after all.

It is worthy of note that Dennis Woodhead, fresh out of the RAF, made his League debut in the game with Newcastle. In later years, Woodhead was to have a spell at Chesterfield, and, by coincidence, his first away match in Wednesday colours was at Saltergate in a game which earned a place in the record books. This game, completed on Saturday June 7, had little at stake except pride. Oliver gave Chesterfield the lead after three minutes, but goals by Slynn and Hunt saw Wednesday in front by the early stages of the second half. Then came the 22-minute spell which made this match special. In that time, Chesterfield right-back George Milburn hammered three penalty-kicks past Roy Smith: the first two being given when Swift's sliding tackles upended Linacre, the third being conceded by Packard for a handling offence. The hat-trick feat gave Wednesday fans something else to talk about during the summer besides that tense battle against relegation. Incidentally, Milburn was the uncle of Jack Charlton, who became Wednesday's manager in later years.

In 1947-8 Wednesday's fortunes took a turn for the better: they finished the season in fourth place, only five points behind Newcastle United, who were promoted with Birmingham City. Indeed, but for a point dropped in each of their last three matches, another they let slip at West Brom, and a defeat at Newcastle, all on the final lap of the campaign, they could have been celebrating a dramatic return to the First Division.

Wednesday collected seven home points more than in the previous season, and nearly trebled their away tally; yet, curiously enough, they scored one goal fewer than in 1946-7. Of course, this time they made the goals count more often . . .and the "goals against" column showed a reduction of 35. One key to the upwards progress was consistency of team selection. Eight players missed fewer than 10 games: indeed, Westlake and Swift at back, and half-back Witcomb were all ever-presents; Cockroft played in 41 matches, Froggatt 39, and Turton and Woodhead 36 each.

The most important newcomers signed during the season were Eddie Quigley, from Bury, and Clarrie Jordan, from Doncaster Rovers: forwards with big reputations. Quigley was not unfamiliar to Wednesdayites, for, the previous Christmas, he had helped Bury achieve a double with a 4-2 win at Gigg Lane and a 5-2 success at Hillsborough; and, soon afterwards, Quigley scored all the goals in Bury's 5-2 defeat of Millwall. Yet the dark-haired marksman had started that season as a back, only being switched to attack in an emergency. He did not play at back again! Jordan, tough and tenacious, was always a centre-forward,

12. Heroes of 1947. . . (back row) Doug Witcomb, Cyril Turton, Frank Westlake, Albert Morton, Hugh Swift, Joe Cockroft; (front row) Frank Slynn, Arnold Lowes, Jimmy Dailey, Redfern Froggatt, Dennis Woodhead.

and had been the sensation of the 1946-7 campaign with 44 League and Cup goals making him the hero of a Doncaster side which won the Third Division (North) title with a record 72 points.

Quigley scored on his home debut on October 18, when a 40,000 crowd saw Luton beaten; and he went on to score 23 goals in 30 games, including four in the 5-3 defeat of West Ham on Boxing Day—a game also remembered because Slynn, who had only just returned to the side, broke his leg as early as the tenth minute. Jordan's arrival in February coincided with the beginning of the run in which Wednesday lost only one of their final 15 games. In fact, Jordan scored only three goals in this spell, but his astute distribution and his ability to hold the front line together helped create many openings from which Quigley and Froggatt benefitted.

Quigley's arrival led to the demotion of Arnold Lowes, who was subsequently used as a makeweight in the Jordan deal. Lowes was not the only man for whom this season marked the end of the line. George Hunt fell out of favour after only three outings; and the coming of Jordan put Jimmy Dailey back in the reserves. Yet, in early September, Dailey had shot himself into the club's record books by scoring five goals against Barnsley. The Scot was to make only five more senior appearances before, in February 1949, he joined Birmingham City for a £9,500 fee.

The only other major change involved the goalkeeping position. Albert Morton was the first-choice at the start of the season, but, after a run of 23 matches, he was displaced by Roy Smith; and then, 12 games later, Dave McIntosh, a young Scot who had been in the Yorkshire League side for most of his six months with the club, was thrust into senior action. McIntosh went on to make some 290 League appearances in Wednesday's goal over the next nine years; and while Smith moved to Notts County, Morton eventually joined Rochdale. When McIntosh made his home debut for Wednesday against Doncaster Rovers, the attendance was 51,467—the best of the season.

Between the end of the 1947-8 campaign and the start of the new season, there were one or two events of interest worth recording. In May a Sheffield derby was staged at Douglas, Isle of Man—the result a 2-2 draw, with Collindridge and Sloan on target for United and Quigley getting Wednesday's goals. In June it was learned that the former Olive Grove idol, Fred Spiksley, had died suddenly; and in August, Tommy Ward, one of the club's saviours in 1946-7, was transferred to Darlington.

Compared with the previous season, 1948-9 proved a disappointment, for Wednesday finished in eighth place, well out of the running for promotion. They were let down by poor away form; and the fact that they conceded only 17 goals at home was not sufficient to make up the difference between them and promoted West Brom and Fulham, who each won four more home games and five more away games than Wednesday. McIntosh and Swift were ever-presents, and Westlake, Turton, Witcomb, Froggatt and Woodhead did not miss many games; while the leading scorers were Quigley (18), Woodhead (14), Jordan (13) and Froggatt (10).

Wednesday began the season with only two wins in their first eight games, but the team remained unchanged until late October. Then Keith Bannister replaced Joe Cockroft, and the captaincy passed to Witcomb. Three weeks later came the sudden transfer of Cockroft to Sheffield United. "It happened right out of the blue," he recalled. "I was flabbergasted. I don't think I really wanted to go, but United's manager, Teddy Davison, said I could do a job for them." Wednesday could hardly say no to an offer of £4,000 for a player five months past his 37th birthday. When Cockroft lined up for United against Preston, he became the oldest player ever make his First Division debut. In his first game he helped United end a sequence of 14 games without a win, but he was unable to turn the tide which swept them to relegation; and, indeed, he had left to become player-manager of Wisbech Town before the end of the season.

Not long after parting with Cockroft, Wednesday signed Kilshaw from Bury, and then, in March, Eddie Gannon, Notts County's Eire international wing-half, was obtained for a fee of £15,000. Unfortunately, the newcomers were unable to end the team's tendency towards inconsistency in results. Wednesday simply could not string together more than two or three good results without a couple of slips; and, on the season's last lap, they had a run of nine matches in which they won only once—hardly promotion form. Early April, in fact, was really quite dismal, and to add to Wednesday's woe, Kilshaw dislocated a knee in the home game with FA Cup finalists Leicester City. He was an experienced

13. Eddie Quigley. . . signed for £12,000 from Bury, sold for £26,000 to Preston.

and clever player who promised to make a lasting impression; but, sadly, he never played again. Kilshaw's injury blow, and the premature retirement of Alf Rogers and Hugh Swift in later seasons, were unfortunate developments for the players and the club.

Wednesday's best home attendance in 1948-9 was 59,924 for the game with West Brom on December 27; but, in retrospect, what seems much more remarkable was that, in February, a crowd of 49,980 should turn up for a County Cup semi-final between Wednesday and United. Quigley scored twice that day, but United won 4-2, with Hutchinson, Hagan, Brook and Fred Smith their scorers.

The 1949-50 campaign was memorable for Sheffield football followers because it saw Wednesday and United involved in one of the most exciting promotion races in the history of the Second Division. In the end, Wednesday pipped United and Southampton on goal-average; and there was a touch of irony in the fact that Wednesday clinched their return to the First Division on the same date, May 6, that United had pipped them in the promotion race 11 years earlier. And, by a remarkable coincidence, the opposition each time was Tottenham. In 1950, however, Spurs came to Sheffield already assured of the Second Division title; and, under the management of Arthur Rowe, they were one of the most attractive and successful teams in the land. That Spurs team included a player later destined to become manager of Wednesday: Vic Buckingham.

It was a remarkable season in that it provided a number of sensations, a touch of tragedy, several setbacks, and plenty of talking points. Wednesday began reasonably well, while United started off so badly that by early October they were languishing close to the foot of the table. The major surprises of this period were provided by United, for first their idol and captain Jimmy Hagan was dropped, and then coach Dug Livingstone lost his job. In October Wednesday began a 13-match run in which they won seven games and drew six, and by Christmas they were six points better off than their city rivals. However, at the start of the new year Wednesday hit a lean patch and did not chalk up their first win in 1950 until March 18, by which time United, enjoying a run of good results, had shot into second place—four points better off than the Owls. Then, between mid-March and the end of the season, Wednesday collected 15 points while United's tally in the same period was 11; the fact that the Hillsborough side had three matches in hand proving the decisive factor at a time when both teams concluded their programme with a burst of consistency.

Wednesday began the season with a 3-1 defeat of Leicester, but lost Woodhead with a broken right leg. Woodhead's absence throughout the first half of the campaign enabled Tomlinson to begin one of his best runs; though, in fact, half of Tomlinson's 22 outings were at inside-left as deputy for the injured Froggatt; and Marriott or Rickett also had spells at outside-left when the other was playing on the right flank. Oscar Fox wore the number seven shirt nine times.

September was a good month, for Wednesday lost only once, at Tottenham, and chalked up four notable victories. Quigley bagged all four goals in the defeat of Chesterfield, and, soon afterwards, Jordan also scored four in the 6-2 victory over Hull City. A lone goal by Quigley earned both points at Plymouth, and Quigley and Jordan got the goals which defeated Sheffield United on September 17. This city derby attracted a crowd of 55,555 to Hillsborough, and United sprang a big surprise before the game by bringing veteran goalkeeper Jack Smith out of retirement to play in place of the injured White. After Hutchinson put United ahead in the eighth minute, Jordan equalised; but Wednesday's winning goal was a controversial affair, for Smith was adjudged to have brought down Froggatt. Quigley made no mistake with the resulting penalty kick.

Quigley, however, was approaching the end of his short stay at Hillsborough. After the 1-4 defeat at Grimsby on October 8, he was replaced by Alf Rogers, and remained on the sidelines until his record-breaking transfer to Preston North End in mid-December. A fortnight after the Grimsby defeat, Wednesday went to Preston for a game which was noteworthy on two counts: "Shadow" Tomlinson got the only goal of the match *12 seconds* after the kick-off; and Walter Rickett made his debut. Rickett, at 5ft 4½in, was a Tom Thumb of a player, but what he lacked in height he amply compensated for in sheer enthusiasm and courage. He had made his name with Sheffield United, who had discovered him in the war years; and, indeed, he had had the distinction of scoring for the Blades in the first minute of his very first match . . . against Wednesday! In December 1947 he moved to Blackpool, for whom he played in the 1948 FA Cup final. Following his £6,000 transfer to Wednesday, wee Walter was to make 95 League appearances over four seasons before moving on to Rotherham.

In November and December, Wednesday dropped home points against Southampton, Luton and Bradford (PA), but were compensated by victories at Barnsley (4-3) and Chesterfield (2-1); and the sequence which brought them 20 points from a possible 26 included a 2-1 win against West Ham remembered for a remarkable solo goal from Edgar Packard. The centre-half carried the ball nearly the length of the field unchallenged before shooting into the net. It was in this season that Vin Kenny, a local product, established himself as regular right-back. "Mick", as he was known to his colleagues, missed only two games (the result of a dislocated shoulder injury suffered in the January FA Cup tie at Arsenal), but, significantly perhaps, Wednesday lost them both. A week after the Cup setback, Wednesday's unbeaten home record was ended by Plymouth Argyle, who won 4-2; and a trip to Bramall Lane on the following Saturday saw United win 2-0 thanks to goals by Harold Brook and Roy Warhurst.

In February and early March, Wednesday struggled desperately to recapture their early-season form. A point was dropped at Hull, where Jordan suffered a knee injury; then they lost by three clear goals at Coventry, where skipper Hugh Swift's jaw was fractured, causing him to withdraw as captain of the England "B" team against Holland. The biggest blow of all, however, was the sudden death of trainer-coach Bill Knox, who died at the age of 44 after a heart attack.

Soon after the Coventry defeat, Wednesday signed "iron man" Gerald Henry, from Bradford. When Wednesday had played Bradford at Christmas, the feature of the game had been the return of Woodhead at outside-left. The winger celebrated with a late equalising goal, but what he remembered best about the match was the way in which Henry left his mark on proceedings; and it was plain that this tough and fearless, thick-set man was a great asset at the heart of any team. On Henry's debut, against Brentford, Wednesday trailed by two goals at one stage, but an 88th-minute effort from Jordan salvaged a point which was to prove vital at the end of the season. Before the next game (at Queens Park Rangers), Eric Taylor made another signing: but on his debut Hugh McJarrow, at the time Chesterfield's leading scorer, was unable to help Wednesday get back to winning ways.

When Wednesday played the return game with Preston on March 11, Froggatt resumed after injury, but now Jordan was back on the sidelines. Attempts to persuade George Robledo, Newcastle United's ex-Barnsley centre-forward, to return to South Yorkshire failed, and, in the end, a chance was given to 20-year-old Derek Dooley, who had scored 14 goals in 13 Central League games. Unfortunately, the big, raw-boned youngster had a miserable day, and Richard A. Sparling, writing in the *Sheffield Telegraph,* commented: "Dooley is not yet ripe for League football." A headed goal by Tom Finney gave Preston a 1-0 victory, and Wednesday slipped to fifth place in the table.

McJarrow was given the number nine jersey for the trip to Swansea on March 18, and he and Marriott scored the goals which gave Wednesday their first win in eight games. The following Saturday saw Leeds beaten 5-2 (McJarrow 2, Henry 2, and Rickett); and in April Wednesday's only defeat in eight games was a crucial one at Southampton. In fact, Wednesday won only three times in that busy April, but, in the final analysis, what mattered most was that they did not concede a goal in five of the eight matches. The 4-0 defeat of Grimsby on April 26, when Rickett got a hat-trick, was probably the most important result of all in that it provided a timely boost to their goal-average. On April 29 Sheffield United concluded their League programme with a 5-0 victory over Hull, while Wednesday drew 2-2 at West Ham. The difference between the Sheffield clubs was one point, while Southampton trailed United by two points. All depended on what happened in the Wednesday-Spurs game and the Southampton-West Ham clash, both on May 6.

A crowd of 50,883 saw Wednesday and Spurs draw 0-0, while at The Dell Southampton scrambled to a 3-2 victory; and it did not take long to realise that Wednesday's total haul of 67 goals gave them the edge over the Hampshire club, while, having conceded one goal fewer than United, they had pipped their city rivals by virtue of a goal-average superior by .008! Had Wednesday's game with Spurs ended in a 1-1 draw, they and United would have had to stage a play-off to decide the promotion issue. On the day, however, Wednesday could not score, but neither could Spurs—though, late in the game, Bennett gave the home supporters a scare when he skimmed the bar with one effort. Wednesday's team in this game was: McIntosh; Kenny, Swift; Gannon, Packard, Witcomb; Rickett, Henry, McJarrow, Froggatt, Woodhead.

Incidentally, a closely-guarded secret in the days before the game was the desperate struggle being waged to get Woodhead fit. The winger had returned from West Ham the previous weekend with a poisoned toe, and, 24 hours before the Spurs game, seemed certain to have to cry off. Overnight, however, he made a sudden recovery. The top of the Second Division at the end of the 1949-50 season looked like this:

		Home			Away			Goals		
	P	W	D	L	W	D	L	F	A	Pts
1. Tottenham.........	42	15	3	3	12	4	5	81	35	61
2. Wednesday	42	12	7	2	6	9	6	67	48	52
3. Sheff United.......	42	9	10	2	10	4	7	68	49	52
4. Southampton	42	13	4	4	6	10	5	64	48	52

It is worthy of note that this was the second successive season in which Southampton had missed out on promotion. In 1948-9 they had actually led the table by eight points, but then stumbled after losing their star forward Charlie Wayman.

A week after the Spurs game, Wednesday defeated United 2-1 in the final of the County Cup, a crowd of 65,979 seeing Tomlinson and McJarrow get the goals. The attendance could hardly have been greater had the match been the play-off which was so nearly necessary.

An interesting aside to the League programme in this campaign was provided by two representative games staged at Hillsborough in 1950. In January a crowd of 40,053 saw England "B" defeat Switzerland "B" 5-0. Wednesday skipper Hugh Swift and leading scorer Froggatt were in the England side; and so was Rickett, who came in as a late deputy for the injured Jimmy Mullen (Wolves). In April Wednesday hosted a schoolboy international, England v Wales, and it is an indication of the enthusiasm for football in those days that a crowd of 40,000 turned up to watch such stars of the future as Johnny Haynes, Ray Parry and Cliff Jones.

4 The yo-yo years: (1) relegation on goal-average, 1950-51

Exactly one year after dramatically clinching promotion to the First Division on goal-average, Wednesday were relegated back to Division Two in similar circumstances. They went down despite a late-season revival climaxed by a remarkable and unforgettable six-goal victory in their final match. Wednesday, their six-goal victims Everton, and Chelsea all finished with 32 points, but the London club's goal-average, superior by .044, enabled them to escape.

There were times when luck was against Wednesday, but, in the final analysis, they had only themselves to blame for their fall. Eleven matches were lost by a one-goal margin, and vital points were dropped in games in which they had held the initiative but let it slip. True, there were matches in which the team had shown considerable fighting qualities, but they did not repeat this kind of form often enough.

A leaking defence conceded 83 goals (including fours in seven games and a five in another), and only Everton (86) and Huddersfield Town (92) let in more. Yet, ironically perhaps, Wednesday scored more goals than 10 of their First Division rivals—and this despite further problems at centre-forward caused by Clarrie Jordan's continuing knee trouble. McJarrow (14), Froggatt (13) and Woodhead (13) were the leading scorers; with Woodhead getting eight of his goals in the season's last nine games after being converted into an emergency leader of the attack—the fifth to fill the position in this season.

Wednesday spent most of the season in the bottom three places in the table, but their fate was in the balance until the last kick of the last match. In the end, the campaign was classed as a big disappointment, but, even so, it was not without its compensations. In retrospect, the 1950-1 season can be seen to have marked the starting point of a number of individual success stories, for it saw the introduction of such promising youngsters as Alan Finney, Albert Quixall and Norman Curtis, while George Davies and Keith Thomas, both acquired from Oswestry Town, were given their first taste of League football; and Keith Bannister and Norman Jackson were given chances to establish themselves. Finney and Quixall, both 17, were regarded as outstanding prospects. Finney was to go on to make more than 450 appearances; while Quixall, the ex-schoolboy international from Meynell Road, was to make more than 250 League and Cup appearances before, in 1958, he became Britain's costliest footballer with his transfer to Manchester United. Norman Curtis, signed from Gainsborough Trinity, was to make more than 300 League appearances at back, and made himself a name as a penalty kick specialist: "Cannonball" used to run all the way from his position in defence and, without stopping, belt the ball in the direction of the net.

An especially significant "signing" was not a player, but an addition to the training staff. Alan W. Brown, a product of the North East, arrived in January 1951 as trainer-coach. Brown had been in League football since the mid-thirties, having begun his career at Huddersfield, but making his name as a fearless centre-half and captain in the Burnley team which gained promotion from the Second Division and reached the FA Cup final in 1947. After leaving Turf Moor in 1948, he had a brief spell with Notts County, but had left the game to run a cafe when Eric Taylor offered him a position at Hillsborough. Brown was to become a principal figure in the Wednesday story in his two spells with the club—the first from 1951 to 1954, the second from 1964 to 1968.

It was soon after Brown's arrival that Wednesday were involved in the two events for which the 1950-1 season is best remembered by many supporters: the unsuccessful attempt to sign Jimmy Hagan, and the subsequent capture of Jackie Sewell for a record £34,500 fee.

If Wednesday had signed Hagan in February 1951, it would have gone down as the most sensational inter-club transfer in Sheffield's football history—and would probably have been the most controversial, too. Hagan was one of the greatest inside-forwards Sheffield United ever had, and Bramall Lane regulars simply worshipped him. United had paid

£2,500 to get him from Derby County in 1938, and, by 1951, he had made around 200 League appearances and scored 65 League goals. Even at 32, he still had six or seven years of top-class football ahead of him. There had been rumours about the possibility of his leaving Bramall Lane, but many Unitedites would have regarded it as unthinkable that he might move to Hillsborough. However, a chance conversation between United chairman, G. E. Marlow, and Wednesday vice-chairman, James Longden, on a train journey opened up the possibilities of a transfer becoming a reality. Eric Taylor was poised to clinch the scoop of the century when United's board accepted Wednesday's offer of £32,000. Unfortunately, the player himself brought negotiations to a dramatic end. He said he preferred to remain with United, not because he didn't want to join Wednesday—but because of a personal problem he didn't feel he would be able to resolve if he moved to Hillsborough. In fact, Hagan had been chosen to tour Australia with a Football Association party in the summer, and, before going, wished to take time off in the spring to have an operation on a damaged thumb. United might be prepared to let him miss eight games, but clearly Wednesday could not be expected to break the transfer record and then manage without their costly signing when so much was at stake.

Little more than a month after the Hagan deal fell through, Eric Taylor went to the Victoria Hotel, Nottingham, and broke the British transfer record by signing 24-year-old Notts County inside-forward, Jackie Sewell. In fact, the Wednesday secretary-manager had set up what was then a staggering £52,250 double deal, but his hopes of getting Jesse Pye from Wolves were dashed when the Treeton-born centre-forward's wife said she didn't want to move to Sheffield.

Sewell, however, was delighted to make the switch that would take him into the First Division and enhance his chances of gaining international recognition. A product of Kells, Cumberland, the dark-haired young forward had been at Meadow Lane seven years, having been taken there by Major Frank Buckley, a man who knew a promising youngster when he saw one. In little more than four seasons as a first-team regular, Sewell, aided by the influence of former England leader, Tommy Lawton, had emerged as a great favourite with the County fans. In around 200 League and Cup outings for County, he had scored about 100 goals; and, in 1949-50, had helped them win the Third Division (South) championship. He was to remain at Hillsborough for nearly five years, and in that time gain six England caps and score around 90 League and Cup goals at an average of one every second game. But, amid all the excitement of the Sewell deal, an outgoing move is also worth remembering: Charlie Tomlinson joined Rotherham United.

In their first season in the top grade since 1937, Wednesday never quite made up for a poor start and struggled in vain to escape from the bottom places in the table. Their first nine games produced a mere four points—two from drawn matches with Stoke, two from the defeat of reigning champions Portsmouth. For their tenth game, at Huddersfield, several changes were made. Johnny Jordan was signed from Birmingham City and came in at inside-right; Tomlinson and Froggatt were switched to outside and inside-left respectively; and Marriott returned at outside-right. Rickett and Woodhead were dropped.

The re-shuffle paid an immediate dividend, for Wednesday registered their first-ever victory at Leeds Road—and they did it after being behind three times! Nightingale gave Huddersfield the lead after 15 minutes, and though McJarrow equalised on the half-hour, Hassall gave Town a 2-1 advantage before the interval. Froggatt made it 2-2 after 65 minutes, but Metcalfe soon restored Town's lead. However, then came a late surge by Wednesday, and goals by Marriott (86 min) and McJarrow (88) clinched a fine win. Former Hillsborough favourite, David McLean, an unexpected spectator at the match, can only have been impressed by his old team's fighting qualities. Johnny Jordan began well but failed to make a lasting impression, and played in only 10 games.

Unfortunately, Wednesday did not repeat their Huddersfield form in their next three away matches—games in which they conceded a total of 12 goals. And the two home fixtures which followed the Huddersfield trip saw more vital points dropped: one in a goal-less draw with Newcastle, and another against Wolves after Wednesday had twice held the lead. However, the team ended October on a bright note, with Froggatt claiming the first hat-trick of his League career in a 4-1 defeat of Liverpool.

On the day Wednesday beat Liverpool, the big football story nationally was the £30,000 record transfer of Aston Villa centre-forward, Trevor Ford, to Sunderland. Ford made his debut in the game at Chelsea, where he faced an uncompromising John Harris and was unable to save Sunderland from defeat. A week later the tough Welsh international made his home debut at Roker Park, where Wednesday provided the oppostion. Ford not only scored a hat-trick in his side's 5-1 triumph, but, towards the end of the game, was involved in the collision in which Edgar Packard's jaw was broken.

The injury ended Packard's run of 65 consecutive League and Cup appearances, and, in the following week's game with Aston Villa, Turton returned at centre-half after 18 months in the reserves. The Villa match saw Gerald Henry tried at centre-forward, and he scored twice in a welcome 3-2 win.

Unfortunately, Turton's return was not a success, and when Bolton visited Hillsborough in late November, Swift was handed the number five shirt—a switch which led to 22-year-old Norman Curtis being given his League debut at left-back. Swift did not have a happy day, and while Curtis did well enough to retain his place, Wednesday slipped to another home defeat. Only two minutes after the kick-off, McIntosh failed to gather a Bobby Langton corner-kick, and Webster put Bolton in front. However, Froggatt soon equalised, and an own-goal by Howe gave Wednesday the lead. But then goals by Lofthouse (22 and 65 min) and Webster (52) left the visitors with a 4-2 advantage. Henry got a third goal for Wednesday, but it was a disappointing day.

When they visited Blackpool in early December, Wednesday were twice in front through goals by McJarrow and Froggatt, but the home side hit back to win 3-2. In the home match with Spurs, Wednesday led

14. Wednesday 1950-51. . . (back row) Keith Bannister, Cyril Turton, Dave McIntosh,
Norman Curtis, Redfern Froggatt, Doug Witcomb; (front row) Walter Rickett,
Hugh McJarrow, Eddie Gannon, Gerald Henry, Dennis Woodhead.

through a McJarrow goal, but an error by Morton (deputising for flu
victim McIntosh) let in Bennett for the equaliser. To add to Wednesday's
woe, when the Chelsea match was postponed in mid-December, they
slipped into bottom spot in the table: they could boast only four wins and
13 points from 21 games. Even when they completed a Christmas
double over West Brom, they remained in 22nd place.

Early in the New Year, Eric Taylor stepped up his efforts to strengthen
the team. However, his only acquisition of note was the appointment of
Alan Brown. When his dramatic bid to sign Hagan failed, he decided to
give youth a fling, and, in the re-arranged game with Chelsea at
Hillsborough, introduced a new right-wing pair, Finney and Quixall.
Finney, a product of Armthorpe, had signed professional forms in the
previous October and been doing well in the reserves; Quixall, a
blond-haired baby-faced local lad with a liking for short shorts, had been
attached to the club since leaving school, and, in fact, had earlier played
with the first-team in a friendly and a County Cup tie against Sheffield
United. In their first League game together, Quixall probably outshone
Finney; but, in fact, Finney was to return to the side towards the end of
the season and make a considerable impact.

In the light of later events, the Chelsea game on February 24 was
significant in that Wednesday conceded yet another vital home point.
Dickson gave Chelsea the lead after 15 minutes, but Wednesday finally
hit back in the second half. Hughes deflected a Woodhead shot into his
own net, then Quixall marked his debut with a goal for which the unlucky
John Harris was partly responsible. However, after 65 minutes it was
Harris who levelled the scores—from the penalty spot. Twelve years

earlier, in his days as a Swansea player, John Harris had missed a vital penalty against Wednesday; but he made no mistake this time. Two days later Wednesday conceded four goals to visitors Manchester United.

For the game at Wolverhampton, Wednesday made three changes: Rickett was tried at centre-forward, Thomas was given a chance at inside-left, and Jackson came in at right-back because injury had ended Bannister's 19-match run. Jackson was to retain the number two shirt to the end of the season, but his first senior outing in the position (he had previously played twice at half back) brought him up against the brilliance of Jimmy Mullen. It wasn't a happy day: Wolves won 4-0.

Wednesday's next match, at Liverpool on March 17, saw the arrival of Britain's most expensive player, Jackie Sewell. He scored on his debut, but Liverpool won 2-1. However, in the next nine games Sewell was to contribute five goals and help the Hillsborough side collect 12 points.

For the match in which Sewell made his home debut, against Sunderland, McIntosh returned in goal after being absent since December, but, more significantly, Woodhead was switched to lead the attack, with Rickett recalled at outside-left. A crowd of 48,467 saw Wednesday win 3-0, with Woodhead, Rickett and Froggatt the marksmen.

Four vital points were dropped in the next three games, but at Bolton on April 14 Wednesday registered their first away win since Christmas—the lone goal a header from Woodhead following a neatly placed cross from Finney.

Now nerves were beginning to plague the team, a point illustrated by the performance against Derby on April 18. For this game Gerald Henry made his first appearance since mid-February, and his first at right-half since September. Things looked good for Wednesday when Woodhead shot them in front and then Oliver, intercepting a Rickett effort that was going wide, only succeeded in deflecting the ball past his own goalkeeper. Big Jack Stamps pulled one back for Derby, but Woodhead converted a penalty to give Wednesday a 3-1 lead after 25 minutes. Now came an attack of jitters, and Lee grabbed two goals to make the score 3-3. Fortunately, Sewell snatched the winning goal 10 minutes before the end.

Four days later, Hillsborough's largest crowd of the season—53,420—saw Wednesday defeat Blackpool 3-1, with Woodhead, Sewell and Witcomb on target. With two matches remaining, hopes of escaping relegation were higher than ever . . .

In retrospect, the date April 28 1951 was probably more significant than May 5 in the story of how Wednesday's fate was decided. For on that day the Sheffield team visited Tottenham, the new League champions, and lost by a single goal. In another part of London, at Craven Cottage, Fulham were meeting Chelsea. On paper it looked a home banker, but Chelsea won 2-1 . . . and now, if they could win their last match, at home to Bolton, the London club still had an excellent chance of staying in the First Division.

The situation on the morning of Saturday May 5 was that Chelsea and Wednesday had 30 points, while Everton, visiting Hillsborough, had 32. If

15. Two Jacks. . . Marriott (left), a bargain buy from Midland League Scunthorpe United, and Sewell, signed for a British record fee from Notts County.

Everton won or drew, Wednesday and Chelsea would be doomed no matter what happened at Stamford Bridge. If Wednesday and Chelsea both won, which of them would join Everton in the drop would depend on the scorelines. It was calculated that Wednesday would need to win by at least six clear goals.

Astonishingly, Wednesday achieved that six-goal target in a match so remarkable that Richard A. Sparling, the doyen of local critics, said: "There will probably not be another one like this for 50 years." Wednesday's team was: McIntosh; Jackson, Curtis; Henry, Packard, Witcomb; Finney, Sewell, Woodhead, Froggatt, Rickett.

The early play gave little warning of the fireworks to come, and it was not until the 26th minute that Woodhead broke the deadlock. Four minutes later he got a second, and Sewell headed number three after 33 minutes. In the first minute of the second half, Woodhead missed the chance of a hat-trick when his penalty-kick was saved by Burnett. However, two minutes later, Finney scored his first League goal, and Rickett made it 5-0 after 63 minutes. Sewell got the sixth goal just before the end.

Unfortunately, the scoreboard on the roof of the Leppings Lane enclosure did not suggest that the signs were good for Wednesday. The news it finally brought was a 4-0 win for Chelsea. Wednesday had needed not six goals but ten! Chairman William Fearnehough took the news philosophically. "We went up last year on goal-average," he said, "so we can't complain at the same system causing us to go down. But on today's display we shouldn't remain long in the Second Division."

Incidentally, Everton's centre-forward in that decisive last match was a man called Harry Catterick. He didn't get much of a look-in that day, but the time would come when he would make a big impact at Hillsborough—as team-manager.

5 The yo-yo years: (2) Dooley, triumph and tragedy, 1951-53

From time to time in the course of a club's history a short phase will see one player step from the shadows and so dominate the scene that he makes the period his own. An unknown, obscure or previously discarded youngster will suddenly and unexpectedly blossom into a star, and the years he spends in the limelight will forever afterwards be associated with his name. At Sheffield Wednesday a classic example of this is the case of Derek Dooley, whose brief but spectacular success in the early 1950s, and the tragic circumstances in which his playing days were brought to an end, made him a very special hero—one of the legendary figures of football in Sheffield.

In the seasons of 1951-2 and 1952-3, several Wednesday men achieved much of note, and two or three enjoyed outstanding personal success; yet it is Dooley's name which dominates the memory of those years. We are apt to forget that Jackie Sewell and Redfern Froggatt both finally gained international recognition—Sewell collecting his first England cap against Ireland in November 1951; Froggatt being honoured for the first time against Wales in November 1952. We forget, too, that 1951-2 was the campaign in which Wednesday were led to the Second Division championship by Keith Bannister, the local lad whose career touched its brief peak when he was given the captaincy halfway through the season. And we tend to overlook the fact that the recall of Dooley was only one of a number of changes which brought about the transformation of Wednesday from also-rans into a table-topping team. Mick Kenny, George Davies, Alan Finney, Albert Quixall and Walter Rickett all came back into the side in the autumn. Perhaps we should remember, too, that while injury caused Doug Witcomb to miss the middle part of the season, he returned to play in the final 11 games; and Curtis and Froggatt bounced back after enforced spells on the sidelines; while Ralph O'Donnell made his debut in November, and kept Turton out for a time.

Yet Dooley is the man whose story captures the imagination when we survey this brief period in the Wednesday records. The flame-haired centre-forward, 6ft 3in and wearing size 12 boots, was the sensation of the day, the most controversial player of his time, and the League's most successful marksman. Dooley burst upon an unsuspecting football world suddenly and unexpectedly and claimed 46 goals in 30 League matches between October and the end of April in 1951-2. By February 1953 he had brought his tally to 62 goals in 60 games when his career was brought to a swift and tragic end: his right leg, broken in a match at Preston, became infected and had to be amputated to save his life.

Anyone who was not around then will find it difficult to appreciate the

16. Goal King. . . Derek Dooley, the sensation of 1951-52.

full impact which Dooley made on the footballing public of his time. His great run spanned a mere 17 months—14 if you discount the summer break—and yet he became a kind of folk hero. It is probably fair to suggest that his scoring feats ensured him a lasting place in the record books, but it was the tragic ending of his career when he was only 23 and at his peak which put him a category of his own. It is a source of continuing speculation to wonder what Dooley might have achieved but for that untimely accident, and the fact that circumstances prevented him from even growing old as a player lent a touch of immortality to his name.

Few better descriptions of Dooley were ever penned than this by the late Don Davies, who wrote in the *Manchester Guardian* under the guise of 'An Old International': "As a centre-forward Dooley defies conventional classification. He hurls himself into the fray like a man possessed . . . woe-betide the centre-half back who has no previous warning of his coming: to face him must be like trying to stop a runaway steer. His ball-control at times would shame a baby and he seems just about as innocent of deceit, but once let him get his eye on the ball and away he goes . . . the great thing is to be there first. Should two or three attempt to bar his path a crash will occur, bodies will reel in all directions, then lie disordered, like shattered trunks in the track of an avalanche. And after all you cannot blame Dooley for cutting straight to the heart of things any more than you can blame a snow plough or a Centurion tank, or even a hippopotamus. That is the way they are made."

What make Dooley's story special are the facts of his scoring and the manner of the blow which ended his career, but it is also remarkable in that it serves to emphasise the part that chance can play in the life of a footballer and in the fashioning of a team's success. When the 1951-2 season began, Dooley was not even in the reckoning for a first-team place, and perhaps if Eric Taylor had not been desperately seeking a means of ending an unexpectedly poor spell, the young centre-forward might never have emerged from the shadows. He had had two previous chances, in 1950 and 1951, and failed, and his hopes of making the grade seemed so remote that Wednesday were prepared to let him go for a small fee—but nobody rushed forward to sign him. True, he had been scoring goals with startling regularity in the club's Yorkshire League and Central League sides, but at 21 he seemed to lack that extra bit of something necessary to enable him to make his mark in the Football League. He was big, fast, fearless and aggressive, but he lacked finesse, ball-control and a certain vision, and if his dashes down the middle of the field struck terror into the hearts of defenders at reserve and third-team levels, he seemed unlikely to ever be able to command such respect in the higher grades—or such was the opinion in the opening weeks of the 1951-2 campaign.

The son of a Sheffield steelworker, Dooley had first gained attention in local junior football circles as a free-scoring 15-year-old with the YMCA. "Pop" Bennett, who ran the team, had wanted to cast the young giant in the role of centre-half, but Dooley said he was a centre-forward or nothing. Even in junior football, he created havoc in opposing goalmouths, and was soon playing occasional games with Lincoln City reserves in the Midland League. It was in a match against Denaby United that Dooley came face to face with Walter Millership, and the tough old defender known as "Battleship" was so impressed with the lad that he told Eric Taylor about him. "He's the most awkward young devil I've ever played against . . . he's just like a ruddy tank!" Taylor noted the name.

But for the unusual circumstances prevailing at the end of that 1946-7 season, Dooley, now 17, might easily have been a part-time professional with Lincoln. They had offered him terms, but Dooley, still playing with the YMCA whenever he could, wanted to remain an amateur long enough to continue helping the Sheffield and Hallamshire CFA side in its bid to reach the final of the Northern Counties championship. By the time Sheffield faced Doncaster in the final, in June 1947, Dooley's registration with Lincoln had lapsed. Tommy Walker, Wednesday's trainer, was at the match and saw Dooley score four goals; and the upshot was an invitation to Dooley to meet Eric Taylor. Wolves and Nottingham Forest were both showing an interest, but when Dooley knew that Wednesday wanted him on part-time forms no other club came into the reckoning.

In the next four seasons, with Johnny Logan his taskmaster, Dooley scored 55 goals in 38 appearances in Wednesday's Yorkshire League side, and also hit 37 goals in 49 outings in the Central League team. On one occasion he bagged eight goals in a third-team game. With Wednesday struggling to find a centre-forward, he could not be ignored. But, first against Preston in March 1950, and then against Charlton the following January, he flopped. He had begun to fear that he might never get a third chance.

Having been relegated from the First Division on goal-average in 1951, Wednesday were confident of bouncing back in one season. Unfortunately, their results in the early weeks of 1951-2 hardly suggested the optimism had been justified. They won three of their first five matches, but lost four and drew two of the next six. Nine points from 11 games was not promotion form. Two defeats had been particularly painful: Sheffield United's 7-3 win at Bramall Lane, and Rotherham's 5-3 triumph at Hillsborough. And it hurt that Sheffield United, with twice as many points as Wednesday, were sitting on top of the Second Division. In a bid to turn the tide, Eric Taylor had brought back Kenny and Finney, and Davies had come in for the injured Witcomb. Three men had been tried at centre-forward; Woodhead, the most successful with seven goals in seven games, was then injured, and neither McJarrow nor Rickett solved the problem. When the team for the home match with Barnsley on October 6 was announced, Quixall replaced Thomas, Rickett was switched to outside left, and Dooley, who had scored 13 goals in nine Central League matches, was given the number nine shirt. It should be added that, on the morning of the game, Curtis cried off with a poisoned toe, and Bannister was given his first senior outing for eight months.

When Wednesday found themselves trailing to a tenth-minute penalty against Barnsley, it looked like another disappointment was in store; but, suddenly, five minutes after the interval, the picture changed. Gannon laid on the pass from which Dooley equalised; and after 77 minutes

Sewell set up the chance which brought a second goal for the centre-forward. "He'll Dooley All Right!" proclaimed the front page headline in that evening's Sheffield *Green 'Un.* It was the beginning of a very interesting phase.

In fact, Dooley claimed only one more goal in the next three matches, but Wednesday picked up five points. Then, at the beginning of November, the big centre-forward found the goal-touch which was to make him the sensation of the season. He hit 22 goals in nine successive matches! He began the sequence by equalling the feat of Trotter and Dailey in scoring five goals in the 6-0 defeat of Notts County. That day the former Wednesday goalkeeper Roy Smith wondered what hit him in the second-half when Dooley scored in 50, 62, 68, 78 and 82 minutes. Dooley then scored twice in each of Wednesday's next four games, got a hat-trick at West Ham, settled for one at Doncaster, and then hammered four against Everton on the Saturday before Christmas. In the Everton match he again waited until after the interval before opening his account; and it was typical of him that, earlier, he had squandered two gloriously simple chances.

By the turn of the year Dooley's haul was 27 goals in 15 games. Wednesday had won 10 of those matches and lost only two; and they were sitting pretty on top of the table. The only home game Wednesday had not won was the Christmas morning clash with Nottingham Forest when a crowd of 61,187 saw Dooley fail to score for the first time in two months.

When Wednesday began the New Year with a home match against Sheffield United, the city clubs had undergone such a remarkable turnabout of fortunes that Wednesday were the odds-on favourites to win. It was even suggested that United should take the cricket scoreboard from Bramall Lane to help keep count of the goals Dooley was bound to score! United had won only two of their previous 12 games.

However, as is so often the case in Sheffield derby games, the form-book was turned upside down. A crowd of 65,384 saw United, for whom Graham Shaw was making his League debut, win 3-1 with Ringstead (2) and Hutchinson their scorers. Redfern Froggatt had a penalty saved by Ted Burgin, and while Dooley got a goal he was unable to escape the attentions of wily old Harry Latham long enough to score more.

That setback against United was the first of three successive defeats. They went out of the FA Cup at Bradford, where Dooley scored, and lost at home to Leeds. In fact, they did not return to winning ways until early February, and when a 4-2 victory over Cardiff City gave them their first victory of 1952, Dooley was absent injured. Sewell scored all four goals. A week later Wednesday were involved in a nine-goal thriller at Oakwell, where Barnsley won 5-4 and Dooley claimed one goal but had another controversially disallowed.

However, "Dreadnought" Dooley began March with a bang, hitting four goals in the 6-0 defeat of Hull City. Sewell got the other two, and, incidentally, scored both goals in the 2-1 defeat of QPR a fortnight later. But after two games without a goal, Dooley proceeded to get eight in the

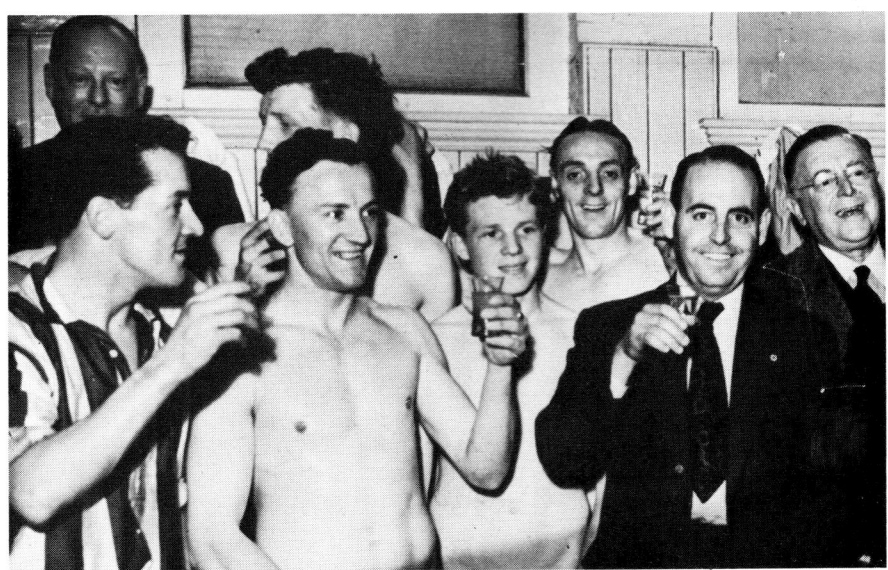

17. *Toasting a Second Division Championship triumph, 1952... Secretary-manager Eric Taylor and chairman William Fearnehough join players Sewell, Dooley, Curtis, Quixall and Gannon in a dressing room celebration after the final match of the season.*

next four games—and his two against Luton at the beginning of April enabled him to pass the 37-goal record held for 25 years by Jimmy Trotter. He followed this with a hat-trick at Brentford, where the opposing centre-half was Ron Greenwood—later to earn fame as manager of West Ham and, of course, the team-boss who took England to the 1982 World Cup finals in Spain.

It was two goals from Dooley at Coventry on April 19 that gave Wednesday the points which clinched promotion and the Second Division title; and, symbolically perhaps, Dooley's 88th-minute goal in the final fixture, against West Ham at Hillsborough, not only saved Wednesday from an embarrassing defeat but brought their tally in the League to exactly 100.

When Wednesday's players went on tour to Switzerland in the summer of 1952, it was fitting that they should take time off to watch the Austria-England match in Vienna, for the national team included Jackie Sewell, whose contribution to the promotion triumph had been significant. Sewell's first full season at Hillsborough had seen him claim 23 goals, and it had been at the Wednesday ground in October that he had played for the Football League against the Scottish League, the match attracting a crowd of 49,075. Sewell had not let the tag of "Britain's most expensive player" affect his game, and he didn't mind being overshadowed in the scoring stakes by the new sensation called Dooley.

After winning the Second Division championship, Wednesday found success a good deal harder to achieve when they returned to the top grade in 1952-3; and Dooley, discovering that life was considerably tougher against uncompromising First Division defences, took some time to adjust and learn to live with the extra attention his reputation brought with it. Wednesday collected only one point from their first five matches, and though they then enjoyed an unbeaten run of 10 games, they ran into difficulties in the second half of the season when a mere five wins in 21 matches put them under the threatening shadow of relegation; and only a last-match victory enabled them to finish one point better off than Stoke City, who went down with Derby County.

Of course, everyone wanted to see how Dooley would fare in the First Division, and a crowd of over 55,000 turned up for the season's opening match, in which the opposition was provided by FA Cup holders Newcastle United. On a warm, sunny afternoon in August, Dooley, unfortunately, found himself completely overshadowed by the giant Scot, Frank Brennan; and Wednesday, two goals down after only 20 minutes, just managed to salvage a point thanks to goals from Sewell and Froggatt in the last seven minutes.

No goals and no points came Wednesday's way in the next four games, and, to add to their problems, goalkeeper McIntosh broke an arm in the home match with Liverpool, and local-born giant Ron Capewell, known to his pals as "Lofty", was given his first taste of League football in the home clash with Charlton. Dave McIntosh was not, however, the only favourite absent when Jimmy Seed's team came north—so was Dooley. Eric Taylor, explaining the decision to drop the big centre-forward, said: "We're doing it to give him a chance. We think he's not had fair treatment, and we don't want to break his heart."

It was intended that Dooley would be twelfth man for the Charlton game, but the deposed leader argued that sitting on the sidelines would not help him re-discover his goal-flair; and Taylor agreed to let him play for the Central League side at Sheffield United. It is a fair indication of the interest that this decision created to note that the attendance at Bramall Lane that September afternoon was 8,531. And, while the first-team was falling to another defeat, Wednesday's reserves came from behind to win 3-1, with Dooley ending his "famine" with two goals scored in the space of a minute ten minutes or so before the end. Four days later, Dooley hit a hat-trick against Liverpool reserves at Hillsborough. Was the lower grade of competition the sole reason for Dooley's re-discovery of his goal-touch? Dooley accorded some credit to his old boots. He had begun the season with a new pair, but, when he was dropped, he dropped the new boots, too; returned to the old pair, and found they still had the comfortable familiarity of carpet slippers while retaining the "magic" which helped put him back on the goal-standard!

When Dooley returned to the first-team for the home game with Spurs on September 13, he wasn't the only man recalled. Kenny came in at right-back, George Davies at left-half, Finney on the right wing, and Woodhead on the left. Dooley didn't get a goal, but Sewell and Finney did, and Wednesday were left celebrating their first win of the campaign.

It was four days later that Dooley finally broke the deadlock, and when he got his first goal in Division One in the 70th minute of the game with

Middlesbrough, the enthusiasm with which the 41,456 spectators greeted it was astonishing. Dooley would never forget that moment. Hats and caps flew into the air, the cheering lasted several minutes, and every one of Dooley's team-mates shook his hand.

The ice broken, Dooley went on to score 16 goals in 24 games—not a sensational record, but satisfactory; and it was noted that, as the season progressed, he was slowly developing his game, acquiring polish and becoming more of a team man. When the critics began hinting that Dooley might yet gain international recognition one day, they were no longer regarded as fools. One leading critic, Edgar Turner, writing after the 3-1 win at Stoke, said: "Dooley is improving his technique. He is waiting less for the ball, using the field more, and has a greater appreciation of open space." As well as scoring twice at Stoke, Dooley got doubles against Aston Villa, Cardiff City and Newcastle; but, directly and indirectly, he was creating space and opportunities for his colleagues to exploit. The return match at Newcastle in late December served to emphasise Wednesday's improvement, for they won a remarkable game 5-2, with Sewell and Marriott benefitting from Dooley's tenacity. The following match, against West Brom at Hillsborough on Boxing Day, was even more remarkable: at one stage Wednesday led 4-2, but the 59,839 spectators then saw them slip to a 4-5 defeat—and Gannon and Curtis each put the ball into his own net!

However, though Dooley began to acquire a little polish, he was still, above all, the dashing, fearless centre-forward who created chaos in the opposition's penalty area. And he was, from the outset, a marked man destined to take a good deal of rough treatment, not all of which was within the rules. In two matches, fouls on Dooley brought Wednesday not one penalty but two; so that Curtis's haul of six successful spot-kicks in the season included two doubles converted in his own inimitable manner. But Dooley did not always find referees whose judgement was unclouded by his reputation; and, on away grounds, his very presence induced strong emotions among rival supporters. J. L. Manning, reporting on Wednesday's visit to Old Trafford, noted: "When Dooley was badly tripped, many of the season ticket holders in front of me jumped to their feet and applauded." At Tottenham Dooley was booed as he left the field at the end of the game, and a spectator was only prevented from attacking him by virtue of a policeman's flying tackle.

Dooley was nothing if not a figure of controversy, but he had many supporters. Critic Alan Hoby wrote: "There are some people who think that Dooley is a dirty player. All I can say is that they must be blind or crazy." Charlton manager Jimmy Seed commented: "I'd rather have Dooley on my side than against me. He's one of the most dangerous centre-forwards in the country, and he'll get better." Spurs manager Arthur Rowe said after the match at White Hart Lane in late January: "Dooley used his weight pretty freely, but I don't think there was anything vicious about his play. He is the sort of player who never gives up, and his persistence is always likely to lead him into situations not encountered by a less tenacious player." Ironically, it was in that Spurs game that Dooley scored his last goal for Wednesday, and Rowe's comments came only three weeks before Dooley suffered the accident which ended his playing days.

At the start of 1953, Wednesday drew at Middlesbrough and beat Cardiff 2-0 thanks to goals from Dooley; but then suffered five successive defeats, including a home fall in the FA Cup, when Blackpool beat them 2-1 before a crowd of over 60,000. (Blackpool, of course, went on to win the Cup). So when Wednesday visited Preston on February 14, team changes included the promotion of Tom McAnearney, the young Scot who had played only twice before; Quixall, on leave from National Service with the army, returned after missing four games; McIntosh resumed in goal after being absent for 23 games; and, with Woodhead injured, Bill Shadbolt, an outside-left signed from Oswestry, was given his debut. The team spent a couple of days at Blackpool, but there was so much ice and snow about that there were serious doubts whether Deepdale would be fit.

However, referee Arthur Ellis declared the pitch playable. At the time Preston stood in fourth place in the table, but only two points behind the leaders West Brom. Deepdale had never been a lucky ground for Wednesday, who had lost 17 times in 23 League visits, so they were pleased to reach half-time with the scores still level. During the interval, coach Alan Brown said that if through balls were played to make use of Dooley's speed, he was confident Preston's off-side trap could be beaten.

It was in the 14th minute of the second half that Quixall provided the pass which led to a typical chase. Dooley, having the advantage of facing Preston's goal and forewarning of what Quixall intended to do, left the home defenders flat-footed. It was a straight race between him and North End's goalkeeper, George Thompson, with the odds slightly on Thompson. But the goalkeeper hesitated, and, with the ball outside the penalty area, Dooley had high hopes of being the first to reach it. In fact, Thompson got his feet to the ball just an instant ahead of Dooley, but the inrushing centre-forward deflected it across the depth of the penalty area . . . and watched it roll agonisingly the wrong side of the post as, in the same moment, he and Thompson collided. Dooley knew instantly that his right leg was broken: a hospital x-ray revealed a double fracture.

After seeing Dooley carried into an ambulance, Wednesday secretary-manager, Eric Taylor, was just about to return to his seat in the stand when he was called to the telephone. He was told that the club's chairman, William Fearnehough, had died earlier in the day in the Sheffield Royal Infirmary. The team returned to Sheffield rather subdued by the turn of events. A goal by Tom Finney had pushed the Owls to another defeat.

Dooley spent the weekend in Preston Infirmary, expecting to be discharged on the following Monday, but when he was making plans for his departure the discovery was made which shattered the centre-forward's world. He asked a nurse to sign the "pot" on his leg, and when she caught his toes accidentally but noticed he had shown no reaction, she suggested the "pot" might be too tight. A doctor was called, and he found the leg seriously infected. It transpired that, at the time of the

18. *Front Page News. . . How the Sheffield Star reported the dramatic news of goal-king Dooley's hospital drama, Preston, 1953.*

The Star

No. 20,658

TUESDAY, FEBRUARY 17, 1953

A KEMSLEY NEWSPAPER   2d

Police Cars in Dash to Hospital With Drugs, Then

DOCTORS FIGHT FOR LIFE
OF DOOLEY

Wife's vigil at bedside

FROM OUR OWN CORRESPONDENTS

DEREK DOOLEY, Sheffield Wednesday centre-forward, is dangerously ill in Preston Royal Infirmary, and doctors are fighting to save his life.

Complications have set in following the breaking of his leg against Preston North End on Saturday, and an emergency operation has been carried out.

An official statement from Preston Infirmary early this afternoon said—

"MR DOOLEY'S CONDITION HAS BEEN COM-PLICATED BY A DANGEROUS TYPE OF INFECTION, FOLLOWING THE EMERGENCY OPERATION, HIS CONDITION REMAINS GRAVE."

Later statements described Dooley as "still gravely ill." His wife, Sylvia, who had remained in Preston over the week-end, is keeping vigil at Dooley's bedside, all other visitors have now been banned.

MRS DOOLEY

RANDOLPH IS

BOATS SUCKED THROUGH CAP, CAPSIZE

Man Drowns, 6 Saved
In Flood Breach

A⁸ Aldeburgh, Suffolk, lifeboatman—Daniel Mann is feared drowned during the first attempt today to plug a 35-yard breach in the River Alde wall.

DEREK DOOLEY

injury, Dooley had got some dirt in a small scratch at the back of the leg; and it was this which had caused gangrene to develop. The disease was spreading rapidly, and the painful decision was taken to amputate the leg in order to save Dooley's life. The news shocked the football world, and, in Sheffield, the club's supporters were stunned.

After the loss of Dooley, Wednesday won only three of their remaining 12 games. For the home match with Stoke on February 21, Jordan was recalled, but it was Sewell who got the goal which clinched two vital points. In mid-March Woodhead was tried at centre-forward; then Sheffield-born Ronnie Codd, signed from Bolton, had two outings in the number nine shirt; but, finally, Sewell was handed the role. Sewell obliged with six goals in the final six matches, and he grabbed a hat-trick in the last match, when a crowd of over 45,000 saw Wednesday beat Sunderland 4-0 to escape relegation and finish in 18th place.

As was the case in the previous campaign, the name of Dooley had again dominated the 1952-3 season, but, again, there had been others whose personal achievements gave them reason to remember the year with some degree of satisfaction. Redfern Froggatt gained international honours, being capped by England against Wales, Belgium and Scotland, all at Wembley, and going on England's close-season American tour. Froggatt also played for the Football League against the Scottish League at Ibrox; while Sewell was in the League XI which heavily defeated the Irish League at Wolverhampton. On the domestic front, only Curtis had been an ever-present; and, of several newcomers introduced during the season, the one destined to make the most lasting impression was 22-year-old Tom McAnearney, the tall, intelligent half-back who had come from Dundee with his younger brother, Jim. Tom established himself as a regular by about 1955, and went on to make around 375 League and FA Cup appearances before leaving to join Peterborough in 1965. Jim McAnearney, an inside-forward, was not quite so fortunate in that, as a player in a position where competition was fierce, he was to make only about 40 appearances between 1953-4 and 1958-9; though it is interesting to note that both Tom and Jim were later to return to Hillsborough as members of the coaching staff, and, in the meantime, Tom had a successful spell as manager of Aldershot, while Jim managed Rotherham United.

6 The yo-yo years: (3) struggle and fall, 1953-55

For Sheffield Wednesday 1953-4 brought neither promotion nor relegation, and it wasn't even one of those seasons in which they kept everyone in suspense until the last match before scrambling to safety. In some ways, it was a term of comparative stability: for though Wednesday finished fourth from the bottom of the First Division, they ended up six points better off than 21st-placed Middlesbrough, who were relegated with Liverpool. And, in a campaign which saw the Sheffield clubs together in the top grade for the first time since 1933-4, Wednesday finished one place above United, who avoided the drop into Division Two by three points.

Yet, for Hillsborough regulars, 1953-4 was anything but uneventful. What lent a little extra lustre to the season was Wednesday's unexpected success in the FA Cup, for they surprised many people by reaching the semi-final for the first time in 19 years. And nobody could say they did it the easy way. They drew at home in the third, fourth and sixth rounds before winning the replays against the odds on opponents' grounds. Unfortunately, the only time they failed to rise to the occasion on the Cup trail was at the last hurdle before Wembley. The superior skills and greater aggression of Preston North End won through, and Wednesday reserved their poorest Cup performance for that Maine Road semi-final which attracted a crowd of over 75,000.

In retrospect, that remarkable Cup run may seem to dominate the memory of this season, but, in truth, it forms only part of the story of a campaign which provided many talking points and notable incidents even before the team started on the Wembley trail. A number of League matches provided moments of high drama and acute disappointment; and, as usual, the season produced a crop of tales of individual triumph and disappointment.

The new faces introduced in this year included Brian Ryalls, a goalkeeper thrust into the first-team after a mere six games in the reserves; backs Tony Conwell and Ivor Seemley were each given a senior run; and Barrie Butler, a part-timer serving his time as an apprentice draughtsman, stepped in for 11 games at centre-half after Ralph O'Donnell broke a leg in December. Jim McAnearney also made his senior debut; while Jack Shaw, a close-season signing from Rotherham United, took time to settle before establishing himself at centre-forward.

Military service limited Albert Quixall's appearances in the opening weeks of the season, but his form was such that he gained international recognition. After playing for the Football League against the Irish League at Belfast in September, he was capped against Wales and FIFA in October and Ireland in November. Jackie Sewell, too, gained further caps, playing for England in two unforgettable clashes with Hungary— the first at Wembley in November, the second in Budapest in May. The Hungarians won the first 6-3 and the second 7-1!

But if it was a happy season for Quixall and Sewell in particular, it was, on the whole, a disappointing one for Redfern Froggatt, Dave McIntosh and Norman Curtis, as well as for the unlucky O'Donnell. Froggatt had a long spell out of favour, largely due to Quixall's success, and he went so far as to seek a transfer; but, fortunately perhaps, a proposed move to Sheffield United failed to get beyond the talking stage, and Froggatt survived a difficult phase to remain a one-club man to the end of his career. Curtis had the indignity of being dropped in mid-season, and so lost the captaincy; but he bounced back quickly, none the worse for the experience.

For the second season in succession, McIntosh suffered a serious injury: ironically, it was on Wednesday's first visit to Preston after the accident to Dooley that the goalkeeper broke his left arm and was put on the sidelines for six months. That Deepdale match was not one of Wednesday's happiest, for Preston beat them 6-0. The injury to McIntosh occurred in the 20th minute, and Norman Curtis took over in goal, where he had the distinction of saving two penalties—one from Finney, the other from Baxter. When McIntosh left the field, Wednesday were trailing to an early goal from Baxter; but though Curtis wasn't beaten until after the interval, Baxter went on to complete a hat-trick, with Wayman, Foster and Tom Finney getting the other goals.

Ron Capewell was the initial replacement for McIntosh, but after four games he was dropped, and when Wednesday visited Bramall Lane in September for the first Sheffield derby in the First Division for 19 years, they sprang a big surprise by promoting an unknown 20-year-old, Brian Ryalls, who had been a part-time professional for only eight months. Indeed, less than a year before, Ryalls had been playing with Grimethorpe Colliery in the Sheffield Association League. On his debut the youngster fared reasonably well, but finished on the losing side: United won 2-0, with Hagan, in brilliant form, scoring the first after 21 minutes and setting up the second for Hawksworth nine minutes later. However, Ryalls survived the ordeal, and remained first-choice goalkeeper until mid-February.

It was around the turn of the year that Kenny displaced Conwell, Seemley was given the left-back spot, and Davies returned to the side, with Tom McAnearney dropping out. And Jack Shaw finally enjoyed a long run at centre-forward. For some time after Dooley's accident, Wednesday searched in vain for a permanent replacement. Shaw arrived at Hillsborough with a big reputation, but it is fair to suggest that he had spent his best years at Rotherham, where he had scored around 120 goals in 260 League games and, in 1950-1, had established a club record with 44 League and Cup goals. In the first half of 1953-4 he managed only eight appearances and three goals, but, following his recall in early January, he settled much better and claimed 14 goals in 26 League and Cup games; and at the end of the season only Woodhead (21) and Sewell (19) had more goals to their credit.

When the FA Cup third-round draw was made it paired Wednesday with Sheffield United for the first time since 1928. As Wednesday had never beaten their city rivals in the competition, their supporters in the 61,250 crowd probably thought that home advantage would provide them with the ideal opportunity to end the sequence. However, that man Hagan again proved to be the player who dashed their hopes, for it was following a brilliant run and shot by the United idol that Toner put the visitors in front after half-an-hour. Two minutes after the interval, however, Quixall, Finney and Sewell were involved in the move which saw Jack Shaw equalise; and Shaw thought he had hit the winner in the last minute, but his effort was disallowed because he had kicked the ball out of Burgin's hands.

United went into the replay without skipper Harold Brook, but still remained the favourites; for, wartime matches excepted, Wednesday had not won at Bramall Lane since 1933. And, the way the first-half went, Wednesday were soon seen to appear right out of the reckoning. With the wind in their favour, United dominated proceedings. In the opening stages they squandered several chances, before, after nine minutes, Davies handled to give them a penalty. Toner put the spot-kick straight at Ryalls, and Wednesday breathed again. But eight minutes before half-time United scored: Ryalls appeared to have a 25-yard shot from Hawksworth covered, but let the ball slip from his grasp and over the line.

All the fireworks came after the interval. In the 52nd minute, Alan Finney grabbed the equaliser, and the tension touched a peak. Referee Jack Clough called the rival captains, Joe Shaw and Jack Sewell, together and issued a warning about rough play; but, barely five minutes later, following a clash with Hagan, Kenny was sent off. Remarkably, it was in the 28 minutes that they played with 10 men that Wednesday struck their best form. 10 minutes from the end, Davies cracked a 25-yard shot past Burgin; and, with three minutes remaining, a flash of brilliance from Sewell brought a third goal to seal a memorable victory. The teams in this replay were:

United— Burgin; Coldwell, Ridge; Joe Shaw, Johnson, Rawson; Ringstead, Hagan, Toner, Wragg, Hawksworth.
Wednesday— Ryalls; Kenny, Seemley; Gannon, Butler, Davies; Finney, Quixall, Jack Shaw, Sewell, Woodhead.

Incidentally, 10 days later Wednesday met United again in a League match at Hillsborough, and Sewell was the hero of a 3-2 victory, scoring the first goal and setting up two for Jack Shaw.

Wednesday were without Woodhead for the home clash with Chesterfield in the fourth round, but the winger's absence was no excuse for the side failing to beat their Third Division (North) neighbours. In fact, in conditions which proved a great leveller, the Derbyshire side had the best of a goal-less draw and fully deserved to take their First Division opponents to a replay.

The Saltergate replay has gone in the records as Quixall's match. The blond forward, well supported by Finney, produced one of his most memorable performances. And yet, it was not until the last half-hour that his brilliance, and Finney's, swung the game Wednesday's way. For though Shaw put them ahead after only 15 minutes, the Sheffielders were pegged back soon afterwards and, early in the second-half, found themselves trailing 1-2. It was not until the 70th minute that a flash of magic from Finney and Quixall enabled Shaw to get the equaliser. Then Sewell and Woodhead got the goals that snuffed out Chesterfield's challenge.

A Hillsborough crowd of 65,000 saw Wednesday go through at the first attempt in the fifth-round clash with Everton. The game was only two minutes old when Shaw gave them the lead. Hickson equalised for the visitors soon after half-time, and it began to look as though yet another replay was inevitable. However, in the last five minutes, first Sewell and then Woodhead scored, and Wednesday were in the quarter-finals.

Wednesday were paired with Bolton at Hillsborough in a sixth-round clash which provided excitement and talking points aplenty. Just before the interval Woodhead had the ball in the net but a colleague was adjudged to be off-side; however, after 75 minutes, the same man had better luck when he headed Wednesday in front from a cross by Finney. Then Butler was penalised for pushing Lofthouse, and everybody remembered that, earlier in the season at Burnden Park, Bolton had beaten the Owls with a hotly-disputed, late penalty. However, in this instance, the groans soon turned to cheers, for Moir shot wide with his spot-kick! Wednesday were just three minutes away from a place in the semi-finals when McIntosh, playing in only his fifth game following his return to the side, made his one mistake of the match. Moir only half-hit a shot, but, astonishingly, the home goalkeeper allowed the ball to pass into the net.

Gannon was the star of the replay, but it was one of those matches in which Wednesday had only a handful of attacks and yet emerged 2-0 winners. Gannon, Davies and Woodhead were involved in the move which led to Sewell getting the first goal after 59 minutes, and Jack Shaw sealed victory with the second just before the end.

Wednesday reserved their most disappointing performance for the semi-final, and, but for some fine work by McIntosh, Preston might have won by a greater margin than 2-0. Tom Finney was North End's brightest star, setting up the goals for Wayman (69 min) and Baxter (80); but the key to Wednesday's failure was the way in which Quixall and Sewell were completely subdued by Forbes and Tommy Docherty. Sewell took a heavy knock midway through the second half, was off the field for 10 minutes, and afterwards reduced to the role of passenger; and a painful afternoon for Quixall was summed up when, somehow, he managed to get his shirt ripped when Docherty made one of his typically full-blooded tackles on the Wednesday man. So the final glory eluded them, but Wednesday at least had the consolation of a share of aggregate gate receipts of £60,052 from their eight Cup games.

The close-season of 1954 had barely begun when the club suffered an unexpected blow with the untimely death of chairman James Longden, a popular local building contractor who had been a director since 1936. Initially, Colonel R. L. Craig succeeded to the chairmanship, but ill-health caused him to resign after a year; and, in May 1955, Dr. Andrew Stephen became Wednesday's fourth chairman since the war. Dr. Stephen, a quiet-spoken Scot, had moved to Sheffield from Aberdeenshire in the early 1930s, and, through his older partner, Dr. Ian Rhind, had become associated with the club as its medical officer. A director since 1949, Dr. Stephen was destined to be Wednesday's chairman for more than 18 years, spanning one of the most eventful and sometimes traumatic periods in the club's history; and, in 1967, he began a nine-year spell as chairman of the Football Association, being knighted in 1972 for his services to the game.

However, Dr. Stephen did not become chairman in the happiest of circumstances, or at an ideal time. For Wednesday had just suffered another fall. The season of 1954-5 proved disastrous: the club finished bottom of the First Division—nine points adrift of their relegation companions, Leicester City. It was a term during which several experienced players began to fade, and a number of youngsters made their bow: so the team often lacked depth of character and maturity, and only eight League matches were won—with three of these victories (including a 5-0 defeat of West Brom) having little real significance in that they did not come until *after* their relegation fate had been sealed. Wednesday lost 24 League matches and had the miserable distinction of being the first club since Grimsby Town in 1947-8 to concede a century of goals in a First Division campaign.

With only one win in the opening five games, and just two victories in the first 10 fixtures, Wednesday were in trouble virtually from the outset. And when they went from mid-October to mid-March without a win, collecting a mere six points in 22 games, they were as good as doomed to the Second Division. The team struggled in almost every position. Curtis missed only one game, and McIntosh three, while Sewell (top scorer with 14 goals) and Quixall were not often absent; but the side seldom remained unchanged for more than three or four games in a row. It sums up the amount of chopping and changing to note that five men filled the back positions, eight different wing-halves were used, eight players figured at centre-forward, seven appeared on the wings, and three appeared at centre-half. The only consolation from a dismal season was probably the fact that a number of bright youngsters emerged; and some of these—notably Stalybridge-born winger, Derek Wilkinson, and Sheffield products Tony Kay and Keith Ellis—were to enjoy a fair measure of success in future years.

Another pointer to the future provided by this season was the opening of the club's floodlights in March. They were used for the first time in the Derek Dooley testimonial match, in which an International XI beat a Sheffield XI 5-1 before a 55,000 crowd; and, a fortnight later, a "B" international between England and Germany was staged under the Hillsborough floodlights. Football, of course, moved into a new era with the introduction of floodlit matches, and it was not long before Wednesday were attracting some of the leading foreign teams to Sheffield for friendly games which were the forerunners of the European competitions accepted as a normal part of the domestic season within a few years. Here, it is probably appropriate to note that, between 1955 and 1960, Wednesday's floodlit friendlies involving foreign visitors included matches against Vasas Budapest (lost 1-7), San Lorenzo (won 9-0), Zagreb, Gwardia Poland, Juventus, Torpedo Moscow, and Tbilisi Dynamo.

The 1954-5 season provided early evidence of Wednesday's weaknesses in defence: 11 goals were conceded in the first three games; and at the end of October began a run of seven matches in which 26 goals were put in to the Wednesday net—including six at Preston (again!). In January, seven goals were conceded at Tottenham, and a five-goal defeat was suffered at Newcastle in April.

This was the last season for a number of older players, including Dennis Woodhead, Eddie Gannon, Mick Kenny, Jackie Marriott, Clarrie Jordan, and George Davies; and for Tony Conwell and Barrie Butler, too.

Woodhead subsequently continued his career with Chesterfield and Derby, managing to take his goal-tally past the century mark before hanging up his boots; Gannon left to become player-manager of Shelbourne; and Marriott and Conwell joined Huddersfield Town in an exchange deal which was to bring Ron Staniforth and Roy Shiner to Sheffield. It was from Huddersfield, in December 1954, that Wednesday made the most significant signing of the season, paying £15,000 for centre-half Don McEvoy.

By coincidence, McEvoy's final appearance for Huddersfield had been at Hillsborough in the previous September. That day Wednesday had won 4-1 and McEvoy suffered the injury which caused him to lose his place to Ken Taylor. After nearly 150 League appearances with Town—he had helped them to win promotion in 1953—the solidly-built McEvoy brought some stability to Wednesday's defence, but, such were the team's problems, he had played in 10 games before he had the pleasure of finishing on the winning side! McEvoy went on to play in over 100 games for Wednesday before moving to Lincoln City in 1958.

Kenny played in only two games before bowing from the scene, and his successor, Conwell, also failed to hold his place beyond February, when he handed the number two shirt to Jack Martin, a product of Dundee and the grandson of an old Wednesday hero, Bob Petrie. Martin remained at Hillsborough for some time, but never really established himself.

Gannon and Davies were the most regular half-backs, but both had spells on the sidelines, and both dropped out for good towards the end of the season. Eventually, Tom McAnearney was brought back; Michael Turley was tried in three games; and teenager Tony Kay was promoted for the final six matches. Kay did not establish himself immediately, but he was eventually to become a key figure and make over 200 appearances.

In attack Wednesday had a troubled season. Finney and Marriott filled the wing positions in the majority of games; but Froggatt, unable to displace Quixall or Sewell for long, had an early-season run at outside-left, while Woodhead had 10 outings there but was in and out, and youngsters Ron Greensmith and Peter Howells were tried. It was in November that an 18-year-old ex-Manchester League amateur, Derek Wilkinson, was given his debut in the game at Cardiff. In fact, Wilkinson played only twice, but, like Kay, he was regarded as an outstanding prospect, and, subsequently, was to become a regular, making some 225 League and Cup appearances.

Of the many players used at centre-forward, veteran Jack Shaw was the most consistent choice, and he managed nine goals in 18 outings in the position; but he had several games at wing-half, too. Wednesday even tried Froggatt as leader of the attack, and three teenagers—Arthur Hukin, Jack Watson and Keith Ellis—each had a brief run. When Hukin, a 17-year-old ex-Sheffield Boys player, was introduced in November, he was hailed as another Dooley, for he was over six feet tall and had red hair. He scored twice on his debut at Leicester, but returned to the reserves after six matches. Ellis, 19, ideally built for a centre-forward, was given his chance in mid-March, when Preston visited Hillsborough; and while he, too, returned to the reserves after a few games, he was destined to come back into the League side and make over 100 appearances in later seasons, scoring over 50 goals.

Unfortunately, the promise of such players as Kay, Wilkinson and Ellis was insufficiently developed in 1954-5 to give Wednesday the immediate lift they needed; and, after relegation had become a fact, it was clear that the club would have to obtain experienced players at back, half-back, centre-forward and outside-left if they were to make an early return to the top grade. In the summer of 1955, men were acquired for all these positions; and Wednesday did, indeed, bounce back to the First Division within 12 months . . .

7 The yo-yo years: (4) up again . . . down again, 1955-58

Eric Taylor knew exactly what he wanted when he went shopping in the transfer market in the close-season of 1955. The signings he made—Staniforth and Shiner from Huddersfield Town, Broadbent (Notts County), Gibson (Manchester United), and Bingley (Bolton)—paid off handsomely, for Wednesday won the Second Division championship with style in the new season; and the key to their success was fire-power in attack and stability and character in defence—exactly the qualities that had been lacking in the previous campaign.

In that 1955-6 season, Wednesday took the title with 55 points—three more than runners-up Leeds United. In fact, Leeds had the better home record, and, overall, won 23 games compared with Wednesday's 21; but the Sheffield club's away form was considerably superior. Furthermore, Wednesday had the edge in the scoring stakes with 101 goals, 41 of which were scored in away games.

Each of the five new signings contributed to the success in varying degrees, but it is fair to suggest that the one who had the biggest initial impact, Roy Shiner, was, at the time of his signing, the one newcomer of whom the least was known or expected. A product of the Isle of Wight, he had joined Huddersfield in 1951 from Cheltenham, but in nearly four seasons at Leeds Road had managed only 21 League appearances and scored six goals. He was one of those never-say-die players who will run until they drop, but the young centre-forward was overshadowed by the many stars on Huddersfield's books in the early 1950s. However, one of Shiner's few outings with the senior side happened to be at Hillsborough in 1954, and, though he was played out of position at outside-left, he made an impression on at least one spectator—Eric Taylor. In his first season with Wednesday, Shiner was an ever-present and scored 33 goals; and he went on to score 93 goals in 152 League appearances between 1955 and 1959.

Shiner arrived in the deal which also brought Ron Staniforth, who was one of the best-known players in the game. Indeed, in 1954, Staniforth had collected no fewer than eight England caps; and the tall, cultured full-back came with the experience of more than 300 League games behind him. He had spent six seasons at Stockport County before enjoying a short but remarkably successful run with Huddersfield, whom he had helped to win promotion in 1953. Staniforth missed only five games in 1955-6, and went on to make around 100 appearances in a stay of four seasons at Hillsborough.

Of the other pre-season signings, wing-half Don Gibson had played in over 100 First Division games with Manchester United, and was to make a useful contribution in his first six months with Wednesday before injury ended the run; Walter Bingley returned to his native Sheffield and had a run of 21 games at left-back between September and December; and Albert Broadbent, bubbling with energy and enthusiasm, missed only one match and provided a temporary solution to the left-wing problem.

Wednesday began the season with O'Donnell (who was soon to revert to a part-time contract) at centre-half, Tom McAnearney at left-half, and Froggatt at outside-right. Subsequently, McEvoy resumed at the middle of the defence and assumed the captaincy, with O'Donnell eventually returning at left-half, and McAnearney coming back at right-half for the last 14 games following the loss of Gibson. It was in November, incidentally, that Peter Swan, the six-foot South Elmsall product destined to become an England player, had his first taste of League football. Sewell had scored 13 goals in 16 matches before, at the beginning of December, he was transferred to Aston Villa in a £20,000 deal which was good business for Wednesday; for Froggatt was able to resume his old place at inside-left, and Finney returned at outside-right. With Sewell's departure, Finney and Quixall resumed their right-wing partnership, and, within less than three months, were playing together in the England Under-23 side which met Scotland's Under-23s at Hillsborough. Finney soon afterwards played for England "B" against Scotland "B" in Dundee.

Wednesday made an excellent start to the season, losing only two of their first 17 matches. They kicked off with a 5-2 home win against Plymouth Argyle, with Sewell claiming a hat-trick, while Quixall, who got the other two, gave an early warning of his intention to get among the goals. In fact, the blond-haired inside-forward went on to score 17 times, which was five more than he had scored in all the previous five seasons put together!

If Sewell was the early pacemaker in the scoring stakes, Shiner was hardly slow on the uptake. His first goal came in the 3-0 win at Liverpool in August, and he claimed doubles in the defeats of Bristol Rovers, Leeds United and Barnsley, and in the drawn game at Blackburn; and by mid-January he had 20 goals to his credit in 27 games. Wednesday clinched their return to the top grade by picking up 16 points out of 20 in their last 10 matches, and Shiner contributed 11 goals to this late push—including a hat-trick in the final match of the campaign, at home to Lincoln.

Wednesday started and finished the season with five-goal perfor-mances, and, overall, scored four or more goals in a match on no fewer

*19. Second Division Champions 1955. . . (back row) Froggatt, O'Donnell, Broadbent,
McIntosh, T. McAnearney, R. Staniforth, Bingley; (front row) Jack Marshall (trainer-coach),
T. Whitham, Shiner, McEvoy, Curtis, Finney, Quixall, E. W. Taylor (secy-manager).*

than 10 occasions. They conceded a total of 62 goals, but only two other
clubs in the grade had a better defensive record; and only one team,
Bristol Rovers, scored four goals against Wednesday. McIntosh missed
nine games through injury, but his deputy, Len Williams, was on the
losing side only once. Froggatt enjoyed one of his best seasons for some
time, for he missed only one game and his 14 goals brought his career
tally to 89—and, for the record, he went on to reach a century of League
goals in the match at Tottenham towards the end of the following
campaign.

Another interesting personality point is that 1955-6 marked Jack
Marshall's first full season as Wednesday's trainer-coach. He had
arrived in January 1955 after Alan Brown left to manage Burnley.
Marshall, who had previously been with Bury and Stoke as a trainer, was
a jolly, likeable Lancastrian who had once been a promising full-back
with Burnley until his playing days had been prematurely ended by
injury.

Wednesday's return to the First Division in 1956-7 was sound rather
than spectacular. They finished in mid-table, and, despite a run which
brought a mere two wins in 13 matches between early February and
mid-April, were well clear of the relegation zone. At home they won 14
and lost only four games, but could not match this form on their travels,
where they won only twice and suffered 16 defeats.

The 1956-7 campaign was notable in that it virtually marked the end of

McIntosh's long run as first-choice goalkeeper when he was displaced by another Scot, Charlie Pllu, in April. McEvoy missed only five games, but Swan proved a capable deputy; and other youngsters given a taste of life in the First Division included a former Sheffield and Yorkshire Boys defender, Brian Hill, and a promising Geordie, Gerry Young. Shiner added another 15 goals to his League tally, but leading marksman was Albert Quixall (22). Finney's 13 goals included a hat-trick in the 4-1 defeat of Spurs in November; and it is noteworthy that a hat-trick by Ellis in the last match of the season brought his personal tally to six in six games. Incidentally, Quixall's 39 goals in two seasons had taken his career total past 50, and, with two goals in the FA Cup, his 24 in 1956-7 was to prove his best for a season in all his 17 years as a League player.

Quixall's FA Cup goals came in the third-round "marathon" with Preston North End. After a 0-0 draw at Deepdale, Quixall and Shiner were on target for Wednesday in the Hillsborough replay, which ended 2-2. With Froggatt absent in the second replay, at Goodison Park, Jim McAnearney came in, and so the brothers McAnearney figured in the senior team together for the first time. Unfortunately, it was not a match of happy memories: Wednesday suffered their heaviest FA Cup defeat since 1890, for Preston won 5-1.

If Wednesday's staff and supporters believed that 1957-8 would mark the beginning of a brighter phase, or at least see the team consolidate its place in the First Division, their hopes were soon dashed. The club's 90th anniversary celebrations were overshadowed by a flu epidemic! The new season was little more than a week away when the flu struck, and no fewer than 16 players found themselves confined to bed. The newspapers referred to Eric Taylor's "sniffle" group (skiffle was all the rage at the time), but the situation was anything but funny. Wednesday successfully appealed to the Football League for postponement of their first two matches, at Manchester City and Newcastle, and finally began their League programme a week behind schedule. Pllu, Staniforth, Bingley, O'Donnell, Quixall, Jim McAnearney and Ellis recovered in time to play in the opening match, at home to Nottingham Forest; but it was a weakened team in more ways than one which slipped to a narrow defeat.

It is fair to suggest that Wednesday never quite recovered from a late and disappointing start to the campaign, and they went on to suffer relegation for the third time in six First Division seasons. A late bid to beat the drop failed, Wednesday finishing bottom on 31 points and going down with Sunderland, who had one point more. That Portsmouth and Newcastle only escaped on goal-average, while Leicester were only one point clear, serves to emphasise that Wednesday went close to clinching safety—and might have been in a better position to do so had they only made a better start to the season.

In fact, Wednesday won more home games than any of the other bottom eight clubs, but failed to win a single away fixture and collected only five points on their travels. Of course, all the blame for their fall could not be attributed to their late start. They lacked consistency in every department, and suffered a number of alarming defeats at home, where, in one run, they conceded 14 goals in three matches. Injuries and other problems caused the team to be chopped and changed. Finney alone played in every League match, and Quixall missed only four games; but, of the rest, only O'Donnell and Tom McAnearney managed more than 30 appearances. This was the season which saw Wilkinson finally establish himself as a regular at outside-right, and Finney's switch to the left flank marked the end of Broadbent's run. Froggatt did not regain a regular place until towards the end of October; while McAnearney, Hill, Gibson, O'Donnell and Kay all figured at wing-half. The full-back positions caused problems, too, for Staniforth managed only 14 outings and Curtis 24; so Peter Baker, a 22-year-old Londoner, had a short run; Bingley and Martin also played; and, in December, Peter Johnson was signed from Rotherham United. Shiner led the attack in 29 games, but was dogged by injuries; and it was in the famous FA Cup fifth-round tie with Manchester United that defender Johnson was given the number nine shirt. The same match saw Swan begin his run as first-choice centre-half.

However, goalkeeper was the position which caused the most trouble, and the problem was not finally resolved until just before the transfer deadline in March. Pllu began the season as first-choice, but badly damaged a finger in a remarkable game at Tottenham in late September. That day Wednesday led 1-0, then lost Pllu, and, with first Gibson and then Bingley taking over the green jersey, slipped to a 2-4 defeat which hardly reflected their spirit or abilities under the pressure of playing with 10 men for much of the time. Ryalls had a run of five games; Pllu returned but had the misfortune to damage an ankle; and McIntosh was called from the wilderness but lasted only three games, being dropped after Aston Villa had won 5-2 at Hillsborough in early December. It was then that amateur international, Mike Pinner, was given a run, but, alas, in five games Wednesday conceded 21 goals; so Ryalls was restored to the side in January, and played in the 11 League and Cup games before Eric Taylor went out and signed Ron Springett from Queen's Park Rangers for £10,000.

It has often been said that if Springett had arrived sooner than mid-March, Wednesday would not have been relegated. That is a matter of speculation, but what is beyond doubt is that 22-year-old Londoner Springett was to prove one of the finest signings Eric Taylor ever made. Many other clubs were taking note of Springett's progress, and at the time of his move north he had made around 90 Third Division appearances. Taylor promised Springett that if he joined Wednesday he would play for England within a year or so—and, remarkably, the promise was fulfilled. Indeed, Springett went on to play in 33 internationals between 1959 and 1966, thus becoming the club's most-capped player. He also played nine times for the Football League. Springett was soon established as a favourite with supporters, hailed as the club's best goalkeeper in the post-war era, and destined to remain at Hillsborough until 1967, in the meantime clocking up more than 380 appearances.

Springett's arrival came in the same period that saw the introduction into the team of another player who was to write his name into the club's record books. John Fantham, a slim, dark-haired inside-forward, the son of a former professional footballer and a product of Burngreave, made his League debut in February 1958 and totalled only six appearances between then and the end of the season. But he was clearly one for the future, and, in fact, went on to succeed Froggatt as the holder of Wednesday's post-war League scoring record with 147 goals.

It was in the same month as Fantham's League debut that Wednesday were involved in an FA Cup tie which can only be described as historic: the fifth-round clash with Manchester United. The background to this game will be familiar to every student of football. It was on February 6 1958 that the greatest tragedy in British soccer history, the Munich Air Disaster, occurred. The crash, which happened when Manchester United were returning from a European Cup game with Red Star Belgrade, cost the lives of eight players, four club officials, and eight newpapermen; and among the injured were manager Matt Busby and a future hero of England, Bobby Charlton.

The tragedy stunned and staggered the nation, and the first match that United played after the disaster happened to be against Wednesday. On the evening of February 19 a crowd of nearly 60,000 packed into Old Trafford, and, not surprisingly, the atmosphere was unlike anything ever before experienced at a soccer match. The night was super-charged with emotion, the sense of sadness and sympathy simply overwhelming. It was a unique occasion, quite unforgettable; and nobody who was present will deny that Wednesday were in an unenviable situation, for no visiting team could have hoped to win the game. The hearts and voices of the great bulk of spectators were totally committed to United's makeshift team; the crowd was in mourning for those who had died at Munich and was at the same time willing their successors to a victory which would symbolise a re-birth of "Busby's Babes". The tempo of the game was all too frantic, the mood so unreal, and goals by Brennan (2) and Dawson gave United a 3-0 victory.

Only two of the Munich surviviors played: Harry Gregg and Bill Foulkes; and marksman Brennan was one of two youngsters making his debut—the other being Mark Pearson (who, later in his career, was to have a spell at Hillsborough). United's team also included two of acting manager Jimmy Murphy's "emergency" signings: Ernie Taylor, the veteran inside-forward from Blackpool; and Stan Crowther, the Aston Villa half-back. The case of Crowther was quite remarkable, for he was not signed until barely an hour before the kick-off, and, in fact, had played for Villa in an earlier round. But, to help the Manchester club, the FA waived the rules which said that no player could appear for two clubs in the competition in the same season, and which required a 14-day qualification period.

In later seasons Wednesday were to score two memorable FA Cup victories at Old Trafford, but they were never again faced with the unique circumstances of that unforgettable night in 1958. For the record Wednesday's team on that occasion was: Ryalls; Martin, Baker; Kay, Swan, O'Donnell; Wilkinson, Quixall, Johnson, Froggatt, Cargill. A foot injury caused Shiner to drop out, with Johnson being switched into a role he had filled on a few occasions at Rotherham; while McEvoy and Finney were dropped, this being the only match that Finney missed all season, and one of only two senior appearances that Cargill made throughout the term.

An intriguing footnote to the occasion is provided by the fact that, on the night Wednesday were playing at Old Trafford, Sheffield United were engaged in a replay at West Brom. The sixth-round draw had paired the winners of these games; but, in the event, the dream of a Sheffield derby in the quarter-final was soon shattered. But then, the dream of a season of consolidation for Wednesday did not survive either. Yet, if 1957-8 ended on a glum note, there were, as always, optimists prepared to wager that the Owls would bounce back quickly; and some were ready to suggest that the last full season in the 1950s might mark the end of those wretched yo-yo years . . .

Part 7
Wednesday After 1958

1 The Catterick years, 1958-61

Wednesday's fall from the First Division in 1958 provoked a flood of angry criticism, most of it heaped upon the heads of the club's directors. Chief target of the critics was Dr. Andrew Stephen, a man who endured many less than happy moments in his years as chairman: the annual meeting of 1958 proved to be one of the stormiest with which he had to cope, but the tenacious Scot survived the ordeal, remaining to fight another day despite calls from some shareholders for his resignation. Events had inspired a revival of activity within the Shareholders Association, who put up four candidates in opposition to the retiring directors. The ballot was postponed for a week, and in the end all four directors (E. G. Flint, R. R. Gunstone, Sir James Turner and R. Pilifent) were re-elected, with the Association's most successful contender, Alderman Percy Kirkman, more than 100 votes short of the number required.

Ahead of this dramatic struggle and the noisy affair which led to some remarkable scenes at the meeting, Wednesday had not been inactive, nor had the board been unmindful of the need for change. Following relegation, Dr. Stephen and his colleagues took stock of the situation and decided upon a course of action which they hoped would silence the critics and, more importantly, lead to an improvement in the club's fortunes. Eric Taylor became general manager and secretary, and the club advertised for a team-manager. In fact, the new team-chief was named shortly before the annual meeting, but, surprising as it may seem in retrospect, the announcement was received without much enthusiasm, and it did little to stem the tide of criticism. The successful applicant for the newly-created post was a young North Easterner called Harry Catterick.

Darlington-born Catterick was destined to become one of the most successful managers of the 1960s, but he arrived in Sheffield virtually unknown. His name was, of course, familiar, but he was best remembered as a tough centre-forward who had spent 14 years with Everton. He had joined the Goodison Park club as a 17-year-old in 1937, but much of his career had been spent in the shadow of the likes of Tommy Lawton and Jock Dodds, and the war had interrupted his progress. He left Everton in 1951 to begin his management apprenticeship at Crewe, and it was while serving as player-manager there that he discovered and encouraged the talents of an ex-schoolboy star called Frank Blunstone, who was later transferred to Chelsea and was capped by England. Catterick left Crewe after two years, spending the next five years as manager of Rochdale, and the experience of operating on a shoe-string with precious few facilities fashioned him into a hard, uncompromising individual, a manager blessed with a strong streak of realism, directness and determination.

Many famous and better-known figures were among the applicants for the Hillsborough post, but Catterick's forthright personality, his confidence and enthusiasm, and his obvious determination to succeed earned him the unanimous vote of the Wednesday directors when he came to Sheffield for the interviews. Dr. Stephen and his colleagues felt that here was a young man who knew where he was going, and were convinced that he would not remain an unknown manager for long. Events were to prove them right, though they were not to know until much later that the young man's ambition and sense of purpose would cause him to feel frustrated and limited in Sheffield and prompt his departure within three years.

When Catterick was released by Rochdale (his contract had two years to run) in time to begin his duties at Hillsborough on September 1 1958, few could have envisaged the success Wednesday would enjoy under his team-management in the next three seasons. In 1958-9 they captured the Second Division championship; a year later they came fifth in the First Division and reached the FA Cup semi-finals; and in 1960-1 they finished runners-up to League champions Tottenham, also reaching the last eight in the FA Cup, with the reserves winning the Central League title.

Catterick's comparatively short stay coincided with the club's most successful spell since the early 1930s, and statistics show that of 126 League matches played in the period 70 were won and only 27 lost. Wednesday were defeated only five times at home, where they conceded only 50 goals in 63 League fixtures. Remarkably, this outstanding record was achieved without one major signing, for the costliest acquisition made by the new manager was Bobby Craig, bought for £6,500 from Third Lanark. This is not to suggest that Catterick did not seek to be more active in the transfer market: it was a source of considerable frustration to him that he could not spend as freely as he would have liked in that direction. It is well-known that, in later years, he looked back upon his time at Hillsborough as a period of lost opportunity, feeling that two or three signings at the right time would have put Wednesday among the honours. It is generally acknowledged that his biggest disappointment was the failure to sign Hibernian's English-born centre-forward, Joe Baker, in 1960-1. Wednesday's £50,000 offer was rejected, and Catterick felt that if only he had got Baker the League championship could have been brought to Sheffield.

As it was, Catterick's success was largely achieved with the players who had been on the club's books at the time of his arrival. His strength as a manager was his ability to command the respect of his players and his capacity to inspire them to extend themselves and play to their full potential. He was a hard taskmaster and a tough disciplinarian, direct and determined, a man whose no-nonsense attitude left no-one in doubt about what would happen if he didn't get what he wanted. He also refused to accept any interference in what he regarded as his domain.

It was in the Catterick years that Springett, Swan and Kay won international recognition, while Wilkinson, Fantham and Megson also gained representative honours. There is no doubt that all these players, and others, owed much to the new manager. Kay, for instance, was a player who made dramatic progress under Catterick's influence, while Don Megson, later to become a notable Wednesday captain, has often said that the decision which changed the course of his career was made by Catterick. Megson, a product of Sale, had arrived at Hillsborough in late 1952 as an amateur outside-left. He went through a phase when he played in every position in the Central League side, and seemed destined to settle at centre-half. However, when he completed his National Service and became a full-time professional, Megson was encouraged to have a run at left-back, Catterick indicating that this role offered the best chance of early progress. After 15 games at left-back in the reserves, Megson was promoted to the first team, and went on to make around 450 appearances.

The success of Johnson and Megson at full-back marked the end of the road for Staniforth and Curtis, who gradually drifted from the scene and moved into management—Staniforth at Barrow and Curtis at Doncaster. Of the other established players, Shiner moved to Hull City soon after Wednesday's return to the top grade; while the faithful Froggatt eventually lost his place to Craig (though not until he had completed a successful spell as captain). Under Catterick, Tom McAnearney, Swan and Kay emerged as perhaps the best half-back line since the 1930s heyday of Strange, Leach and Marsden; Wilkinson and Finney supplied power from the wings; and the scoring flair of Fantham developed rapidly, complemented by the scheming abilities of Craig.

Within two weeks of moving in, Catterick had made two of his most important managerial decisions—one passing virtually without comment, the other prompting the full blaze of publicity.

The move which provoked little interest outside the club was the appointment of Tommy Eggleston as trainer-coach. Jack Marshall left to succeed Catterick as manager of Rochdale, and Eggleston, an astute, efficient and friendly North Easterner, was brought to Sheffield. A former player with Derby County, Leicester City and Watford, Eggleston had turned to coaching after injury curtailed his playing days; and had served an apprenticeship at Brentford and Watford prior to being recruited by Catterick. At Hillsborough Catterick and Eggleston established a formidable partnership and provided a brand of tough discipline and professionalism which formed the basis of the success which followed in the next three years.

It was Catterick's decision to sell 24-year-old Albert Quixall, the club's captain and golden-boy, which provided the first sensation of the new era. Exactly 18 days after the new team-manager moved in, Quixall moved out—joining Manchester United to become the first signing made personally by Matt Busby after Munich. Busby's first offer for Quixall was

£35,000, but he needed to raise the figure to £45,000 and break the British transfer record before he got his man.

Quixall's departure was not entirely a surprise, for Wednesday's relegation had left him pondering his future. He felt that Second Division football would hinder his hopes of further international recognition, and was keen to capture some of the game's honours at club level. It was no secret that Busby was a great admirer of the blond forward's talents, while Catterick's view was that Quixall tended to over-elaborate and lacked the consistency that he demanded from a player.

The initial contender for the vacancy created by Quixall's departure appeared to be Jim McAnearney, who had recently become a full-time professional. However, within a couple of weeks, young John Fantham was recalled, and the ex-Burngreave schoolboy took his chance so well that McAnearney remained in the shadows and subsequently moved to Plymouth Argyle. Fantham played to his strengths and quickly displayed a remarkable talent for goalscoring. After being recalled for the home derby against Sheffield United on October 4 1958, he went on to claim 48 goals in 114 League games in the next three seasons, easily taking the prize as the team's most prolific marksman in the Catterick era. Quixall's successor as captain was Froggatt, who thus had the opportunity of emulating his father by leading Wednesday to the Second Division championship. Froggatt's contribution to the success the team enjoyed in the first season under Catterick cannot be overstated, for, in addition to his inspiring captaincy, he managed 26 goals in 37 appearances—and only Shiner, with 28, scored more.

The facts of Wednesday's Second Division title triumph of 1958-9 are that their 62 points left them two points ahead of runners-up Fulham and nine in front of third-placed Sheffield United. They scored 106 goals, including 68 at home; lost only once at Hillsborough; and claimed 10 away wins. Their biggest victories brought them seven goals against Lincoln, six against Sunderland and Grimsby Town, and five against Rotherham and Barnsley. Their best away wins, both by a 4-1 margin, came at Derby and Scunthorpe; and they suffered their heaviest defeats at Fulham (2-6) and Swansea (0-4). Their success was based on the consistency of team-selection, scoring power in attack, and strength in defence (especially at home, where they conceded only 13 goals). Curtis was the only ever-present; but Springett, Tom McAnearney, Finney, Fantham, Shiner and Froggatt were seldom absent. In addition to the 54 goals contributed by Shiner and Froggatt, Wilkinson (12), Fantham (12) and Finney (11) all reached double figures; and Wilkinson, in the middle of his best run with the team, was chosen to play for the Football League against the Scottish League in October and against the League of Ireland in March.

Wednesday began the campaign in promotion style, losing only one of their first 13 games and dropping just three points. After falling at Stoke in their first away match, they did not slip again until the visit to Liverpool at the end of October; and the unbeaten run of 11 games included the six-goal victories over Sunderland and Grimsby. The September clashes with Sunderland merit attention for different reasons: the trip to Roker saw a piece of history made when Wednesday had the Wilkinson twins, Eric and Derek, in their forward line; and the return game a week later marked Quixall's 261st and final appearance.

The Roker game proved disappointing for Wednesday. For a start, on the journey north, Don Gibson was taken ill, and travelling reserve Ron Staniforth was unexpectedly drafted in at left-half. However, during the match Staniforth had to switch to right-back when Martin was injured. By the 54th minute, goals by Froggatt (2) and Shiner had given Wednesday a 3-1 advantage, and they retained the lead until seven minutes from the end. Then Sunderland scored twice in the space of three minutes, the equaliser coming from the penalty spot.

When Sunderland visited Sheffield a week later, the match provided one of the highspots of a memorable campaign. Wednesday chalked up a brilliant 6-0 victory in a game in which everyone knew that Quixall was probably appearing in the club's colours for the last time. The newspapers on the morning of the match had revealed that the Hillsborough captain had made a formal request for a transfer. Quixall said farewell with an outstanding performance, and notched his team's second goal; but it was Froggatt, who scored three times in the space of 10 minutes soon after the interval, who was hailed as the man-of-the-match.

It was little more than a fortnight later that Fantham came in at inside-left (with Froggatt switching to inside-right) to begin a run which was to see him miss only four of the next 116 games. Fantham claimed his first League goal in his second game, at Brighton; bagged his first double in the 5-0 defeat of Rotherham on November 1; and got another couple in the 7-0 victory over Lincoln on Boxing Day, when Froggatt (2), Shiner (2) and Finney were the other scorers.

The trip to Cardiff in late November was significant in that it saw Catterick fit another vital piece into his jigsaw of success. For some time, Tony Kay had been telling Gibson: "I'll soon be having your shirt, mate!" Now he was given it, and the McAnearney-Swan-Kay line was launched. Catterick never ceased to enthuse about this trio. McAnearney and Kay were sharply contrasting wing-halves, but complementary in that what one lacked the other had. McAnearney, though not always appreciated by the crowd, had the tactical sense and the character to provide the stabilising influence which was foreign to Kay's game. Kay contributed the energy, flamboyance and fire; he had the arrogance, the hardness of tackle, and the drive which lifted his colleagues (and which later prompted Catterick to give him the captaincy). Kay's return at Cardiff coincided with the debut of another youngster, Billy Griffin, for whom this game was his only senior outing of the season. Griffin never became a first-team regular, yet, whenever he played, he nearly always scored a goal; he scored 14 in 19 games under Catterick.

Wednesday's chief rivals in the promotion race were Fulham, and, in the final analysis, the only difference between the sides was a margin of two points. Fulham, indeed, were the only team to take three points out of four from Wednesday, and it was at Craven Cottage in late March that Catterick's men suffered their heaviest defeat. This was the first of 10 games that Springett missed, and it proved an unhappy day for deputy Pinner. Fulham scored six times, with Jimmy Hill grabbing three goals in the final 15 minutes. When Fulham visited Sheffield for the return on the following Monday, Pinner was replaced by Roy McLaren, the goalkeeper signed from Bury earlier in the season.

The Second Division title was clinched thanks to an unbeaten eight-match run which began immediately following the Fulham setback; and promotion became a reality with the 1-0 defeat of Liverpool at Hillsborough on April 14. Perhaps it was appropriate that the marksman on this occasion was Froggatt. The captain followed up with two goals in the 5-0 defeat of Barnsley in the final home match, bringing his total tally to 26—almost twice as many as his previous best haul for a season. By the way, many of Froggatt's goals were scored with his head: he was one of the best headers of the ball in the game in his time.

Their first season back in the top grade saw Wednesday finish in their highest position in the First Division for 25 years. They ended the 1959-60 campaign in fifth spot with 49 points—six fewer than League champions Burnley. And, to complete a highly satisfying year for supporters, they also reached the FA Cup semi-final.

Yet, though they began their programme with a notable 1-0 victory at Arsenal—Fantham got the goal—Wednesday's early-season form was moderate; and a 5-0 defeat of Blackpool in mid-September was the highspot of a start which brought only seven points from their first nine games. However, in early November they began a run which swept them up the table and into the last four of the FA Cup: they lost only three of 27 League and Cup games.

A feature of the club's return to the First Division was that it helped bring recognition to a number of players. In September, Springett was chosen to play for the Football League against the Irish League in Belfast; and, soon afterwards, Wednesday had three players—Springett, Swan and Kay—on duty in the Football League v League of Ireland game at Blackburn. In November, Springett made his England debut against Northern Ireland, and Swan gained his first Under-23 cap; while, in March, both Swan and Kay were in the England Under-23 side for the games with Scotland at Ibrox and Holland at Hillsborough; and, in May, Swan gained the first of his 19 England caps when he was chosen for the clash with Yugoslavia at Wembley.

Springett's selection for the Ireland match was especially satisfying to Eric Taylor, who had promised the goalkeeper he would be capped within approximately a year of joining Wednesday. When Springett reached the Wembley dressing room, a pile of telegrams awaited him, one reading: "What did I tell you?" from the club's general manager. Springett marked his international debut with a penalty save from Jimmy McIlroy. He went on to enjoy a long run as an automatic choice for England, and when he played against Scotland at Hampden Park in 1960 he became the first Wednesday goalkeeper to appear in this fixture since Jack Brown 32 years earlier. Over the years he spent at Hillsborough, Springett was a model professional. He continued to live in London throughout his Wednesday career, and this agreement,

20. Wednesday, 1959-60. . . (back row) T. Walker (trainer), E. W. Taylor (general manager),
Bob Lyttle (physio), Peter Swan, Jack Martin, Ron Staniforth, Ron Springett, Roy McLaren,
Don Gibson, Peter Johnson, Tony Kay, Tommy Eggleston (coach), Harry Catterick
(manager), Johnny Logan (trainer); (front row) Roy Shiner, Norman Curtis,
Jim McAnearney, Redfern Froggatt, Tom McAnearney, John Fantham, Alan Finney,
Derek Wilkinson.

negotiated at the time of his transfer in 1958, was later an occasional source of frustration to managers from Catterick to Alan Brown; but Springett never abused the privilege, and never let the side down.

Wednesday's improved form in the autumn of 1959 coincided with a number of changes. Around the end of September, Kay returned after missing eight games; and when Shiner dropped out and left for Hull, first George Kirby and then Keith Ellis took over at centre-forward. However, the team's revival really began following the introduction of two new faces—defender Don Megson and forward Bobby Craig. Megson made his senior debut in the home match with Burnley on November 14; and a week later Craig, signed from Third Lanark, arrived in time for the trip to Leeds. Megson's speed and tenacity earned him a regular place, and veteran Curtis departed from the scene. Craig was an astute, skilful player with an unhurried style and a quick football brain; and he made an important contribution to the Wednesday story. Craig's arrival marked the end of Froggatt's long run as a first-choice; though, in fact, Froggatt did return to the side towards the end of the season, and, playing at centre-forward, scored two goals to bring his career tally in the League to 140.

Craig's home debut, against West Ham, coincided with one of Wednesday's best performances of the season. At the time West Ham led the First Division, but the Sheffield team knocked them off their pedestal with a superb 7-0 victory. Fantham, Ellis and new captain Alan Finney each scored twice, and Craig claimed his first goal for the club. Craig's first five appearances in Wednesday's League side saw the team grab 21 goals—three at Leeds, four at Chelsea, five against Arsenal and two against Preston in addition to the seven put past West Ham. If one includes the 2-1 victory in the friendly with Torpedo (Moscow), Wednesday's record between mid-November and the end of February shows they lost only one of 19 matches.

The early months of 1960 were dominated by the FA Cup, and for some time it looked as if Wednesday were destined to make it all the way to Wembley. They started with a 2-1 home win against Middlesbrough in the third-round—Tom McAnearney setting them on the victory trail with a 36th-minute penalty, and later providing the free-kick which led to Ellis scoring the second. Craig scored twice in the 2-0 defeat of Jimmy Hagan's Peterborough in the fourth-round, and it was another McAnearney penalty which brought victory on the visit to Manchester United at the next stage. Megson, recalling this Old Trafford game, observed that Wednesday enjoyed a stroke of fortune: "Peter Swan cleared a shot from Albert Quixall that had gone *over* the goal-line. Fantham collected the clearance, took on Maurice Setters, who gave away a penalty, and McAnearney made no mistake from the spot. All in a flash we could have been a goal down but instead were in front." Setters had been with Manchester United only a few weeks; and the previous October had been sent off while playing for West Brom at Hillsborough. At the time he may not have had happy memories of games with Wednesday, but, many years later, he was to join the Sheffield club's training staff.

Fortune again smiled on Wednesday in the quarter-final clash with neighbours Sheffield United at Bramall Lane. "We were only in the game for about 15 minutes in the first half," said Megson, "but in that time Derek Wilkinson scored twice. After that we felt certain that our name was written on the Cup!"

Unfortunately, as in 1954, the Maine Road semi-final proved to be the end of the line for Wednesday, and their luck ran out when they faced Blackburn Rovers before a crowd of over 74,000 on the Manchester ground. Irishman Derek Dougan gave Rovers the lead after only 11 minutes. Soon afterwards Finney had the ball in the net, but referee Williams of Nottingham ruled "no goal" because he said that Wilkinson was off-side. Dougan made it 2-0 after 71 minutes, and though Fantham headed in from a McAnearney free-kick four minutes later, it wasn't to be Wednesday's day.

Of the team which played in this semi-final, only three men survived to figure in the Wednesday side which was to defeat Blackburn on the way to Wembley six years later—Springett, Megson and Fantham. However, it is relevant to add that two other players destined to go to Wembley with Wednesday in 1966 played in a few League games in 1959-60: Gerry Young and Johnny Quinn. Young made six appearances—three at inside-right, two at outside-left, and one at centre-forward—and teenager Quinn, a product of St. Helen's and signed from Prescot Cables, played twice at outside-right. Young's only goal of the season came in his first outing, the home match with Spurs in September, when Wednesday chalked up an excellent 2-1 victory. One of Young's other outings came in a remarkable home game with Bolton in late February. After only 17 minutes, Bolton lost goalkeeper Joe Deans with a dislocated shoulder, but Deans' deputy, Hennin, was not beaten until the 54th minute when Finney got the only goal of the game. Five minutes later the emergency goalkeeper saved a McAnearney penalty, and it was the award of this spot kick which led to the incident in which skipper Joe Higgins became the first Bolton player to be sent off for 23 years.

Wednesday's first season back in Division One saw Swan and Fantham the only ever-presents, but Springett and Finney each missed only two games, and Tom McAnearney three. Fantham topped the scoring lists with 16 League goals, while Ellis claimed 13 in 22 outings. With Ellis having established himself at centre-forward, at least for the time being, Kirby was transferred to Plymouth in January, when Jim McAnearney also moved to the Devon club.

In 1960-1, much to the delight of their supporters, Wednesday improved upon their performance of the previous season. They finished as First Division runners-up—their highest placing since the title-winning campaign of 1929-30. Wednesday collected 58 points, and a year earlier this would have been enough to give them the League championship. It is probably fair to say that in *any* ordinary year Wednesday's record would have earned them the title. Alas, this just happened to be the year of that extraordinary team, Tottenham Hotspur, who not only took the championship with 66 points (equalling Arsenal's feat in 1931), but went on to become the first club since Aston Villa in 1897 to complete a League and Cup double. Spurs were magnificent, but Wednesday stayed hard on their heels until the last weeks of the season.

It was a memorable and colourful campaign. As well as making a big push for League honours, Wednesday had a triumphant run in the FA Cup before falling to Burnley in a sixth-round replay. The season also brought further individual successes, for both Springett and Swan were England regulars; while Fantham—the club's top scorer with 23 League and Cup goals—gained an Under-23 cap against Italy in November; and Megson played for the Football League against the Italian League, also in November. The year brought tragedy, too, for Duggie McMillan, a promising 19-year-old inside-forward who had made one senior appearance in a County Cup-tie, had to have a leg amputated following an accident when the first-team's coach crashed on the return journey from Highbury in late December.

This was also the season which saw the demolition of the old North Stand and work started on the building of a new £150,000 cantilever stand. The money was raised by the issue of debentures, and supporters rallied splendidly in the bid to make Hillsborough one of the best equipped grounds in the country. In subsequent years, Wednesday were often accused of making ground improvements at the expense of strengthening the team, but it is important to note that the money raised on this occasion was forthcoming because it was solely for the purpose of building the new stand. In truth, this was a remarkably astute stroke of business, for the terms negotiated meant that the stand cost around £13 a seat—a fact which was to sound quite astonishing within only a few years.

If ever there was a time in the post-war era when Wednesday seemed poised to reach a pinnacle of achievement, it was in the early months of the 1960s. Unfortunately, the season which saw the team shoot to within touching distance of the League title also marked the end of the Catterick years. The team-manager actually quit Hillsborough a week before the championship was conceded to Tottenham.

Wednesday began the season with a remarkable run of 12 games without defeat, their first fall coming at Wolverhampton on October 22. Three weeks later, in one of the season's most memorable Hillsborough matches, Wednesday became the first team to topple mighty Tottenham. Three successive defeats followed, but in early December Wednesday began an unbeaten run of 19 League games. Of course, it had to be Tottenham who ended the sequence, and they did so on the night they clinched the title. In fact, Wednesday won only one of their last seven games, and would have conceded second place in the table to Wolves had not the midlands club suffered a surprising home defeat against Fulham in their final match. Wolves completed their programme with 57 points, and Burnley, the previous year's champions, were fourth with 51 points.

Wednesday actually had a better home record than Tottenham, at least in that they lost one game fewer and conceded 11 fewer goals. But Spurs' 16 away victories put them in a class of their own—Wednesday won eight and drew eight. It is interesting to note that Spurs, Wolves and Burnley all topped a century of goals, while Wednesday's tally was 78; but the Sheffield side had a better defensive record than all three, and Wolves and Burnley conceded 28 and 30 goals more than Wednesday.

In their first 15 games Wednesday collected 24 points (10 more than in the corresponding period in the previous season), their record being made up of eight home victories and two wins and four draws in away matches. In the same period Spurs played 16 games, dropped *one* point and scored 53 goals! Not surprisingly, when the teams met at Hillsborough on November 12, the clash was billed as a battle of giants, and a crowd of 56,363 turned up for the game. Wednesday limbered up for the big occasion by crushing the touring Tbilisi Dynamo 5-0 on the previous Monday, with Fantham getting four of the goals.

Wednesday faced Spurs with McLaren deputising for the injured Springett, and the teams lined up thus:

Wednesday— McLaren; Johnson, Megson; T. McAnearney, Swan, Kay; Griffin, Craig, Ellis, Fantham, Finney.

Tottenham— Brown; Baker, Henry; Blanchflower, Norman, Mackay; Jones, White, Smith, Allen, Dyson.

McLaren turned in one of his best performances, and two of his saves, from Smith and Allen, were among the outstanding features of the match. Indeed, it was his save from Allen five minutes before half-time which started the attack which brought Wednesday's first goal—crashed into the net by Billy Griffin. However, Norman headed Spurs level from a free-kick soon afterwards. Wednesday's winning goal came after 68 minutes at the end of a move started by Megson: Ellis got his head to the ball, and when it rebounded off the legs of a defender, Fantham pounced to shoot past Brown. It was a great triumph!

After this delightful dose of glory, Wednesday lapsed into a comparatively ordinary phase, and won only one of their next seven games—a sequence which saw them slide down to fifth place. Immediately following the Spurs match, they lost at Leicester, Aston Villa ended their home run, and a third defeat was suffered at Everton. In early December, with 19-year-old Bobby Lodge making his League debut and Young a last-minute deputy for McAnearney, Wednesday returned to winning ways with a 5-4 victory over Blackburn Rovers. But what a close affair it proved to be! After 12 minutes Dougan shot Rovers in front, but Fantham soon pulled Wednesday level. Wednesday then slipped into top gear, and goals from Craig (2) and Lodge (2) helped them race to a 5-1 half-time lead. What Jack Marshall said to his Rovers team at the interval has not been recorded, but the visitors cracked three goals in the second-half . . . and Wednesday greeted the final whistle with a huge sigh of relief.

That shaky success launched Wednesday on a run which saw them go 16 League and Cup matches without defeat. The fourth game of this sequence was a 1-1 draw at Arsenal on Boxing Day, and it was on the journey home that tragedy struck. The team's coach crashed on the Great North Road at Alconbury Weston, near Huntingdon. Duggie McMillan, who had travelled to Highbury as reserve, was standing in the entrance door well at the front of the coach at the time of the crash, and, trapped in the wreckage, had to have his right leg amputated before he could be freed. Others injured included Peter Swan (fractured shoulder) and skipper Tony Kay (concussion).

Wednesday began the New Year with a 2-0 defeat of Leeds United in the FA Cup, Quinn and Ellis getting the goals. A 1-1 draw in the League fixture at West Ham followed, and then Wednesday began a five-match sequence which brought them 23 League and Cup goals.

The run started at Fulham in a game which earned a place in the record books because Wednesday went 1-0 up in the first minute without one of their players having touched the ball! Home half-back Alan Mullery thumped the ball back to his goalkeeper, but Macedo missed it as it sped into the net. Fulham equalised soon afterwards, but McAnearney restored Wednesday's lead after 21 minutes; and, with further goals from Ellis (2), Fantham and Finney, they emerged 6-1 winners.

On the following Saturday, Wednesday drew their home fourth-round FA Cup tie with Manchester United, and it seemed they had conceded the initiative. However, in the replay they created a major surprise, not because they won, but by the size of their victory. The winning margin was 7-2! The man who made all the difference to Wednesday was Bobby Craig, who returned after being injured since Christmas. Fantham put

Wednesday ahead after only two minutes, and though Mark Pearson grabbed a quick equaliser, Finney restored his side's lead on the half-hour. Two goals from Ellis left Wednesday with a 4-1 advantage at the interval. Second-half goals came from Fantham, Ellis and Finney for Sheffield, and Dawson for Manchester.

Three days after this triumph, Wednesday beat Preston 5-1, with Fantham (2), Griffin (2), and Ellis on target. A trip to Burnley followed, and a late penalty from McAnearney clinched a dramatic 4-3 victory. Burnley were to gain their revenge 25 days later.

Goals by Fantham and Ellis gave Wednesday a fifth-round Cup win at Leyton Orient, but in the quarter-final Catterick's men failed to cash in on home advantage against Burnley. In the replay Wednesday gave John Frye, a young forward from St. Mirren, his senior debut, but though Burnley were second-best in the first-half, they never looked back once Jimmy Robson had put them in front soon after the interval. McIlroy made it 2-0 to Burnley with a 64th-minute penalty.

Despite this setback, team-spirit was high in the Hillsborough camp, a point emphasised by Fantham's decision in mid-March to forego a second Under-23 cap in order to play for Wednesday at Blackpool on the same evening. Perhaps it was fitting that the only goal of the game came from Fantham, who was duly rewarded within a week of the Blackpool trip when he joined Springett and Swan in the Football League side which met the Scottish League at Ibrox.

The Blackpool match, incidentally, saw Wednesday try Gerry Young at centre-forward. Ellis, who had at one stage 19 goals to his credit in 26 League and Cup games, was left out after failing to score in five matches. In his third game in the number nine shirt, Young claimed a hat-trick, the victims of a 5-1 triumph being Manchester United.

The defeat of Manchester United left Wednesday three points behind Spurs at the top of the table. Unfortunately, it was just at this time that the Hillsborough side's challenge lost its impetus, for while they picked up only five points from their next four games, Spurs added eight to their tally. Wednesday won at Newcastle, but dropped points at Blackburn and at home to Newcastle and Leicester. So when the Sheffielders visited White Hart Lane on the evening of April 17, they trailed the London club by six points, both clubs having four games left.

With Wednesday having everything to play for, and Spurs determined to avenge that November upset, it proved to be another remarkable match. After half-an-hour Megson's first senior goal for the club gave Wednesday the lead, but Smith and Allen both scored for Spurs in a quick burst just before the interval, and the Londoners held on to their 2-1 advantage to end the Sheffield club's 19-match run without defeat and clinch the League championship.

Wednesday had gone into this vital game without a manager, for Harry Catterick had resigned in the previous week. Within a matter of days he had replaced Johnny Carey as manager of Everton; and, by one of those strange coincidences which football frequently produces, Catterick's first match in charge of the Goodison Park club brought him straight back to Hillsborough. To add a touch of irony to events, Everton won

2-1—only the second team to inflict a home defeat on Wednesday all season.

Not surprisingly, perhaps, Catterick's departure was the subject of considerable debate among Wednesday's supporters, and there was some regret at the loss of a man who had achieved so much in such a short time. The Catterick era had seen Wednesday enjoy their best phase for 30 years, and the club's followers wondered if the impetus could be maintained without the man who had inspired it. With the benefit of hindsight, we know that the team never touched the same peaks again—and distance has lent enchantment to the memory of those three seasons under Catterick.

The full details of the circumstances surrounding Catterick's resignation will probably remain forever unknown, but it seems fair to suggest that his departure was inevitable. The fact that, within a matter of days of quitting Sheffield, he should be appointed manager of Everton lends substance to the theory. Of course, Carey was still in residence at Goodison Park at the time Catterick left Hillsborough. Whether Catterick's sudden availability precipitated developments at Everton, or, indeed, if the knowledge that Carey's days at Everton were numbered influenced Catterick's actions, those who know may never choose to reveal. We can be sure that Catterick had good reason to be confident that he would not be out of a job long. During his spell at Sheffield at least two clubs had tried to tempt him away. Catterick had become disenchanted at Hillsborough, partly because he wanted greater personal rewards for himself, partly because he wanted to spend more money on strengthening his squad, and also as a result of a not entirely unexpected personality conflict with general manager Eric Taylor. Catterick and Taylor were both strong-willed, determined men, each outstanding in his own specialist area. Catterick, who had, quite literally, stepped from obscurity and achieved a great deal in a very short time, felt he deserved greater rewards and recognition. So he was frustrated. However, even if this had not been the case, it seems unlikely that he could have resisted the lure of Everton, and, by virtue of his record at Hillsborough, it seemed certain that the call would come from Goodison Park sooner or later. Not only was Everton his old club, with whom he had been a player for 14 years; but, with Pools millionaire John Moores as chairman, the Merseyside club offered huge personal rewards and tremendous scope to an ambitious manager. Catterick wanted full authority, and he knew he could have it at Goodison Park.

So, perhaps there was a sense of the inevitable in his move to Merseyside. Maybe, with the benefit of hindsight, we can recognise that there was some truth in his suggestion that his Sheffield years were a time of lost opportunity, but history shows that Hillsborough turned out to be only one eventful chapter in the Catterick story, just as Catterick was limited to providing a colourful and memorable chapter in the longer story of Sheffield Wednesday Football Club.

2 The Buckingham style: 1961-64

The early 1960s were eventful years. It was a time of great change—not only in football, but throughout society. In some ways the change was so considerable and so dramatic that it constituted a kind of revolution, and the effects were to be far-reaching. Styles and attitudes were transformed, if not overnight, certainly quickly and suddenly.

Football, of course, is "the people's game", and it has often been said to reflect society at large. So in the early 1960s the game began to move in new directions, swept along on the tide of change, echoing the mood of the times on and off the field. Ordinary people had now begun to enjoy greater affluence and increased freedom, and they not only had the means to make better use of their leisure, but faced an ever-widening choice of alternative forms of entertainment upon which to spend their time and money. Ironically, perhaps, this was just the moment when the maximum wage was abolished, and worried officials of football clubs looked at declining attendances and wondered how to relate them to the increased expenditure that the "new deal" would create. It was in 1961 that the first £100-a-week footballer arrived; and, within two years, the Eastham case saw the retain and transfer system declared illegal in the High Court. In the sea of progress upon which the game was swept forward, those two early developments, great though they were, proved to be only the first of a series of waves which would wash away the old ideas and philosophies. Football would never be quite the same again, and the process of change would not be without its problems.

As was noted in the previous chapter, Harry Catterick's last season at Hillsborough was rather eventful for the club, and there was plenty happening to engage the attention of supporters. However, that 1960-1 campaign produced a number of important developments within the game nationally, and these provoked widespread comment about the direction in which professional football seemed to be moving. The Football League, for instance, had elected to launch its own Cup competition. This was not received with enthusiasm by all clubs, especially those in the higher grades; and, indeed, some—Wednesday among them—chose not to participate. However, if the new League Cup failed to capture the headlines, one event which did so without any trouble was the threat of a players' strike. The maximum wage, £14 in 1951, had been raised to £20 in 1958, but now the PFA, under the leadership of Jimmy Hill, wanted to see the maximum abolished. They got their way, and the start of the 1961-2 campaign marked the beginning of a new era for the professional footballer. Clubs adapted to this change in various ways, and it is interesting to note that Wednesday were the first club to introduce a wage structure based on a bonus system related to attendances. This unique formula was highly acceptable to the players, for at that time Wednesday's average gates were among the best in the country.

It was amid this atmosphere of change at the start of a new phase in football history that Wednesday recruited a new team-manager. In fact, they found the man they wanted within a month of Catterick's departure.

He was brought from Holland, and his name was Vic Buckingham.

At the time of being told by a friend that a vacancy had arisen at Hillsborough, Buckingham was in Amsterdam and nearing the end of a successful two-year spell as coach to Ajax, the Dutch First Division club. He had led them to League and Cup success, but was now planning a return to English soccer. Indeed, only a few weeks previously, at the prompting of his friend Bernard Joy, Buckingham had verbally committed himself to becoming manager of Second Division Plymouth Argyle as from June 1. However, he never moved to Devon. Instead, at midnight on May 8 1961 he formally accepted the appointment as Catterick's successor at Hillsborough, having first obtained release from his unsigned agreement with Plymouth.

Buckingham was not unknown to the football-going public, and, within the game, was widely recognised as an outstanding and astute coach whose teams played with adventure and style. Born at Greenwich, he had spent all his playing days with Tottenham Hotspur, making his debut with them as a 20-year-old in 1935, and quickly establishing himself as a clever, intelligent full-back. After war service in the RAF, he returned to White Hart Lane, and remained there until 1950. This proved to be an important period in his life, for it was now that he turned to coaching, and a spell with the Middlesex FA brought him under the influence of Walter Winterbottom. When he finally quit as a player, he became coach to Pegasus, guiding them to a famous victory in the FA Amateur Cup final of 1951. He had his first taste of management with a League club in the unlikely setting of Bradford Park Avenue, but, in early 1953, took charge of West Bromwich Albion. He had been at The Hawthorns barely a year when Albion won the FA Cup—and, incidentally, if Wednesday had beaten Preston in the 1954 semi-final they would have met Buckingham's team at Wembley. It was in 1959 that Buckingham quit Albion, handed over his duties to his loyal assistant Gordon Clark, and set off to try his luck in Holland.

Buckingham probably ranks as the most colourful personality to hold the team-manager's job at Hillsborough. After Catterick, he certainly presented a stark contrast, in his personal style, his management methods, and his football philosophy. Tall, elegant and sophisticated, Buckingham was an easy, almost nonchalantly confident extrovert who had about him a style and manner of the cultivated and successful man of the theatre—indeed, one felt that he would have been quite at home among a group of Shakespearian actors. This was the London influence, and, not surprisingly, many of his friends were stars of the stage and screen. The suggestion of culture was not without foundation, for he had a reputation as a football intellectual, and had, after all, mixed with university footballers at Pegasus. Buckingham's thinking, and his attitude towards tactics, were of a newer school, and, in 1961, he was, perhaps, ahead of his times. This was largely the influence of Winterbottom, but also partly due to his close contact with Continental football.

The new manager was, too, a man of ready wit and quick intelligence, given to summing up much in a few well-chosen words—words often accompanied by a look or a shrug of the shoulders, gestures which spoke volumes. In the Wednesday dressing room, Buckingham was quickly categorised as something of a character. He brought a new style of management, and a breath of London and the Continent swept through the corridors of Hillsborough. As a manager, however, he knew exactly what he wanted from his players, but he saw them as experienced professionals and credited them with the intelligence to do some of their own thinking. He encouraged them to express themselves, and wanted to see them creating excitement and drama, using their skills to provide entertaining football. He was an idealist. Behind the apparently easy-going appearance of his wise-cracking flamboyance, he was deadly serious about encouraging talent. Buckingham didn't believe in making a team fit a plan, but sought to formulate a plan to fit them. He recognised that he had inherited a squad of seasoned players, and while one or two were approaching the veteran stage, felt that the disciplines they had acquired under Catterick would provide a firm basis, and if they were encouraged to express themselves they could only get better. If Buckingham arrived in the dressing room before a match, pushed his trilby onto the back of his head, and asked "how do you want to play it today?", he was not suggesting he didn't know the answer, but indicating that he expected his players to have ideas of their own so they could adapt to any situation, unexpected or otherwise, which might develop on the field.

Buckingham remained with Wednesday for three seasons, and the team reached sixth place in the table in each term. In one, the first, they went to the fifth round of the FA Cup and the quarter-finals of the new European competition the club had helped launch, the Fairs Cup. The major transfer deals completed by Buckingham included the departure of Tony Kay to Everton and Bobby Craig to Blackburn Rovers, while Keith Ellis joined Scunthorpe and Billy Griffin left for Bury; and new arrivals in David Layne (Bradford City), Eddie Holliday (Middlesbrough), and Mark Pearson (Manchester United). The period also saw the introduction of a number of promising youngsters. These included Colin Dobson, a skilful inside or wing forward; Peter Eustace, who ultimately emerged as a graceful wing-half; Vic Mobley, destined to succeed Swan at centre-half; John Hickton, a defender who would make a big impact as a centre-forward in the post-Buckingham era; and Robin Hardy, a half-back from the Worksop area. It was following the sale of Tony Kay in December 1962 that Buckingham successfully converted Gerry Young into a left-half; and discoveries at junior level in this period included future successes in Wilf Smith and David Ford.

A manager has to have luck to succeed with his signings, said Buckingham, and he has since quoted the case of David Layne to illustrate his point. Layne, who scored 54 League goals in 74 games, plus five goals in the Fairs Cup and one in the FA Cup, emerged as the club's most successful centre-forward for years following his £16,000 move from Bradford in the summer of 1962. He was spotted by Gordon Clark, who had quit West Brom and rejoined his former boss at Sheffield in the autumn of 1961. Clark, a former Manchester City player who had later served a managerial apprenticeship with Hyde United, Distillery and Aldershot, was a chief scout with a knack of discovering talent in unexpected places; and he told Buckingham that he thought Layne could make the transition from Fourth to First Division football. The manager at Valley Parade at the time was Bob Brocklebank, a man who, following an earlier spell at Birmingham City, had been given some temporary scouting work by Buckingham during the latter's West Brom days. So they were old friends. A chat soon revealed that Layne was available, and a deal was set up. "But it was a gamble," said Buckingham later, "and Layne gets all the credit for what he achieved at Sheffield. He played far better than I had expected. I was lucky that time!" Perhaps it was an example of getting a pay-off because the player was encouraged to express himself.

Under new management, Wednesday began the 1961-2 campaign with four wins in their first five games, followed this with a run of five matches without a win, and then won four of the next five fixtures. It was a pattern which set the trend for the Buckingham era: alternate bursts of brilliance and mediocrity. In February and March they won only one of seven League fixtures, but ended the season with four successive victories to finish in sixth place with 46 points—one fewer than city rivals, Sheffield United, and 10 behind champions Ipswich (managed by Buckingham's old Spurs colleague, Alf Ramsey).

By coincidence, Buckingham's first League match as Wednesday's manager took him back to West Brom, where, thanks to goals from Ellis and Finney, the new chief kicked off with a victory. Wednesday also won their first home game, defeating Bolton Wanderers 4-2; but this fixture, played on the evening of August 23 1961, had a special place in the Hillsborough club's records because it coincided with the opening of the new £150,000 North Stand by Sir Stanley Rous, secretary of the Football Association. This magnificent structure, 360 feet in length and designed by a Sheffield firm, Husband & Co., constituted a major success for the club. The work of gradually demolishing the 60-year-old existing stand and replacing it with the new one had been completed in just under a year. With 10,008 seats in 48 rows providing a view of the playing area unobscured by pillars or posts, the cantilever stand brought Hillsborough's seating capacity to 16,000—an increase of 7,000. Now it was clear that Wednesday would be equipped to house more big matches, and, significantly, in October 1962, they staged a full international for the first time in over 40 years; and, around the same time, it was revealed that the Sheffield ground had been chosen as one of the venues for the World Cup matches scheduled to be played in England in 1966. Naturally, the overriding hope was that Wednesday would themselves fill the ground by virtue of the success they achieved in League and Cup competitions.

Wednesday followed the defeat of Bolton with a splendid 5-2 win against Birmingham City, the feature of the match being a hat-trick by Fantham, whose third goal was a brilliant flying header. A week later came another memorable victory—at, of all places, Everton. Goals by Kay, McAnearney (penalty), Craig and Ellis earned a 4-0 scoreline against Harry Catterick's side, and the game was watched by former Hillsborough hero, Ellis Rimmer, who had taken time off from working at his Liverpool hotel to attend. "I haven't seen football like that from an English team for years," said Rimmer, who probably didn't realise that he had been in the Wednesday team the last time they had won at Goodison Park—way back in September 1933.

Unfortunately, Wednesday now endured a long run of seven games in which they managed only one victory. Two of the defeats suffered in this spell came against the newly-promoted pair, Ipswich Town and Sheffield United. The match at Bramall Lane was the 75th League meeting between the Sheffield clubs. Wednesday, following a half-time request from referee Kevin Howley, played in white shorts instead of their usual black after the interval. United's winner came from "Doc" Pace just before the end.

A generally disappointing September was brightened by two events: the arrival in the team of a 21-year-old forward who had graduated through the junior teams; and Wednesday's first appearance in the Fairs Cup. Colin Dobson, a product of the North East, had been on the club's books for six years, but, because he wanted to complete a shipbuilding apprenticeship on his native Teesside before devoting himself exclusively to football, had only been a full-time professional six weeks when he made his League debut against Arsenal. Red-haired Dobson, a small but clever player, quickly made his mark in the side, and, in 1963, was to gain an England Under-23 cap. His success was to encourage Wednesday to let Craig go. Dobson went on to make more than 170 League appearances, but, though his contribution was significant, it is fair to suggest that he never went as far as many had predicted when he burst upon the scene in 1961.

Dobson's introduction to the first team actually came eight days after Wednesday had played the first leg of their Fairs Cup-tie with Lyonnaise in France. At one stage in this game the Sheffield side trailed 0-3, but rallied and lost by a 2-4 margin; and Dobson was one of the heroes of a fighting performance in the second leg. When the French team visited Hillsborough on October 4, they quickly extended their lead to 5-2, but Wednesday staged a dramatic recovery to take the tie on a 7-6 aggregate. Fantham, playing at centre-forward for the first time, sparked off the revival with a headed goal, and he later scored the winner with another of his diving headers. The other goals came from Griffin, Dobson and McAnearney (with another penalty).

By coincidence, three days after the Fairs Cup triumph, Wednesday returned to winning ways in the League—and, yet again, success was achieved only after the opposition had been given the initiative. Chelsea led 2-0 after 17 minutes, but goals from Fantham and transfer-listed Craig pulled the home side level by half-time; and a 10-minute burst soon after the re-start saw Dobson, Fantham and Griffin give Wednesday a 5-2 advantage. Tambling notched his third goal for Chelsea later, but the Owls pocketed the points.

Fantham's outstanding form—he finished the season with 25 goals—earned him a place in the Football League side in the games with the Irish League and the Italian League; and late September brought him the only "full" international cap of his career in England's World Cup qualifying match with Luxemburg at Highbury. Many lesser players than Fantham have gained more honours. Incidentally, Swan and Springett added to their haul of England caps in this period; and both were in the squad which went to the World Cup finals in the summer of 1962, but Swan had the misfortune to suffer an untimely attack of tonsillitis, and it brought his international career to a premature end.

In the last weeks of 1961, Wednesday maintained their progress in the Fairs Cup with a 4-0 defeat of Roma at Hillsborough. Gerry Young was recalled to the troublesome centre-forward spot for this game, and celebrated with a hat-trick. In the return in Italy a fortnight later, Roma could only manage a 1-0 victory.

The arrival of 1962 saw Buckingham and his men turn their attention to the FA Cup. A goal by Finney gave them a 1-0 victory in the home third-round tie against Swansea, and Craig and Ellis were on target in the 2-0 success at Nottingham Forest in the fourth round. When Wednesday shared a goal-less draw with Manchester United at Old Trafford in the next round, the signs looked good. Indeed, they felt they had been denied an obvious penalty when Ellis had been brought down by Setters; but they were confident that home advantage would bring them success in the replay. Unfortunately, a crowd of 65,000 (receipts topped £12,700) saw Manchester United earn a place in the quarter-final with goals from Johnny Giles and Bobby Charlton.

A week after their FA Cup exit, Wednesday returned to the Fairs Cup trail with a home first-leg fixture against Barcelona in the quarter-final. Twice in arrears, twice they pulled level, with Fantham heading the first equaliser and Finney shooting the second; and a second-half goal from Fantham left them with a 3-2 advantage to take to Spain. Unfortunately, that one-goal margin was not enough: Barcelona won the second leg 2-0.

In between the various Cup games, Wednesday won only one of seven League matches in February and March, and just before the transfer deadline Buckingham attempted to add pep to the team's attack by signing 22-year-old Middlesbrough winger, Eddie Holliday, who cost £26,500. Holliday, a product of Royston, near Barnsley, had played three times for England in 1959. His arrival at Hillsborough coincided with a run which saw Wednesday win six and lose only three of 11 games, and so climb up the table. A few weeks after Holliday arrived, Craig departed for Blackburn. Holliday was destined to remain in Sheffield for three seasons, in which time he made around 50 League appearances and scored 12 goals; and in 1965 he returned to Middlesbrough, later playing with Hereford, Workington and Peterborough.

With the 1961-2 campaign behind him, Buckingham spent the summer months seeking means of strengthening his team and training staff. He had the good fortune to solve the centre-forward problem with the acquisition of David Layne, and followed this with the "signing" of Jack Mansell as trainer-coach.

Layne was a local man who had escaped the attention of the city clubs when he played in the same Sheffield Boys team as John Fantham and Gordon Banks. He had made his Football League bow with Rotherham United, who had introduced him as an 18-year-old in 1957; but, after 11 senior outings with the Millmoor club, was allowed to move to Swindon, where he became a full-time professional and scored 28 goals in 51 League appearances before being transferred to Bradford City in December 1960. At Valley Parade he began to hit the headlines, claiming 44 goals in 63 League matches, including a club record 34 in 1961-2.

Mansell was a coach who shared the Buckingham philosophy in terms of being an advocate of attractive football with the emphasis on encouraging skill. A former England "B" full-back, Mansell was a product of Salford, and had once been an amateur on Manchester United's books. However, it was with Brighton that he had become a professional, and they were responsible for converting him from a winger into a defender. Mansell made his name with Cardiff City and Portsmouth, playing in over 150 First Division games with these clubs before turning to coaching as manager-coach of Eastbourne United. At the time of his arrival at Hillsborough, he had spent a year broadening his experience with Blau-Wit, the Dutch First Division club.

The 1962-3 season coincided with the worst winter for bad weather since 1947, and, because of a "big freeze" which began shortly before Christmas, a full programme of League soccer was not completed on any Saturday from mid-December to the first week in March. This was the season when the Pools Panel, comprising football experts, sat for the first time to create imaginary results to keep the punters happy on those blank Saturdays!

For Wednesday, who began the campaign wearing "butcher's apron" shirts (so named because of a broader blue stripe and narrower white stripe), this was another of those disappointingly inconsistent seasons. After losing two and drawing two of their first four matches, they won four games on the trot and actually went on to lose only one in nine; but, between October and December, they had a 12-match run without a victory. In the second half of the season two separate spells which brought five successive victories proved sufficient to push them into sixth place by the end of the campaign; but they finished 13 points behind the new League champions, Catterick's Everton. It was in this year that Wednesday struggled to dispose of Third Division Shrewsbury Town in the FA Cup third round, scrambling through by a 2-1 margin after extra time in the Hillsborough replay; but then losing in the fourth round at Arsenal.

Features of the season included the staging at Hillsborough of a European Nations Cup match between England and France, and the memorable visit of World Club champions, Santos—both games being played in October. The international, the first leg of a first-round tie, proved a disappointment: England could not master a moderate French team and only salvaged a 1-1 draw with a lucky second-half penalty. It is appropriate here to refer to the second-leg match, played in Paris in February, because France beat England 5-2, and Ron Springett, for whom this game was a nightmare, was subsequently dropped by new

England team-manager Alf Ramsey. It would, perhaps, be interesting to know what Ramsey said to his old colleague, Vic Buckingham, on the subject; and, for that matter, what the Wednesday boss said in reply. In any event, Ramsey called up Gordon Banks, the Sheffield lad who was to remain England's first choice for a long time.

The Santos match was a much happier occasion, and a crowd of 49,058 enjoyed a feast of good football, with Pele the shining star in a brilliant Brazilian team. Coutinho got both goals as Santos established a 2-0 lead in the first half-hour, but Griffin and Layne pulled Wednesday level by the 35th minute. Unfortunately, Layne then retired injured. Young deputised. Just before the interval Coutinho completed his hat-trick; but the most unforgettable moment came when Pele made it 4-2 to Santos with an astonishing penalty kick. Recalling the incident years later, Eric Taylor said: "Pele did the fox-trot, a two-step and a tango as he stepped up to the ball. He then stopped dead and sent poor Springett the wrong way. No goalkeeper in the world could have saved that penalty." Springett's after-the-match comment was: "I nearly had him going the wrong way!" It was one of those floodlit occasions the memory of which supporters savoured for years.

Two months later Tony Kay was transferred to Everton. By coincidence his last game for Wednesday was in the home fixture with Harry Catterick's team on December 22, and, soon afterwards, the Goodison Park club agreed to pay £55,000 for Kay. The fee was at the time a British record for a wing-half. The departure of Kay saw opportunity knock for 18-year-old Peter Eustace. The Stocksbridge youngster, who had had an 11-match run as McAnearney's deputy at right-half early in the season, was now recalled at left-half. However, after seven games he was replaced by Young for the trip to Blackpool on March 16, and the Geordie quickly made the number six shirt his own. As for Eustace, his return to the reserves was only temporary, for within 18 months, he would become a first-team regular in the number four shirt.

Dobson had by now established himself at outside-left, his switch enabling Johnny Quinn to settle at inside-right, where the popular Lancastrian enjoyed his longest run to date. Only Springett (41), Swan (42) and Layne (39) played in more games than Dobson, while only Layne scored more goals. Dobson's tally was 14; and Layne proved an outstanding success in his first season, scoring 30 times in League and Cup—his record including a hat-trick against Manchester City and seven doubles, two of them notched against Sheffield United.

The 1963-4 campaign saw Wednesday make their poorest start for six years, with a mere six points from the first eight games. In late September they showed one brief flash of better things when they celebrated their return to the Fairs Cup with a 4-1 victory over DOS Utrecht in Holland; but, in fact, it was mid-October before they put together a substantial run of good results. They went nine matches without defeat between October 12 and December 7, and after 21 games boasted 25 points—the best they had achieved in the first half of a season under Buckingham. Results in this period included a 5-0 defeat

21. Wednesday in the early 1960s. . . (back row) O'Donnell, Eustace, McLaren, Ron Springett, K. Ellis, Johnson, Hardy, Megson; (front) D. Wilkinson, Finney, John Quinn, Swan, Layne, Fantham, Dobson, Holliday.

of Wolves and a remarkable 4-4 draw at Stoke—where they had trailed 0-3 eight minutes before half-time. Unfortunately, Wednesday's improvement in the League was not matched in the Fairs Cup; for though they won the home return with DOS Utrecht 4-1, with Layne getting a hat-trick, they were KO'd at the next stage, FC Cologne winning 3-2 in Germany and 2-1 at Hillsborough. Indeed, the home defeat in the Fairs Cup was soon followed by a fall-off in League form, the team slipping back into the old pattern of inconsistency. Typically, perhaps, within the space of eight days in January, Wednesday suffered the embarrassment of being beaten 3-2 at Fourth Division Newport County in the FA Cup, and followed up with a fine 4-1 victory at Ipswich, where Layne grabbed what was to prove the last hat-trick of his Wednesday career.

Throughout 1963-4, Wednesday were dogged by injuries, and only Megson and Young were ever-presents. Johnson, Holliday, Dobson, Fantham and Springett all spent spells on the sidelines. Fantham, in fact, had one of his most frustrating seasons, for he played in only 19 League games; while Johnson, reduced to 10 senior outings, saw injury cause him to concede his place to Brian Hill. Springett missed 14 games, including the FA Cup tie at Newport. It was at the time Fantham dropped out at the beginning of October that Buckingham signed Mark Pearson, the Manchester United forward, for £20,000; but though Pearson made 28 League appearances in his first season, he did not enjoy a long spell at Hillsborough.

Despite the absence of Springett, Fantham and McAnearney, Wednesday chalked up a notable 3-0 win against Sheffield United at

Hillsborough in January, with Derek Wilkinson (2) and Layne adding to their haul of goals in derby games. The absent trio all returned in February, but Wednesday endured another lean spell, with only two wins in nine games. However, at the end of March Blackburn were defeated 5-2 and a sequence which saw Wednesday lose only one of their final seven games enabled them to finish in sixth place for the third season in succession. Wednesday had a good home record, and it was poor away form which had cost them the chance of making an impression in the title chase. Their 49 points left them eight points adrift of champions Liverpool, but only four points behind runners-up Manchester United.

However, by the time the curtain fell on the season, the club's supporters had other things to discuss besides whether greater consistency or better away form might have put them among the honours. For April 1964 turned out to be one of the most traumatic months in Wednesday's history. And all the drama came off the field.

It was towards the end of March that rumours began to circulate suggesting that Vic Buckingham's three-year contract would not be renewed at the end of the season. Speculation in the Press started to gather momentum around the time that the board rejected a transfer request from Springett; and it was soon apparent that changes were in the offing. However, for the moment, it was business as usual for Buckingham, and on April 4 he introduced a 20-year-old centre-half called Vic Mobley into the team for the game at Wolverhampton. Barely 24 hours after this match, it was learned that assistant manager, Gordon Clark, was leaving Wednesday to manage Peterborough United—Clark getting the appointment ahead of his Hillsborough colleague, Jack Mansell, who had been regarded as favourite for the job. Clark's move was later to have important implications for Tom McAnearney, who was to join Peterborough in 1965 and subsequently move to Clark's former club, Aldershot, as player-coach.

Four days after Clark's new appointment had been announced, the speculation about Buckingham's future became a matter of fact: following a board meeting on the evening of Thursday April 9, Wednesday revealed that the manager's engagement would not be renewed and the position would be advertised as being vacant from May 31. Buckingham took the decision philosophically. Soon afterwards he rejoined Ajax; and when he went back to Amsterdam and entered the Dutch club's dressing room for the first time in three years, he felt immediately at home—his old track-suit was still on the same peg where he had left it on moving to Sheffield!

The weekend was only a few hours away when the Hillsborough board meeting broke up following the Buckingham decision. On the Friday morning, chairman Dr. Andrew Stephen and vice-chairman Harold Jessop boarded a train for Glasgow, bound for the following day's Scotland-England match. No doubt they discussed the managerial situation now existing at the club, but they could not have foreseen that the choice of Buckingham's successor would be strongly influenced by a newspaper story which would drop upon them like a bombshell before they came home to Sheffield little more than 48 hours later. On the

Sunday morning after the international, Messrs Stephen and Jessop caught the train for home, and so much of the journey was taken up with conversation that they were more than half-way to Sheffield before Harold Jessop began to idly scan the newspapers. When he picked up a copy of *The People,* his eyes fell upon a story which made his heart miss a beat. It was a story which had already left thousands of Wednesday supporters in Sheffield stunned with disbelief.

The story contained allegations that three Wednesday players—Swan, Layne and Kay—had been involved in a betting coup in December 1962, with one of the games concerned being the Ipswich-Wednesday match played at the beginning of that month.

With regard to the players involved, it is not necessary here to go into further detail except to note that they were subsequently banned by the Football Association, as were a number of others. What is relevant in the context of Wednesday's history is the effect of the affair on the club. Of course, Wednesday lost the services of two of their best players (the third had been transferred), and an international defender and one of the game's most successful forwards could not be, and were not, replaced readily or easily. The loss of two key players was to have long-term effects; but more important, perhaps, was the damage done to the club's reputation and morale. Eric Taylor described the business as "horrifying" and said: "This is the biggest blow the club has ever received"—and, indeed, it was many years before Wednesday fully recovered from the setback. We shall probably never know all the implications, just where and how the shock waves reached to influence and alter the course of history. Within the game it was widely recognised that Wednesday had been the innocent victims, and that what had happened was foreign to the club's principles and its name as an organisation which did everything above-board. But, naturally perhaps, Wednesday had to suffer alone the painful reality of the whole affair.

By coincidence, little more than 24 hours after the sensational news had burst upon unsuspecting club officials, Wednesday had a home match with Tottenham Hotspur. They won the game 2-0, with deputy centre-forward Derek Wilkinson scoring both goals in the first half; but the occasion was memorable for the way in which the 31,377 spectators responded. From the kick-off they got right behind the team, and, after listening in silence to a half-time message broadcast by Eric Taylor, who asked them to "bear with the club in this most tragic affair", the supporters broke into a roar which proclaimed their loyalty and faith. Those who were present on this emotional evening could have no doubts that Wednesday would survive the ordeal. It might take a long time, but they would erase the memory of this dark moment in club history and emerge with pride and trust restored.

Perhaps it was significant that when they got down to the business of choosing a manager, Wednesday looked for two important qualifi-cations: they wanted someone they knew, and the chosen man would have to have a reputation as a tough disciplinarian. The man whom they decided fitted the bill best was Alan W. Brown, the former Hillsborough coach who had been manager of Sunderland since 1957.

3 Alan Brown—man with a mission, 1964-68

When, after an absence of nearly ten years, Alan Brown returned to Hillsborough in the summer of 1964, he arrived in Sheffield a man with a mission—his goal to lift morale and help restore some of the pride and prestige which had taken a heavy knock with the shattering revelations of the previous April. The big North Easterner was well suited to the task in hand, and it was typical of the man that he immediately threw himself into action with the same drive and fierce determination which had made him such a forceful and respected player.

Now in his late forties, Brown retained an energy and vigour which was the envy of many men half his age; and personal fitness was an essential part of his creed. He had been in professional football for around 30 years, and, having been raised in a hard, practical school at Huddersfield and Burnley, there was precious little that he didn't know about the game. As a tall, commanding centre-half and captain, he had been bold and fearless, a man who never held back in his quest to be a winner. Brown hated to lose, even in a six-a-side or a tennis match played for fun, and defeat almost invariably left him silent and pensive, preoccupied by the business of analysing where he might have failed. The same tough, single-minded approach and uncompromising spirit had marked his style as a coach and manager. He came back to Sheffield with a reputation as a rugged disciplinarian. The Press had dubbed him the "iron man".

However, while he was recognised within the game as an unyielding manager, his abilities as a tactician were widely acknowledged and his opinions not only highly regarded but frequently sought. It was said, for instance, that few managers could assess the strengths and weaknesses of an opposing team more quickly or accurately. And loyalty to his club and players was the cornerstone of his philosophy. His former assistant, Jack Marshall, described Brown as "a terrific worker" whose energy seemed to know no bounds. To the outside world the public face of the apparently ice-cold man with the stony stare and the inscrutable expression may have supported the "iron man" image portrayed in the Press; but there was another side to Alan Brown, and he had the capacity to inspire his teams. Another former colleague, David Smith, has said that Brown "was terrific for the players", and several of the men who played under him have said he was a manager for whom they would willingly have run through a brick wall.

When Brown had left Sheffield in late 1954 after three years as trainer-coach on Eric Taylor's staff, it was to return to Burnley, his old club, to begin a career in management. He arrived at Turf Moor in a transitional phase in the Lancashire club's history, but kept Burnley among the leading clubs in the First Division; and, replacing fading stars with a number of promising youngsters, laid the foundations for the side which won the League championship in 1959-60, by which time, of course, he was working elsewhere.

The sensation of the football world in 1957 was the so-called "Sunderland scandal", when the Roker Park club faced allegations of illegal payments. Amid the turmoil they began to look for a new manager who suited the needs of the time. They chose Alan Brown. By coincidence, as a boy Brown had stood long and often on the Roker terraces, and Sunderland was a club for which he had a special affection.

At this time Sunderland had never been out of the First Division since joining the Football League, and this unique record was a source of considerable pride on Wearside. Alas, in Brown's first full season in charge, he was unable to steer them clear of the fall into the Second Division—relegated on goal-average with Sheffield Wednesday. That fall was only the beginning of an acutely difficult phase for Brown. In 1959 Sunderland finished 15th in the lower grade, and 16th a year later. However, in 1960-1, things began to improve, and they climbed to sixth place. More frustrations awaited them, for in 1961-2 they missed promotion by a point, and in 1962-3 were pipped on goal-average. The team that pushed them out of second place in 1963 was Chelsea; and perhaps Brown recalled that the same club had sent Wednesday to relegation on goal-average 12 years earlier, in his days as trainer-coach at Hillsborough. Chelsea were to figure prominently in the Alan Brown story in later years.

Sunderland's first-ever spell in the Second Division finally came to an end in the spring of 1964. This time they made no mistake, gaining promotion as runners-up to Leeds United. (An ever-present in the Sunderland team that year was Len Ashurst, one day to become Wednesday's manager). So Brown achieved his goal, having re-built the side and taken Sunderland back to the First Division. However, just when he might have been expected to take time off and enjoy his moment of glory, he elected to quit the Roker scene and move south. He started out for Sheffield, where he was to experience all the pleasure and pain of football management in a period of change—a period which was to prove rather eventful and, at times, very exciting.

★ ★ ★

In a stay of a little under four years at Hillsborough, Alan Brown stamped his personality on the club and the team. He brought a new look to Wednesday, on and off the field, injecting discipline and formality into the daily routine, and transforming the team and the training staff. It was in these years that Wednesday dispensed with their traditional striped shirts, replacing them with blue jerseys with white sleeves; but of much greater consequence was the manager's decision, taken in his second season, to adopt a 4-3-3 style of play.

Brown's major transfer deals saw the arrival of Brian Usher (Sunderland), Jim McCalliog (Chelsea), Peter Springett (Queen's Park Rangers) and John Ritchie (Stoke City); and the departure of Eddie Holliday, Mark Pearson, Alan Finney, Tom McAnearney, Colin Dobson, John Hickton, Ron Springett and Johnny Quinn. In terms of what he spent and what he recouped, Brown broke about even. The period also saw the introduction of such youngsters as Howard Wilkinson, Peter

Wicks, Wilf Smith, David Ford, Graham Pugh, Sam Ellis and Jack Whitham. Brown, incidentally, also gave John Hickton, a reserve centre-half, his first senior chance at centre-forward—a move the astuteness of which was only recognised after the player matured and achieved great success with Middlesbrough.

Off the field, Brown brought in a new trainer-coach, David Smith, a former Burnley and Bristol City player who had been working in Libya; but later he dispensed with the services of Smith plus the long-serving Tommy Walker and Johnny Logan. In their stead came the trio dubbed the "M Squad"––Lawrie McMenemy (later to earn fame as Southampton's manager), Ian McFarlane, and Jack Marshall.

Brown's first season in charge saw Wednesday finish eighth in the table, a reasonable beginning. In the following year he introduced new tactics, but if the 4-3-3 plan did not endear him to all, his critics were quickly answered by the success the team enjoyed in going all the way to the FA Cup final. Amid the euphoria induced by this achievement, the critics overlooked the fact that the team had finished in 17th place in the First Division. Indeed, at the time of Wednesday's Wembley defeat, the general view was that a bright and successful future beckoned Brown's re-shaped team of blended youth and experience. In that summer of 1966, Hillsborough staged a number of World Cup matches, England won the Jules Rimet trophy, and unlimited promise seemed to await the likes of Sheffield Wednesday.

Unfortunately, the promise remained unfulfilled. Slowly but surely the golden dream faded and, though it was not to happen until after the end of the Brown era, the dream became a nightmare.

In 1966-7 Wednesday seemed at one stage destined to make a quick return to Wembley, but their hopes were dashed by a last-minute goal in the quarter-final at Chelsea; and it was Chelsea who were to deliver the KO blow in the fifth round a year later. FA Cup success had awakened an awareness of the rewards of European competition, and now Wednesday made a belated entry into the Football League Cup, the winning of which earned the prize of a place in Europe. Unfortunately, as if the gods were punishing them for having delayed their entry so long, Wednesday's early experience of the competition was less than even reasonably successful. Meanwhile, their League form left much to be desired. After finishing in mid-table in 1967, they slumped to 19th place a year later—ending up only two points better off than their city rivals, Sheffield United, who were relegated with Fulham.

Alan Brown was a complex man who has been described by some of his friends as a Jekyll and Hyde, a deep thinker whose motives and the source of his motivation were not always easy to fathom. He was regarded as a bit of a loner, a man who, consciously or not, set himself apart. Yet, if he seemed to erect around himself a barrier which was difficult to penetrate, he commanded respect and admiration from his players. As the Wednesday men soon found, the "iron man" was not without his faults, but he certainly had a heart. In the beginning he won them over because, although his rule was rigid and strict, he demanded from his players only what he himself was prepared to give—100 per cent loyalty and dedication. The new manager made a big impression because, in training, he led by example. He may have been twice as old as most of his players, but he participated, often with furious energy, in practice sessions, seemingly determined to pit himself physically against the fittest of his men. A lesser man might have sought an excuse to avoid the risk of failing and losing face in front of his players.

He was a man of many contradictions, and even his best friends have admitted that it was difficult, if not impossible, to get close to him. Yet, if a player did what Brown demanded, he had no better ally or supporter than the boss. The manager's loyalty to those players who were, in his eyes, fulfilling their obligations, was at times quite remarkable. A player suddenly caught up in a personal tragedy, for instance, would find Brown ready to offer not merely sympathy or understanding, but help which took forms which went beyond the call of duty or concern for a colleague. One player recalled being in hospital after an operation, and remembered how Brown had provided a regular taxi service—personally delivering the man's family at visiting times, and returning them home afterwards. At a training session, Brown might have disagreed quite strongly with the training methods of a coach, and may not have spoken to the man again all day. But that night, learning that the wife of that same coach had been taken ill, Brown would turn up and take charge of nursing arrangements so that his colleague could be sure of getting a good night's rest.

Brown was not the kind of man to court popularity, yet, even years after his spell in Sheffield, his former players talk about him with great affection. His very presence seemed to instil in his men a confidence and self-reliance. He frequently told them that 11 men could climb Everest, but no man could do it alone. He insisted that a vital key to success was to develop the right habits in training as well as in an actual game. He was a firm believer in minute preparation, planning ahead in great detail, and making his players work relentlessly on variations in moves at free-kicks and corner-kicks. The combination of his overall philosophy and his careful attention to detail frequently brought a pay-off which was unexpected to all except Brown and his staff. The classic example, of course, was provided by the FA Cup run of 1966, when Wednesday, the outsiders in almost every round, turned the form-book upside down—and never with more aplomb than in the semi-final defeat of Chelsea and the first 50 minutes or so of the final against Everton.

If Brown had a fault it was, perhaps, his inflexibility once he had made his mind up about something or someone. At times he took decisions which, on the surface anyway, seemed to defy logic; but he adamantly refused to explain his reasoning. If anyone once got the wrong side of him, if he felt that for some reason his trust had been abused or betrayed, Brown could be an unforgiving man. On this subject, it is not necessary to cite instances, but a number of players over the years felt the effects of this aspect of Brown's character. There were probably occasions when Brown's loss was as great as the player's, though not often, but once he had made his mind up it was the end of the matter. At least no player was ever able to take Brown for granted or rest on his laurels: every man was always on his toes!

The Press never found Brown an easy man to deal with, yet there were times when he provided reporters with better "copy" and quotes than many a manager who more readily sought publicity. Typical of the reticence in Brown which frustrated the sportswriters was the occasion when he pulled out of a proposed deal with Bolton which would have brought Wyn Davies, the Welsh international centre-forward, to Sheffield. Brown's interview with Davies took place in the manager's vehicle in the car park of a Manchester hotel. It lasted about two minutes. The reporters, sensing a good story, remained puzzled by the sudden turn of events, but Brown refused to enlighten them. Yet, in 1966, those same Pressmen were to find Brown relaxed, friendly and talkative—and the manager even publicly thanked them for helping to relieve the boredom for his players in the pre-Cup final residence at lonely Lilleshall. Brown did not suffer fools gladly, and, in dealing with journalists, had no time for the usual preliminary courtesies. When you interviewed Alan Brown you got to the point—quick! Yet, though he made life difficult for the sportswriters, few managers have provoked so much discussion among journalists; and the writers had such respect for him that they consciously took the trouble to refrain from swearing in his presence!

An example of the apparent contradictory nature of Alan Brown's thinking was provided in the 1965-6 season. Before it began, he returned to his former club, Sunderland, and acquired Brian Usher. This meant that he now had in his first-team squad two natural wingers—Usher and Colin Dobson. Alas, within a matter of weeks, Brown began to ponder on the introduction of a 4-3-3 system—which made wingers obsolete! Usher never became a favourite with the crowd in any event, but was handicapped within months of his arrival because he found his style did not fit in with the team-pattern. Dobson was allowed to leave for Huddersfield.

Brown's influence, therefore, was considerable, and, in his first two seasons, he seemed to have laid the foundations for a successful future. Unfortunately, the promise was never fulfilled, and in early February 1968 Wednesday found themselves without a manager. Brown had packed his bags, and, within 24 hours, it was revealed that he had turned up back at Sunderland.

There are times when things do not go according to plan, when hard work and effort do not bring the expected reward. The fate of an individual at these times seems to be influenced by circumstances over which he has no control. Those twists of fate which affected a number of individuals at Hillsborough in the post-Wembley period may not add up to the whole story, nor may they entirely explain the team's gradual decline. But certainly they serve to indicate some of the key factors which saw the club's progress on and off the field hampered by external circumstances.

In the spell which followed Wembley, injuries to Graham Pugh, Peter Eustace and David Ford proved crucial. Ford, who was injured in a road accident, was desperately unlucky, and Wednesday's misfortune was that they lost his services just when he and £70,000 newcomer John Ritchie had struck up a highly-promising partnership in attack. The period also brought changes in the club's training staff.

If the 1966 Wembley team seemed to offer high hopes for the future, the basis of success had to be, initially at least, the opportunity for them to remain together long enough to ensure that the younger men could mature together. It is important to remember that the optimism did not necessarily have its roots in firm foundations: officials pinned their hopes on a team which had won *five* successive away matches in the FA Cup. That team was hardworking and disciplined, and the fact that Mobley, Ford and McCalliog gained international honours indicated that there was talent in the ranks; but there was a danger of overstating the promise. There was, too, a danger of failing to recognise how easily the bubble could burst. Two or three injuries at the wrong time, a loss of impetus, and it might prove difficult to regain a foothold on the tightrope of success. This is what happened.

Initially, the decline was not as serious as it became later, and, while Brown remained at the club there always seemed to be the likelihood that he would pull the team upwards again. His financial resources were rather restricted, even though he was able to pay a club record fee for Ritchie six months after Wembley; but the manager had already shown what could be achieved by discipline and organisation. Unfortunately, Brown did not remain long enough to achieve all that might have been, and his successors were left with an awesome task without having his capacity to get the best out of his players.

There were other developments of significance in this period. Dr. Andrew Stephen, the club's chairman, became chairman of the Football Association in January 1967. Two months earlier, general manager Eric Taylor had rejected the opportunity to become director-general of the North American Soccer League. Alas, in July 1967, Taylor narrowly escaped death in a car crash in which he was the innocent victim. He subsequently recovered sufficiently from serious injuries to resume his Hillsborough duties, but the accident left its mark on him.

4 1966 and all that

Wednesday knew well in advance that 1966 would be an important year for the club as well as for English football. For the first time, the World Cup finals were to be staged in England, and Hillsborough was one of the selected venues for the matches. Eric Taylor and his staff knew they were going to be very busy, the club's administrative resources put to the test. When Eric England said to Development Fund organiser, Derek Dooley, in the summer of 1965, "It'll be just like us to get to Wembley and win the FA Cup in this of all years", he could not have known how close to the truth he would be. Wednesday *did* get to Wembley, and though they didn't win the Cup, the excitement of that 1966 run helped to make it an unforgettable year in club history.

With the World Cup in view, the years following the completion of the new North Stand saw further ground improvements undertaken and the planning of extended facilities at Hillsborough. It is, incidentally, worth noting that when the North Stand had been planned, Eric Taylor had the foresight to fix on its roof exactly the number of flagpoles required for a World Cup venue! (The first man to notice this was Sir Stanley Rous on the day he visited the ground to open the stand). Main developments which followed included: conversion of the South Stand terracing to provide open seating for 3,310; building the £100,000 West Stand, containing 4,465 seats, at the Leppings Lane end of the ground; erection of a gymnasium behind the North Stand (it was used as a Press centre during the World Cup); and building a restaurant behind the main offices. In the year before the World Cup, some £250,000 was spent on improvements, with part of the cost offset by a Government grant made available to all the clubs whose grounds were to host fixtures on this important occasion.

The story of Wednesday's run to the FA Cup final of 1966 really begins nearly two years earlier, at the time Alan Brown took charge of playing affairs. The new manager's influence was quickly apparent, and his first season saw a number of changes, some of which were very significant in the long term. This campaign marked the end of the line for long-time regulars Tom McAnearney, the captain, and Alan Finney; while Holliday and Pearson also bowed from the scene. McAnearney was succeeded at right-half by Peter Eustace, while former Abbeydale Grammar schoolboy and Youth international Howard Wilkinson was tried in Finney's outside-right position in 14 games. Springett's one absence during the year provided a debut of historical interest, for his deputy, Peter Wicks, became the then youngest player ever to appear in the League side, being 16 years 247 days old when he faced Liverpool at Anfield on January 16 1965.

Vic Mobley, the blond giant who had made the centre-half spot his own, gained the first of his 13 England Under-23 caps, while Gerry Young's consistency finally earned him international recognition with a call into the England team for the match with Wales at Wembley in November. Soon afterwards Young had the misfortune to suffer an injury which kept him out of the Wednesday side for most of the second half of the season, costing him further honours; and his absence saw the introduction at left-half of 18-year-old Wilf Smith, a former Sheffield Boys and Yorkshire Schools player.

Perhaps one of the most significant of the early developments in Brown's first months took place in Denmark in late September: the captaincy changed hands at half-time in a friendly game with Aarhus GF. The Danes beat Wednesday 4-1, and, in the first-half especially, the Sheffielders were given a run-around. McAnearney was the victim of a youthful opponent, and came under fire in the half-time dressing room discussion. The upshot was that Brown threw the ball to Megson and told him to lead the side out for the second half. Megson led the side into the next League match, at Everton, and Eustace took over McAnearney's number four shirt.

Wednesday finished 1964-5 in eighth place. They lost only three

League matches at home, with a 5-1 defeat of Burnley (Fantham got a hat-trick) in September and a 5-2 win against Birmingham in October the biggest of 13 Hillsborough victories. But they struggled in away games, registering only three wins—at West Ham, Sheffield United and Blackburn. They conceded four goals at Liverpool, Burnley and Stoke; and it was to be significant that in the game at Stoke all the home side's goals were scored by John Ritchie.

Perhaps the most interesting switch made by Brown in this first season involved John Hickton, the Brimington, Chesterfield, product who had joined the club as a left-back. Hickton, now 20, had played twice in the first team at right-back in March 1964, but was the Central League side's centre-half. There were those who regarded Hickton, a strong, solidly-built young man good in the air, as the best centre-half on the club's books; and some considered him unlucky not to have been given the first chance to succeed Peter Swan. However, there were others who felt that the blond-haired Hickton could make the grade as a centre-forward. Derek Dooley was Hickton's keenest supporter. In the days of Harry Catterick, when Dooley had been looking after Wednesday's juniors, Hickton had been tried as leader of the attack, and the youngster had scored eight goals in one game and five in another. Significantly, though Hickton had now reverted to centre-half, he was the reserve team's leading scorer, largely because he often found the target with his head after moving into the attack for corner-kicks.

At the start of the season the versatile Johnny Quinn had worn the number nine shirt, but in late September it had passed to Derek Wilkinson. Then in early November, Hickton was brought in against Fulham, and he celebrated with a goal in a 1-1 draw. Hickton went on to score 10 goals in 26 outings that season; and only Fantham (whose 19 took him past a century of League goals) managed more.

Megson and Mobley were ever-presents in 1964-5, while Springett, Fantham and Dobson each missed only one game. Quinn made 40 appearances and Hill played 39 times at right-back. Springett and Hill were absent injured when Wednesday were put out of the FA Cup by Everton in a third-round replay which attracted a crowd of 50,080 to Hillsborough. A teenage back, Andy Burgin, had his first taste of top-class football in the two games with Harry Catterick's team.

★ ★ ★

At the start of the 1965-6 campaign, nobody could have predicted that the season would see Wednesday enjoy their best FA Cup run since 1935. A realist would have said the evidence indicated an ordinary year—which, indeed, is what it would have been but for the run of five away victories in the FA Cup.

In looking at this season, one needs to remember that it saw the introduction of the rule permitting substitutes, and also marked the beginning of a greater tactical awareness within the game. At the outset, the decision to permit substitutes limited their use to that of replacements for injured players; so in 1965 it could not really be said that League football had become a 12-man game. As for tactics, this was the year when we began to hear football people talking about back fours, midfielders and strikers. In the beginning, many spectators (and some football writers, too) were bemused by the new language of football. It was some time before the terms became familiar. In the context of the Wednesday story in this period, it is important to note that although Graham Pugh and Johnny Quinn took over the number seven and number eleven shirts respectively towards the end of 1965-6, they were *not* playing on the wings. They were the first of a new breed of midfielders.

Wednesday's only major signing in the 1965 close season was Brian Usher, the Sunderland winger. Ironically, perhaps, he was an early victim of Alan Brown's decision to adopt a 4-3-3 system. The other victims were Dobson, Brian Hill and Hickton. Hill lost his place at right-back to Smith, largely because Smith was not only a coming player but had the speed required of backs in the new era. The backs now became supplementary wingers in the sense that, when the team was pushing forward, they were expected to "overlap" down the flanks and cross the ball into the opposition goalmouth. Usher and Dobson were simply unlucky in that the new system dispensed with the old-fashioned winger, but both contributed to Wednesday's Cup run before losing out. Hickton's case was probably different in that, despite reasonable success, he still lacked the flair and consistency which were to become his hallmark after his move to Middlesbrough. Smith, Quinn, Pugh and Ford were all suited to the new pattern. Smith had defensive qualities and speed, and Ford was a quick, direct striker who at one stage promised to become a world-beater; while Quinn had the experience and adaptability which made him an ideal midfielder, and Pugh had the tenacity, the terrier-like qualities which ideally contrasted with the delicate styles of other youngsters like Eustace and McCalliog.

The introduction of these youngsters—Pugh was 18, McCalliog and Smith 19, and Eustace, Ford and Mobley 21—lent a certain impish zest to the side; and, bearing in mind that almost all the Cup rounds were played on heavy grounds, the team's qualities of youthfulness and boundless energy saw them through to Wembley. It was no small achievement that a side containing so much inexperience should reach the FA Cup final, but it is important to remember that the team's reputation was built on what it achieved in six matches—and the manner in which they slipped to defeat in the sixth match, at Wembley, after leading 2-0 served to indicate that, in reality, they still had much to learn. They deserved all the praise they got, but perhaps those who anticipated great things from them afterwards expected too much.

Wednesday kicked off 1965-6 with two home wins and three away defeats in their first five games; then, between mid-September and early November, won only one of eight matches. At the end of October, Brown made the signing which was probably the first important piece in the new tactical plan he was formulating: he acquired 19-year-old Chelsea inside-forward, Jim McCalliog. Few of the club's supporters had heard of the slim young Scot, which is hardly surprising for he had played in only three League games and a few League Cup ties for Chelsea, yet the fee Wednesday paid—£37,500—was at the time a British record for a teenage player. McCalliog was destined to make 150 League appearances and gain international honours in his four-season stay at Hillsborough, but he had several spells when he was unsettled; and he subsequently played with Wolves, Manchester United and Southampton. McCalliog made his debut at Aston Villa on the same day that David Ford was given his first full outing after having been substitute a week earlier. Significantly, perhaps, Ford and McCalliog were appearing together in the side for only the second time when Wednesday registered a notable victory at Tottenham on November 13. What made this 3-2 win worthy of special mention was that it was Wednesday's first away success for 10 months, and Tottenham's first home defeat after an unbeaten run of 34 matches.

Hickton regained his place at Ford's expense in December and January, and in that time brought his tally of goals for the season to 11; so that when he grabbed a fine hat-trick in the Christmas defeat of Arsenal, few could have foreseen that he would figure in only eight more first-team games. One of those eight games was the match which saw Wednesday begin their memorable run to Wembley—the third-round tie at Reading in late January, when Usher and Dobson were also on duty.

Wednesday did not go into that Cup duel at Elm Park with abundant confidence, for a visit to a Third Division ground is not the easiest of challenges at the best of times—and these were not the best of times for Don Megson and his men. Wednesday had won only one of their previous six matches, and their away form was considerably less than encouraging. In the event, they scrambled through thanks to a last-minute goal from Fantham. It was Fantham who had put them in front after 25 minutes, but Reading had battled bravely and equalised on the hour; and though McCalliog then headed his first goal for Wednesday, Reading had quickly pulled themselves level a second time.

It is said that there is a world of difference between the League and the Cup, and Wednesday provided an illustration of the truth of this in early February. When they visited Newcastle in a First Division match, they lost 0-2; but a week later they won 2-1 at the same ground in the FA Cup fourth round. This tie provided the first clue to Wednesday's stamina. It also gave supporters some indication of Alan Brown's thinking, for both Hill and Hickton were left out for this game, with Smith and Ford coming in.

Conditions at Newcastle were dreadful, but Wednesday overcame the snow and mud and survived a snowstorm to emerge triumphant. A speculative effort from Dobson put the Sheffielders in front after 25 minutes, and a few minutes later Megson hammered a free-kick hard and low into the Newcastle goalmouth, where home defender McGrath deflected the ball into his own net. Lucky? Perhaps. But Brown had had Megson and the others working on moves designed to exploit conditions and circumstances. Suddick got Newcastle's late consolation goal.

In the fifth round at Huddersfield, Wednesday were a goal down after less than a minute, and it was not until eight minutes into the second half that Ford snatched an equaliser. Ten minutes remained when Fantham provided the cross from which Usher scored the winner.

Without a home draw for five years, Wednesday hoped for a change of luck in the quarter-final. They didn't get it, and were paired with Blackburn at Ewood Park. This game saw Quinn make his first Cup appearance of the season, with Dobson, having previously missed only two matches all season, stepping down. McCalliog returned to the side after missing a couple of games through injury, and though the Scot was not fully fit, the gamble paid off. Conditions were again appalling, with the Blackburn pitch more suited to water-polo than soccer. Fantham was responsible for setting up Wednesday's first goal, scored after 11 minutes by Ford. Byrom equalised for Rovers on the half-hour, but nine minutes after the interval Wednesday went 2-1 up. The home goalkeeper stopped but could not hold a hard shot from Young, and Ford pounced to whack the loose ball into the net.

In the interval between the sixth round and the semi-final, Usher lost his place, and Graham Pugh, only six weeks past his 18th birthday, was thrust into the side. In the space of a few short months, Wednesday's team had been transformed; and when the semi-final draw paired Wednesday with Chelsea at Villa Park, the Sheffielders were not considered to have much chance against a team which contained many experienced stars and which had reached the penultimate stage of the competition a year earlier.

Geoffrey Green, football correspondent of *The Times,* described the Villa Park playing surface as "a black treacle pudding of a pitch". The conditions suited Wednesday better than their rivals, and Brown's instructions to keep play simple and straightforward paid off. Wednesday's 2-0 victory was little short of sensational. The main incident in a rather dull first half was a crunching clash between Vic Mobley and Chelsea's George Graham, with both players suffering painful injury. It was not until after the game that the extent of Mobley's injury was known: he played for 60 minutes with badly damaged ligaments in his right ankle. Substitutes were not permitted yet in the FA Cup. The big defender remained at centre-half until the interval, and spent the second-half hobbling at centre-forward.

It was in the 56th minute that Wednesday made the breakthrough. Again Fantham was the goal-maker, with his cross to the far post being headed back into the goalmouth by Ford. Mobley tried in vain to provide the finishing touch, but it was left to Pugh to celebrate his Cup debut with the goal which put Wednesday on the way to Wembley. A minute before the final whistle, McCalliog headed a second goal, the former Chelsea player adding a final touch of irony to a game in which the underdogs had enjoyed a magnificent triumph.

The only cloud on Wednesday's horizon in the three weeks before the Cup final clash with Everton was the injury to Mobley. It was quickly evident that the man who had been denied a full international cap a year earlier through injury was not going to be fit to play at Wembley. Mobley's misfortune provided a dream chance for 19-year-old Sam Ellis, a lanky red-haired defender in his first season as a professional. Ellis had at this point played in only four first-team games, but Brown made it plain that the lad from Ashton-under-Lyne was favourite to wear the number five shirt at Wembley. There were those who argued that Hickton, now back at centre-half in the reserves, was the best man for the job, but Brown had made up his mind.

However, before their date at Wembley, Wednesday had the not unimportant job of catching up on their League programme. In fact, they concluded their First Division season with only two wins in the last 10 games. Fortunately, those points were enough to keep them out of trouble. They finished with 36 points, while Northampton, with 33, were relegated at the same time as Blackburn Rovers.

The FA Cup final of 1966 has gone into the record books as one of the most exciting ever seen at Wembley. On paper, the experts believed there was only one team in it—Everton. But Alan Brown told his players: "You've no chance . . . of losing!" Wednesday's underdogs rose to the occasion in magnificent style, and for so long in an unforgettable game seemed destined to win. Then the great prize was snatched from their grasp suddenly and dramatically.

The team which Don Megson led onto the pitch on that sunny May afternoon included six players 21 or under. Two of the players, Pugh and Ellis had each made only nine senior appearances, with Ellis making his FA Cup debut; and Ford and McCalliog had both played in fewer than 30 first-team games. Wednesday's opponents just happened to be a club managed by ex-Hillsborough chief, Harry Catterick, who had built an experienced, talented and costly side. Everton played in their usual blue shirts and white shorts; Wednesday appeared in what had become their adopted Cup outfit, all white. The teams lined up:

Wednesday— Springett; Smith, Megson, Eustace, Ellis, G. Young, Pugh, Fantham, McCalliog, Ford, Quinn.

Everton— West; Wright, Wilson, Gabriel, Labone, Harris, Scott, Trebilcock, A. Young, Harvey, Temple.

Megson won the toss for choice of ends, the first Wednesday captain to do so in an FA Cup final since 1890—ironically, the only one of the club's previous four final appearances in which they had suffered defeat. Fortunately, none of the Sheffielders in the crowd was conscious of the fact, so nobody was troubling about proceedings having started with a possible ill-omen. After four minutes, no Wednesdayite in the 100,000 crowd cared tuppence for omens—for Wednesday had scored! Eustace took a throw-in on the left, Ford slipped the ball across to McCalliog, and the Scot saw his shot glance off Wilson's leg and spin into the net with goalkeeper West looking on in agonised helplessness. After that, Wednesday's narrowest escape was probably in the 18th minute when Alex Young crashed to the ground as Springett went to make a save. "Penalty!" yelled the Everton fans, but referee Jack Taylor took no notice.

Eleven minutes after half-time, Wednesday went 2-0 up. Alex Young was caught in possession, and Fantham powered away with the ball. As he neared goal, the Wednesday striker struck a hard shot. West stopped the ball but couldn't hold it. Ford dashed in and shot it into the net. Surely now the Cup was destined for Sheffield!

Within two minutes, however, Everton pulled one back. Gabriel

22. *F.A. Cup final team, 1966. . . (back row) Jim McCalliog, Peter Eustace, Ron Springett, Gerry Young, Sam Ellis, Wilf Smith; (front row) Graham Pugh, John Fantham, Don Megson (captain), David Ford, Johnny Quinn.*

flighted the ball into the Sheffield penalty area, Temple got his head to it and set up a chance for Mike Trebilcock. The young Cornishman, a late and controversial choice in place of Pickering, hit the ball first time . . . and it squeezed past Springett. Six minutes later, Eustace conceded a free-kick, unluckily thought some. Scott punted the ball into the goalmouth, it came out again, but only as far as Trebilcock. He shot, somehow the ball swerved through the gap between the players, the net bulged . . . Everton, incredibly, were level!

But the cruellest blow was still to come. It arrived in the 73rd minute. Everton skipper, Brian Labone, hit a long ball out of defence. No danger. Gerry Young had it covered, and it was poised to fall on his good left foot. In the same situation hundreds of times before, the ever-dependable defender had always trapped the ball easily and safely. This time he trapped a ball that wasn't there: for some inexplicable reason, the ball eluded his boot and bounced past him. The hand of fate was at work. Temple now pounced on the ball and sped forward. Seconds later the Mersey roar burst forth as Temple's shot hit the net. The Cup was bound for Goodison Park.

Poor Gerry Young! He lay full length on the Wembley turf, a picture of dejection. Later Alan Brown consoled him: "It's the sort of thing that could have happened to anybody." Years after the event, Young had learned to live with the memory of that single mistake. "It was still a great experience to have played in the match," he said. "I'll remember the occasion as long as I live, and, as for Everton's third goal, it was fate."

"Yes," said John Fantham, "it was fate. Cup finals are all about your name being on that trophy. Our name was never on it, even when we led 2-0. Everton might have looked a beaten side at one stage, but once the tide turned everything dropped perfectly for Everton. I've studied that match on film many times, and I'm convinced the fates were on their side not ours. The two goals by Trebilcock came from snap shots which went in. In each instance, if the ball had been placed a foot further to the left or to the right, Springett would have got his hand to it, or it would have gone past the post. And as for Temple's winner, it had to be fate. The ball was falling on Gerry's best foot, but I'm convinced that Temple knew he was going to miss it. When Temple came running in, he knew he wasn't near enough to make a challenge. Normally in that situation a forward will hesitate and slow down almost unconsciously. But Temple simply kept going. He *knew* what was going to happen. And when it happened, he was there. He shot from 20 yards when many players would have gone closer, and, just as he was ready to shoot, the ball lifted slightly and he was able to strike it just right."

To have fallen to defeat after having had one hand on the Cup was a shattering experience for the Wednesday men, but, at Megson's call, they rallied round, lifted their heads and urged their weary limbs on a lap of honour round the stadium—the first time a losing side had ever done that.

On the day after the game, the players returned to Sheffield and were given an astonishing welcome by their supporters and the people of Sheffield. The players were applauded and cheered as they passed through the city centre poised on the roof of a bus; and later, speaking from the Town Hall balcony, Megson vowed: "We'll bring the Cup back next time." Nobody doubted him at that moment, but, sadly, the passing of the years did not see fate decree that Wednesday's name would be written on the most coveted trophy in football—a trophy made little more than a couple of hundred yards from the balcony upon which Megson and his colleagues stood that Sunday afternoon.

In 1965-6 Wednesday's season ticket sales had been down slightly on the previous year, but, thanks to the FA Cup run, match receipts and average attendances improved as the year progressed. Then, naturally, 1966-7 brought a substantial increase in season ticket sales, and the average League gate climbed from just over 22,000 to over 30,000. Even so, Wednesday reported a loss at the annual meeting of 1967. The club's wage bill had gone up by £14,000, and total expenditure had risen by £58,000; but the loss was largely due to a £60,000 deficit on transfers. Six months after the Cup final Wednesday had paid a club record fee of £70,000 for John Ritchie.

Wednesday began the 1966-7 campaign with promise, remaining unbeaten in their first seven games. However, between September 3 and December 17, they managed only two victories in 17 League matches. The post-Wembley honeymoon was over. Ironically, Wednesday's first defeat of the season came in the club's first-ever League Cup tie, a home fixture with Second Division Rotherham United, at the time managed by former Hillsborough coach Jack Mansell. A late goal by Frank Casper KO'd Brown's men. Four days later West Ham came to Sheffield and won 2-0. Two other matches played in the early weeks of this season merit a mention for historical reasons. On September 24 Wednesday and United met in the 200th Sheffield derby, a game in which Fantham was making his 300th League appearance, and a crowd of 43,557 saw the teams share a 2-2 draw. A week later, at Southampton, Wednesday lost 2-4, but one of their goals, converted by Eustace, earned a place in the records because it came from the first penalty awarded to the team in 81 games.

In September Alan Brown transferred John Hickton to Middlesbrough for £20,000. 'Boro manager, Stan Anderson—he had been captain under Brown at Sunderland—actually signed Hickton as a centre-half, but it wasn't to be long before he converted his new player into a centre-forward; and Hickton was destined to score more than 200 goals for Middlesbrough. Derek Dooley urged Brown not to part with Hickton, and, indeed, some years later Dooley was to offer the Teesside club £80,000 for his former junior—but by then he was regarded as beyond price.

The irony of Hickton's departure was that, two months later, in November 1966, Wednesday paid a record fee to Stoke City for John Ritchie in the hope that he would solve the club's centre-forward problem. Ritchie, tall, and built like a guardsman, had scored 64 goals in 110 League appearances for Stoke. He was to score 34 in 88 League matches for Wednesday, plus 10 in the FA Cup and one in the League Cup. His former club eventually bought him back for £25,000.

Ritchie made his debut at Manchester United, but had played in seven games before he had the satisfaction of finishing on the winning side. However, he helped Wednesday end 1966 in fine style with two goals in a 6-1 defeat of Chelsea on New Year's Eve. Ford (2), Fantham and McCalliog got the other goals.

Having won only five of their first 21 games, Wednesday won nine of the second 21. It was hardly a sensational record, but a number of successes hinted that they were capable of touching the heights, and, on their day, could be quite brilliant. In addition to the defeat of Chelsea, notable triumphs included a 4-1 win against Southampton (Fantham hit a hat-trick), a 5-0 defeat of Sunderland, and a 7-0 crushing of Burnley. Ford claimed his first hat-trick against Burnley, but the feature of the game was the introduction of another youngster, Jack Whitham, who made his debut in the role of substitute and scored twice.

Inevitably, Wednesday's return to the FA Cup was awaited with eager anticipation. The third round brought them a home tie with Queen's Park Rangers, and a crowd of over 40,000 turned up for the game—before which, incidentally, a new mascot, Ozzie Owl, was launched. The match brought the Springett brothers, Ron and Peter, up against each other, and gave Hillsborough supporters their first sight of Peter, who was destined to join Wednesday the following May. However, on that January day in 1967 Peter had the disappointment of conceding three goals while

Ron kept a blank scoresheet. John Ritchie scored all Wednesday's goals.

Mansfield Town provided the opposition in the fourth round, and a remarkable (or so it seems these many years later) crowd of 49,000 packed into Hillsborough to see Wednesday win 4-0. Ritchie bagged two goals, with Fantham and McCalliog getting the others. Ron Springett missed this game, and 16-year-old Gary Scothorn, a product of Hoyland, was given an unexpected first-team baptism.

Wednesday were through to the last 16 of the FA Cup, but all was not as well as it might have been in the Hillsborough camp. Injuries to Pugh and Eustace had affected the team's rhythm, and now Gerry Young was out for a long spell with damaged ligaments. It was at this point that Alan Brown decided the time was ripe for a clean sweep in the dressing room, and David Smith, Tommy Walker and Johnny Logan were dismissed from the coaching staff. Jack Marshall, who had recently quit as manager of Blackburn Rovers, returned to Sheffield as Brown's assistant; and, subsequently, Lawrie McMenemy and Ian McFarlane were recruited to the staff. McMenemy, who was later to acquire an outstanding reputation in the game as Southampton's manager, had only limited experience at the time he joined Wednesday: the ex-Guardsman had been working in a local government office in Gateshead while acting as part-time manager of Bishop Auckland. McFarlane was also destined to achieve a fair measure of success in League management: a former Leicester City and Chelsea defender, the big Scot had been connected with Bath City prior to joining Wednesday.

When Wednesday visited Norwich City in the FA Cup fifth round, they enjoyed a comfortable 3-1 win, with Quinn, Ford and Fantham the marksmen. Now the quarter-final brought the Sheffielders a pairing with Chelsea at Stamford Bridge. The Londoners, defeated by Wednesday in the previous year's semi-final and hammered 6-1 in the League in December, finally got their revenge—they KO'd Don Megson and his men with a last-minute goal.

Wednesday lost only two of their remaining seven League games after the Cup exit: it was not an especially auspicious finale, apart from the 7-0 win against Burnley, but the points enabled them to finish up in the respectable safety of mid-table.

Megson alone had played in every match, though Ellis and Smith had each been absent only once, while Ford and McCalliog had missed two and three games respectively. Eustace, however, had played in only 23 matches, and Pugh in 29; and while such youngsters as Symm, Branfoot and Whitham had shown promise, it was evident that Wednesday were still a long way from being more than just a good, hardworking side capable of occasional bursts of brilliance.

This season had seen Mobley recover from the injury which had kept him out of the 1966 Cup final, and the form of the hefty Oxford product earned him a place on the England Under-23 summer tour. David Ford, slight and speedy and already building up a good understanding with Ritchie, had also gained representative honours with two England Under-23 caps; while McCalliog, a clever player whose apparently casual style was deceptive, had earned himself a slice of club history. The dark-haired forward gained his first Under-23 cap in November, and in April was chosen to play for Scotland against England at Wembley—the first Wednesday man to win a Scottish cap for 47 years.

An off-the-field event of great significance in club history had come in January when Wednesday chairman, Dr. Andrew Stephen, now 60 and retired from medical practice at Wisewood, followed in the footsteps of Sir Charles Clegg and was elected chairman of the Football Association. Dr. Stephen had only accepted the chairman's job at Hillsborough with great reluctance, yet now the quietly-spoken Scot found himself in the game's top post. He always said that he owed his progress to the encouragement and tuition of Eric Taylor. Sadly, within barely six months, Stephen's aide, mentor and friend had become the victim of a cruel twist of fate, and the new FA chairman dashed home from a foreign tour on England duty to be at the general-manager's bedside.

✱ ✱ ✱

Wednesday's centenary in September 1967 came in the middle of a 10-month period which was one of the most significant phases in the club's history, and it is probably fair to suggest that some of the things which happened then could later be seen as pointers to the start of the decline which followed in subsequent years.

However, there was still an air of optimism about at Hillsborough in late May when Alan Brown negotiated the unique deal which saw the Springett brothers switch clubs. Ron, who had gained the last of his 33 England caps in October 1965, returned to QPR after nine years with Wednesday; while Peter, aged 21 and regarded as one of the most promising goalkeepers in the game, had played in 139 League matches for QPR, and had just helped the London club win the Football League Cup and the Third Division championship.

Six weeks after this signing had made the headlines on the back pages of the newspapers, Eric Taylor was the subject of a news story which dominated the front pages—having been the victim of a car crash which had occurred as he was driving to the ground from his Fulwood home. Taylor, aged 55, was lucky to escape with his life, emerging from the wreckage with serious injuries, including extensive burns, broken ribs and a badly damaged right hand. The accident was a psychological as well as a heavy physical blow to the general-manager, and he needed to draw deep upon his resources of courage and humour in the struggle towards recovery. He retained his sharp wit and determination after his eventual return to work, but this brush with fate wrought a subtle change in his personality. One immediate effect of Taylor's absence was that Wednesday's 100th anniversary passed with little celebration, although the club did mark the occasion by allowing spectators half-price admission for the home game with Fulham on September 6.

Wednesday began the 1967-8 season with three victories, and, indeed, won five of their first six games, with Ritchie getting seven goals. One of his goals gave Wednesday a 1-0 victory at Sheffield United—only their second League triumph at Bramall Lane since 1933. After starting the campaign as the First Division pacemakers, the Owls remained in the top three until November. By then they had suffered another major blow, for, in September, David Ford was injured in a car crash, and so joined Pugh on the sidelines.

Early in this season Smith, too, had a spell on the injured list, and his absence led to Quinn being switched into the number two shirt. Quinn, versatile and ever-loyal, found himself out of the side when Smith returned; and, at his own request, was placed on the transfer list. He did not remain on the list long, for, within a few days in that November, he was snapped up by new Rotherham United manager, Tommy Docherty. At Millmoor they certainly appreciated their new man, and an appropriate current pop hit "The Mighty Quinn" became Rotherham's theme song. Docherty paid £27,000 and got the bargain of the season.

Gloom began to gather over Hillsborough towards the end of 1967. After beating Southampton on November 4, Wednesday won only three of their next 27 League matches. Yet it was not until Boxing Day that they finally surrendered their unbeaten home record: and it took a controversial penalty from Johnny Giles to give Leeds the distinction of ending the run.

It was in the middle of this disappointing spell that John Fantham established a new post-war League scoring record for the club. Having equalled Redfern Froggatt's tally of 140 with a goal in the 4-2 defeat of West Ham in mid-December, Fantham finally scored goal number 141 on January 6 when the visitors were Sheffield United. The goal came in the 54th minute, but, unfortunately, it did not give Wednesday victory; for, soon afterwards, Mick Hill pulled United level.

Fantham was on target again in the next game, a home clash with Spurs notable not because the Londoners registered their first League victory at Hillsborough since 1937, but for the debut in the Spurs side of Martin Chivers, newly signed for what was then a record £125,000 fee. Chivers had the satisfaction of scoring the winning goal four minutes from the end.

Wednesday again failed to make much impression in the League Cup. Starting with a 5-3 victory at Stockport, they struggled before overcoming Barrow in the third-round match at Hillsborough. Fantham (2) and McCalliog got the goals in a 3-1 victory. Wednesday went out at Stoke in the next round, having first shared a 0-0 draw with them at home.

The FA Cup brought Wednesday a home third-round tie with Second Division Plymouth, and goals by Whitham, Fantham and Ritchie (penalty) saw them safely through. However, before the fourth-round clash with Swindon Town was played, important developments had occurred behind the scenes at Hillsborough.

On Saturday February 3, Sunderland came to Sheffield, and, thanks to a goal by Brand, beat Wednesday 1-0 to register their first victory for three months. Five days later, Sunderland sacked their manager, Ian McColl; and Alan Brown asked Wednesday for his release. At the moment of making his dismissal from the Roker club public, McColl named his successor as Brown. However, when reporters gathered at the Brown family home at Bents Green that same evening, Brown insisted that he knew nothing about the Sunderland vacancy. The next day—surprise, surprise—Brown was formally installed at Roker, beginning his second spell with them.

Jack Marshall, who had just moved into a new house in Sheffield, suddenly and unexpectedly, found himself acting team-manager. "Alan had said nothing to me to indicate that he was about to leave," Marshall recalled. "Of course, I had heard on the grapevine that things were about to happen at Sunderland, and Alan's name had been mentioned. But he didn't tell me he was going there until the day his appointment was announced."

Marshall's first match in charge was the FA Cup-tie with Swindon Town, managed by Danny Williams. A goal down at half-time, Wednesday hit back to win 2-1 with goals by Wilf Smith and Ritchie. By the time of the quarter-final games with Chelsea, Eric Taylor had returned from convalescing in the West Indies and Marshall had been formally appointed as team-manager. A crowd of 49,186 saw Chelsea recover to earn a 2-2 draw at Hillsborough; and goals by Osgood and Tambling gave the Londoners victory in the Stamford Bridge replay.

At the time of Brown's departure, Wednesday had 25 points from 27 games. They collected only nine points from their remaining 15 First Division matches, with only two victories—at Stoke and Wolverhampton. Finishing the campaign with 34 points, they ended up in 19th place. Their city rivals, Sheffield United, were relegated with 32 points. The season had also been an eventful, indeed traumatic, one for the Bramall Lane club; for they had sold two of their young stars, Mick Jones and Alan Birchenall, for £100,000 each. Birchenall, who had previously excelled in Sheffield derby games, was in the Chelsea side which put Wednesday out of the FA Cup. When United went down after losing five of their last seven games, John Harris handed over his team-management duties to Arthur Rowley, but the man who later became Wednesday's assistant manager still had an important part to play in the Sheffield United story.

5 The dark years: 1968-1977

No period in the history of Sheffield Wednesday can quite compare with the years from 1968 to 1977 in terms of dramatic decline, deep depression and desperate despair. The ten years which followed the departure of Alan Brown were tense and traumatic, and Hillsborough was shrouded in almost continuous gloom. In the following pages the spotlight falls on the phase which began on the day Brown walked out in February 1968 and ended when Jack Charlton strode into the manager's office early in October 1977—a span of nine years and eight months—and it is, perhaps, appropriate to begin by noting some of the broad facts of this troubled and sometimes bitter period.

During these years Wednesday suffered a number of unfortunate and embarrassing Cup setbacks—against the likes of Exeter, Bournemouth and Scunthorpe, to name just three—and these served to underline the downward trend. A top club will often fall to a Fourth Division club—once; but not three or four times in the space of a few years.

However, of much greater significance was the manner in which the club slumped from the respectability of a comfortable place in Division One to the foot of the Third Division—with the abyss of Division Four looming dangerously close. The bare facts are that Wednesday were relegated from the First Division in 1970, lost their Second Division status in 1975, and went frighteningly close to becoming a Fourth Division club in 1976, when only a last-match victory kept them in the Third Division. In this dark decade, Wednesday played a total of 411 League matches, of which they won only 113 and collected 342 points out of a possible 822. In 1969-70 they managed only eight League victories, and in 1974-5 a mere five.

It is impossible to convey the sense of hurt that dedicated Wednesdayites felt in these years, or to measure the frustrations and baffled disbelief which those most closely involved in the club's affairs endured during a decline which at one stage seemed never-ending. Wednesday's average home gate in 1967-8 was just under 32,000, and by 1976-7 had fallen to 13,600, having been as low as 11,000 a year earlier. Only the brave and the fiercely loyal stayed with the club throughout those painful years, but a hard core of supporters never lost hope; and, remarkably, despite all the gloom, a new generation of Wednesdayites, too young to remember the brighter days of the early 1960s, came along to cheer . . . and to dream of a time when they might see the club back at the top.

After Brown, Wednesday hired—and subsequently fired—five managers in less than 10 years: Jack Marshall, Danny Williams, Derek Dooley, Steve Burtenshaw and Len Ashurst. As a group they had little in common in terms of personality, background or philosophy; but each in turn failed to guide the club back into the First Division. In fact, each man in some way contributed to changes which created the circumstances from which the eventual revival stemmed; and, if one remembers that success sometimes has to be assessed in direct relation to what happens immediately before and after a particular phase, it is fair to suggest that some managers in this period were more successful than others. All the managers brought their own training staffs, so that perhaps a dozen coaches parade across the stage during the drama of these years; and, as for players, they came and they went, and while some proved costly failures, some left their mark and are still remembered with affection.

Not surprisingly, the club's decline had its effect in the boardroom, where there were wholesale changes in the mid-1970s. The key dates in this respect were December 1973 and September 1975: the first being the time when Sir Andrew Stephen and Keith Gardiner, chairman and vice-chairman, resigned. It was then that Matt Sheppard became chairman, a position which he subsequently handed over to Bert McGee 21 months later when he took on the vice-chairman's role.

It was soon after the end of Sir Andrew Stephen's long term as chairman that Eric Taylor announced his retirement after 45 years' service. Sadly, indeed tragically, he died in the following September. His successor as secretary was Eric England, who had been with the club since October 1936 and who had seen much change in his 37 years at Hillsborough. The new secretary was to see much more change in the next few years, but with Eric England in charge of administration Wednesday knew that they had a man with the knowledge and experience to ensure that consistency was maintained in the day-to-day running of the club throughout the turmoil which was a necessary prelude to a revival of playing fortunes.

✱ ✱ ✱

"Jolly" Jack Marshall's reign lasted barely 13 months, and in that time the team-manager's crown sat uneasily on his head. The 51-year-old Boltonian, a straightforward and likeable man, knew what he wanted, but found the gulf between theory and practice, the dream and the reality, difficult to bridge. It was a tough and painful phase for a man who was not unfamiliar with the frustrations of professional football.

The son of Scottish-born parents who had settled in Lancashire before the Great War, he might have become a poultry farmer had he not made the grade as a full-back with Burnley before the war; and, when injury ended his playing days at 28, he might have settled to life in an engineering works had Bury manager, Bert Head, not brought him back into the game as a trainer. Having managed Rochdale and Blackburn before returning to Sheffield as Brown's assistant, he was not unaware of the size of the task now facing him.

Marshall's first major decision was to throw out the 4-3-3 system and replace it with the more positive 4-2-4. A commendable philosophy in theory proved extremely hard to convert into practice with the desired results. In truth, the old system suited the talents of the available players, while the new required the acquisition of two top quality forwards to fill the wing positions if it were to prove successful; and, at a time of limited financial resources, men of the right calibre could not be bought cheaply. Marshall tried unsuccessfully to get Nottingham Forest winger Barry Lyons, but Lyons rejected the proposed £50,000 move. In the end, Archie Irvine, an unproved youngster who had been a part-timer with Airdrie, arrived at a cost of £24,000; but while Irvine may have qualified as a winger he lacked experience and was unable to establish himself in the top grade. Later, another youngster, Brian Woodall, showed a brief flash of promise; and Jack Whitham returned, emerging as leading scorer with 10 goals, all of which were notched in his first 11 appearances before he found himself confined to the sidelines for 14 weeks with an injury. When Marshall originally adopted 4-2-4, inside-forwards Ford and Fantham were placed on the flanks; but their effectiveness was lessened by their use in unaccustomed roles. Overall, the team's positive tactical framework produced few dividends, for they failed to score in 18 games. Fantham managed only four goals all season, Ford claimed only three, and Ritchie, who became increasingly unsettled as the year wore on, finished with six.

To add to the problems, Marshall's year at the helm coincided with a growing sense of disenchantment among certain players. Mobley, Ellis, Eustace, McCalliog and Ritchie all submitted transfer requests; and the unrest marked the beginning of a period when the club began to lose its sense of purpose, with the seeds of destruction unwittingly sown in the first two years or so after Alan Brown's departure. Mobley and McCalliog were the only ever-presents in 1968-9, and Springett was absent just once; but Megson missed 10 games and Fantham 15, and, towards the end of the campaign, there was a hint that some of the more experienced players were out of favour, with Megson, Fantham and Eustace all dropped into the reserves for one match in April. Incidentally, Smith's form gained him a place in the Football League XI, and Eustace got the call from Sir Alf Ramsey, who brought the Wednesday midfielder into the England squad before the Rumanian international in January. Unfortunately, Eustace ended one of his most successful runs himself when he damaged a knee while skiing on the slopes of Stocksbridge during the heavy snow of February.

The season also brought changes in the training staff. In October, Tom McAnearney quit as player-manager of Aldershot and returned to Sheffield as Marshall's assistant. At the end of November, Lawrie McMenemy left to begin a management career which would take him to Doncaster Rovers, Grimsby and Southampton. At the end of the season Ian McFarlane also moved on.

If the 1968-9 campaign turned sour towards the end, it certainly began well enough, for Wednesday lost only one of their first eight League matches and just two of their first 13. However, it was in this period that the team touched the extremes of success and failure, scaling the heights with a brilliant performance and plummetting to the depths with a shattering and embarrassing defeat—all in the space of four days.

On the last Saturday in August, a 51,931 crowd basked in the sunshine, and Hillsborough presented a magnificent setting for what has been described as "a match of a lifetime", with Wednesday recovering from a 2-4 deficit to beat European champions Manchester United 5-4. Ironically, Marshall was not present, being in hospital recovering from an appendicitis operation. Whitham shot Wednesday in front after only two minutes, but, thanks to the brilliance of Best and Law, United led 2-1 by the 12th minute. Ritchie got a second goal for the home side, but Law and Bobby Charlton made it 4-2 to United by the 37th minute. Then, just before the interval, Whitham pulled one back for Wednesday. In the second half, United's Nobby Stiles headed the ball into his own net—one of the most remarkable own-goals seen in years, for there was not a home player near him; and, finally, after 70 minutes, Whitham completed his hat-trick when he scored the winning goal. "For sheer excitement," said Eric Taylor, "I doubt if there's been a game like that at Hillsborough since 1920, when England beat Scotland 5-4 after trailing by two goals."

Alas, Wednesday followed this great occasion with a defeat which was one of the season's biggest shocks: they crashed out of the League Cup at Exeter. The Fourth Division side won 3-1, and it was a red-faced Sheffield party which returned from Devon. To add to the woe, Ritchie suffered a knee injury which was to keep him out for a long spell; though his absence provided Alan Warboys, a big striker signed from Doncaster in the summer, with the chance to make his First Division bow.

(Incidentally, Usher had gone to Belle Vue in the Warboys deal).

The Manchester United game apart, the match most readily associated with Wednesday's 1968-9 campaign was the third-round FA Cup replay at Leeds in January. At the time Leeds were the Cup favourites, having reached the semi-finals three times in the previous four seasons. In the first match, at Hillsborough, a Lorimer penalty after 16 minutes seemed to signal the end for Megson and co.; but, just before half-time, goalkeeper Sprake misjudged a Ritchie shot and the scores were level. Wednesday then had the best of the second period, but could not turn their pressure to advantage. The Elland Road replay had only been in progress eight minutes when Johannesson put Leeds in front; but Woodall, making his Cup debut in place of the injured Ford, got the equaliser after 36 minutes, then had the delight of shooting Wednesday in front four minutes after half-time. Ritchie later made the score 3-1. Eustace was outstanding in a magnificent team performance. Unfortunately, Wednesday bowed from the Cup at the next stage. Twice behind in the home tie with Birmingham, they earned a replay only thanks to a splendid second equaliser shot from 35 yards by Gerry Young. Birmingham won the replay 2-1.

Meanwhile, Wednesday were struggling in the League. After winning at Wolves on December 23, they failed to win any of their next six games; and on March 1 Arsenal came to Sheffield and won 5-0. It was barely a fortnight after this defeat that Marshall learned that his contract would not be renewed when it expired at the end of the season. He promptly resigned. The players were away at Lilleshall, in the charge of Tom McAnearney; and a telephone call from Eric Taylor informed the 36-year-old Scot of developments. McAnearney, who only a few years earlier had been playing alongside the likes of Fantham, Eustace and Megson, found himself "the boss"—acting team-manager.

The last weeks of the season were not without incident, with local youngster Kenny Burton getting the chance to stake a claim for Megson's left-back position, and former Don & Dearne schoolboy Mick Prendergast making his League debut in place of Ritchie. Wednesday collected only five points from their last 10 matches, and perhaps the most significant development of the tail-end of the season was the signing of Tommy Craig for £100,000 from Aberdeen. Craig, 18, had played in some 60 Scottish League games, and his club's manager, Eddie Turnbull, described him as a midfielder with a brilliant future. When the red-haired Scot made his debut in Wednesday's final match against Tottenham in May, his fellow-countryman, Jim McCalliog, was making his final appearance; and by the time the next season began, would be wearing the colours of Wolves. Ritchie, substitute in that Spurs game, also departed in the summer of 1969, rejoining Stoke. With McCalliog sold for £70,000 and Ritchie for £25,000, Craig's fee was virtually recouped. Now the scene was set for the arrival of Danny Williams . . . and what a time of change Danny's era was to prove to be!

✽ ✽ ✽

The match in which Tommy Craig made his Wednesday debut, against Spurs on May 12, should have been played two months earlier, on March 15; and, had snow not caused a postponement, the game would have been Jack Marshall's last before he learned that his contract was not being renewed. Yet, if that March day in 1969 went down as a blank on the Wednesday calendar, it was not a date without some significance in the club's story: for their immediate future was probably influenced by the result of an event taking place 160 miles away at Wembley on that day—the League Cup final. In a game which went into extra time, Third Division Swindon Town beat First Division Arsenal 3-1. A few weeks later the Wiltshire club won promotion from the Third Division, finishing in runners-up spot behind Watford. Their manager was a 45-years-old former Rotherham United favourite called Danny Williams.

As a youngster, Thrybergh-born Williams had spent five years as a pit-top worker at Silverwood Colliery, and might have remained there but for his emergence during the war years as a promising footballer. Reg Freeman took him to Millmoor, and Williams, a positive, energetic and instinctive wing-half who preferred attack to defence, went on to play in more than 620 first-team games for Rotherham. He was in his 38th year when he finally hung up his boots and succeeded Tom Johnstone as the club's manager in July 1962. He remained in the job until February 1965, when he quit and retired to Bournemouth. That happy-go-lucky Danny could contemplate retirement at such an early age said much about the man and his nature. Though he had passed most of his years as a player in the era of the maximum wage, he had saved his money and invested it wisely; and, with a thriving sports outfitter's business, hardly needed to depend upon football management for a living. However, his retirement lasted barely four months. Swindon sought his services, and Williams couldn't resist the challenge. With some astute buying and selling, he soon built a strong and successful side, and the team's double League Cup and promotion triumph in 1968-9 brought fame to Swindon and made Danny a kind of folk hero. As a manager, he appeared to have a magic touch: and the fact that he could laugh and joke and succeed with such apparent ease, while remaining the same ordinary, down-to-earth and simple-living South Yorkshireman he had always been, lent a note of character and colour to the image.

What Swindon had done under the management of Williams had not gone unnoticed in his native South Yorkshire, especially at Sheffield Wednesday. The Wiltshire club's success touched a peak just at the moment when Wednesday were at their lowest ebb for years. The Hillsborough club had received over 100 applications for the vacant team-manager's job, but the Wednesday board decided that the situation demanded a bold gesture and an appointment which would capture public imagination. They came to the conclusion that the man who could turn the tide was Danny Williams. The first thing Williams knew about it was when he received a telephone call from Eric Taylor. Clearance was obtained from Swindon, and Dr. Andrew Stephen and vice-chairman Keith Gardiner travelled to Wiltshire to discuss the matter. Danny agreed to move back to South Yorkshire. When the appointment was announced, he told reporters: "Wednesday made me an offer I couldn't refuse."

On the face of it, Wednesday had pulled off a major coup in acquiring the services of a successful manager who was a well-known name and a popular personality. Unfortunately, as soon became evident, Danny Williams was no wonder man and was unable to repeat in the First Division what he had achieved in the Third. He remained at Hillsborough only 18 months, and in that time Wednesday's slide did not merely continue but accelerated as they tumbled into the Second Division for the first time in 11 years. Williams transformed the team, parting with 13 players and acquiring nine; and his only consolation was that he made a profit of not far short of £200,000 on the deals. In his defence it seems only fair to note that he argued that he could not make a profit in the transfer market *and* build a team, as, he claimed, he was expected to do.

At Swindon, Williams had had charge of a settled side in unpretentious circumstances, and the benefit of a well-organised staff and a team-spirit which enabled him to make the best use of what he always regarded as his limited talents and abilities. The Swindon team comprised men who played for each other and refused to carry passengers: as someone close to the club said "The lads did all the talking for Danny with what they achieved on the field." At Hillsborough, Williams was given his first taste of life at the top, and he had the misfortune to find himself facing circumstances which exposed him to difficulties he was ill-equipped to overcome. Life in the top grade with a successful team is one thing, but it's something quite different when the team is struggling. He took over a team in decline, a club troubled by unrest and a lack of spirit and discipline both in the dressing room and on the field. It did not take him long to recognise that he was a manager with many problems.

Wednesday lost their first three games of the 1969-70 campaign, won the next two, but then managed only two victories in the following 25—and after 30 League matches they had a paltry 15 points. They picked up only 10 more points in the remaining 12 games, and were relegated with Sunderland at the end of the club's worst season for 50 years. To add insult to injury, they were also dumped out of the League Cup by a Third Division club, Bournemouth; and a Fourth Division club, Scunthorpe United, delivered the KO blow in the fourth round of the FA Cup. Against Bournemouth in September, Wednesday had at one stage led 1-0 in the home match, but an own-goal by Ellis took the tie to a replay; and at Dean Court the Sheffield side never recovered after conceding an eighth-minute goal. The FA Cup clash with Scunthorpe was nothing less than a disaster, for Wednesday led with a Whitham goal after only four minutes, but let Barker and Cassidy notch the goals which put the Lincolnshire club in the fifth round.

At the time of his arrival, Williams learned that Ritchie had returned to Stoke, and McCalliog, having rejected a move to Birmingham, was poised to join Wolves; while Mobley, Smith and Eustace were unsettled and anxious to leave. Mobley was sold to Queen's Park Rangers for £55,000 in early October, and, soon afterwards, Fantham's 13 years at

Hillsborough came to an end when he was transferred to his father's old club, Rotherham United, for a bargain £5,000. In December Ford moved to Newcastle, and Irvine and Branfoot left for Doncaster, with Eustace joining West Ham for £90,000 a few days after Christmas. The Cup defeat by Scunthorpe marked the end of Megson's long run in the first team, and in March he was granted a free transfer to enable him to join Bristol Rovers.

Williams sought to re-shape the team by making a number of signings. In October he acquired Tony Coleman, the former Tranmere, Preston and Doncaster winger, who had played 77 times in Manchester City's League side; and Bill Lawson, a young winger, cost £4,000 from Brechin. Jackie Sinclair, a 26-year-old Scottish-born outside-right, formerly with Leicester, arrived from Newcastle in exchange for Ford in December; and around the same time Harold Wilcockson, a former Hillsborough Boys product who had made over 100 League appearances for Rotherham, was obtained from Doncaster Rovers in exchange for Irvine and Branfoot. Just before Christmas, Rotherham manager, Jim McAnearney, was persuaded to part with 20-year-old Steve Downes, who had scored 22 goals in 63 games, for £38,000. At this time, Downes, a slim, confident young man, was getting a lot of publicity, and being tipped for a great future. Williams had not seen him play, but was convinced by the opinion of members of his scouting staff. The Scunthorpe debacle cost Springett his place, and Williams went out and paid £30,000 for Nottingham Forest's long-serving former England Under-23 goalkeeper, Peter Grummitt.

Danny Williams was an eminently likeable, even loveable character, but he was no psychologist. In his first League match as Wednesday's manager, he quickly recognised the team's shortcomings as FA Cup holders Manchester City swept them aside and coasted to a 4-1 victory. Typically, perhaps, the ever-open, honest Williams admitted in a television interview: "I've only got six good players." It was not a remark geared to raise morale in the dressing room.

Wednesday's decline was swift and seemingly unstoppable. The men Williams bought failed to inspire a revival. Somehow, the signing of Downes in late December epitomised the manager's frustrations. Downes marked his debut with a memorable goal against Sunderland, and Wednesday enjoyed their first win in 13 games; but the youngster failed to score again all season and lost his place after seven games. He did return at a later stage, but injuries pushed him back into the shadows. The idea behind the signing of Wilcockson was to release Smith to add some sting in midfield, but Smith was soon switched to left-back to replace Megson. Williams was not happy with Craig's early form, and the youngster found life at the wrong end of the First Division a great ordeal after success in Scottish League football.

Despite the fact that they dropped into bottom place in the table in late November and then lost six of their next nine games, Wednesday were still not without hope of escaping relegation as the season moved into the later stages. Three successive victories in late February and early March—inspired by the return of Ellis, Young and Warboys—lifted them out of the bottom two for the first time since October. Unfortunately, they then went into a run of eight matches from which they collected a mere four points—yet, astonishingly, they reached the last match of the season still capable of avoiding the drop.

In the last weeks of the campaign, Wednesday seemed fated to fail. In March they won home games against West Brom and Nottingham Forest, but went down at Liverpool, Chelsea and Stoke: at Liverpool, Whitham was carried off, and at Stoke the home side's goals came from John Ritchie (one a penalty). Then Wednesday lost two home games by one-goal margins: Alan Mullery giving Spurs victory, and Everton, the new League champions, scrambling to a lucky victory after the Sheffield side had hammered continuously at their goal without scoring. In their last away game, at Manchester United, Wednesday were two goals down after only 10 minutes, but Coleman reduced the arrears after 40 minutes, and Whitham salvaged a point with a goal in the second half. The fighting performance at Old Trafford led many to believe that Wednesday could yet be saved.

They went into their final game, against Joe Mercer's Manchester City, knowing that nothing less than victory would save them from relegation. Crystal Palace, who had completed their programme, were two points better off, but had an inferior goal-average; and Sunderland were already doomed. On the fateful evening of April 22 1970, the weather was wet, cold and windy, but a crowd of 45,258—the biggest of the season—turned up at Hillsborough. It is fair to suggest that the majority of spectators had every expectation of seeing Wednesday rise to the occasion, pull out all the stops, and grab the two points which would keep them in the First Division. Manchester City had won only twice in 37 League visits to the Wednesday ground, and, with a date in the European Cup Winners' Cup only a week away, Mercer's team were likely to be anxious to avoid risking injuries.

Before the match, there were doubts about the fitness of two key defenders in the home side—full-back Wilf Smith and centre-back Colin Prophett, the six-foot Crewe product who, at 22, had won his way into the team in November and gone on to play in every game. In the event, both Prophett and Smith played, but the decision to risk Smith was a gamble—and it was a gamble which failed. Suffering a recurrence of his thigh strain, the back retired midway through the first half, and, in a re-shuffled line-up, Young was switched to defence from midfield, with Downes coming on as substitute.

The turning point in the game, however, was probably not the loss of Smith, but an injury suffered by City's international forward, Mike Summerbee, also in the first half-hour. The challenge on Summerbee by Prophett bore the stamp of anxiety and inexperience, but losing their star forward hurt City, and, later, when they learned the extent of Summerbee's injury, the visitors seemed to find the "killer" instinct which had been noticeably lacking in their earlier play. Ironically, it was Ian Bowyer, the substitute for Summerbee, who scored the goals which sent Wednesday into the Second Division.

Earlier, City had been awarded a penalty following a handling offence, and their skipper, Tony Book, had run the length of the field to give instructions to Mike Doyle. Amazingly, Doyle's tame shot went straight to Grummitt. If Wednesdayites thought that was a happy omen, they were soon stunned into silent disbelief: for Bowyer, with a long shot which might have gone anywhere, beat Grummitt, who was helpless as the ball swerved through the air and flashed into the net.

Coleman pulled Wednesday level in the second-half with a memorable goal shot from 25 yards at the end of a fine solo run; but again that young man Bowyer popped up to restore City's lead. In the end Wednesday failed miserably. Danny Williams commented: "We didn't play like a team that wanted to win." Eric Taylor described it as the unhappiest night of his career: "City played with their hands in their pockets for most of the game, and still we couldn't win."

Three days after that mournful but historic night, Gerry Young's testimonial match was staged. One of the few players who had shown the character and fighting qualities Wednesday needed, Young could hardly have dropped on a worse moment for his big event. However, with Sheffield United providing the opposition, a crowd of 12,120 turned up for the game—better than might have been expected in the circumstances.

Jack Whitham—Wednesday's leading scorer with 12 League and Cup goals—claimed two goals in the 3-3 draw with United, and a few days later was signed by Liverpool manager, Bill Shankly, for a £55,000 fee. Soon afterwards, Coleman was transferred to Blackpool for £15,000. Williams planned to use the money to solve his midfield problem by acquiring Burnley's Brian O'Neil, but when he and Eric Taylor travelled to Turf Moor hoping to finalise the deal they found that O'Neil had already signed for Southampton. As an alternative, Williams was offered Burnley's 24-year-old Sammy Todd for £40,000. The Wednesday team-boss admitted he had never seen Todd play, but accepted the offer. The problem was that Todd, capped seven times by Ireland, was really a defender, and never settled at Hillsborough, protesting that he was playing out of position in midfield. Later in the close season, Williams obtained John Sissons, an experienced former England Under-23 winger who had made over 200 appearances for West Ham. Sissons, who was 25, cost around £65,000.

Not surprisingly, Wednesday's fall from the First Division provoked a flood of criticism, and the Shareholders' Association highlighted the average supporter's dismay and anger at a number of meetings which were well-publicised in the summer of 1970. At the annual meeting, retiring directors Keith Gardiner, 66, and "Dick" Gunstone, 67, were opposed by Association nominees, Harry Allen, 41-year-old owner of a string of chemist shops, and Roy Whitehead, a 37-year-old businessman who was in engineering. Messrs Gardiner and Gunstone, however, survived the challenge and gained re-election.

When the 1970-1 campaign began, the Hillsborough camp was still troubled by internal problems. Wilf Smith was quite determined to leave, and, after playing in the opening game—a 1-0 defeat of Charlton at Hillsborough—got his way. Smith rejected a move to Chelsea, but on

August 31 signed for Coventry City, and the £100,000 fee made him the game's most expensive full-back. A few weeks after parting with Smith, Williams signed Leicester City's Welsh international back, Peter Rodrigues, for £55,000. Rodrigues, who was 26, had played in over 200 League games for Leicester and his home-town club, Cardiff, and had been capped 22 times by Wales. Williams made him captain.

Wednesday made a disappointing start to their programme, winning only one of their first seven games; and in early October, a week before the arrival of Rodrigues, suffered their heaviest home defeat in the Second Division for 25 years—Luton beating them 5-1, with Malcolm Macdonald scoring three. After this, they won five of their next nine games and lost only two, reaching the halfway stage of the season with 21 points from 21 matches; but it was evidence of the team's problems that Ellis, Prophett and golden-boy Craig were all dropped and recalled in this period, and ex-Liverpool Boys captain, Allan Thompson, was pushed into the side in circumstances less than ideal for a promising teenage defender. Coach Tom McAnearney had left, but was soon back in work as manager of Bury; while Dave Ewing also departed after only a very brief stay with the club.

When Wednesday shared a 1-1 draw with Oxford United a week before Christmas, the attendance of 11,134 was the lowest for a League match at Hillsborough since before the war—clear evidence of rapidly declining support. Alan Warboys, who scored against Oxford, was, in fact, making his farewell appearance, though he didn't know it: a few days later he was transferred to Cardiff City for £42,000. As if to rub salt in the wounds, two weeks later Warboys scored twice for Cardiff in a 4-0 defeat of Wednesday. (Incidentally, two of the players transferred in the Williams era, Ford and Warboys, later returned to Sheffield and played with United.)

A match which summed up Wednesday's problems, underlining their lack of experience and organisation, was the game at Hull City on Boxing Day. The club had been troubled by 'flu, and Jimmy Mullen, an 18-year-old product of the North East, was thrown in for his League debut, and David Sunley, a promising striker who was also 18, came in for only his second League outing. Rodrigues was absent and defender Prophett was given the number nine shirt vacated by Warboys. Remarkably, Wednesday raced to a 4-1 lead, with Sinclair scoring twice and setting up a goal for Prendergast, and Ellis converting a penalty. However, Hull were allowed to claim three goals in the last seven minutes of the game, and if the final whistle had not halted proceedings, Wednesday would almost certainly have lost.

Seven days after the Hull game, Wednesday went out of the FA Cup at Tottenham, and it was three weeks later, on the very weekend when the club had a blank Saturday because of the Cup, that the Hillsborough board decided to dispense with the services of Danny Williams. At the time, Wednesday had 25 points from 26 games and stood in the lower half of the table.

In fact, since the departure of Alan Brown, Wednesday had played 125 League games and won a mere 19. And it was against this background of alarming decline that the club's leading figures, Dr. Andrew Stephen and Eric Taylor, persuaded Derek Dooley to leave the Development Fund office and become Wednesday's sixth team-manager in a little under 13 years. They knew that Dooley was still a legendary figure in Sheffield football 18 years after his playing days had been ended in tragic circumstances; and hoped he would now emerge as the "messiah" who would lead Wednesday out of the wilderness. For Dooley it was like a dream come true, but, sadly, the story was not to have a happy ending.

✱ ✱ ✱

A new generation of supporters had grown up since Derek Dooley's playing days had been cruelly ended by the amputation of his right leg in a Preston hospital in 1953; yet now, in 1971, he was still regarded as a living legend in Sheffield. There was still something special about his name, and, at 41, he was known as one of the great Wednesdayites—an apt and popular choice as President of the Supporters' Club. When his career as a fearless, free-scoring centre-forward had been suddenly halted at the age of 23, he had said: "They can stick me in the ground and use me as a corner-flag, so long as I can stay in the game." Nothing was more certain than that Dooley would not remain long outside the world of professional football. But first he had spells as a telephonist at a local bakery and as a football correspondent for a national newspaper; and later he looked after Wednesday's juniors. Then, in 1962, he returned to Hillsborough to join the permanent staff as organiser of the club's new development fund. An office was built at the Penistone Road end of the ground, and here Dooley found himself close to the game and part of his favourite club—in touch with the professionals and in regular contact with supporters. He was at home among players, training staff and his administrative colleagues; and, in dealing with his band of development fund agents, could sit in his office, smoke his pipe, and debate the fortunes of the club in particular and the game in general with ordinary supporters who reflected the opinion of the man on the Spion Kop and terrace. Dooley had become an integral part of the club, and was a happy, contented man. Of course, occasionally, he dreamed of becoming a manager, and no doubt felt he could do as well as some he had seen. Having played the game, and, in more recent years, watched football at all levels, he didn't doubt that he had the knowledge. But the years passed—and they might have gone on passing had Wednesday's crisis not deepened. On that fateful weekend towards the end of January 1971, Dr. Andrew Stephen (later knighted) said the words which had a magic ring to Dooley: "We want you to become team-manager."

With the benefit of hindsight, it is easy to reflect that Dooley the folk hero was taking a terrific gamble in accepting the job, putting his reputation and legendary name on the line to be shattered by the harsh realities of the modern game and football management in particular. But it was a challenge the man himself could hardly have been expected to resist. It must have seemed to him that he had spent all his life preparing for that moment. He had no doubts that he could make a success of the job. At the time of the appointment, it was not difficult to see it as a step which *could* prove to be a master stroke, but it did not require much perception to recognise that it was a move fraught with potential dangers. Initially, the appointment might capture the imagination of supporters, and stem the mounting tide of criticism; but what if it failed? If Dooley did not achieve the desired success, it would surely mark the end of the "old order" at Hillsborough.

In the event, Dooley was destined to remain in charge for just under three years, in which time the team played 121 League matches, of which 38 were won and 52 lost. The figures indicate an improvement on the previous three years, but the bare figures do less than justice to Dooley, who deserves credit for achievements not necessarily adequately reflected in results. He certainly restored much-needed pride and discipline in the dressing room; and at one stage, in his second full season, Wednesday led the Second Division. He acquired a number of seasoned players, and it seemed that at one point the team was poised to make a significant breakthrough. Alas, the team fell away in the later stages of that 1972-3 campaign, and finished tenth. The following season began badly, a mysterious virus infection swept through the club, and before the after-effects had abated, Dooley found himself dismissed as team-manager when a run of bad results left Wednesday in the relegation zone.

When Dooley took control, Wednesday had 16 games left to play in 1970-1. They won only three and lost eight, collecting 11 points to finish the season in 15th place. Wednesday's first win under Dooley came against Bristol City on February 27, Prendergast getting the goals in a 2-0 win, with Craig, having withdrawn a transfer request, deputising as captain. At Easter, incidentally, the biggest Hillsborough crowd of the season (the biggest in the Second Division that term), 47,592, saw the 90th League derby between the Sheffield clubs. The game ended in a 0-0 draw, and the point helped United clinch promotion to the First Division—and, incidentally, it was following this success that United's board finally decided to remove county cricket from Bramall Lane and make plans to build a new fourth-side stand.

At the end of 1970-1, Gerry Young, after long and loyal service, was appointed to the coaching staff, joining Ron Staniforth, who had returned to the club a year earlier as a junior coach but subsequently graduated to first-team duties. Later in Dooley's period as team-manager, Staniforth went back to looking after the youngsters, and Young became first-team coach.

Dooley's first major signing was John Holsgrove, a six-feet two-and-a-half inch tall centre-back, a former Spurs amateur who had graduated to the professional ranks with Crystal Palace and gone on to make more than 170 League appearances with Wolves. While Dooley was seeking Holsgrove, the Shareholders' Association was continuinig its efforts to put nominees on the Hillsborough board, but at the annual meeting retiring directors Dr. Andrew Stephen and Cecil Turner were both re-elected.

Wednesday began their first full season under Dooley badly, collecting only one point from their first six League games—an especially unfortunate sequence in view of the fact that the club had appointed a firm of marketing consultants to promote the Wednesday image. The team's only success in this spell was a 2-0 win at Rotherham in the League Cup, but they crashed out at the next stage of the competition, defeated 5-0 at Carlisle. The biggest blow was suffered in the first home game, with Wednesday turning in an alarmingly inept performance which enabled visitors Bristol City to cruise to a 5-1 win, with ex-Rotherham man John Galley claiming a hat-trick.

Dooley's immediate reaction was to return to the transfer market. A few weeks earlier he had been unable to conclude a proposed deal involving Wyn Davies, the Newcastle striker, and attempts to persuade Middlesbrough to part with John Hickton proved unsuccessful. But now Dooley clinched a £100,000 double deal which brought defender-midfielder Dave Clements and striker Brian Joicey from Coventry City. Irishman Clements, at 25, had the experience of more than 250 League games and 20 international appearances behind him; while Joicey, if he lacked the skill and versatility of his colleague, was the kind of determined forward Dooley felt he needed. Joicey, who had scored 44 goals for North Shields in 1968-9 and helped them win the Amateur Cup, had claimed 10 goals in 30 League games for Coventry. In fact, Joicey went on to score 53 goals in more than 160 appearances for Wednesday; while Clements was to play in 77 League games before leaving for Everton in 1973—a move prompted by his desire to play in the First Division, and as a midfielder rather than a back.

Clements and Joicey helped Wednesday pull away from the foot of the table. Joicey was on target in the first League victory, against Sunderland on September 18; and though Wednesday lost at Oxford a week later, they followed up with an unbeaten run of eight games. Indeed, between the end of September and the end of December, they lost only one of 15 games. Alas, they then went six games in League and Cup without a win; and it was not until February 19 that they chalked up their first victory of 1972—a 2-1 home win against Watford. Incidentally, a week after the Watford success, Sissons claimed a hat-trick at Burnley, but Wednesday lost 3-5.

Victories over Watford and Preston were, in fact, Wednesday's only successes in a 15-match run, and their cause was not helped by a goalkeeping crisis which saw an unknown local amateur, Trevor Pearson, step in for four games when both Grummitt and Springett were absent injured. However, three wins in their last five games enabled Wednesday to finish the campaign in 14th place—five points better off than Charlton, who were relegated with Watford. In one of those late-season victories, Joicey claimed his first hat-trick, against Orient, and it brought his tally for the campaign to a highly satisfactory 16.

The 1972-3 season was the highspot of the Dooley era, for Wednesday had a spell at the top of the Second Division in the early weeks and enjoyed a notable triumph in the FA Cup in February; and, at one stage, there was reason to believe they might soon be on their way to better things. However, at the end of the campaign which had seen the return of the club's traditional blue-and-white striped shirts, they finished in tenth position, well out of the running for promotion even if three more points would have have put them in the top four.

With Sam Ellis having gone to Mansfield Town, Dooley now transferred Graham Pugh to Huddersfield Town, but, just when it looked as if the last of the 1966 FA Cup final team had gone, Peter Eustace was brought back from West Ham. Eustace had not had a happy time in London, and had been loaned to Rotherham before Dooley's £12,000 offer was accepted. However, Eustace was not the only "old boy" who returned to Hillsborough in 1972. The Football Association lifted the bans imposed on Peter Swan and David Layne in 1964, and Wednesday offered them the chance to make a new start. Swan, now 34, showed himself to be remarkably fit, and enjoyed a successful run of 15 League and Cup appearances, later joining Bury; but Layne was unable to regain a first-team place with his old club, though he subsequently made a happy League comeback with Hereford. Another significant pre-season signing was little Willie Henderson, the former Glasgow Rangers idol who had played 35 times for Scotland; and the Scot enjoyed a stay during which he emerged as a great favourite with supporters who relished his brand of entertaining wing play.

Wednesday began the season with five wins in their first seven games, and remained in the top two places until mid-October. But one point from five games pushed them down to seventh, and at the end of December, with 10 wins in 26 games, 27 points left them in eighth place. Then came a memorable FA Cup interlude. In the third round, goals by Prendergast and Joicey gave them a 2-0 victory over Fulham. The fourth round paired them with Crystal Palace, the big-spending First Division side. Wednesday went into the match without the suspended Joicey, and gambled with a half-fit Prendergast—a gamble which came unstuck when the youngster retired after only 18 minutes. It left young Sunley with the awesome task of battling alone up front. Fortunately, Wednesday had made the best possible start, scoring in the first minute. A typical Henderson dribble led to the wee Scot being brought down in the penalty area, and Tommy Craig made no mistake with the spot-kick. In the second-half, however, Don Rodgers earned the Londoners a replay when he cashed in on a defensive error.

At Selhurst Park in the replay, Wednesday looked to be on their way out of the competition when Phillips gave Palace the lead after 83 minutes; but Sunley, celebrating his 21st birthday, snatched a dramatic 89th-minute equaliser. In the second replay, staged at Villa Park, Wednesday produced a memorable performance which probably provided Dooley with his happiest night as team-manager. Twice behind, Wednesday bounced back, and clinched victory by a 3-2 margin in extra time. Joicey paid another dividend on his £45,000 fee with a splendid hat-trick.

Unfortunately, in the fifth round at Hillsborough, another London side, Chelsea, snatched a 2-1 victory to disappoint home fans in the 46,910 crowd.

Once out of the Cup, Wednesday returned to the League and registered four successive victories. However, in their final eight games they won only twice. One of the games they failed to win, a home clash with Brighton which ended 1-1, is noteworthy because Eustace spent the second-half in goal following an injury to Springett; while the 2-0 success against Orient has a place in the records because Peter Fox, aged 15 years and eight months, became Wednesday's youngest-ever first-team player—and the brave, slightly-built goalkeeper played much of the match with a broken toe.

Joicey enjoyed another successful season with 20 League and Cup goals; and Sunley, whose tally was 12, seemed to offer unlimited promise for the future. Craig, who scored 10 goals, significantly claimed four of them from the penalty-spot. A feature of the campaign was the emergence of Roy Coyle, signed from Glentoran and gaining his first Irish cap after only seven League appearances.

In the summer of 1973, Dooley took further steps to strengthen his squad. With Clements determined to leave, Bernard Shaw, the former Sheffield United back, was obtained from Wolves for £40,000; while Ken Knighton, an aggressive midfielder, cost £60,000 from Hull City. Both Shaw and Knighton had the experience of more than 250 League games. Shaw, a local product and younger brother of former England defender Graham Shaw, had once been an automatic choice at Sheffield United, and had enjoyed success with Wolves; while Barnsley-born Knighton had been with Wolves, Preston and Oldham before joining Hull.

For the first time in three years, Springett began the season as first-choice goalkeeper, while 1973-4 was to see Liverpool youngsters, Allan Thompson and Eric Potts, establish themselves in the senior side. Potts, who had played with New Brighton and Oswestry before his move to Sheffield, was a clever little winger who had been knocking on the first-team door for a couple of years; while former Liverpool Boys skipper, Thompson, had become a regular deputy in defence.

Unfortunately, Wednesday began the season with only two wins in their first seven games. In late September, Prendergast got his first hat-trick in the 4-0 defeat of Crystal Palace at Hillsborough, and Millwall were beaten 3-2 four days later; but only two further victories were achieved in the next 16 League and Cup matches. The biggest setback suffered in this spell came in the League Cup at Loftus Road, where Queen's Park Rangers crushed Wednesday 8-2.

Wednesday's poor form was partly due to circumstances beyond their control—a mystery virus infection which swept through the club and affected no fewer than 16 players over a period between early September and early November. Willie Henderson was the first reported victim, on September 5, and Shaw and Joicey were the last to go down with the illness at the end of October; and at one point 11 players plus Derek Dooley were down with the virus. It was later suggested that the public were not fully aware of the extent of the epidemic until it had passed; and few realised that several key players were troubled by the after-effects for several weeks. Dooley was reluctant to use the virus as an excuse, and knew that supporters were weary of excuses—even though this time they were more genuine than many that might have been made in previous years. It didn't help when the Football League turned down Wednesday's request for postponement of the home match with Notts County on October 27, and, struggling to raise a team, they had no choice but to thrust youngsters Danny Cameron and Eddie Prudham into action. The dressing room area was subsequently closed, sealed off, and fumigated, but it was late November before things began to get back to normal—and by this time the team's situation at the foot of the Second Division had begun to look very serious. With a mere 12 points from 17 games, Wednesday were in 20th place—and nobody needed reminding that the Football League had introduced three-up and three-down from this season. At home matches, supporters were becoming increasingly restless and staging noisy demonstrations—with Dooley, Eric Taylor and Sir Andrew Stephen the chief targets of their chants.

It was on Thursday December 6 that dramatic developments took place, not in the dressing room but in the boardroom. Sir Andrew Stephen resigned, and his vice-chairman, former newspaper editor Keith Gardiner, went with him. Matt Sheppard, a 49-year-old chartered accountant and businessman who had been a director two years, was named as the new chairman. A week later the vacancies on the board were filled by Bert McGee, 56-year-old head of a well-known local toolmaking firm, and 40-year-old Roy Whitehead, who had earlier made an unsuccessful bid to gain a place when nominated to stand as a Shareholders' Association candidate at the club's annual meeting.

The newly-constituted board was named on December 13—Dooley's 44th birthday. Two days later, Wednesday played a home game with Fulham, and a crowd of only 7,925 turned up to see the Hillsborough side slip to a 0-3 defeat—their fourth defeat in six home games. They now had 13 points from 20 matches. On the following Saturday, Wednesday travelled to Crystal Palace, and a 0-0 draw gave them their first away point since mid-October. On Sunday a board meeting was held at Hillsborough. The next day, Monday December 24, Dooley drove to the ground feeling slightly more optimistic than he had been a week earlier. With two home matches over the holiday period, he was sure that the team could get the results which would signal an upturn in fortunes. He found the new chairman waiting at Hillsborough. Mr. Sheppard informed him of the decision taken by the board less than 24 hours earlier. Dooley was no longer team-manager. On Boxing Day, before the match with Hull City, Mr. Sheppard issued the following statement:

"Sheffield Wednesday are a great and famous club, and I, as chairman, and all the members of the board, are determined that the club will regain its rightful place among the top clubs. It was with the greatest reluctance, and after much deep thought, that the board unanimously decided to replace the team-manager, and, in accordance with tradition and good manners, it was my responsibility to formally inform Derek Dooley as soon as possible. It was most regretful that this coincided with Christmas Eve, but in view of our position—only 14 points from 21 matches—it was decided that the club should advertise for a replacement immediately. I speak for myself and all the directors without exception in stating we have a very high regard for Derek as a man and as an excellent employee. Derek has worked extremely hard and conscientiously as team-manager. The playing side has, in our opinion, improved considerably both in spirit and depth under his stewardship. Unfortunately, our position in the Second Division is not satisfactory, and the directors decided a change was necessary. Derek has not been sacked as an employee. His contract will be honoured and discussions will take place to see if a mutually agreed position and terms can be arranged for him."

Gerry Young was appointed "coach in charge of dressing room and playing matters" pending the appointment of a new manager. Dooley did not return to Hillsborough. For a time he worked as a public relations and promotions manager for a Leeds firm, but in November 1974 he joined Sheffield United as commercial manager. Dooley's contribution to the Wednesday story, as player, development fund organiser and team-manager, will not be forgotten, and, in the manner of his departure, he will be remembered as a victim of circumstances. It might have been so different had only he been appointed 18 months sooner, but, then, it might have been another story had the team not been hit by the virus epidemic just when supporters lost patience and began to demand change. It was a traumatic period in club history, and well worth noting in some detail. But the problems were not yet over, and more change was on its way at Hillsborough . . .

✱ ✱ ✱

It was during the period when Wednesday were seeking a successor to Derek Dooley that Eric Taylor confirmed he was to retire. Making the announcement before the FA Cup third-round tie with Coventry City on January 5, he said he would leave in June—a month after his 62nd birthday. Symbolically, perhaps, he posed to be photographed in front of the memorial to Sir Charles Clegg, the first of seven chairmen under whom he had served in graduating from office boy to general-manager in a career spanning 45 years. It was, very clearly, the end of an era in club history.

The events which had led to the departures of Sir Andrew Stephen and Dooley had not, said Taylor, influenced his decision: nor had the criticism to which he and others had been subjected caused him to call it a day. He had always planned an early retirement, though he had hoped that, when it came, it might coincide with a successful phase. Unfortunately, fate had decreed otherwise. But if he was saddened by the current situation, he believed Wednesday would survive and climb again—because the club was greater than any single individual, be he director, official, player or supporter.

Taylor had the consolation of knowing that he had played his part, and, though he didn't say it, knew he would leave behind a lasting memorial to his ambition and achievement in the form of a magnificent stadium which would always bear the stamp "Taylor made". The tragedy of Eric Taylor was not so much that he signed off at a moment when the club's fortunes were at such a low ebb and still in decline, though he was desperately unlucky in that the last days of his career should be passed in an atmosphere of gloom and turmoil which clouded the reality of his considerable contribution to the club's development. Where the fates were especially savage was in that they denied him the quiet and peaceful retirement he surely deserved, and the circumstances meant also that he did not receive the acclaim his achievements merited. At the time he announced he was to bow from the scene, few realized how ill he really was, and nobody knew that he had only a few months more to live. A kinder fate would have spared him to see his beloved Wednesday rise again in the hands of his successors. Eric Taylor was well-known for his sayings, and one of them was "You only get what you deserve"; but, in the final analysis, that is what he didn't get.

Born at Fulwood in May 1912 and brought up at Birley Carr, Eric Woodhouse Taylor was a football fanatic from boyhood and a Wednesdayite from the day he first learned of the existence of Hillsborough. Yet the boy who used to stand outside the ground, waiting for the gates to open so that he could slip in and watch the last 10 minutes of a match, never dreamed that one day the club would become his life and he would be dubbed "Mister Sheffield Wednesday". When he left school in 1926, his first job was in a solicitor's office, but in 1929 he spotted an advertisement for an office boy at an unnamed football club. To his horror, when he was invited to attend for the interview he was told to report to Bramall Lane. He was relieved to discover that the vacancy was at Hillsborough, and delighted to emerge the successful applicant.

Now, nearly 45 years later, Eric Taylor was one of the most famous and respected administrators in football, widely-travelled, a man whose flair was acknowledged and appreciated throughout the game. The greatest single influence on the young Taylor was his first manager, Bob Brown, and he never forgot the principles instilled in him by Brown; so that, in one sense, Taylor remained one of the old school, and this background conditioned a lot of his attitudes, especially with regard to discipline and efficiency. Yet, as he illustrated as he grew in stature and authority, he was essentially a product of his times, a modern, forward-looking man who, at his peak, had a vision which was well in advance of most of his contemporaries. On the day Taylor revealed details of his retirement plans, the general-manager of visitors Coventry City, Joe Mercer, was at Hillsborough; and he said, "Football can ill-afford to lose the wisdom and experience of a man like Eric." In fact, it was intended that Taylor, as long-serving chairman of the Football League Secretaries' and Managers' Association, should continue to serve the game; and Wednesday had plans to offer him a consultancy role. But he became seriously ill and his death in late September 1974 meant he was lost to football sooner than anyone expected.

If Eric Taylor earned lasting praise for his abilities as an organiser, and if his flair and showmanship put him in the spotlight, the man himself admitted that he could never have achieved all he did without the help and support of "the other Eric". So it was fitting that Eric England should subsequently be named as Taylor's successor as secretary.

A product of Shiregreen, Eric England had always wanted to be an engineer until he left school at 14 in 1934 and found jobs hard to get. He became an office boy at a small cutlery firm in Sheffield; and the boss, incidentally, was the same John "Pop" Bennett who was connected with the YMCA, and who would play a part in the Derek Dooley story. Bennett had high hopes that young Eric would one day succeed him in the business, but, by the time he was 16, the boy had decided his future did not lie in cutlery. He wrote after a number of jobs, and one day in the autumn of 1936 received a reply from Sheffield Wednesday. On the following Sunday morning he arrived for an interview, and, after being given a shorthand and typing test by the then 24-year-old Taylor, was appointed office boy at 7s 6d (37½p) a week. It was the beginning of a happy and successful partnership, and if the older Eric got most of the praise and publicity, the part played by the younger man did not go unnoticed where it mattered.

Eric England, too, was a born Wednesdayite, having as a boy cheered on such heroes as Jimmy Trotter and Ernest Blenkinsop from his seat in the old North Stand. Apart from a wartime spell in the RAF, he was destined to spend the rest of his working life at Hillsborough. A quiet, thoughtful man, he was the ideal partner for Taylor, and was content to remain in the background. Promoted to assistant secretary in 1946, he emerged as a key figure in organising big matches when Hillsborough was restored to the semi-final circuit. Indeed, he and Eric Taylor learned together, and actually devised many of the techniques and practices which became an accepted part of the business of arranging ticket distribution and other details in the organisation of big-match administration.

What was important to Wednesday in 1974 was that, in a period of great turmoil and change, they had in Eric England, at 54, a man who not only provided an important link with the past, but whose knowledge, experience and dependability ensured continuity and stability would be maintained in the club's administration. He was well-equipped to ensure that Wednesday's tradition for efficiency and organisation would be handed on to the inheritors in the new era in club history.

✱ ✱ ✱

After Derek Dooley's departure, Gerry Young remained in charge of playing affairs for five weeks. In that time Wednesday lost only one of seven matches—an FA Cup replay at Coventry. During this period John Sissons was transferred to Norwich City and Peter Grummitt joined Brian Clough's Brighton, where he had been on loan since early December. Incidentally, Sammy Todd, unable to regain his first-team place, was loaned to Mansfield in February and so ended his association with the club.

Predictions that Wednesday would recruit an experienced and possibly famous manager to succeed Dooley proved to be wide of the mark, for on January 29 1974 the new man was named as 38-year-old Steve Burtenshaw, a highly-rated coach for whom the Sheffield job was his first managerial post. Burtenshaw had spent all his 17 years as a player with his home-town club, Brighton, had subsequently enjoyed several successful years on Arsenal's coaching staff, and had been chief coach at Queen's Park Rangers just seven months when he became Wednesday's manager.

At the time of Burtenshaw's arrival, Wednesday had 16 games left to play. They went on to win six, and a haul of 15 points proved just sufficient to enable them to escape relegation by one point. In this period they chalked up two of their best wins of the season in successive matches—a 5-1 victory at Notts County and a 5-0 defeat of Cardiff—but also suffered their heaviest-ever setback in the Second Division when Jack Charlton's Middlesbrough crushed them 8-0. And it was during this up-and-down spell that they lost striker Mick Prendergast with a broken leg, suffered at Preston on Good Friday.

Wednesday's first League match under Burtenshaw's management earned a special place in the club's records because it was the first League game to be staged at Hillsborough on a Sunday. The switch to Sunday was part of a development, happily only temporary, prompted by the effects of an energy crisis which gripped the country and created a three-day working week. For the record, Bristol City provided the opposition on that historic February 10; and a crowd of 15,888 saw Wednesday win 3-1, with Joicey, Henderson and Shaw getting the goals. This game, incidentally, marked the debut of Bobby Ferguson, the displaced West Ham goalkeeper; and he went on to play five times for Wednesday during his one-month loan period.

Wednesday went into their final game, at home to Bolton, knowing that victory would save them from the fall into Division Three. Crystal Palace, who also had one match left, could finish with the same points tally as the Sheffield club, but Wednesday's goal-average was superior. Hillsborough's best League crowd of the season—23,264—saw Ken Knighton clinch the vital points with a dramatic 86th-minute goal, and, such was the sense of relief, hundreds of jubilant supporters poured onto the pitch at the end of the game, with skipper Knighton carried shoulder-high from the field. The scene resembled a promotion celebration.

If supporters thought that the face-saving victory against Bolton would prove to be a turning point and that 1973-4 would be the last of the lean years, they were to be bitterly disappointed, for the 1974-5 campaign was to go down as the worst in club history, and this time there would be no escape from the Third Division.

With a mere five wins and a paltry 21 points from their 42 games, Wednesday finished bottom of the Second Division—15 points adrift of the safety mark. They scored only 29 goals, and actually failed to find the net in no fewer than 22 matches. They won only one of their first 13 games, managed nine points from nine matches in mid-season, but then won only one of their last 23 fixtures. At one stage their plight was so alarming that the local evening newspaper, *The Star,* was inspired to launch a "Save Our Owls" campaign; but they dropped it after only a few weeks.

The season saw the arrival of a number of newcomers. They included Irish defender, Hugh Dowd, who cost £30,000 from Glenavon; Colin Harvey, an experienced half-back signed from Everton for £60,000 in September; Phil Henson, a young, slightly-built midfielder who arrived from Manchester City for £45,000 in February; and free-transfer men

Bobby Brown (Chelsea), Fred McIver (Sunderland) and Jimmy Quinn (Celtic). However, perhaps the most successful acquisition was former Irish international, Eric McMordie, who arrived on loan in October and stayed for two months during which time he was on the losing side only three times. McMordie, now 28 and unable to command a first-team place at Middlesbrough, scored six goals in his first six appearances, and, remarkably, was still the club's leading scorer at the end of the season. Because he had business interests in the North East, he could not be persuaded to consider a permanent move to Sheffield.

With Tommy Craig transferred to Newcastle in December, and Coyle, Prudham and Cameron allowed to leave, Wednesday's quest for a winning blend saw them call upon 26 players, and only one—Eric Potts—played in every game. (Potts, taking on the mantle of the now-departed Henderson, was the only man who played in every game in the Burtenshaw era.) Goalkeeper Springett went out of favour midway through the season, losing his place to 17-year-old Peter Fox; Holsgrove, Eustace and Rodrigues were pushed on to the sidelines; while, in attack, no fewer than eight players were tried in endless permutations seeking the right pair for the twin striker roles. Youngsters thrust into action without any lasting success included Wylde, David Herbert and Ronnie Ferguson. Gainsborough product Ferguson, aged 17, headed a memorable goal on his debut, but it was to be the only one he managed in his brief League career at Hillsborough.

By the end of the first week in September, clouds of gloom had begun to gather. With just two points from four League games and a League Cup KO at the hands of Fourth Division Scunthorpe United, the outlook was decidedly grim. Burtenshaw immediately signed 29-year-old Colin Harvey, who had played 380 times for Everton; and at least the newcomer had the consolation of helping Wednesday to victory on his debut at Bolton on September 14. The 20-year-old Plymouth-born Bobby Brown, making his first "full" appearance, scored the only goal of the game. Unfortunately, Wednesday collected only three points from their next eight games.

McMordie arrived on October 16, and three days later the little Irishman notched a goal as Wednesday came from behind to beat Hull City 2-1—their first home win of the season. It was another three weeks before Wednesday managed their next victory: a 3-0 defeat of York City. This was the game during which a naked man streaked onto the pitch; but, in the final analysis, the biggest talking points were Wednesday's goals, each one a gem. Ferguson claimed the first, McMordie volleyed the second, and Potts got the third with a diving header.

A week later, Wednesday shared a thrilling 3-3 draw with Notts County at Meadow Lane. McMordie gave them an early lead, but, midway through the second half, County's Ian Scanlon snatched a hat-trick of goals in the space of only two-and-a-half minutes. The first came from the penalty spot, he shot the second, and headed the third. Potts pulled one back for Wednesday with a spectacular 30-yards shot, and McMordie grabbed an equaliser five minutes from the end.

On December 7 Wednesday were involved in another remarkable

high-scoring drawn match—against Manchester United. A crowd of 35,067 saw a game in which fortunes fluctuated dramatically and a pitch invasion by visiting supporters might easily have led to play being abandoned but for some quick thinking by referee Ken Baker and prompt action by mounted policemen. The game was only seven minutes old when Houston shot United ahead from a free-kick, but Sunley levelled the scores after 19 minutes, and goals by Harvey and Shaw left the home side with a 3-1 advantage after only half-an-hour. United were handicapped by the 15th-minute loss of defender Jim Holton, who suffered a broken shin bone in challenging for a 50-50 ball with McMordie. However, by the time the match was an hour old, Tommy Docherty's side had drawn level at 3-3, Macari and Pearson getting the goals. Sunley restored Wednesday's lead, but a last-gasp effort by Macari made the score 4-4 at the finish.

A week after the Manchester game, Wednesday entertained Oldham Athletic, and a crowd of 13,339 saw a clash which ended in a draw, with Craig missing a penalty. What made this match notable in retrospect is the fact that it marked the final appearance in Wednesday's League side of Springett, Craig and McMordie. Springett was subsequently displaced by Fox, McMordie returned to Ayresome Park, and Craig was transferred to Newcastle. Craig, who had played in some 230 League and Cup matches for Wednesday, cost Newcastle £120,000. He later played with Aston Villa and Swansea City.

At the end of December a goal by Potts gave Wednesday a victory at Southampton—a success which merits a mention because it was to be the last win of the season, even though 17 League games remained to be played. The club moved into 1975 with 18 points from 25 games, and, to add to the gloomy outlook, revealed a bank overdraft of £224,619. At the time Wednesday were losing at least £1,000 a week. If they hoped their financial problems might be eased by a money-spinning FA Cup run, they were soon disappointed. They bowed out in the third round at Chelsea, losing 3-2 after leading 2-0 15 minutes from the end. Wednesday's lack of success in the second-half of the season only added to the economic stress, for the average home gate declined from around 14,600 in the pre-Christmas period to 11,500; with five of the last six fixtures being watched by fewer than 9,000.

A week after their FA Cup exit, Wednesday were pushed to their 13th League defeat by Manchester United, for whom ex-Owl Jim McCalliog scored twice; and another home setback, against Portsmouth in mid-January, sparked off more crowd demonstrations. Burtenshaw acquired 21-year-old Henson, who had played 13 times in Manchester City's first-team; but the youngster was unable to make any significant impact.

Wednesday's continuing lack of goal-power had by now become a source of alarm. Youngsters Wylde and Herbert were thrust into senior action, but without success. When Orient visited Hillsborough on March 15 and walked off with the points, it meant that Wednesday had collected just one point and scored only one goal in a run of eight games. Now the supporters' demands for action were as loud and persistent as they had been 15 or 16 months earlier. Within a few days further boardroom changes were announced. Arthur Broomhead and Stan Ashton resigned and were replaced by Stanley Speight and Cliff Woodward; and Bert McGee was named as Broomhead's successor as vice-chairman.

Wednesday suffered more defeats—and still the goals failed to come. Incredibly, Wednesday managed only one goal in a run of 14 games; and, in one sequence, starting on March 8, they played eight League matches without scoring. Finally, on April 19, a crowd of only 7,444 saw the "famine" ended in the home match with Oxford United. In fact, Oxford had taken the lead in the eighth minute, and Wednesday looked booked for another defeat until Joicey claimed the equaliser in injury time. The goal came in the last desperate fling: Mullen crossed from the left, Sunley got his head to the ball, and it was bound for the net when Joicey stepped forward to make sure. It was Wednesday's first League goal in 14 hours 10 minutes play, and it was the first Second Division goal they had scored at home since December 14. It was only the second goal Joicey had scored all season, though he had missed some 20 games.

Four days later Wednesday completed their home programme with a match against Aston Villa. A crowd of 23,605 saw Villa romp to a 4-0 victory (Wednesday's 11th home defeat) which clinched them a return to the First Division after eight years in the wilderness. At the end, while jubilant Villa supporters invaded the pitch and made themselves at home, Wednesdayites slipped mournfully away and wondered how much longer they would have to wait before the tide turned.

Wednesday's decline in a period of 10 years was emphasised by a feature which subsequently appeared in the *FA Year Book*. The records of all 92 League clubs between 1965-6 and 1974-5 were tabulated: Wednesday's 25.2 per cent return left them bottom of the away table, while a 57.1 per cent return put them in 91st position in the home results list. It presented a staggering picture of collapse, and the manner of their fall into the Third Division for the first time in their history hardly suggested much hope for a bright immediate future.

The end of the 1974-5 campaign saw Wednesday give free transfers to Springett, Eustace, Holsgrove and Rodrigues, all of whom had fallen out of favour in the second half of the season. Springett later joined Barnsley, Eustace moved to Peterborough, and Holsgrove signed for Stockport; but perhaps the most remarkable postscript was provided by Rodrigues. The Welsh international defender illustrated the truth that luck plays an important part in football, and a player will often appear a failure if he's in the wrong place or if the time is wrong, while the same man can be a success in the right place at the right time. Rodrigues was snapped up by Southampton manager Lawrie McMenemy, and, within a year, was Southampton's captain when they defeated Manchester United at Wembley to win the FA Cup. Another ex-Wednesday man, Jim McCalliog, was in the same Cup-winning side.

With the need for drastic economies paramount, Burtenshaw also dismissed chief scout Fred Scott and physiotherapist Geoff Eggington in the close season of 1975. He signed two new players: Coventry's

Lancashire-born goalkeeper, Neil Ramsbottom, and Buxton product Andy Proudlove.

Unfortunately, Wednesday did not begin the new season with any great conviction. They won only two of their first eight games, and struggled in the lower half of the Third Division; and, to add insult to injury, they fell in the League Cup at the first-round stage—KO'd by Fourth Division Darlington, who ended a three-match marathon by winning 5-3 on penalties. In late September Matt Sheppard and Bert McGee switched roles, and the new chairman had been in office only six days when he had the task of telling Burtenshaw that his term as manager was over after 20 months. Gerry Young's 20-year spell at Hillsborough came to an end at the same time—ironically on his birthday. Jim McAnearney, who had returned to the club during Burtenshaw's term, was put in temporary charge of team affairs.

For the record, Burtenshaw had been manager for a period covering 71 League and Cup games, of which only 14 had been won and 41 lost. Incidentally, within four days of Burtenshaw's departure, Sheffield United decided to part company with their manager, Ken Furphy; so Sheffield was left in the remarkable position of having two League clubs without a manager.

✳ ✳ ✳

Barely a fortnight after Burtenshaw left, his successor was named as 36-year-old Len Ashurst, a Liverpudlian who had made his name as a dependable and consistent left-back with Sunderland. As an amateur he had been on Liverpool's books, and, in the meantime, had begun an apprenticeship in the printing trade; but, though good enough to gain several youth international caps, he remained at Anfield only three years. It was following a short spell with Wolves that he got his big break, for in 1957 he was "discovered" by Alan Brown and taken to Roker Park. A year later he made his Football League debut, and was an automatic choice in the red-and-white of Sunderland for the next 12 years. He gained England Under-23 honours and helped the Roker club win promotion to the First Division in 1964. He finally bowed from the League side in 1970—the year Sunderland were relegated to the Second Division with Sheffield Wednesday.

Len Ashurst was one of a number of men who were inspired and encouraged by Alan Brown to seek to continue their careers in football management once their playing days were over. Ashurst elected to begin his managerial apprenticeship at Hartlepool—the toughest possible beginning considering they stood at the foot of the Fourth Division. Yet Hartlepool was where his former colleague Brian Clough had begun, and what had suited Clough was good enough for him. By the time Ashurst left Hartlepool three years later, the club had moved into the top half of the table. In 1974 Gillingham won promotion to the Third Division and lost the services of their manager, Andy Nelson, who moved to Charlton Athletic. Ashurst was named as Nelson's replacement. His first months at the Kent club were less than easy, for the team struggled. But they picked up in the second half of the season and finally finished in tenth place. In the following season, 1975-6, they began well, and by October stood in fifth place. It was at this point that Ashurst applied for the vacancy which had arisen at Hillsborough.

He arrived at Sheffield Wednesday at a critical moment in the club's history. He knew he was moving to a club with an illustrious past—but where the glory days had gone a long time before. He recognised that Wednesday had suffered a rapid and dramatic fall, and while the potential was still great, it was plain that the future could only get bleaker unless drastic action was taken to halt the slide. On his first day in the new job, Ashurst described Hillsborough as "a slumbering giant" in need of a rude awakening. He promised a big shake-up, with no stone left unturned in the bid to dig down to the foundations and begin the task of rebuilding from scratch; but he warned that it would be a painful process demanding time, patience, and, above all, understanding. In their years in decline, Wednesday had seen their financial losses mount at an alarming rate; so Ashurst knew he would have little money to spend—the luxuries to which the club had become accustomed would no longer be available, and the new manager would be charged with the task of pruning the training and playing staff while at the same time seeking to re-build and re-shape the team into a unit capable of climbing the table. Clearly things might get worse before they got better, and Wednesday were poised for changes which would shake the club to its roots but, hopefully, ultimately leave the way clear for a rebuilding programme to be launched free of the inhibitions of past associations.

Ashurst later described his first half-year at Hillsborough as the hardest six months of his life. The team struggled desperately through the rest of the season, winning just nine of 36 League matches and only escaping relegation at the last gasp. In this period came the first of a series of sweeping changes which transformed the club's playing and training staff—with cost-cutting an essential, indeed vital, part of the overall strategy. At the end of October, John Haselden and George McCabe were the first of the "backroom boys" to leave; followed in mid-January by Jim McAnearney and Ron Staniforth. Ex-Marine Commando Tony Toms, who had been associated with Ashurst since his Hartlepool days, followed the new manager from Gillingham; and Ken Knighton hung up his boots and took on responsibility for the reserves and juniors. David Sunley, once rated in the £100,000 class, joined Hull City for £7,500 (the fee having been reduced to that figure from £35,000 by an independent tribunal); Cameron, back after a spell on loan to Peterborough, was transferred to Preston; and the wage-bill was further reduced by outgoing loans involving Ferguson, Wylde and Brown. At the end of the season, free transfers were given to Shaw, Quinn, Thompson, Harvey, McIver, Herbert, Joicey, Brown and Ferguson. Ironically, at one stage after Ashurst's arrival, Thompson had been promoted to captain, but he and McIver lost their places after the Easter defeat at Mansfield. Of the nine released, only Shaw had played in the final match of the campaign.

It is, perhaps, relevant to note that the fall from favour of Thompson—once a youngster of apparently unlimited promise—proved the making of young Jimmy Mullen, who took over the captaincy, and, like his mentor Gerry Young, never failed to set an example in terms of effort and determination. Other, less experienced youngsters pushed to the fore in Ashurst's first months included Rotherham-born defender, David Cusack (a protege of Jim McAnearney's); Boston-born striker Ian Nimmo, who acquired a brief reputation as a scoring substitute; and ex-Sheffield schoolboy, full-back Gary Hull.

The first signings made by Ashurst included two of his former players, Neil O'Donnell and Barry Watling, both obtained on free transfers. O'Donnell, a Scottish-born half-back who had begun his career at Norwich, had been taken to Gillingham by Ashurst. He was destined to make only 40 League appearances with Wednesday before injury ended his playing days. Watling, a goalkeeper who had been on the books of no fewer than seven clubs but closely associated with Hartlepool, actually played only once in Wednesday's first-team. Derek Bell, a striker, had a four-game spell on loan from Halifax; while the only acquisitions costing fees in this period were striker Peter Feeley, from Gillingham, and Richard Walden, a defender who had played in 400 League games for Aldershot. This pair cost a total of £25,000.

Wednesday's first win under Ashurst came in his fourth game—ironically the victims on a wet November 5 were his former club, Gillingham, beaten 1-0, with the 8,235 Hillsborough spectators seeing Joicey score what was to be his last goal for the club. Unfortunately, this was the only win the team achieved in their first 16 League games under their new manager—though, in fact, they did win two FA Cup ties against non-League Macclesfield and Wigan Athletic. The situation was, to say the least, desperate: and Ashurst and Toms decided that desperate remedies were required.

That January was a month of snow and icy winds—and life was pretty unpleasant even if you were confined to Sheffield and its suburbs. Out on the moors beyond the city, it was bleak enough to put one in mind of Siberia. So when Ashurst told his players they were "taking to the hills", there were a few raised eyebrows and shudders down the spine! The name of the game was a "survival exercise" which meant sleeping out in the open, living "rough" far from home comforts: and if that didn't shake them out of their losing ways, nothing would! Fortunately, the players returned to Hillsborough none the worse for their ordeal, and the exercise paid an immediate dividend: Wednesday celebrated their first victory for 12 weeks, goals by Prendergast and Nimmo enabling them to beat Chester 2-0. They went on to collect seven points from their next six games, but four successive defeats in March left them still struggling close to the foot of the table.

In the final analysis, Wednesday saved themselves from what would have been a catastrophic fall into the Fourth Division by winning their last five homes games—a 1-0 margin proving sufficient against Colchester, Crystal Palace, Bury and Halifax. They went into their final match, against Southend United, needing one point to be sure of retaining their Third Division status. In the event, they emerged comfortable winners by a 2-1 margin. The attendance on that Thursday evening in late April 1976 was 25,800—some 15,000 up on the average for the season—and the crowd saw the issue settled by first-half goals from Prendergast and Potts. At the end, there were some remarkable scenes as, for the second time in three years, supporters demonstrated their relief that relegation had been avoided. The win doomed Southend to the drop, and defeat cost their manager, Arthur Rowley, his job, with the position subsequently passing to former Hillsborough coach David Smith. Incidentally, that last-match win of Wednesday's spared Sheffield from what would have been a unique relegation double; for United, now under the management of Jimmy Sirrel, had finished bottom of the First Division.

The 1976-7 campaign brought more important team changes. Fox, who had regained his place in goal at the expense of Ramsbottom half-way through the previous season, now found himself displaced by 17-year-old Chris Turner, an outstanding local product. When, in March 1977, Ashurst obtained Bob Bolder from Dover FC for a small fee, it signalled the end for Fox. Summer signings in 1976 included John Collins, a back from Halifax, but he did not remain long before moving on to Barnsley; and Jeff Johnson, a Welsh Under-23 midfielder acquired on a free transfer from Crystal Palace, who was probably Ashurst's most outstanding capture. In September, Sheffield-born former schoolboy international, Paul Bradshaw, 22, was signed from Burnley for £25,000; 20-year-old Tommy Tynan, another striker, came from Liverpool for £10,000; and Bobby Hope, the experienced former Scottish international midfielder who had played in over 320 League games with West Brom, was snapped up free after returning from a spell in American football. In November, David Rushbury, a back, was brought on loan from West Brom and subsequently signed permanently; and Denis Leman, another midfield player, was signed from Manchester City for a £9,000 fee around the same time. All the arrivals meant that Nimmo, Fox and Feeley were made available to other clubs on loan.

The record books show that Wednesday finished in eighth place in the Third Division in 1976-7, only six points separating them from Crystal Palace, who were promoted with Mansfield and Brighton. (Incidentally, Rotherham missed promotion on goal-average). But for three succes- sive home setbacks in the autumn—including two at the hands of Mansfield and Rotherham—and four away defeats in the last weeks of the season, the much-changed Hillsborough side might well have scrambled into the top three.

They collected 10 points out of a possible 12 from their first six home games, and ended a near two-year run without an away win in the League when they captured both points at Reading on October 16; but then came those three home defeats in the space of 11 days. In the League Cup, Wednesday had kicked off with a 3-0 success at Grimsby, followed this with an impressive 2-1 win at Wolverhampton in round two, and defeated Watford 3-1 at Hillsborough before falling in the fourth round at Millwall; and this run of success seemed to hint at better things for the club. An eight-match run between early November and mid-January saw Wednesday collect 13 points out of 16 and climb into fifth place; but then the sequence came to a sudden and painful end at Walsall, where the Sheffield side conceded four goals in the second half and lost 1-5. In the middle of this run, Wednesday made an exit from the FA Cup—defeated at Darlington, where the only goal of the game was notched by ex-Owl Ronnie Ferguson.

Wednesday concluded the 1976-7 campaign with seven wins in their last eight home games; but though they also won two away fixtures in this spell, six defeats suffered on their travels proved crucial—especially the setbacks against promotion rivals Crystal Palace, Preston and Brighton. Walden was the only ever-present, but Turner only missed one game, while Dowd (38), Wylde (43), Johnson (34), Tynan (38) and Bradshaw (37) ensured a broad base of consistency in team-selection. Wylde, the tall, cultured young forward who had so nearly left Wednesday in the previous season, established himself in the side, and had the satisfaction of emerging leading scorer with 25 League and Cup goals; while Tynan's final tally was a satisfactory 15.

There were only three changes of note in the close-season of 1977—two on the playing side and one on the management staff. Eric Potts, after some 150 League outings, was transferred to Brighton; while Ian Porterfield, a Scottish-born forward, was signed for £20,000 from Sunderland. Porterfield, who had made around 100 appearances with Raith Rovers before going on to play in over 200 League games with the Roker club, had earned lasting fame by virtue of the goal he scored to give Sunderland a memorable victory in the 1973 FA Cup final against Leeds United. He had happy memories of Hillsborough, too, for in that great Cup run, Sunderland had defeated Arsenal in one of the most unforgettable semi-finals staged at the Sheffield ground.

It was in August 1977 that Ashurst made a remarkably astute "signing" when he brought former Sheffield United manager, John Harris, to Hillsborough as chief scout. Harris, who was later to become number two to Jack Charlton, was 59 at the time of his move across the city, and was acknowledged as one of the game's most astute and experienced figures. A former Swansea and Chelsea defender and the son of former Scottish international centre-forward, Neil Harris, he had literally spent a lifetime in football, and had begun his management career 20 years earlier at Chester. In 18 years at Bramall Lane he had built a reputation as a canny and careful team-builder with an eye for budding talent and a bargain; and it was a source of some surprise that United had chosen to dispense with his services. His knowledge and experience were to prove invaluable to Wednesday.

After the relative success in the previous season, hopes were high when Wednesday began 1977-8 with two impressive League Cup victories against Doncaster Rovers. In the home leg, a Wylde hat-trick helped them to a 5-2 success, and goals by Wylde, Tynan and Porterfield booked a 3-0 win in the second leg at Belle Vue. In fact, Wednesday were destined to reach the fourth round of this competition, falling to Everton at the end of November following victories over Blackpool and Walsall.

Unfortunately, Wednesday hit rock bottom in the League. They began with two drawn games, at home to Swindon and Walsall, but collected only three points in their next eight games. After 10 matches they stood at the foot of the table without a single victory and a tally of a mere six points. Once again the spectre of relegation cast a long and threatening shadow across Hillsborough. Indeed, the first days of that autumn of 1977 found Sheffield football again in a state of crisis: for while Wednesday were 24th in Division Three, United were 21st in Division Two. United's failure cost their manager, Jimmy Sirrel, his job in late September. On October 5 Wednesday announced that Len Ashurst's two-year reign was over.

The club's statement read: "The directors of Sheffield Wednesday announced that, as from today, Mr. Len Ashurst will no longer be their manager. Until an appointment is made, Ken Knighton is in charge of team matters. The board wish to record their appreciation of Mr. Ashurst's dedication and application, and it is to be regretted that success was not his reward."

Results had gone against Ashurst at a critical period. "I am leaving the club, but I hope they have a great deal of success in the future, particularly for the supporters, who have been absolutely tremendous," he said. "We gave them a lot to be proud of, but, in six weeks of poor results this year all that has been destroyed." Ashurst's friend and colleague, Tony Toms, commented: "Len was just a spit away from success."

Ashurst had been in charge for 92 League games, of which 31 had been won, with 89 points collected. Overall, it consituted an improvement of around 17 per cent on the results achieved in the previous phase; but statistics had little meaning in relation to the team's precarious position in the table, and the fear that the club might quickly lose any ground that had been gained in the past two years. The hope was that Wednesday might now make use of the base which Ashurst had at least swept clear of cobwebs. Now the goal had to be a manager with a winning touch. The man the directors decided they wanted was soon identified as Jack Charlton.

6 Jack Charlton arrives—and the tide turns: 1977-1982

In that autumn of 1977, Jack Charlton was probably the best-known out-of-work manager in football. Having quit First Division Middlesbrough six months earlier, he had been the subject of constant speculation, with the pundits ever-ready to link his name with every vacancy which cropped up—and even with some that didn't. He was widely regarded as the leading contender for the post as England's team-manager, but, in the event, Ron Greenwood's temporary appointment became permanent—or as permanent as any situation can be in modern soccer. Everybody, or so it seemed, was keen to see Charlton back in business. The man least concerned about everything was Charlton himself. He didn't wish to remain too long out of the game, but was in no hurry to return. Perhaps he felt confident that the right job would turn up in time. Meanwhile, the lanky 42-year-old ex-Leeds United and England centre-half was contented—and fully occupied. He could relax and enjoy his fishing and shooting, and "get away from it all". But, of course, he was "a personality" and, as such, seldom remained long out of the limelight. His reputation as a fluent, forthright speaker ensured he stayed in constant demand as a star attraction at lunches and dinners, and somebody, somewhere, always wanted "Wor Jackie" to open something. Television, too, took up much of his time: with coaching films to be made for young viewers, and regular appearances on panels of experts called in to analyse and comment upon big matches such as Cup finals and internationals. So Charton was not short of something to do. There was no danger of him sinking into obscurity during his temporary retirement from soccer management. And Jack had no fears that the wolf might soon be knocking on his door. Fame had been good to the lad from Ashington, County Durham.

Jack Charlton was, indeed, a big name; a celebrity and an acknowledged expert in his own field; and a man whose reputation as a player and manager had long been synonymous with success. Football to him was not so much a job as a way of life, and fame had given him a privileged place among the giants of the game. His public image was that of a man who knew football inside out and talked about it fluently and fervently, speaking without fear or favour, and using language that the ordinary supporter could understand. If anyone was likely to put into words what others were thinking but wouldn't say, that man was Jack Charlton.

He came from footballing stock. The game was in his blood, for his mother was a Milburn; and, in the North East, the Milburns were a part of the region's football folklore. Four of his mother's brothers had played in the Football League—two of them, George and Stan, with Chesterfield. A cousin, Jackie Milburn, had been the toast of Tyneside in the 1950s. Bobby Charlton, Jack's brother, had emerged as one of the game's all-time greats; and together, Bobby and Jack had made history by becoming the first brothers to play in the same England team since 1899. The Charlton boys had, of course, helped England win the World Cup in 1966.

While Bobby had gone to Manchester United as a boy, Jack had joined Leeds United's groundstaff in 1951. After making his League debut a few days before his 18th birthday in 1953, he had gone on to play in 629 League games for the Elland Road club. In over 20 years he had collected just about every major honour, helping Leeds win the League Championship, the FA Cup, League Cup and the Fairs Cup. He had figured in a few near-misses, too, in a remarkably eventful playing career. One of those near-misses came in 1973, when FA Cup favourites Leeds were beaten in the Wembley final by Second Division Sunderland—for whom Ian Porterfield scored the winning goal. It was within hours of this game that Jack Charlton announced his retirement as a player, and the man who had been capped 35 times by England revealed that he was to become manager of Middlesbrough.

In his first season at Ayresome Park, he guided his new club to the

Second Division championship. They took the title with a staggering margin of 15 points, and Charlton was named Manager of the Year. He remained at Middlesbrough four years, until April 1977, and left simply because he felt he had stayed long enough. He was, he insisted, in no hurry to find another club; but few believed he would remain long on the sidelines.

✻ ✻ ✻

Wednesday's directors were intent upon finding a manager with a reputation as a winner. They also wanted a big name, someone whose arrival was likely to capture the imagination of the public and supporters. Jack Charlton fitted the bill on both counts—if he could be persuaded to take the job. An invitation was extended to him to "come and have a look at us". He accepted, electing to watch Wednesday in action against Chesterfield on the following Saturday—October 8. It was intended that he would watch the game as an anonymous spectator, but that would have been well-nigh impossible anyway—Charlton being one of the best-known and most easily recognised figures in football. In the event, a local radio station ensured that his visit would be anything but secret: they announced that he had been offered the job!

Charlton and his wife, Pat, sat half-way up the North Stand—and hadn't been in their places more than a few minutes before it seemed that every one of the 12,920 spectators in the ground knew where they were sitting. The photographers were more concerned with recording Charlton's visit than the action on the field. For the record, Wednesday registered their first win of the season, Tynan getting the vital goal after 34 minutes. Afterwards, the Charltons walked round the ground to the main entrance, were taken into the directors' reception area, and, little more than an hour later, chairman Bert McGee, wearing a smile as wide as the nearby Five Arches, announced that "big Jack" was the new manager of Sheffield Wednesday.

Charlton told the waiting reporters that he had intended going away to think over Wednesday's offer before making a decision. "But then I thought 'what the hell, let's start now'. I thought 'if I walk away from it now, I might talk myself out of it'." He admitted that the reaction of supporters in the North Stand had influenced his decision. "If anybody convinced me to take the job, it was those fans. About 300 people shouted 'We want you, Jack'; only one said he didn't want me. It certainly wasn't the team that persuaded me to come. There is an awful lot to be done on that score." The new manager warned: "I don't expect instant success. People might not like what they see at first, but I hope they'll stay with us."

Within a week of his arrival, Charlton was facing the sharedolders at the annual meeting. Wednesday had revealed another loss, smaller than in previous years but at £43,966 still substantial; and, with the team at the foot of the Third Division, the gathering at the Phoenix Rooms, Rotherham, could have been a stormy affair. In the event, the appointment of Charlton said all that needed to be said about what the board was doing in a bid to improve the club's situation. A few blunt, carefully chosen words from the new manager helped generate a new sense of optimism.

In fact, the appointment of Jack Charlton was only one piece in the jigsaw—a vital piece, but not the whole picture of the changes being made by Bert McGee and his colleagues. In the years between 1971 and 1977 inclusive, Wednesday's accumulated losses topped half-a-million pounds. The club was bleeding to death. In the next few years the trend was not simply halted but reversed; and when Wednesday reported a surplus of £219,553 on the year ended May 31 1981, with assets of over £300,000, Mr. McGee described the club's financial report as one of the finest in the Football League. In describing how the transformation had been achieved, the chairman said: "We stopped spending and started earning. We kept a tight control on all overheads, instituted rigorous, sensible housekeeping, appointed sound management, and let them get on with it." The turnabout really began when, under Len Ashurst, the staff had been cut back to the bare essentials; in 1976 came a new share issue, which provided a timely "blood transfusion"; and in late 1977, a new lottery was launched to supplement the existing Development Fund. In the latter case, commercial manager Dennis Woodhead was a key figure. The overall realism in the club's approach to spending, and to making the best use of its resources, paid dividends; and, of course, with the stadium having been already rebuilt in previous years, redevelopment was no longer a pull on finances other than in terms of paying off outstanding debts.

✻ ✻ ✻

Jack Charlton's arrival did not bring instant success on the field, and, as he had forecast, improvement was slow and gradual. Wednesday won only two of their first 10 League games under the new manager, and it was not until around the turn of the year that things began to improve. A goal by Mick Prendergast gave them a 1-0 victory over Rotherham on December 27, and that was probably the day when Charlton could first perceive a sign of light at the end of the tunnel. Wednesday collected 33 points from the remaining 25 games, and, losing only one of their final 12 matches, finished in 14th place.

Charlton made changes in the team, and perhaps the most significant of these in 1977-8 were the promotion of Bob Bolder and Dave Grant, two teenagers, from the reserves, and the acquisition of Brian Hornsby from Shrewsbury in March for £45,000. Incidentally, Peter Fox and Mick Prendergast were sold to Stoke and Barnsley respectively to help pay for Hornsby. A blow to the club at this time was the loss of Bradshaw, whose career was prematurely ended by injury. Bolder, who had cost £1,000 from Dover in the previous March, came into the side in December, and quickly established himself as first-choice goalkeeper. A big, well-built young man, he had a long spell on the sidelines in 1978-9 through injury, and endured a difficult phase in the early part of 1979-80 when he was dropped for a time; but he had chalked up more than 160 League appearances by the end of 1981-2. Defender Grant, too, settled into the side relatively quickly, and the former Sheffield Boys youngster had played in over 130 games before falling out of favour in 1981-2.

Charlton's first season in charge, 1978-9, saw other youngsters given their first taste of League soccer: they included ex-Barnsley Boys midfielder, Kevin Taylor; defender Peter Shirtliff, from Hoyland; and Brian Cox, a former Sheffield Boys goalkeeper. The summer of 1978 produced a number of important changes on and off the field: Walden left to join Newport—an independent tribunal placed a paltry £3,500 fee on his head—and Ray Blackhall, who had played 37 times for Newcastle, was signed for £25,000 to fill the right-back spot. Maurice Setters, the former Doncaster Rovers manager and one-time West Brom and Manchester United half-back, was added to the staff, joining trainer Tony Toms and John Harris, who had been promoted to the manager's number two almost as soon as Charlton arrived at Hillsborough.

Early in the new season, Tommy Tynan was transferred to Lincoln and David Cusack moved to Southend, and in October the bulk of the money was used to acquire central defender Mick Pickering from Southampton. Pickering, now 22, had started out with Barnsley, for whom he had made his League debut at the age of 18. After 100 appearances, he had been sold to Southampton for £35,000 in May 1977. He missed only one game in the Hampshire club's successful Second Division promotion campaign of 1977-8, but lost his place after a few matches in the top grade, and Wednesday paid £65,000 to obtain his services. It is interesting to note that Pickering, who became captain, had the distinction of having played in all four grades of the Football League when making his Third Division debut in Wednesday's game at Rotherham.

Wednesday's form in the early part of 1978-9 was moderate, and there was evidence that much was still to be done if they were to be more than a mid-table outfit. Though they collected seven points from the first seven away games, they only won two of their first 11 matches at home. They lacked consistency: between early November and early March, they went 10 Leagues games without a win; then they collected nine points from five games; and this was followed by a run which brought only one win in 11 matches. They finished the season in 14th place.

The highlight of the season was provided by the FA Cup. In the first round a replay was needed to dispose of Scunthorpe, and two attempts were also required before Tranmere Rovers were defeated at the next stage. The third round paired Wednesday with FA Cup holders Arsenal at Hillsborough.

The Arsenal saga was destined to extend over a 16-day period which saw the teams meet five times. The first game only went ahead after volunteers had worked long and hard to clear snow from the pitch. The Londoners led after only 10 minutes, but Jeff Johnson pulled Wednesday level soon after the interval. At Highbury, Wylde put the Owls in front just before half-time, and a major shock looked on the cards until Brady snatched a last-minute equaliser. The second, third and fourth replays were all staged at Leicester. Arsenal led twice in the first Filbert Street clash, but Hornsby twice pulled Wednesday level. Two days later, the fourth meeting of the teams ended in a 3-3 draw. Rushbury headed the first goal after 59 minutes, Stapleton equalised for Arsenal six minutes later, Young headed the Londoners in front after 75 minutes, Lowey made it 2-2 after 85 minutes; and in extra-time Stapleton scored for Arsenal, with Hornsby shooting Wednesday level again from the penalty spot. In this game Turner saved a penalty. The marathon finally ended after 540 minutes, when Arsenal won the fifth meeting 2-0, with goals by Gatting and Stapleton. The Londoners went on to reach the final again, and lost to Second Division West Ham at Wembley; but for Wednesday the epic had boosted morale and provided an important financial fillip, too.

The Cup saga over, Charlton returned to the transfer market. Ian Fleming, a forward, was obtained from Aberdeen, but the Scot was not destined to remain long in Sheffield, and was transferred to Dundee within a year. In March, however, Wednesday made a signing which was to prove highly significant in the bid to build a team capable of winning promotion—Terry Curran, a clever if controversial winger, was acquired from Southampton for £100,000. Curran, then 24, had made 170 League appearances with four clubs, but had never seemed to entirely fulfil his promise at any. He had started out with Doncaster Rovers, at the time managed by Maurice Setters, and later had spells with Nottingham Forest and Derby before joining Southampton. In the next four seasons, Curran was to make more than 120 League appearances for Wednesday, scoring nearly 40 goals—including 22 in his first full season when the decision to give him a free forward role paid dividends. A later decision to given Curran additional responsibilities saw his form suffer, the upshot being his eventual move to Sheffield United in the 1982 close season.

In the summer of 1979 Wednesday followed up the capture of Curran with further signings of considerable importance. Andy McCulloch, a six-foot-two solidly-built centre-forward, was acquired from Brentford for £70,000; and Ian Mellor, a lanky midfielder, was brought from Chester for £60,000. In August Charlton bought again, bringing Jeff King from Walsall for around £30,000. All three men possessed skill and experience. McCulloch, at 28, had made 258 League appearances and scored 91 goals in a career which had seen him at QPR, Cardiff and Oxford before joining Brentford; Mellor, 29, had started with Manchester City and been with Norwich and Brighton as well as Chester, and had 230 League appearances to his credit; and King, a Scottish-born forward, had been with Derby before Walsall—and, indeed, the previous season, had scored a memorable goal *against* Wednesday. Outgoing moves which came in this period saw Rushbury join Swansea (£60,000), Nimmo (£20,000) and Dowd (£15,000) move to Doncaster, and Turner transferred to Sunderland for £90,000. Wednesday subsequently sold Fleming, and in February Rodger Wylde left for Oldham Athletic, with Wednesday pocketing an £80,000 fee for the young striker.

✱ ✱ ✱

1979-80 was the season when Wednesday finally turned the corner, beginning the long climb upwards by gaining promotion after five years in the Third Division. Yet, early in the campaign, they had looked anything but strong contenders for a place in the Second Division. It was

23. Hillsborough squad 1979-80, the year Wednesday won promotion from Division
Three. . . (back row) Jack Charlton (manager), J. Honey (physio), Brian Strutt,
Terry Curran, Rodger Wylde, Ian Porterfield, Ian Fleming, Bob Bolder, Ray Blackhall,
Andy McCulloch, Hugh Dowd, Peter Shirtliff, Ian Mellor, Maurice Setters (coach),
Tony Toms (coach); (front) Jimmy Mullen, Jeff Johnson, Denis Leman, Brian Hornsby,
Mick Pickering, Gordon Owen, John Lowey, David Grant, Kevin Taylor, Mark Smith.

thanks largely to an unbeaten run of 16 games which began in
mid-January, and a vital win at Blackburn in late April, that they finished
in third place—pipping neighbours Chesterfield by one point and going
up with Grimsby Town and Blackburn Rovers.

Though they began the season with a 3-0 win at Barnsley—McCulloch
and Mellor each marking his first appearance with a goal—Wednesday's
form in the first months of the campaign left much to be desired. Home
defeats against Blackburn, Brentford, Barnsley and Exeter highlighted
the team's shortcomings. In the Blackburn game, which Rovers won 3-0,
Bolder had one of those nightmare afternoons which occasionally
plague young goalkeepers, and lost his place for a time to Cox; but,
ultimately, he bounced back, having survived the ordeal of heavy
barracking. Wednesday were also handicapped by injuries which
caused McCulloch to miss 13 games between October and December
and Pickering to be absent throughout September and October. Lowey,
a Manchester product who had had a spell in American football,
deputised for McCulloch with limited success; while Mullen returned for
his last senior run as stand-in for Pickering. By early December,
Wednesday had collected 24 points from 22 games and stood in eighth
place. Leaders at this stage were Sheffield United with 28 points.

When Wednesday visited Reading on December 21, 17-year-old
Charlie Williamson, a former Waltheof Comprehensive schoolboy, was
thrust into action as deputy for the suspended Grant, but with McCulloch

back it was the attack which captured all the attention as goals by Curran and Mellor completed a victory which was to mark the start of a run which saw Wednesday lose only one of 19 games.

Five days after the Reading trip came the "match of the season"—the first League meeting of the Sheffield clubs in eight and a half years, and, in fact, the 100th city derby in League and Cup. United, having been relegated from the Second Division at the end of the previous season, were already looking hot favourites for promotion; while Wednesday's form was uninspiring. The Boxing Day clash attracted a crowd of 49,309—a record for a Third Division game. Mellor shot Wednesday ahead with a superb 25-yards drive five minutes before half-time, and after 63 minutes McCulloch set up a chance for Curran to head number two. A couple of minutes later, Hornsby and Curran were involved in the move which ended with King making it 3-0; and three minutes before the final whistle, Mark Smith, the Shirecliffe lad who had firmly established himself in a defensive partnership with Pickering, shot home a fourth goal from the penalty spot. The defeat marked the beginning of a surprising fall-away by United, who eventually ended up in twelfth place in the table. The teams in this game are worth noting for posterity:

Wednesday— Bolder; Blackhall, Williamson, Smith, Pickering, Hornsby, King, Johnson, McCulloch, Mellor, Curran.

United— Richardson; Speight, Tibbot, Kenworthy, MacPhail, Matthews, de Goey, Bourne, Butlin, Garner, Sabella. Cutbush substituted for the injured Speight after 57 minutes.

A couple of weeks before the United match, Jeff Johnson had regained his senior place, and such was to be his impact in the second half of the campaign that he was subsequently voted "Player of the Year" by supporters. By coincidence, he displaced the previous year's "Player of the Year", Ian Porterfield; and, on the first day of 1980, Porterfield—who had missed only 12 games in two and a half seasons at Hillsborough—was appointed manager of Rotherham United. He was destined to enjoy immediate success in soccer management, leading the Millmoor club to the Third Division title in 1981. He then left Rotherham almost immediately to join Sheffield United, and guided the Bramall Lane club to the Fourth Division championship in 1982.

Wednesday started the New Year of 1980 with a home defeat against Plymouth on January 12—but that was to be their last setback until they visited Bury exactly three months later. The next home game was significant on two counts: Wednesday returned to winning ways with a 3-0 victory against Colchester (Smith got two goals from the penalty spot), and 19-year-old Kevin Taylor was recalled and siezed the chance to establish a regular place. The defeat of Colchester was followed with a 5-1 crushing of Bury (Curran 2, Grant, Taylor and Smith, pen, were the scorers); and McCulloch bagged a hat-trick in the 5-0 win against Rotherham. Away wins at Swindon (2-1), Carlisle (2-0) and Oxford (2-0) helped push the Hillsborough side up the table, and though they had a spell in which five out six games ended in a 1-1 scoreline, they stayed in the thick of the promotion chase.

One of those 1-1 results came in the return clash with Sheffield United at Easter, when a crowd of 45,156 saw the Blades take the lead on the stroke of half-time through MacPhail, with Wednesday salvaging a point thanks to a brilliant goal from Curran—a goal enshrined on film thanks to the attendance of BBC-TV's "Match of the Day" cameras and commentator John Motson.

Two days after the Bramall Lane game, Mark Smith's 11th penalty goal of the season in League and Cup gave Wednesday two more points from the home clash with Gillingham, and another home win against Chester ensured that Jack Charlton's side maintained its impetus. However, with Chesterfield hard on their heels, Wednesday went to Blackburn on April 22 knowing they could ill-afford to lose. Things didn't look good when Brotherston gave Rovers the lead four minutes before half-time. But, in the second period, the Sheffield side rose to the challenge magnificently. After 62 minutes Taylor cracked in the equaliser, and eight minutes from the end Mellor grabbed the winner with a diving header. Ray Blackhall set up both goals with telling crosses from the right. Victory was sweet, but even sweeter was the news that Chesterfield had lost at Chester on the same evening: promotion was now a virtual certainty.

Though Wednesday lost at Exeter in their final away fixture, a draw in the final home match against Carlisle enabled them to finish a point above Chesterfield; and the 32,734 spectators at Hillsborough that day roared their delight when skipper Mike Pickering and his colleagues took a bow from the directors' box at the end of the afternoon. Curran, thanks to a slight change of role, had emerged leading scorer with 22 goals in 41 games; while McCulloch had contributed 12 and Mellor 11. Smith had missed only two games, and his nine League goals from the penalty spot had been an important contribution; while Grant, absent only three times, had also enjoyed a successful term. Mullen, whose 14 outings had brought his career total of League appearances to 230, held his testimonial match a few days after the season's final game. Soon afterwards he joined his former colleague Ian Porterfield, and at Rotherham Mullen was destined to win a Third Division championship medal in his first season.

✱ ✱ ✱

Wednesday's first season back in the Second Division was satisfactory rather than sensational. They did very well following promotion, but could, perhaps, have done even better. They finished in tenth place, eight points behind Swansea City, who were promoted to the First Division along with West Ham and Notts County. Wednesday's average home attendance in the League was some 5,000 more than Swansea's, and almost double Notts County's, but, in the final analysis, they lacked what really mattered—the number of points to take them into the top grade. Yet they could easily have climbed into a promotion place with just a little more consistency. They lost only three home games, but managed only three away victories, and it was poor away form which cost them the chance of clinching what would have been a remarkably rapid return to the First Division. In truth, there was a good deal of inexperience in the side, and Jack Charlton admitted that a lack of experience had cost vital points in matches they needed to win.

The important thing was that Wednesday were moving in the right direction, and, not surprisingly, 1980-1 had seen a further re-shaping of the team. After Mullen's departure, 22-year-old John Lowey, who had scored four goals in 42 League outings, was transferred to Blackburn Rovers; and Wednesday "imported" Yugoslavian international midfielder, Ante Mirocevic at a club record fee of £200,000. Mirocevic made 22 League appearances in his first season, and 20 in his second; showing splendid skills but finding it difficult to hold a regular place. In early November, Pickering dropped out with an injury, and Peter Shirtliff began his longest run to date at the heart of defence; while 19-year-old ex-Sheffield Boys defender, the strongly-built Mel Sterland, also enjoyed an extended spell as a regular. When Hornsby found himself confined to the sidelines with a recurrence of his old injury, Leman was brought back.

At the start of the season, incidentally, Wednesday met their old rivals, United, for the first time in the Football League Cup. Goals from Johnson and Taylor earned Wednesday a 2-0 win in the home leg, and the second leg at Bramall Lane ended in a 1-1 draw. Wimbledon were disposed of by a 4-3 margin over two legs in the second round, but Watford came to Sheffield in the third round and delivered the knock-out.

No player appeared in every League match in 1980-1, though Blackhall and the fast-improving Smith were absent just once, and Bolder and McCulloch missed only three games. McCulloch's 18 goals (including a hat-trick against Cambridge) made him top scorer, while Curran, who had taken over responsibility for penalty kicks, claimed nine goals in the Second Division and two in the League Cup. Unfortunately, Curran missed three games in September after being sent off in the match at Oldham. The sending off occurred in the 27th minute following an incident involving Athletic's former Sheffield United striker, Simon Stainrod. Sadly, when Curran was given his marching orders by referee George Tyson, it sparked off astonishing scenes as a section of the crowd at the visitors' end of the ground poured onto the pitch. Play was held up for over half-an-hour, and manager Jack Charlton and chairman Bert McGee were involved in trying to restore order. A mindless minority inspired the trouble, and the incident, not surprisingly, captured the headlines. Wednesday disassociated themselves from the hooligan element among their followers, but it was, nevertheless, the club who were left to foot the bill; for subsequently standing areas at Hillsborough were closed for four games, and Wednesday's followers were banned from the next four away games with the home clubs compensated financially to the tune of £3,000 each, plus VAT.

✱ ✱ ✱

In 1981-2 Wednesday went within a point of gaining promotion to the First Division. In their final fixture they beat Norwich City, but it was the Norfolk club who went up. Ironically, this season had seen the introduction of a new points system—three for a win, one for a draw—and, had the old system been retained, Wednesday and not Norwich would have been promoted with Luton and Watford. Though

24. The "team" in the boardroom. . . (back row) Eric England (secretary), Geoff Hulley, Keith Addy, Jack Charlton (manager), Ernest Barron, Cliff Woodward; (front row) Matt Sheppard (vice-chairman), Bert McGee (chairman), Stan Speight.

Norwich won two more games than Wednesday, they lost 15 matches compared with the Sheffield club's 12; but, under a system which devalued the drawn game, Wednesday paid the price for drawing eight of their home fixtures. Another interesting point is that promotion would have made Wednesday Yorkshire's only First Division club, for Leeds United's long run in the top grade came to an end in 1982.

Before the start of the season, Wednesday transferred Jeff Johnson to Newport for £60,000, and signed three new players—Jim Holton and Gary Bannister from Coventry, and Gary Megson from Everton. Holton, the former Manchester United defender, obtained on a free transfer, never made the first team and, indeed, was subsequently released; but Bannister and Megson, who each cost around £100,000, both settled in quickly and well. Striker Bannister, indeed, played in every match and topped the scoring charts with 21 goals; and such was his form that he joined Smith and Pearson in the ranks of Wednesday's Under-21 internationals. Megson, a 22-year-old midfielder, was the son of the man who captained Wednesday in the 1966 FA Cup final; he had started his career with Plymouth Argyle, and had the experience of 100 League games before his move to Hillsborough.

Wednesday started the season in splendid style, winning their first four games without conceding a goal—and the manner in which they romped to a 3-0 victory at Luton on September 12 had even the most cautious critics tipping Jack Charlton's side for promotion. At Luton, with the BBC's "Match of the Day" cameras present for the clash of the

Second Division's pacemakers, Curran's form inspired suggestions that he ought to be playing for England; and the controversial forward had a hand in the goals scored by McCulloch, Megson and Bannister as the Owls chalked up their first victory at Luton for 21 years. Unfortunately, Curran subsequently endured a lean spell, was left out of the side for several games in mid-season, and finished the campaign with only three League goals to his credit. (Curran, controversial to the end, virtually negotiated his own transfer to Sheffield United at the end of the season, and Hillsborough officials were dismayed when an independent tribunal set the fee at half Wednesday's valuation.)

When Wednesday dropped their first points in the home game with Derby in mid-September—a late goal by Megson salvaged a draw—and then suffered their first defeat when a 35-yard "thunderbolt" from Banks gave Barnsley the points at Oakwell, optimism was still high. But a 0-3 defeat against struggling Wrexham and victories scrambled after coming from behind against Cardiff and Oldham, at Hillsborough in October, indicated that the team still had a long way to go. A setback against bottom-of-the-table Orient and another home defeat, at the hands of QPR (for whom Stainrod got a hat-trick), served to emphasise that the youthful Wednesday still lacked experience and maturity.

Curran was left out for the home game with Blackburn in mid-January, but though McCulloch and Megson gave them a 2-0 lead, Wednesday ended up drawing 2-2—two more vital points squandered. Wednesday began February with a vital 3-2 win at Norwich, where they didn't play well but a Bannister double and a goal from Peter Shirtliff clinched the three points. Three days later came the return fixture with leaders Luton, and the result—a 3-3 draw—illustrated how two promotion-chasing sides could give everything, serve up an exciting, entertaining game and yet both lose two points. Indeed, in the circumstances, Wednesday's fighting performance earned a draw which would have been regarded as an excellent result a year earlier. Wednesday were twice behind, with Luton's second goal coming from a disputed penalty; but they rallied and seemed to be heading for a 3-2 win. Alas, in "injury time" Megson got himself sent off, and Luton went upfield and snatched an equaliser.

A home defeat against struggling Bolton, and costly points dropped in home games with Grimsby, Shrewsbury and Charlton saw Wednesday reach mid-March with the promotion dream wearing a faded look. But, then, optimism suddenly returned. The presence of BBC's "Match of the Day" cameras coincided with another sparkling Wednesday performance at Oldham, where goals by Megson, Bannister and substitute Pearson clinched a 3-0 victory. This win was followed by successive home victories against promotion rivals Leicester City and Ken Knighton's struggling Orient. In the Orient game, incidentally, another newcomer, 24-year-old midfield player, Gary Shelton, made his debut as substitute for Curran. Shelton, who came initially on loan, was subsequently signed for a £50,000 fee from Aston Villa.

A defeat at QPR at the end of March was followed by three successive victories—at Shrewsbury, and in the home games with Newcastle and Cambridge. An Easter Monday crowd of 29,917 saw Wednesday come from behind to beat Newcastle, with new hero Shelton snatching the equaliser and Pearson claiming the winner. The 2-1 defeat of Cambridge was less than convincing, but Wednesday were still very much in command in the chase for that third promotion place.

On the last Saturday of April the final fade-out began when they crashed to their heaviest defeat of the season—beaten 4-0 by Watford. It meant that Wednesday went into May with a three-points lead over Leicester and Norwich and a five-point advantage over FA Cup finalists QPR: but Leicester and QPR both had matches in hand.

A goal-less draw against Chelsea at Hillsborough on May 1 was followed by another draw at Rotherham. Frustration was the name of the game in the first match; luck went against Wednesday in the second—with Rotherham being awarded a penalty which was dubious to say the least. It was the second time Sterland had been the victim of a harsh decision. However, despite the loss of four more points, Wednesday were still in the race—just. In their final away fixture, at Bolton, they had the boost of an early goal, but let Bolton bounce back to win 3-1. There would be no promotion celebrations at Hillsborough.

Wednesday's last home match, against Norwich, could have been the big promotion decider, but now the Norfolk side came to Sheffield seeking one point to be sure of booking their return to the First Division. A few weeks earlier, Norwich had seemingly been right out of the race, but a run of victories had pushed them back into contention. In the event, Wednesday denied City the draw they wanted, with McCulloch and Bannister on target in a 2-1 win. But, at the end, the visitors learned that rivals Leicester had dropped two points, which meant Norwich had clinched that final promotion spot. A tally of 71 points, just one more than Wednesday, had proved sufficient: how Wednesday regretted those points they had squandered in so many home games!

Perhaps in the final analysis the team had again paid for its lack of experience, but maybe the consolation was that the progress of so many youngsters promised a brighter future. Mel Sterland, 20, had finally become first-choice at right-back in preference to Blackhall, and Williamson, at 19, had shown promise at left-back; and, on many occasions, Wednesday had fielded a back-four with an average age of 20 until Pickering, 25, returned to play in 24 matches. In midfield, Mirocevic, Mellor and, later, Shelton, raised the average age, but red-haired Megson was only 22 and Taylor celebrated his 21st birthday during the season. Up front Bannister, at 21, was the bright star, and McCulloch and Curran the "veterans". But McCulloch had been unlucky again with injuries, and 18-year-old John Pearson, a lanky ex-Wisewood schoolboy, made 21 appearances (including nine as substitute) and claimed eight important goals. With Blackhall, Grant, Leman, Mellor and Hornsby released in the summer of 1982, clearly the future was in the hands of the young inheritors from Bolder to Bannister, though, significantly, one newcomer for 1982-3 was the experienced Mick Lyons from Everton.

As it happened, it was the very young who brought a note of success to Wednesday on the eve of the final League match of 1981-2, for the club's juniors won the Northern Intermediate League Cup, beating Barnsley 3-0 at Oakwell. At half-time in the Norwich game, chairman Bert McGee drew attention to this achievement by presenting the NIL Cup to one of the successful youngsters, Tony Simmons. The 17-year-old Simmons, who had scored one of the goals at Oakwell, had finished the campaign with a remarkable haul of 41 goals; and his reward was to be named as substitute for the first-team game against Norwich. Perhaps we could detect a note of symbolism in the moment, a few minutes from the end of that final match, when Simmons was sent on, replacing the soon-to-depart Curran. The future was beckoning.

For the record

As at May 1982, Sheffield Wednesday had spent 79 seasons in the Football League—51 in the First Division, 23 in the Second, and five in Division Three. Wednesday's honours:

Division One
Champions, 1902-3, 1903-4, 1928-9, 1929-30
Runners-up, 1960-1

Division Two
Champions, 1899-1900, 1925-6, 1951-2, 1955-6, 1958-9
Runners-up, 1949-50

Division Three
Promoted (3rd) 1979-80

FA Cup
Winners, 1896, 1907, 1935
Runners-up, 1890, 1966
Losing semi-finalists, 1882, 1894, 1895, 1904, 1905, 1930, 1954, 1960

Wednesday's accumulative League record (1892-1982):

	P	W	D	L	F	A	Pts
Division One.......	1982	771	444	767	3169	3197	1986
Division Two.......	958	396	240	322	1481	1268	1052
Division Three	230	83	76	71	297	266	242
	3170	1250	760	1160	4947	4731	3280

Big Matches at Hillsborough

Internationals

April 10 1920	*England 5*	*Scotland 4*	25,536 (£4,278)

This match was described as one of the best internationals seen for years, played on a pitch made ankle deep in mud by several days of rain. *Cock* gave England the lead after 10 minutes, *Miller* quickly equalised, but *Quantrill* restored England's lead after 15 minutes. Then Scotland hit back, and after *Wilson* equalised, goals by *Donaldson* and *Miller* gave them a 4-2 advantage. England's recovery began after 67 minutes when *Kelly* got number three. *Morris* levelled the scores a minute later, and *Kelly* got the winner in the 73rd minute. The teams were:

England— Hardy (Aston Villa); Longworth (Liverpool), Pennington (West Brom); Ducat (Aston Villa), McCall (Preston), Grimsdell (Spurs); Wallace (Aston Villa), Kelly (Burnley), Cock (Chelsea), Morris (West Brom), Quantrill (Derby).

Scotland— Campbell (Liverpool); McNair (Celtic), Blair (Wednesday); Bowie (Rangers), Low (Newcastle), Gordon (Rangers); Donaldson (Bolton), Miller (Liverpool), Wilson (Dunfermiline), Patterson (Leicester), Troup (Dundee).

October 3 1962	*England* 1	*France* 1	35,380
	Flowers(pen)	Goujon	

England— Springett (Wednesday); Armfield (Blackpool), Wilson (Huddersfield), Moore (West Ham), Norman (Spurs), Flowers (Wolves), Hallawell (Birmingham), Crowe (Wolves), Charnley (Blackpool), Greaves (Spurs), Hinton (Wolves).

"B" Internationals

January 18 1950	*England "B"* 5	*Switzerland "B"* 0	43,053
	Gray, Bailey, Rickett, Briggs, Froggatt.		
March 23 1955	*England "B"* 1	*Germany "B"* 1	23,630
	Swinbourne	Jushowiak (pen)	

Under 23 Internationals

February 8 1956	*England U-23* 3	*Scotland U-23* 1	40,000
	Haynes 2, Harris	Hamilton	
September 24 1958	*England U-23* 4	*Poland U-23* 1	38,525
	Charlton 3, Greaves	Gadecki	
March 16 1960	*England U-23* 5	*Holland U-23* 2	21,163
	Baker 2, Greaves, Paine, Eastham (pen)	Prins 2	

Youth International

November 1957	*England* 2	*Belgium* 0	

Inter-League

October 1951	*Football League* 2	*Scottish League* 1	49,075
	Lofthouse, Finney	Hamilton	
October 1955	*Football League* 4	*Scottish League* 2	37,788
	Lofthouse 2, Turner, Finney	Smith, Collins	

Schools Internationals
1930: England 3 Scotland 1. 1950: England 6 Wales 1. 1957: England 2 Scotland 0. 1965: England 0 Wales 0.

World Cup matches at Hillsborough (July 1966)
West Germany 5 (Held, Haller 2, 1 pen, Beckenbauer 2), *Switzerland* 0;
Spain 2 (Sanchio, Amaro), *Switzerland* 0; *Argentina* 2 (Artime, Onega),
Switzerland 0; *West Germany* 4 (Held, Beckenbauer, Seeler, Haller),
Uruguay 0. The last match was a quarter final game.

FA Cup semi-finals
The first FA Cup semi-final to be staged at the Wednesday ground was
the West Brom-Blackburn Rovers replay on April 3 1912, when a crowd
of 20,050 paid £1,232 and saw an extra-time goal from Pailor give Albion
victory and a place in the final against Barnsley. In fact, the final that year
ended in a draw, and the replay was staged at Bramall Lane, where
Barnsley beat West Brom 1-0 with the winning goal coming in the last
minute of extra-time. Hillsborough was the setting for two FA Cup
semi-finals in the years between the wars—in 1921 and 1922, when the
teams on both occasions were Tottenham and Preston. In 1921 Spurs
came from behind to win 2-1, Bliss getting both their goals, with the
match watched by 43,320 (receipts £4,506 19s 4d). In 1922 it was
Preston's turn to win, with Rawlings and Roberts getting the North End
goals, and Seed (later to play for Wednesday) replying for Spurs. A
crowd of 49,282 paid £4,687 7s 2d. Details of the 25 FA Cup semi finals
staged at Hillsborough since 1946 are as follows:

1946	*Derby C* 1 Carter	*Birmingham* 1 Mulraney	65,000 (£14,250)
1948	*Man United* 3 Pearson (3)	*Derby C* 1 Steel	65,000 (£14,250)
1949	*Man United* 1 Mitten	*Wolves* 1 Smyth	62,250 (£15,297)
1951	*Wolves* 0	*Newcastle* 0	
1952	*Blackburn* 0	*Newcastle* 0	65,000 (£15,975)
1955	*York City* 1 Bottom	*Newcastle* 1 Keeble	65,000 (£16,300)
1956	*Birmingham C* 3 Kinsey, Astall, Brown	*Sunderland* 0	65,000 (£16,407)
1957	*Birmingham C* 0	*Man United* 2 Berry, Charlton	65,000 (£16,848)
1959	*Nott'm Forest* 1 Quigley	*Aston Villa* 0	65,000 (£16,484)
1962	*Tottenham H* 3 Greaves, Jones Medwin	*Man United* 1 Herd	65,000 (£27,580)
1963	*Liverpool* 0	*Leicester C* 1 Stringfellow	65,000 (£32,680)

1964	*West Ham* 3 Boyce (2), Hurst	*Man United* 1 Law	65,000 (£32,680)
1965	*Leeds United* 0	*Man United* 0	60,000 (£32,413)
1967	*Tottenham H* 2 Greaves, Saul	*Nott'm Forest* 1 Hennessey	55,000 (£47,500)
1969	*Leicester C* 1 Clarke	*West Brom* 0	53,207 (£47,500)
1970	*Man United* 0	*Leeds United* 0	54,000 (£65,017)
1971	*Arsenal* 2 Storey (2) 1 pen	*Stoke City* 2 Smith, Ritchie	55,000 (£78,200)
1972	*Birmingham C* 0	*Leeds United* 3 Jones (2), Lorimer	55,000 (£82,250)
1973	*Arsenal* 1 George	*Sunderland* 2 Halom, Hughes	55,000 (£82,280)
1974	*Newcastle* 2 Macdonald (2)	*Burnley* 0	55,000 (£101,500)
1975	*Fulham* 1 Mitchell	*Birmingham* 1 Gallagher	55,000 (£107,000)
1976	*Derby C* 0	*Man United* 2 Hill (2)	55,000 (£140,000)
1977	*Leeds United* 1 Clarke (pen)	*Man United* 2 J. Greenhoff, Coppell	55,000 (£140,660)
1980	*Arsenal* 0	*Liverpool* 0	50,174 (£192,159)
1981	*Tottenham H* 2 Archibald, Hoddle	*Wolves* 2 Hibbitt, Carr (pen)	50,174 (£192,162)

League Cup semi-final
January 1972   *Stoke City* 0   *West Ham* 0   42,424

League Cup final (replay)
March 1977   *Everton* 1 Latchford   *Aston Villa* 1 Kenyon o.g.   (after extra-time) 52,135 (£109,299)

Wednesday's Internationals
England— W. Betts (1); E. Blenkinsop (26), F. Bradshaw (1), E. Brayshaw (1), T. Brittleton (5), J. Brown (6), H. Burgess (4), H. Burrows (3), E. Catlin (5), J. C. Clegg (1), W. E. Clegg (2), T. Crawshaw (10), H. Davis (3), E. Davison (1), J. Fantham (1), W. Felton (1), R. Froggatt (4), J. Hudson (1), F. Kean (9), T. Leach (2), W. Marsden (3), W. Mosforth (9), A. Quixall (5), E. Rimmer (4). J. Robinson (4), H. Ruddlesdin (3), J. Seed (5), J. Sewell (6), F. Spiksley (7), R. Springett (33), R. Starling (2), G. Stephenson (3), J. Stewart (3), A. Strange (20), P. Swan (19), G. Wilson (12), G. Young (1).

Scotland— J. Blair (2), J. Campbell (1), J. Lyall (1), J. McCalliog (3), D. McLean (1), G. Robertson (3), A. Wilson (6).

Wales— H. Hanford (3), T. Jones (1), P. Rodrigues (16), R. Williams (4), D. Witcomb (1).

Ireland— D. Clements (13), R. Coyle (3), W. Gowdy (1), E. M'Connell (5), S. Todd (3).

Eire— W. Fallon (2), E. Gannon (11).

Full details of "B", Under-23, Youth, Under-21 and amateur internationals are contained in the club's handbook, published annually.

Acknowledgements

The writing of this new history of Sheffield Wednesday was not embarked upon until September 1981, and was completed within nine months; but, in fact, preparations for the book began as long ago as 1966—and perhaps before. I could say I started preparing myself for the task the first time I stood on the Kop at Hillsborough in 1947. But the important foundations were laid after I joined the sports department of the *Morning Telegraph*. At the outset I began compiling records and statistics with the sole purpose of equipping myself to become an informed sportswriter who could see the present in an historical context. However, in researching old matches and meetings and interviewing old players, the idea of doing a book began to take shape. The late Eric Taylor has not lived too see it completed, but it was he who first suggested that it might be done. Taylor's successor as club secretary, Eric England, was responsible for sparking off the resolve to set about the task. Mr. England not only provided important additional background, but checked the work as it progressed; and much is owed to his encouragement and that of chairman H. E. McGee.

Thanks are also owed to the staff of the Local Studies Division of Sheffield City Libraries; to former Wednesday players Gerry Young, Don Megson, John Fantham, John Quinn, H. H. C. Hill, Joe Cockroft, Jim McAnearney, Frank Melling, and Dennis Woodhead; to former managers Vic Buckingham, Jack Marshall, Derek Dooley and Len Ashurst; and ex-coach David Smith. Journalist friends Peter Cooper, Peter Harvey and Dick Williamson have supplied information and help; as did Harry English (Husband & Co.) and former director Stan Ashton.

Richard A. Sparling's *Romance of the Wednesday* was an invaluable source of material, but the study of the period covered by this volume was researched anew with the aid of the files of the *Sheffield Daily Telegraph, Sheffield & Rotherham Daily Independent* and the *Sheffield Mail.* Later periods were studied with the aid of the *Sheffield* (later *Morning*) *Telegraph,* and additional material was gleaned from the *Manchester Guardian* and *The Times,* plus various football annuals, including those produced by the *Sheffield Telegraph, Playfair, News of the World,* and *Rothmans.* Among books referred to, especially helpful were *The Jimmy Seed Story,* Billy Walker's *Soccer In The Blood,* and Frank Swift's *Football From The Goalmouth,* plus Geoffrey Green's *Official History of the FA Cup.*

A debt of gratitude is also owed to Edith and Billy Hoyland, who have provided invaluable domestic assistance in a period when my typewriter supplanted the cleaner as the most important piece of equipment in my home. Thanks also to Miss Linda Lax for assistance in proof-reading, to Sheffield Newspapers for permission to reproduce photographs, also Wednesday's official photographer Steve Ellis.